WALLACE STEVENS

A CELEBRATION

WALLACE STEVENS

A CELEBRATION

EDITED BY

FRANK DOGGETT AND ROBERT BUTTEL

PRINCETON UNIVERSITY PRESS

PRINCETON, NEW JERSEY

1980

THIS BOOK HAS BEEN COMPOSED IN LINOTYPE ELECTRA
DESIGNED BY BRUCE CAMPBELL

CLOTHBOUND EDITIONS OF PRINCETON UNIVERSITY PRESS
BOOKS ARE PRINTED ON ACID-FREE PAPER, AND BINDING
MATERIALS ARE CHOSEN FOR STRENGTH AND DURABILITY

PRINTED IN THE UNITED STATES OF AMERICA BY PRINCETON
UNIVERSITY PRESS, PRINCETON, NEW JERSEY

811.5
W187d

210829

... there is a blue peacock, blue and green and all the denser modulations of these colors, with gold and silver fans, which it turns to and fro as if to exhibit the brilliance of its mere presence and thereby to command. On the peacock's head, there is a diamond crown, like a coxcomb of darting light and darting fire. As this image of the imagination passes us, we are impressed by the manner of its attendant persons, silent and obedient, as if they were grateful for some expectation of their labor, of which they seem to feel sure.

WALLACE STEVENS
From the second draft ending to
"A Collect of Philosophy"

CONTENTS

PREFACE

IN THE CENTENNIAL YEAR OF WALLACE STEVENS'
birth, Stevens' art still seems fresh and elusive, but less pre-
cious and less eccentrically modern than it did more than
fifty years ago when his first book appeared. Since then, the
rich and memorable language of *Harmonium* has been aug-
mented by the equally memorable, if more abstract, phrases
in the later books. It is now assumed that the imagery de-
rives from eternal or universal human situations and rever-
berates with echoes of philosophic implications. The poetry
still imparts its special quality of withheld thoughtfulness.
The effect of its subtly qualified, seemingly abstruse state-
ments is to suggest that the poet may be amused, even skep-
tical of their never quite formulated profundities. Along with
this implicit questioning, each poem's discourse contem-
plates in exacting language the shadings of its idea. "Words
are thoughts," Stevens says, and with this concept of lan-
guage his poetry, as so many critics have noted, involves a
movement of thought, an activity of mind. This activity is
stimulated by intimations beyond the plain statements in
poems. The poems exert the fascination of what may be rec-
ognized as theory and what may be realized at the same time
as the poet's intuition of a person in a time, a season, and a
place, a setting.

Stevens has taken his place among the other cherished
figures of our literature as part of an inheritance rather than
as the isolated phenomenon he seemed to be in earlier days.
Many critics now regard him as one of the major figures in
the romantic tradition, and his relationship to Wordsworth
and Keats, discussed in these pages, will be easily accepted by
most of his readers. Yet he has not receded into a general
background of romantic poetry. He is still the individualist,
the master of his own style. Stevens' individuality attracts

and overcomes parody. And because he is inimitable, his in-
fluence has been minimal for a poet of his monumental
reputation.

From the first, the uniqueness of the poems has provoked
curiosity about the poet. Alfred Kreymborg and Carl Van
Vechten produced sketches of the man who was writing *Har-
monium,* and later a thin factual biography was included in
William Van O'Connor's *The Shaping Spirit.* However, the
major biographical events for students of Stevens' life and
poetry have been, first, the publication of Holly Stevens' se-
lection from her father's letters and then the publication of
his journal in *Souvenirs and Prophecies.* No subsequent vol-
umes can rival these two in importance for readers and critics
of Stevens' work. The first critical biography of the poet,
Samuel French Morse's pioneering *Wallace Stevens: Poetry
as Life,* appeared between publication of the letters and the
complete journal.

For a poet generally conceded to be one of the truly origi-
nal figures in American literature, the amount of biographi-
cal material published so far is very small. Except for brief
passages in his letters, little information has been available
about the creating poet and the poet involved in the prob-
lems of publication and public acceptance. And in spite of
the prodigious amount of idle astonishment that has been
wasted on Stevens' role as an insurance executive, no account
of the nature of his work or glimpse of the man in his office
has been printed except in the pages of *The Wallace Stevens
Journal.* Usually Stevens has been depicted as a solitary fig-
ure, like the man in "Esthétique du Mal" who thinks of two
worlds, "The peopled and the unpeopled. In both, he is /
Alone. . . ."

In this volume celebrating Stevens' one hundredth birth-
day, the essays concerned with the human figure of the poet
see him at ease and at work with other men. The one excep-
tion to these accounts of Stevens in the world of men and
affairs is Holly Stevens' "Holidays in Reality," which shows
the poet at play and at rest in companionship with his wife
and child. In contrast, Wilson E. Taylor contributes the

recollections of an especially favored younger business associate, offering an informal portrait of the poet in his office and in pursuit of such pleasures as the New York World's Fair, pastries, college football, and walking. A selection from Stevens' letters to Taylor suggests the flavor of his more casual correspondence and includes some business letters. An interesting supplement to Taylor's reminiscences is the medley of impressions collected by Peter Brazeau. These memories of the poet by some who joined in his search for pleasure during visits to New York City were selected from a large mass of tape recordings that will eventually become an oral biography of Stevens.

Concluding the section of biographical material is George Lensing's history of Stevens' difficulties with British publishers and British acceptance. Stevens' reputation has had a slow and intermittent growth in England. Even today he stands about where he did in America before publication of "Notes toward a Supreme Fiction": a few admire him greatly, but the majority of the educated public still does not know his name. This account of Stevens' dealings with publishers is revealing of the poet who was also a man of business.

Of particular note in this volume is Stevens' early version of "The Comedian as the Letter C," titled "From the Journal of Crispin." In preparing the poem for inclusion in *Harmonium*, Stevens made extensive changes, the most dramatic ones being deletions of a number of long passages. Only rarely has it been possible to catch this poet in the act of revising his work and thus become aware of how he arrived at the polish and seeming inevitability of his completed poems. It is instructive to perceive the strictness of the standards that prescribed the excisions; he had a sharp eye by this time for his own dead wood. In his essay accompanying the printing here of the whole of "From the Journal of Crispin," Louis Martz examines the poem in light of the aesthetics of American painting and poetry at the time.

Also published here for the first time are the several endings for "A Collect of Philosophy," which were written in perplexity about how to conclude an essay on poetry and philosophy. These variant conclusions are especially interesting because they reveal some of his thoughts about his own creative processes and contain a brilliant and suggestive image of the imagination as a peacock. Peter Brazeau gives an account of the inspiration for and composition of the endings and conjectures their significance for Stevens.

Additional new Stevens material is made available here in the sizable number of previously unpublished *Adagia* items that A. Walton Litz has edited and annotated; he has also provided a complete chronology of all of the *Adagia*. In his commentary Professor Litz discusses the poet's lifelong fascination with epigrams, adages, and proverbs and his habit of collecting quotations congenial to his outlook and also setting down in compact form philosophic and aesthetic aperçus of his own, ready to be absorbed into his emerging poetic theory or to provide succinct matter for his poems.

In probing the poet's biography, especially the influence of the father-lawyer-poet Garrett Stevens on his son, and then in discerning the effect of the biographical roots on the poetry, Richard Ellmann's essay creates a bridge between the biographical materials that precede it and the critical and theoretical essays that follow. Professor Ellmann finds evidence for his case in Holly Stevens' *Souvenirs and Prophecies* (as well as in the *Letters*), but J. Hillis Miller in his essay takes a counterposition. What we learn in *Souvenirs and Prophecies*, he says, is of interest and does anticipate some of the later developments. "Nevertheless," he maintains, "the authentic voice of Stevens as a poet is not touched by such explanations" as can be based on information in that book. Indeed, the search in any source for the origins of that voice are futile; the origins will remain a mystery.

However much the essays in this collection vary in approach and point of view, they nevertheless speak to one another, at times in complementary and at other times in differing or qualifying ways. Helen Vendler's essay considers the constant and germinating effect of Keats' "To Autumn"

on Stevens' consciousness as he absorbed, imitated, and
played variations upon the inexhaustible implications of this
particular romantic poem throughout his career. Isabel G.
MacCaffrey, on the other hand, scrutinizes the subtleties of
meaning in one central Stevens poem, "Le Monocle de Mon
Oncle," revealing some of Stevens' affinities with Words-
worth. Irvin Ehrenpreis traces Stevens' exploitation of the
sounds of nonsense in his poems to achieve the "strange
relation" of meaning and effect, the curious mixture of the
absurd, the haunting, and the meaningful. John Hollander
is also concerned with the subject of sound, specifically, the
element of music in the poet's work. He places Stevens' pro-
found absorption in the musical in the context of the interest
in the idea of music shown by earlier American writers such
as Emerson. Whereas Richard Ellmann's concern is with
the youthful, formative years of the poet, Frank Kermode
dwells on Stevens' last years, when he had become "a poet
of thresholds" (as in the magnificent poem on Santayana),
meditating poignantly and with serene assurance on final
things, expressing an interest in Heidegger and Hölderlin.

Three essays concerned chiefly with Stevens' thought and
poetics from a theoretical point of view illustrate his intricate
elusiveness and the intensity of his search for what would
suffice in an age without a central ordering myth. J. Hillis
Miller considers both the theoretical in the poet—his view,
for instance, that the theory of poetry is the life of poetry
and his quest for a unified theory—and that which evades
theory, concluding that Stevens' "essential poem at the cen-
ter of things . . . may be neither named, nor seen, nor pos-
sessed theoretically." Joseph Riddel is also intrigued by what
lies at the center of Stevens' poetry. His essay examines why
for Stevens there could be only *notes toward* a supreme fic-
tion, for the attempt to discover a stable center leads back
through a series of displacements of central metaphors to a
point beyond any possible knowledge of origins, of clear-cut
beginnings. Given this dilemma, a "total book" with a fixed
correlation between language and reality, between thought
and its figurations, becomes an impossibility. At the center of

Stevens' conception of things is an abyss wherein is revealed
(in "The Auroras of Autumn") a tantalizing, elusive, corus-
cating serpent: "In the turnings of the serpent, a 'serpent
body flashing without the skin,' the 'master of the maze' is
revealed as only another image, itself without origin."

Roy Harvey Pearce's contrasting approach nevertheless
complements Professor Riddel's, stressing not an infinite
process of metaphorical "staging" (that is, one metaphor dis-
placing another in a series of attempts to define and fix in
place what exists ever elusively at the center), but rather the
process of negation/decreation, which brings the mind to an
unflinching apprehension of "The weight of primary noon, /
The A B C of being," the mystery at the center. He traces
Stevens' movement from the predominant strategy in *Har-
monium* of the imagination's transformations of reality, to-
ward the decreative process that cuts through evasions to ex-
pose that "A B C of being," to finally, in the late poems, a
point beyond decreation, that "of being recreated and re-
creating." Here Stevens achieves, says Professor Pearce,
"what I can only call transcendence."

Frank Kermode has a similar conception of the role that
Stevens arrived at in his last poems, when he says with ref-
erence to the ending of "The Auroras of Autumn," "Hölder-
lin would have called this poet a servant of the wine god,
bearing all such care, seeing that blaze on behalf of all,
imagining everything for them, including death." This is to
suggest the human value of Stevens' poetry. He has often
been thought of as being detached from human concern—
unfeeling, austere, aloof behind the protective barrier of a
mannered wit. And there appears to be some validity to this
estimate: at the personal level he seems to have withheld a
good part of himself. Also, as Auden said of Yeats, he could
be "silly like us," not above triviality, as some of the bio-
graphical details in these pages indicate. Professor Kermode
calls our attention to the poet's taste for exquisite bookbind-
ings, implying a slightly indulgent sensibility counter to the
nobility of his poetic aims. But it is in those aims and in their
accomplishment that the humanity of Stevens is evident. He

believed devoutly that poetry should help us live our lives. As he sought relentlessly the "blissful liaison" between mind and nature, as he shed, one after the other, easy refuges for the imagination and stretched the mind to the furthest reaches of what it might be possible to know without falsification, he demonstrated the mind's ability to arrive at points of accord, however fleeting, with reality. "Poetry as manifestation of the relationship that man creates between himself and reality"—this is how he defines the role of poetry in one of his *Adagia*, and this role attaches to poetry, as his own poems prove again and again, a profound human significance. One measure of that significance is the depth of response among readers who come to know the poetry. Another is the diversity of that response; the poems in their rich complexity accommodate varying interpretations and allow readers to reach new syntheses of understanding as they assimilate these interpretations. The noble accents and human implications of Stevens' thought, as well as the inescapable rhythms of his poems, are what give his work the important place it holds today and assure that it will be read long after the occasion of his centenary.

The editors wish to thank those who have granted permission to reprint published and unpublished Stevens material: The Huntington Library, San Marino, California, for permission to quote from letters from Stevens to Henry Hull Church, Alfred A. Knopf, Nicholas Moore, Thurairajah Tambimuttu, Herbert Weinstein, and Oscar Williams, an unpublished letter from Stevens' father to Stevens, and Stevens' notebooks, Adagia I & II and Sur Plusieurs Beaux Sujects I & II; Alfred A. Knopf, Inc., for permission to quote selections from *The Collected Poems of Wallace Stevens* (New York, 1954), © 1954 Wallace Stevens, *Letters of Wallace Stevens*, selected and edited by Holly Stevens (New York, 1966), © 1966 Holly Stevens, and *Opus Posthumous*, edited by Samuel French Morse (New York, 1957), © 1957 Elsie Stevens and Holly Stevens; New Directions Publishing Corporation for permission to quote from *Kora in Hell: Im-*

provisations (Boston, 1920), © 1954 William Carlos Williams, and *The Complete Collected Poems of William Carlos Williams, 1906-1938* (Norfolk, Conn., 1938), © 1938 New Directions Publishing Corporation; Holly Stevens for permission to print thirteen unpublished letters from Stevens to Wilson Taylor and R. Dorsey Watkins, © 1978 Holly Stevens, and "From the Journal of Crispin," © 1978 Holly Stevens; and the Collection of American Literature, Beinecke Rare Book and Manuscript Library, Yale University, for permission to print the unpublished parts of "A Collect of Philosophy."

CHRONOLOGY

1879	Born October 2
Sept. 1897- June 1900	At Harvard, where he knew Santayana, edited *The Harvard Advocate*, and published verse and prose sketches
1900-1901	Works as a journalist in New York City
1901-1903	Attends New York Law School
1903	Hunting and fishing expedition to British Columbia
1904	Admitted to New York State bar
1909	Marries Elsie Moll
1913	Attends Armory Show
1914	"Carnet de Voyage" published in *Trend*
1915	"Sunday Morning" published in *Poetry*
1915-1917	Writes three verse plays
1916	Begins career with the Hartford Accident and Indemnity Company
1921-1922	"From the Journal of Crispin" written and revised as "The Comedian as the Letter C"
1923	Visits Havana, Cuba, in February
1923	*Harmonium* published, September
1923	Cruise with his wife to California, October-November
1924	Holly Stevens born
1932	Buys house in Hartford
1934	Becomes vice president in the Hartford Accident and Indemnity Company
1934-1938	Letters on poetry to Ronald Lane Latimer
1935	*Ideas of Order*
1936	*Owl's Clover*
1937	*The Man with the Blue Guitar*
1938-1945	Letters on poetry to Hi Simons
1942	"Notes toward a Supreme Fiction" written between January 28 and June 1
1942	*Parts of a World*

1944	"Esthétique du Mal" written between June 17 and July 28
1945	Elected to National Institute of Arts and Letters
1947	*Transport to Summer*
1949	"An Ordinary Evening in New Haven" written for the 1000th meeting of the Connecticut Academy of Arts and Sciences
1950	*The Auroras of Autumn*
1950	Receives National Book Award
1950-1954	Letters on poetry to Renato Poggioli
1951	*The Necessary Angel*
1953	*Selected Poems* published in England
1954	*Collected Poems*
1955	Wins Pulitzer Prize, National Book Award
1955	Dies August 2
1957	*Opus Posthumous*
1966	*Letters of Wallace Stevens*, selected and edited by Holly Stevens
1977	The complete journal published in *Souvenirs and Prophecies: The Young Wallace Stevens*, by Holly Stevens

ABBREVIATIONS

CP   *The Collected Poems of Wallace Stevens* (New York: Alfred A. Knopf, 1954)

L   *Letters of Wallace Stevens*, selected and edited by Holly Stevens (New York: Alfred A. Knopf, 1966)

NA   Wallace Stevens, *The Necessary Angel: Essays on Reality and the Imagination* (New York: Alfred A. Knopf, 1951)

OP   Wallace Stevens, *Opus Posthumous*, ed. Samuel French Morse (New York: Alfred A. Knopf, 1957)

SP   Holly Stevens, *Souvenirs and Prophecies: The Young Wallace Stevens* (New York: Alfred A. Knopf, 1977)

WALLACE STEVENS

A CELEBRATION

LOUIS L. MARTZ

"FROM THE JOURNAL OF CRISPIN": AN EARLY VERSION OF "THE COMEDIAN AS THE LETTER C"

ON DECEMBER 21, 1921, WALLACE STEVENS WROTE TO Harriet Monroe, describing his strenuous efforts to create a poem worthy of submitting for a new prize offered by the Poetry Society of South Carolina, which had been announced a few weeks earlier in the December issue of *Poetry*:

> I return your greetings, most sincerely, and in these Mrs. Stevens joins, although possibly, in her case, rather gingerly, for I have made life a bore for all and several since the announcement of the Blindman prize in your last issue. To wit: I have been churning and churning, producing, however, a very rancid butter, which I intend to submit in that competition, for what it may be worth, which, at the moment, isn't much. But what's the use of offering prizes if people don't make an effort to capture them. My poem is still very incomplete and most imperfect and I have very little time to give it. But I am determined to have a fling at least and possibly to go through the damnedest doldrums of regret later on. (*L*, 224)

Since the announcement declared that "All poems entered in this competition must be in the hands of the Secretary of the Society not later than January 1, 1922," Stevens was writing furiously against time. He evidently sent the poem off less than ten days after his letter to Monroe. Amy Lowell, judge of the prize, awarded it to Grace Hazard Conklin, but Stevens received an honorable mention for his poem "From the Journal of Crispin." No poem by Stevens was ever published under this title, and the manuscript he submitted was thought to have disappeared.

But in 1974 a Connecticut minister, the Reverend John Curry Gay, gave a group of manuscript poems by Wallace Stevens to the Beinecke Rare Book and Manuscript Library of Yale University, along with an account of how he came to acquire them:

> The house which my Grandmother built at 735 Farmington Avenue in West Hartford was divided into three apartments by my Mother and Father. Mr. Stevens rented one of the apartments and lived there with his wife and daughter Holly for some time—exactly how long I do not know. I do remember them well especially Miss Stevens. My parents became very close friends with Mr. Stevens. . . .
>
> My parents were very appreciative of Mr. Stevens' talents and always looked forward to the notes which accompanied his monthly rental cheques—the only example I have is the one in the brown leather wallet enclosed. Once in a while my Mother would grab a few pages from the trash can that were obviously Mr. Stevens' work—that is the source of the enclosed material. She thought it a very unlady-like thing to do, while at the same time she thought they might some day be of value. We always liked to think that some very important work of Mr. Stevens might have been written in our house.

The collection contains a nineteen-page, double-spaced typescript of "From the Journal of Crispin," along with a carbon copy that lacks three pages but is important for two variants. Above the title of the original is typed "Submitted for Blindman Prize," and in the upper right-hand corner, in pencil, are the words "Honourable Mention." The typescript represents an early version of the first four parts of "The Comedian as the Letter C," with 128 lines that were not included in *Harmonium* (1923) and hundreds of lesser variants scattered throughout. (The complete text of "From the Journal of Crispin" follows; the excised lines are enclosed in brackets, while minor variations have been left for the reader to explore.)

As they stand, the four sections have a completeness of their own. As the fifteen excised lines indicate at the very close, the poem exists in a tentative present:

> His colony may not arrive. The site
> Exists. So much is sure. And what is sure
> In our abundance is his seignory.
> His journal, at the best, concerns himself. . . .
> . . . .
> As Crispin in his attic shapes the book
> That will contain him, he requires this end:
> The book shall discourse of himself alone,
> Of what he was, and why, and of his place,
> And of its fitful pomp and parentage
> Thereafter he may stalk in other spheres.

The verbs throughout are usually cast in the present tense, while in the final version the whole poem has been put in the past tense, in keeping with the retrospective view of the "fatalist" comedian in the fifth and sixth sections that appeared in *Harmonium*. Did these added sections, with their wry "defeat" of the hero, form any part of Stevens' original plan? He told Harriet Monroe, "My poem is still very incomplete and most imperfect"; perhaps, then, a germ of something further might have been in Stevens' mind. And yet one wonders. A hundred lines have been excised from sections three and four of the "Journal," and these hundred lines create an effect quite different from that of the final version, which has been redesigned to lead toward the settling down of Crispin into the acceptance of his comfortable domesticity.

In the early version Crispin's discoveries in section three are more emphatic, more extensive, more adventurous, as a glance at some of the excised lines will show:

> The poet, seeking the true poem, seeks,
> As Crispin seeks, the simplifying fact,
> The common truth.

Hence Crispin becomes dissatisfied with "moonlight," with "Chanson evoking vague, inaudible words."

> Crispin is avid for the strenuous strokes
> That clang from a directer touch, the clear
> Vibration rising from a daylight bell,
> Minutely traceable to the latest reach.
> Imagination soon exhausts itself
> In artifice too tenuous to sustain
> The vaporous moth upon its fickle wings.

It is true, however, that Crispin cannot bring himself utterly to forgo the possibility that he has earlier described in this section, in lines preserved in *Harmonium*:

> Perhaps the Arctic moonlight really gave
> The liaison, the blissful liaison,
> Between himself and his environment,
> Which was, and is, chief motive, first delight,
> For him, and not for him alone.
>
> (CP, 34)

So now, in a passage retained with some significant revisions, Crispin goes on to describe what he "conceives his Odyssey to be":

> An up and down in these two elements,
> A fluctuating between sun and moon,
> A sally into gold and scarlet forms,
> As on this voyage, out of goblinry,
> And then retirement like a sinking down
> To sleep, among its violet feints and rest
> And turning back to the indulgences
> That in the moonlight have their habitude.

Nevertheless, he knows that he can never be satisfied to rest within these "backward lapses." Both the "moonlight fiction" and the "gemmy marionette" of spring are renounced (for a time) by the "searcher for the fecund minimum," the seeker after a "sinewy nakedness." This is the quality that he has earlier called "the umbelliferous fact"—that is, the fact that bears a flowery diadem.

Then begins a passage of eight lines that is retained, with some revisions, in the final version:

> A river bears
> The vessel inward. Crispin tilts his nose
> To inhale the rancid rosin, burly smells
> Of dampened lumber, emanations blown
> From warehouse doors, the gustiness of ropes,
> Decays of sacks, and all the arrant stinks
> That help him round his rude aesthetic out.
> He savors rankness like a sensualist.
> He notes the marshy ground around the dock,
> The crawling railroad spur, the rotten fence. . . .

One thinks here of the poem "Smell!" by William Carlos Williams, which appeared in his volume of 1917, *Al Que Quiere*:

> Oh strong-ridged and deeply hollowed
> nose of mine! what will you not be smelling?
> What tactless asses we are, you and I, boney nose,
> always indiscriminate, always unashamed,
> and now it is the souring flowers of the bedraggled
> poplars: a festering pulp on the wet earth
> beneath them. With what deep thirst
> we quicken our desires
> to that rank odor of a passing springtime!
> . . . .
> Must you taste everything? Must you know everything?
> Must you have a part in everything?

Stevens suggests in the "Journal" that he is willing, for a time at least, to follow Williams in this exploration of the local, using the kind of detail that Williams himself was constantly exploring:

The crawling railroad spur, the rotten fence,
That makes enclosure, a periphery
Of bales, machines and tools and tanks and men,
Directing whistles, puffing engines, cranes,
Provocative paraphernalia to his mind.
A short way off the city starts to climb,
At first in alleys which the lilacs line,
Abruptly, then, to the cobbled merchant streets,
The shops of chandlers, tailors, bakers, cooks,
The Coca Cola-bars, the barber-poles,
The Strand and Harold Lloyd, the lawyers' row,
The Citizens' Bank, two tea rooms, and a church.
Crispin is happy in this metropole.

But of course Stevens can never use these details in Williams' way, to evoke the concrete, stark presence of a living thing ("no ideas but in .the facts"). No, Crispin pauses to ponder and to question what these details may mean, allowing for the possible magical transmutation of the fact by the old "goblinry," the old "moonlight":

If the lilacs give the alleys a young air
Of sentiment, the alleys in exchange
Make gifts of no less worthy ironies.
If poems are transmutations of plain shops,
By aid of starlight, distance, wind, war, death,
Are not these doldrums poems in themselves,
These trophies of wind and war? At just what point
Do barber-poles become burlesque or cease
To be? Are bakers what the poets will,
Supernal artisans or muffin men,
Or do they have, on poets' minds, more influence
Than poets know? Are they one moment flour,
Another pearl? The Citizens' Bank becomes
Palladian and then the Citizens' Bank
Again. The flimsiest tea room fluctuates
Through crystal changes. Even Harold Lloyd
Proposes antic Harlequin.

Thus Crispin, the dismayed "short-shanks" of section one, is resurrected in an American guise. And so, in a passage significantly revised in the final version, we find that Crispin has indeed been "made new":

> Crispin revitalized
> Makes these researches faithfully, a wide
> Curriculum for the marvelous sophomore.
> They purify. They make him see how much
> Of what he sees he never sees at all.
> He grips more closely the essential prose. . . .

The drastic removal of so much detail and so much pondering creates quite a different effect in the final version:

> He marked the marshy ground around the dock,
> The crawling railroad spur, the rotten fence,
> Curriculum for the marvelous sophomore.
> It purified. It made him see how much
> Of what he saw he never saw at all.
> He gripped more closely the essential prose. . . .
>
> (CP, 36)

"It purified. It made him see. . . ." The word "it" refers to the general "curriculum"; but "they" in the first version refers to his "researches" into the much broader range of experiences, which include observations of machinery, Coca Cola bars, barber poles, and Harold Lloyd. The "essential prose" in the first version therefore stresses much more specifically the American place. The result is the much more "local" significance of Crispin's action at the outset of the next section, when he reverses the opening statement of his journal ("Nota: Man is the intelligence of his soil . . ."), even though nothing is changed in the final version except the tense:

> Nota: His soil is man's intelligence.
> That's better. That's worth crossing seas to find.
> Crispin in one laconic phrase lays bare
> His cloudy drift and plans a colony.

> Exit the mental moonlight, exit lex,
> Rex and principium, exit the whole
> Shebang. Exeunt omnes. Here is prose
> More exquisite than any tumbling verse,
> A still new continent in which to dwell.
> What was the purpose of his pilgrimage,
> Whatever shape it took in Crispin's mind,
> If not, when all is said, to drive away
> The shadow of his fellows from the skies,
> And, from their stale intelligence released,
> To make a new intelligence prevail.

The chief effect of the early version of section three, then, is to stress Stevens' alliance with the other writers who had stayed home in America, and who had, as Williams reports, sought to create American art and literature through cultivation of the "local." Williams is speaking of the era, in 1922, just before the publication of Eliot's *The Waste Land*: "There was heat in us, a core and a drive that was gathering headway upon the theme of a rediscovery of a primary impetus, the elementary principle of all art, in the local conditions. . . . I felt that we were on the point of an escape to matters much closer to the essence of a new art form itself—rooted in the locality which should give it fruit."[1]

The "Journal of Crispin" shows Stevens as wholly aware of this movement, which was represented by Alfred Stieglitz and his famous 291 (Fifth Avenue) Gallery. This movement was well described in a remarkable essay by Paul Rosenfeld that appeared in *The Dial* for December 1921,[2] the very month in which Stevens was pondering his entry for the Blindman Prize. Indeed, the "Journal of Crispin" seems to follow the voyage of the American artist, as described by Rosenfeld, not because Stevens necessarily read the essay (though he was a steady reader of *The Dial*), but because Rosenfeld sums up the movement toward contact with the local that had been the "slowly shaping drive" of letters and art in America from the outset of the century.[3] Rosenfeld begins his essay with a long discussion of the effort to discover what Williams calls "the essence of a new art form," as represented in the paintings of Albert Pinkham Ryder, where "the fanfares of romance breathe through the tender mysterious tones, the sensitive foaming forms" (p. 649). Here, says Rosenfeld, "For the first time, paintings speak to the American of what lies between him and his native soil. In them, for the first time since the pictorial art began to be practised among the European colonists of America . . . a painter has succeeded in digging down through sand to the sea."

Three generations of sober craftsmen had sought to spade their way through Reynolds and Constable, through Munich and Barbizon, had painted the valley of the Hudson and the hill walls of Lake George, the Rockies and Niagara Falls, chintz and girl graduates and candied Monets, quite vainly. Their little ponds float nothing save paper boats. But, in the Ryders, the ocean moves: we are set afloat beyond our depth, without intellectual compass and chart, and challenged to find our way across the tide to the unknown other shore. (pp. 649-50)

Just so, Crispin, in the opening section of both versions of this poem, makes his way from European "salad-beds" and "jupes" to his devastating vision of the sea:

Crispin,

The lutanist of fleas, the knave, the thane,
The ribboned stick, the bellowing breeches, cloak
Of China, cap of Spain, imperative haw
Of hum, inquisitorial botanist,
And general lexicographer of mute
And maidenly greenhorns, now beholds himself,
A skinny sailor peering in sea-glass.
What word split up in clickering syllables
And storming under multitudinous tones
Is name for this short-shanks in all this brunt?
Crispin is washed away by magnitude.

Crispin in his European guise evokes the courtly elegance and cleverness of his archetype in seventeenth-century French comedy: the valet whose descendant is Figaro. Costumed in cape, tall boots, knee breeches, ruff and cuffs of delicate lace, and a round hat, wittily given to fanfaronade, essentially timid but capable of appropriating heroic passages from Corneille's *Le Cid*, valet in command of every devious device, playing the roles of scholar, teacher, musician, poet, or doctor, judging and classifying all the terms and conditions of the greenhorns whom he plans to dupe—such a figure, Stevens implies, is the outmoded representative of an age when man conceived himself to be "the intelligence of his soil." Such is the point of view that lies between the modern artist and his native soil—a point of view that Stevens, with his affection for modern French poetry, may have seen as continuing into the modern era in the writings of Verlaine and his contemporaries.[4]

But this movement from the "foreign" to the "local" is not a simple matter of choosing to deal with "American" materials, such as the landscapes of Maine or New Mexico, the Ford factory, or the figure five on the fire engine. It involves the removal of "foreign," inherited ways of seeing and apprehending, or the absorption of these ways into the inner self in such a manner that the individual imagination of the artist can freely conceive and reconceive the object. To apprehend what Stevens calls the "early and undefiled American thing" requires not only seeing the thing "as it is," but also recreating the thing within the self. This, according to Rosenfeld, is what Ryder did: "For life, at length, had brought forth in the west a painter able to work from what he perceived upon his eyelids when his eyes were shut. Ryder was what the others were not, a poet. . . . And so, while the others, weak in imagination, were dependent always on the material facts which started their vision . . . Ryder could study the image in his brain" (p. 650). The passage bears a striking affinity with the action in Stevens' poem "Stars at Tallapoosa," which was published six months after Rosenfeld's essay appeared:

The mind herein attains simplicity.
There is no moon, no single, silvered leaf.
The body is no body to be seen
But is an eye that studies its black lid.

                                    (*CP*, 71)

Such interior apprehension, for Ryder, occurred "only as the
world became a few lines and areas of soft hue, and the
moon shone watery and glamorous over the roof-lines." Only
then "did the waves of warm wet flow against his skin again,
to make the hour plastic" (p. 651). Thus in "Stars at Talla-
poosa" the speaker urges the listener to seek within the mind
the lines that "are straight and swift between the stars," for
"in yourself is like: / A sheaf of brilliant arrows flying
straight. . . ."

> Or, if not arrows, then the nimblest motions,
> Making recoveries of young nakedness
> And the lost vehemence the midnights hold.

In describing this interior movement as represented in
Ryder's art, Rosenfeld seems also to describe the essential
"motions" of *Harmonium*:

> And consequently, when he gave forth again in sombre
> and argent mass the objects which he had ached to seize
> and possess within himself, it was part of himself that he
> issued on to the canvas. It was the world, or whatever
> portion of the world it was that he, the child of transcen-
> dental New England, was able to perceive, that, arranged
> in conformity with his own personality, his own physical
> order, was deposited in opaque colour by his brush. The
> mystic hues of sundown were combined in accordance
> with the desires of the artist; the flying mists moved at the
> dictation of his spiritual rhythms; the old windmill in the
> citron-coloured moonshine, the white horse in his stall,
> gave again the beat of his blood, the tingle of his nerves.
> A world had come into a man, and been recorded through
> him. The consciousness of a man at a given moment of
> life in America; the thing real as any object created before

humanity or without it, had come to stand, rich and
sumptuous and dreamy, among the other natural things.[5]
(pp. 650-51)

The very phrasing in places reminds one of Stevens, as the
vision here mirrors the essential discovery of Crispin as he
meets the ocean and becomes "an introspective voyager." As
Rosenfeld says:

> Slowly, painfully, the minds began to turn towards self-ex-
> pression, towards acceptance of self, of the vague and men-
> acing American future. . . . Of that first, difficult, steep,
> contact with local conditions, contact with what for want
> of a closer term one calls "the soil," the art of Ryder is the
> breath, the suspiration. In its very essence, it is the sign of
> a reality that is only an edge, a fine rim, and threatens at
> any moment to waver and disappear into non-being. The
> pigment of these moony canvases vibrates. . . . (p. 651)

Ryder's work, like that of Stevens, balances on an edge be-
tween the soil and the shadow: "There is always the refrain
of a shadowy and unreal life, of solitary wandering, of vain
search, in Ryder's art. He is Jonah, cast into the ravening
black sea; calling in vain for help, in the jaws of the monster,
upon the faint legendary god shining afar. He is the Flying
Dutchman, a ghost peering over the rail of a phantom ship
that bears him over the wastes of ocean . . ." (p. 653). Like-
wise, Crispin sees the vestiges of the old mythology disap-
pearing, as Triton disappears into the waves of the sea. "And
then," Rosenfeld continues:

> like a pendant to all this unsubstantial life, the brush
> paints itself into the yearned-for world of the releasing, the
> resting, palpable moment. . . . He dreams himself in a
> world of soft colour, colour soft as the sky at evening over
> the Jersey bluffs, tenderer than the winds of a spring night
> in the deserted city streets. He is back again, in the land
> of his childhood, in a New England where it is always
> golden fall, always apple-scented afternoon, and where
> mountains stand sweet and soft and protecting, like huge
> mothers. (pp. 653-59)

This movement back toward what Stevens calls "the ro-
mantic" or the "moonlight," says Rosenfeld, is inevitable
in the American writer of the time: "For we of the new
world, do we not all of us strain away into some dim land?
How many of us are there who can perceive the wonder of
the world of humdrum familiar things? Our being steers
away always into some pearly and mournful distance scarcely
visible to the naked eye. . . . No American is happy
in a room, happy over a tiny hill, happy over what little he
has, contented to sit and watch three trees growing in the
yard before his house" (p. 654). Is that last sentence perhaps
the germ of sections five and six of the "Comedian"? And
does it perhaps bear some relation to Stevens' lines in "Of
the Surface of Things"?

> In my room, the world is beyond my understanding;
> But when I walk I see that it consists of three or four hills
>   and a cloud.

(CP, 57)

But now, says Rosenfeld, a later generation "has come to
occupy the scene" (p. 655), that is, the generation of Mars-
den Hartley, whose paintings are described by Rosenfeld in
terms that remind one of the "savage color" found by Cris-
pin amid the "Thunderstorms of Yucatan." Rosenfeld finds
in Hartley's work "the expression of a gigantic power, an in-
tense and mordant sensuality . . . passionate colour drowned
in black." Here are "daring and voluptuousness" that never
quite reach fulfillment, never "accomplish quite a work of
art." Hartley, he says, "is often-times likest a cadaver covered
with a profusion, a hill, of the most tropic and devilish
bloom. . . . Or, a cold and ferocious sensuality seeks to satisfy
itself in the still-lives, with their heavy stiff golden bananas,
their dark luscious figs, their erectile pears and enormous and
breast-like peaches. A sensuality become almost morbid
writhes in the terrible landscapes of the New Mexican period
. . ." (pp. 657-58).

So Crispin, as he stops "in the land of snakes," becomes
"intricate / In moody rucks, and difficult and strange / In

all desires, his destitution's mark." He seeks to find "coolness for his heat"

> in the fables he would write
> With his own quill, in its indigenous dew,
> Of an aesthetic tough, diverse, untamed,
> Incredible to prudes, the mint of dirt,
> Green barbarism turning paradigm.
>
> . . . .
>
> Making the most of savagery of palms,
> Of moonlight on the thick cadaverous bloom
> That yuccas breed, and of the panther's tread.

Turning next to the art of Kenneth Hayes Miller, Rosenfeld finds here too, though in a different way, "the American incompleteness" (p. 658). Miller's insecure grasp of "the immediate" suggests to Rosenfeld that Miller "had the transcendental strain in his blood, always felt the distance more beautiful than the near; and that, in order to overcome the yearning tendency left in him by puritan and pioneer forebears, had sacrificed much of his fantasy, his dream, in the hope of first achieving the immediate contact with life, and then, later, of re-uniting dream and reality" (pp. 559-60). Something of this sort seems to be happening in sections three and four of the "Journal of Crispin," where the search for the "relentless contact he desires" follows upon the nostalgia for the moonlight with which section three had opened:

> The book of moonlight is not written yet,
> Nor half begun, but, when it is, leave room
> For Crispin, fagot in the lunar fire,
> Who, in the hubbub of his pilgrimage
> Through sweating changes, never can forget
> That wakefulness, or meditating sleep,
> In which the sulky strophes willingly
> Bear up, in time, the somnolent, deep songs.
> Leave room, therefore, in that unwritten book

For the legendary moonlight that once burned
In Crispin's mind above a continent.

That is why Crispin must conceive his voyage as "an up
and down in these two elements," the sun of reality and the
moon of romance. As Rosenfeld goes on to say, "it is not
strange that one should find in the company of the modern
Americans certain painters who have achieved, or are upon
the point of achieving, the unification of their personalities,
and bringing the entire man, dream interpenetrated with
reality, and reality with dream, to the composition of their
works. There are amongst us workmen with feet planted
firmly upon the ground. There are, among others, John
Marin, Arthur Dove, Georgia O'Keeffe" (p. 663). And, one
must add, Wallace Stevens in the fourth section of Crispin's
"Journal." As with Marin, Stevens was "one of those whom
the life at 291 Fifth Avenue benefitted hugely," either di-
rectly or indirectly.

> The Puckishness has never left him [Marin]. But, beside
> the boy, there has come to be a very self-conscious and
> robust adult. The wash has become freer, deeper, more
> biting and powerful. Fused with the French delicacy, there
> has come to exist a granite American crudeness. . . . Na-
> ture is felt in her endlessness, her indifference, her vast
> melancholy fecundity. The conscious and the unconscious
> mind interplay in this expression. Flashes of red lightning,
> pure ecstatic invasions of the conscious field, tear through
> the subdued and reticent American colour of the wash.
> The deep blues and browns become strangely mystic. The
> realism turns very suddenly, inexplicably, into unrealistic,
> ghostly expressionistic art. (p. 664)

Such is the kind of art propounded in a long passage of
section four of the "Journal," which was excised in *Har-
monium*:

> Crispin delineates his progeny:
> A race of natives in a primitive land,
> But primitive because it is more true

> To its begetting than its patriarch,
> A race obedient to its origins
> And from the obstinate scrutiny of its land,
> And in its land's own wit and mood and mask,
> Evolving the conjectural resonance
> Of voice, the flying youthfulness of form,
> Of a spirit to be singer of the song
> That Crispin formulates but cannot sing.
> It comes to that. This late discoverer
> Discovers for himself what idler men
> And less ambitious sires have dawdled with.

And so, in a passage mostly retained in the final version, Crispin goes on to develop his theory that "the natives of the rain are rainy men," and "in their music showering sounds intone." Likewise, in an excised passage Stevens develops the same theory:

> Virgins on Volcan del Fuego wear
> That Volcan in their bosoms as they wear
> Its nibs upon their fingers. They adorn
> Their weavings with its irridescent threads.
> They shut its fury in each bangle-blaze.

Thus he comes to speak "Commingled souvenirs and prophecies," for he realizes clearly that these "fictive flourishes" are "Related in romance to backward flights." However he may try to escape the "dreamers buried in our sleep,"

> The apprentice knows these dreamers. If he dreams
> Their dreams, he does it in a gingerly way.
> All dreams are vexing. Let them be expunged.
> But let the rabbit run, the cock declaim.

Such is the oscillation between "reality" and "dream" that constitutes the central theme of Stevens' later poetry. It is from this point, at the end of section four of the "Journal of Crispin," that Stevens' major career proceeds.

Sections five and six were apparently composed during the summer of 1922, when, as Stevens related to Harriet Monroe, he revised the poem and gave it the final title, "The Comedian as the Letter C" (*L*, 229-30). Stevens' repeated explanation of the significance of the letter *c* as sound first appears in a letter of 1935.[6] The examples of the *c* sounds that Stevens cites come from sections five and six; but a frequent stress upon the sounds of *c* can also be heard in the original version, even in portions later excised. Thus one may assume that, consciously or unconsciously, the poem was in its early form set in "the key of C." But one should not, I think, attempt to find any symbolical or allegorical meaning in this use of sound; it is rather an organizing, unifying factor that helps, by sonic emphasis and coalition, to create the character of Crispin. As Stevens says, "You have to read the poem and hear all this whistling and mocking and stressing and, in a minor way, orchestrating, going on in the background. . . . The natural effect of the variety of sounds of the letter C is a comic effect" (*L*, 352).

The comic vision of Crispin's collapse into domesticity in the two added sections should not be taken as representing Stevens' view of his own probable future; rather, it is a way of discarding the mask of Crispin, as Ezra Pound said farewell to the nineties in the character of Hugh Selwyn Mauberley.[7] The placement of the "Comedian" in *Harmonium* supports this view. During the summer and fall of 1922, as his letters show, Stevens went through an agony of selection in order to make up the volume *Harmonium*, for which the manuscript was ready in November 1922 (*L*, 231-32). Stevens discarded dozens of his poems, some of them quite good. At the same time, his deployment of materials in *Harmonium* is, as usual, far from random. (Even in his periodical publications he was deeply concerned with the order of his poems, especially for "a good beginning and a good end.")[8] In his directions to Knopf (October 16, 1930) for the second edition of *Harmonium* he took particular care with the placement and order of the group of fourteen added poems: "The order of the poems in the original edition of Harmonium is satisfactory," he wrote. "In the new edition I should like to omit The Silver Plow Boy, on page 78, Exposition of the Contents of a [Cab], on page 98, and Architecture, on page 121." "The new material," he added, "is to be inserted after page 138 [that is, after "Nomad Exquisite"] in the following order." He then lists the order as it appears in the second edition and in his *Collected Poems*. Finally, he says, "After this new material the book is to be closed with the two poems in the original edition, entitled A Tea, on page 139, and To The Roaring Wind, on page 140" (*L*, 259-60).

Clearly, Stevens was not keeping to any chronological order of composition in making this arrangement: the first of the added poems dates from 1921, the next three from 1918, and the last from 1917, while the two poems that he chose for his "good end" in both editions date from 1915 and 1917. This neglect of chronology, this care for a significant arrangement of the poems, to suggest, apparently, a meaning that lies beyond the realm of biographical interpretation—all this holds too for the entire first edition of *Harmonium*, which likewise ignores chronology of composition, putting, for example, some seventy pages between "The Snow Man" and "Tea at the Palaz of Hoon," which were originally published side by side in *Poetry* (1921). Among the intervening poems we find "The Comedian as the Letter C," placed early in the volume, although it was then a very recent poem. What is the meaning of Stevens' original arrangement?

The poems in *Harmonium* seem to be placed to create an effect of oscillation, undulation, or contrast. Thus, whereas the book opens with "Earthy Anecdote," the next poem, "Invective against Swans," has the soul soaring off into the skies. Yet such transcendental poems are not frequent among the twenty poems chosen to precede the "Comedian." These are mainly poems of earth and sea, concretely grasped, with the Paltry Nude starting her voyage "on the first-found weed." "Domination of Black" brings fear in the cry of the peacocks, while the Snow Man, with his ruthless reduction of being, beholds "Nothing that is not there and the nothing that is."[9] If things rise toward the heavens they tend to rise only as high as "the red turban / Of the boatman" in "The

Load of Sugar-Cane," or the "flaming red" of "Hibiscus on the Sleeping Shores." And when a star is seen, it is urged in "Nuances of a Theme by Williams" to

> Shine alone, shine nakedly, shine like bronze,
> that reflects neither my face nor any inner part
> of my being, shine like fire, that mirrors nothing.
>
> (CP, 18)

Or, on the other hand, the star is seen mirrored in the sea in "Homunculus et La Belle Etoile," which immediately precedes the "Comedian": "Good light for drunkards, poets, widows, / And ladies soon to be married" (CP, 25), a light that also conducts "The movements of fishes," and finally, a good light too for those

> That know the ultimate Plato,
> Tranquillizing with this jewel
> The torments of confusion.
>
> (CP, 27)

The major poem among those preceding the "Comedian" is appropriately "Le Monocle de Mon Oncle," a poem that narrates these very torments of confusion and despair, as the middle-aged speaker feels his loss of erotic power:

> Our bloom is gone. We are the fruit thereof.
> Two golden gourds distended on our vines,
> Into the autumn weather, splashed with frost,
> Distorted by hale fatness, turned grotesque.
> We hang like warty squashes, streaked and rayed,
> The laughing sky will see the two of us
> Washed into rinds by rotting winter rains.
>
> (CP, 16)

Thus the thirty pages of poetry that precede the "Comedian" set the scene for the problem posed at the outset of that poem, where "The World Without Imagination" overwhelms the representative of traditional civilized rationality, just as the death of a loved one overwhelms "Another Weeping Woman":

> The magnificent cause of being,
> The imagination, the one reality
> In this imagined world
>
> Leaves you
> With him for whom no phantasy moves,
> And you are pierced by a death.
>
> (CP, 25)

Crispin's voyage explores the ways of recovering from the death of the imagination, by returning to fact in order to discover a new kind of "romantic" derived from a concrete grip on things as they are.[10] Sections five and six of the poem contemplate the possibility of failure: "So may the relation of each man be clipped." *May*, not *will*, or *must*. Let Crispin go: he is happy in his way. But the remaining seventy pages of poetry, including "Sunday Morning" and "Peter Quince at the Clavier" (both from 1915) tell of the imagination's constant struggle with mortality and motion, and of its frequent, though always temporary, victories. As Stevens told Williams in the famous letter of April 9, 1918, quoted in the prologue to Williams' *Kora in Hell*, the secret of recovery for Stevens lies in maintaining a constant point of view by which the imagination controls the undulations of being.[11] "The Place of the Solitaires" puts it well. A solitaire is an island bird, of Rodriquez or Jamaica, a precious stone, a diamond, or a solitary, retiring person: all of these meanings converge in the poem to create the motion of a mind that controls the motions of physical existence:

> Let the place of the solitaires
> Be a place of perpetual undulation.
>
> Whether it be in mid-sea
> On the dark, green water-wheel,
> Or on the beaches,
> There must be no cessation
> Of motion, or of the noise of motion,
> The renewal of noise
> And manifold continuation;

And, most, of the motion of thought
And its restless iteration,

In the place of the solitaires,
Which is to be a place of perpetual undulation.
(CP, 60)

This poem helps to explain why Stevens objects to the "casual character" of Williams' poems in *Al Que Quiere*, the volume published in December 1917 that provoked his letter.

My idea is that in order to carry a thing to the extreme necessity to convey it one has to stick to it; . . . Given a fixed point of view, realistic, imagistic or what you will, everything adjusts itself to that point of view; the process of adjustment is a world in flux, as it should be for a poet. But to fidget with points of view leads always to new beginnings and incessant new beginnings lead to sterility. . . . A single manner or mood thoroughly matured and exploited is that fresh thing. . . .[12]

All this, of course, represents a misunderstanding of Williams' variety of postures in *Al Que Quiere*. For Williams, the role of the poet as observer tends to be set in some very particular place or movement:

Well, mind, here we have
our little son beside us:
a little diversion before breakfast!

Come, we'll walk down the road
till the bacon will be frying.
("Promenade")

You sullen pig of a man
you force me into the mud
with your stinking ash-cart!
("Libertad! Igualidad! Fraternidad!")

At ten A.M. the young housewife
moves about in negligee behind

the wooden walls of her husband's house.
I pass solitary in my car.
　　　　("The Young Housewife")

In brilliant gas light
I turn the kitchen spigot
and watch the water plash
into the clean white sink.
　　　　("Good Night")

I have discovered that most of
the beauties of travel are due to
the strange hours we keep to see them. . . .
　　　　("January Morning")

Rather notice, mon cher,
that the moon is
tilted above
the point of the steeple
than that its color
is shell-pink.
　　　　("To a Solitary Disciple")

For Williams, the point of view is directed from the street
or the road or the sink or the ferryboat across the Hudson.
He works from a shifting *physical* point of view, a series of
camera angles, in order, as he says in the prologue to *Kora
in Hell*, "to draw a discriminating line between true and
false values":

> The true value is that peculiarity which gives an object a
> character by itself. The associational or sentimental value
> is the false. Its imposition is due to lack of imagination,
> to an easy lateral sliding. The attention has been held too
> rigid on the one plane instead of following a more flexible,
> jagged resort. It is to loosen the attention, my attention
> since I occupy part of the field, that I write these improvi-
> sations. Here I clash with Wallace Stevens.[13]

And indeed, though both poets use the "local" object, there is a divergence in their principles of creation. With Stevens, the solitaire, the point of view arises and moves within the center of the mind, as that "monstered moth" arises in "Hibiscus on the Sleeping Shores," or as in "Tea at the Palaz of Hoon":

> Out of my mind the golden ointment rained,
> And my ears made the blowing hymns they heard.
> I was myself the compass of that sea:
>
> I was the world in which I walked, and what I saw
> Or heard or felt came not but from myself;
> And there I found myself more truly and more strange.
>
> (CP, 65)

Or, with greater attention to the mingling of outer and inner worlds, we have the "Anecdote of Canna," where, whether in dream or in daylight, the mind clings to the contemplated object, so that the canna "fill the terrace of his capitol"—his head—sleeping or waking:

> Huge are the canna in the dreams of
> X, the mighty thought, the mighty man.
> They fill the terrace of his capitol.
>
> His thought sleeps not. Yet thought that wakes
> In sleep may never meet another thought
> Or thing. . . . Now day-break comes. . . .
>
> X promenades the dewy stones,
> Observes the canna with a clinging eye,
> Observes and then continues to observe.
>
> (CP, 55)

Only in this way, for Stevens, can a new "romantic" be discovered, where the inner and the outer worlds are fully realized in "a single manner or mood thoroughly matured."

But the undulations continue, the "ambiguous undulations" of "Sunday Morning," or the evenings that die, for Peter Quince, "in their green going, / A wave, interminably flowing," or in the "Thirteen Ways of Looking at a Black-

bird," observing and observing, or in this vision in one of the
"Six Significant Landscapes," where the imagination, despite
its reachings, is made to measure itself finally by the limita-
tions of mortality:

> I measure myself
> Against a tall tree.
> I find that I am much taller,
> For I reach right up to the sun,
> With my eye;
> And I reach to the shore of the sea
> With my ear.
> Nevertheless, I dislike
> The way the ants crawl
> In and out of my shadow.
>
> (CP, 74)

Undulations, oscillations, between dream and fact, inner
and outer, bleakness and splendor, extinction and vitality—
so the measures flow throughout the poems that follow the
"Comedian." Such supreme fictions as "Stars at Tallapoosa"
are in the latter half of *Harmonium* intermingled with the
warning of "The Jack-Rabbit," the meeting with Berserk,
the "sorry verities" of "The Weeping Burgher," the malady
of "Banal Sojourn," and the "human, heavy and heavy, /
Who does not care" of "The Wind Shifts." Yet the domi-
nant tone of the poems that follow the "Comedian" is not
one of defeat or resignation. Rather, it is a mode of constant
rebeginning, rededication, rebuilding, as in the poem "Archi-
tecture," which Stevens later discarded from the edition of
1931, thus removing a work that shows perhaps too easy an
optimism:

> Let us build the building of light.
> Push up the towers
> To the cock-tops.
> These are the pointings of our edifice,
> Which, like a gorgeous palm,
> Shall tuft the commonplace.

These are the window-sill
On which the quiet moonlight lies.

. . . .

Only the lusty and the plenteous
Shall walk
The bronze-filled plazas
And the nut-shell esplanades.

(OP, 17, 18)

The key poem of the last few pages of *Harmonium* is, how-
ever, "To the One of Fictive Music," a poem that shows
the mind's creative power with all its undulating complexity
—evasive, precarious, yet there, in the mind's center. This is
a poem for which a corrected typescript exists among the
papers preserved by Stevens' neighbor, and the precariousness
of the point of view here may be suggested by Stevens' many
attempts to find a proper title. At first he typed "To the
Fictive Virgin," a title that clearly, indeed, too clearly,
stresses the element of secular parody of traditional hymns to
another Virgin, which provide much of the imagery in the
poem. This title is crossed out, and penciled above and
around it are various suggestions: "Souvenir de la Muse
De la Belle Terre"; "De la Terre Belle et Simple"; "Souvenir
of the Muse of Earlier, Simpler Earth"; "Souvenir of the
Muse of Archaic Earth"; "Souvenir of the Archaic Muse";
"Souvenir of A Muse"; "Of Fictive Music"; "To the ["Fic-
tive" crossed out] One of Fictive Music." The poem is the
perfect offspring of the tendencies revealed in the "Journal
of Crispin," and still, in a muted way, conveyed in the first
four sections of the "Comedian." The poem celebrates the
fictive power by which the archaic earth of our physical
world (including our physical selves) is transmuted into the
"crystal" of the mind:

For so retentive of themselves are men
That music is intensest which proclaims
The near, the clear, and vaunts the clearest bloom,
And of all vigils musing the obscure,

That apprehends the most which sees and names,
As in your name, an image that is sure,
Among the arrant spices of the sun,
O bough and bush and scented vine, in whom
We give ourselves our likest issuance.

(CP, 88)

The security and firmness of the language here does not sug-
gest despair but rather an assurance that the cry at the close
of the poem will be answered by a renewal of creative power.
The "seignory" of that power within the mind is emphasized
in this poem's typescript version, where the "Unreal" is asked
to give back not "what once *you* gave" but "what once *we*
gave": "The imagination that we spurned and crave."
  So, in 1923, the "good end" of *Harmonium* presents a ris-
ing movement:

You dweller in the dark cabin,
Rise, since rising will not waken,
And hail, cry hail, cry hail.

(CP, 89)

Rising will not waken because dream and fact can be com-
mingled in the mind, waking or sleeping, as this whole poem,
"Hymn from a Watermelon Pavilion," is designed to dem-
onstrate, following immediately after "To the One of Fictive
Music." The cry of "hail" is answered three poems from the
end of *Harmonium* in the brilliant "Nomad Exquisite," in
which the motions of inner and outer worlds are perfectly
matched in an expression of Stevens' powerful capability for
physical response. The "Forms, flames, and the flakes of
flames" in this poem suggest "the reverberations in the
words" of Crispin's "first central hymns," as described in the
fourth section of the "Journal."
  After this the quiet, very brief poem "Tea" shows how
the imagination need not always live amid the solitary
splendors of Hoon, but can at times, especially in autumnal
times, be content with a civil room and a meet ceremony:

When the elephant's-ear in the park
Shrivelled in frost,
And the leaves on the paths
Ran like rats,
Your lamp-light fell
On shining pillows,
Of sea-shades and sky-shades,
Like umbrellas in Java.

(*CP*, 112-13)

Then the volume's final poem, "To the Roaring Wind,"
reaches out toward the future with the imagination still
seeking to speak the word that will express "the span / Of
force, the quintessential fact," as Crispin heard it in the
thunderstorms of Yucatan:

And while the torrent on the roof still droned
He felt the Andean breath. His mind was free
And more than free, elate, intent, profound
And studious of a self possessing him,
That was not in him in the crusty town
From which he sailed. Beyond him, westward, lay
The mountainous ridges, purple balustrades,
In which the thunder, lapsing in its clap,
Let down gigantic quavers of its voice,
For Crispin to vociferate again.[14]

The volume's final poem shows that the quest of Crispin
here continues, in another voice:

What syllable are you seeking,
Vocalissimus,
In the distances of sleep?
Speak it.

WALLACE STEVENS

FROM THE JOURNAL OF CRISPIN

I.

THE WORLD WITHOUT IMAGINATION.

Nota: Man is the intelligence of his soil,
The sovereign ghost. As such, the Socrates
Of snails, musician of pears, principium
And lex. Sed quaeritur: Is this same wig
Of things, this nincompated pedagogue,
[The sceptre of the unregenerate sea?]
Crispin at sea creates a touch of doubt.
An eye most apt in gelatines and jupes,
Berries of villages, a barber's eye,
This eye of land, of simple salad-beds,
Of honest quilts, the eye of Crispin, hangs
On porpoises, that hung on apricots,
And on silentious porpoises, whose snouts
Dibble in waves that are mustachios,
Inscrutable hair in an inscrutable world.

One eats one paté, even of salt, quotha.
It is not so much that one's mythology
[Is blotched by the sea. It was a boresome book,
From which one trilled orations of the west,
Based on the prints of Jupiter. Rostrum.]
A snug hibernal from this sea and salt,
This century of wind in a single puff.
What counts is the mythology of self.
That's blotched beyond unblotching. Crispin,
The lutanist of fleas, the knave, the thane,
The ribboned stick, the bellowing breeches, cloak

Of China, cap of Spain, imperative haw
Of hum, inquisitorial botanist,
And general lexicographer of mute
And maidenly greenhorns, now beholds himself,
A skinny sailor peering in sea-glass.*
What word split up in clickering syllables
And storming under multitudinous tones
Is name for this short-shanks in all this brunt?
Crispin is washed away by magnitude.
The whole of life that still remains in him
Dwindles to one sound strumming in his ear,
Ubiquitous concussion, slap and sigh,
Polyphony beyond his baton's thrust.

Can Crispin stem verboseness in the sea,
The old age of a watery realist,
Triton, dissolved in shifting diaphanes
Of blue and green? A wordy, watery age
That whispers to the sun's compassion, makes
A convocation, nightly, of the sea-stars,
And on the clopping foot-ways of the moon
Lies grovelling. Triton incomplicate with that
Which made him Triton, nothing left of him,
Except in faint, memorial gesturings,
That are like arms and shoulders in the waves,
Here, something in the rise and fall of wind,
That seems hallucinating horn, and here,
[And everywhere upon the deep, in caves,
And down the long sea-eddies, his despair,]
That is a voice, both of remembering
And of forgetfulness, in alternate strain.

* *sea-glass.* The original typescript here reads "sea-grass," but on the
carbon copy, where Stevens has made corrections in his own hand,
"grass" is corrected to "glass." This is almost certainly not a revision
but a correction of a typist's error, as are nearly all the changes made
by Stevens on the carbon. The typist seems to have worked from dicta-
tion, for some of the errors suggest mishearing: "And I" for "An eye";
"divocation" for "divagation." On the original typescript these changes
are made with the typewriter.

Just so an ancient Crispin is dissolved.
The valet in the tempest is annulled.
Bordeaux to Yucatan, Havana next,
And then to Carolina. Simple jaunt.
Yet Crispin, mere minuscule in the gales,
Appoints his manner to the turbulence.
The salt hangs on his spirit like a frost,
The dead brine melts within him like a dew
Of winter, until nothing of himself
Remains, except some starker, barer self
In a starker, barer world, in which the sun
Is not the sun because it never shines
With bland complaisance on pale parasols,
Beetles, in chapels, on the chaste bouquets.
Against the shepherds' pipes a trumpet brays
Celestial sneering boisterously. Crispin
Becomes an introspective voyager.

Here is the veritable ding an sich, at last.
Crispin confronting it. A vocable thing,
But with a voice belched out of hoary darks
Noway resembling his. A visible thing,
And excepting negligible Triton, free
From the inescapable shadow of himself,
That lies elsewhere around him. Severance
Is clear. The last distortion of romance
Deserts the insatiable egotist. The sea
Severs not only lands but also selves.
Here is no help before reality.
Crispin beholds and Crispin is made new.
The imagination, here, no more evades,
In poems of plums, the strict austerity
Of one vast, subjugating, final tone.
The drenching of stale lives no more descends.
What is this gaudy, gusty panoply?
Out of what swift destruction does it spring?
It is caparison of wind and cloud
And something given to make whole among
The ruses that are shattered by the large.

II.

CONCERNING THE THUNDERSTORMS OF YUCATAN.

[They say they still scratch sonnets in the south,*
The bards of Capricorn. Medicaments
Against the weather. Useful laxatives.
Petrarch is the academy of youth]
In Yucatan. The Maya sonneteers
Of the Caribbean amphitheatre,
In spite of hawk and falcon, green toucan,
And jay, still to the bulbul make their plea,**
As if raspberry tanagers in palms,
High up in orange air, were barbarous.

But Crispin is too destitute to find
[In any book the succor that he needs.
He is not padre in a curricle,***
Thumbing opuscules, brooding on their musk.]
He is a man made vivid by the sea,
A man come out of luminous traversing,
Much trumpeted, made desperately clear,
Fresh from discoveries of tidal skies,
To whom oracular rockings give no rest.
Into a savage color he goes on.

How greatly has he grown in his demesne,
This auditor of insects! He that saw

* *sonnets.* This scorn for sonnets and sonneteers recurs in two later
passages that Stevens excised. Such explicit rejection of bookish models
is carried out in other excised passages of sections three and four, as in
the allusions to Virgil, Ariosto, and Camoëns. Stevens himself (like
Ezra Pound) was addicted to the writing of sonnets in his college years,
and he wrote at least one sonnet to Elsie as late as 1909. See *SP*, 29-35,
210.

** *bulbul.* In some ways the original reading seems better than the
revision "night-bird," since "bulbul" is an exotic, Persian word that
smacks of nineteenth-century Orientalism. Tennyson consecrated the
word in "Recollections of the Arabian Nights."

*** *curricle.* This must be an error for "cubicle," as the context indi-
cates. Note the heavy stress here on the sounds of the letter *c*.

The stride of vanishing autumn in a park
By way of decorous melancholy; he
That wrote his couplet yearly to the spring,
As dissertation of profound delight,
Stopping, on voyage, in the land of snakes,
Finds his vicissitudes have much enlarged
His apprehension, made him intricate
In moody rucks, and difficult and strange
In all desires, his destitution's mark.
[Qua interludo: Crispin, if he could,
Would chant assuaging Virgil and recite
In the oratory of his breast, the rhymes
That drop down Ariosto's benison.]
And be in this as other freemen are,
Sonorous nutshells. This he cannot do.*
His violence is for aggrandizement
And not for stupor, such as music makes
For sleepers halfway waking. He perceives
That coolness for his heat comes suddenly,
And only, in the fables he would write
With his own quill, in its indigenous dew,
Of an aesthetic tough, diverse, untamed,
Incredible to prudes, the mint of dirt,
Green barbarism turning paradigm.
Crispin foresees a curious promenade
Or, nobler, senses elemental fate,
And elemental potencies and pangs,
And beautiful barenesses, as yet unseen.
[These are the snowy fables he would write,]
Making the most of savagery of palms,
Of moonlight on the thick, cadaverous bloom
That yuccas breed, and of the panther's tread.

* *This he cannot do.* The revision here drastically changes the mean-
ing and seems to create an inconsistency: "He was in this as other free-
men are, / Sonorous nutshells rattling inwardly." But the point of the
original is that Crispin here has undergone a change and can no longer
find comfort in traditional things. The word "freemen" seems to be
causing difficulty here.

[An artful, most affectionate emigrant,
From Cytherea and its learned doves,
Or else nearby, become a loyal scribe.]
The fabulous and its intrinsic verse
Come like two spirits parleying, adorned
In radiance from the Atlantic coign,
For Crispin and his quill to catechize.
But they come parleying of such an earth,
So thick with sides and jagged lops of green,
So intertwined with serpent-kin encoiled
Among the purple tufts, the scarlet crowns,
Scenting the jungle in their refuges,
So streaked with yellow, blue and green and red
In beak and bud and fruity gobbet-skins,
That earth is like a jostling festival
Of seeds grown fat, too juicily opulent,
Expanding in the gold's maternal warmth.

So much for that. [For one compelled to nose
Through much locution for the savory sense,
Crispin is tireless at the task. He hears]
A new reality in parrot-sqwawks.*
But let that pass, [since Crispin aims at more,
An umbelliferous fact.] Now, as this droll
Discoverer walks round the harbor streets
Inspecting the cabildo, the façade
Of the cathedral, making notes, he hears
A rumbling, west of Mexico, it seems,
Approaching like a gasconade of drums.
The white cabildo darkens, the façade,
As sullen as the sky, is swallowed up
In swift, successive shadows, dolefully.
The rumbling broadens as it falls. The wind
Tempestuous clarion, with heavy cry,
Comes bluntly thundering, more terrible
Than the revenge of music on bassoons.
Gesticulating lightning, mystical,

* *parrot-sqwawks.* Probably the typist's error.

Makes pallid flitter. Crispin, here, takes flight.
An annotator has his scruples, too.
He kneels in the cathedral with the rest,
This connoisseur of elemental fate,
Aware of exquisite thought. The storm is one
Of many proclamations of the kind,
Proclaiming something harsher than he learned
From hearing signboards whimper in cold nights
Or seeing the midsummer artifice
Of heat upon his pane. This is the span
Of force, the umbelliferous fact, the note
Of Vulcan, that a valet seeks to own,
The thing that sanctions his most eloquent phrase.

And while the torrent on the roof still drones
[Crispin arraigns the Mexican sonneteers,]
Because his soul feels the Andean breath.
[Can fourteen laboring mules, like theirs,
In spite of gorgeous leathers, gurgling bells,
Convey his being through the land? A more condign
Contraption must appear. Crispin is free,]
And more than free, elate, intent, profound
And studious of a self possessing him,
That was not in him in the crusty town,
From which he sailed. Beyond him, westward, lie
The mountainous ridges, purple balustrades,
In which the thunder lapsing in its clap,
Lets down gigantic quavers of its voice,
For Crispin to vociferate again.

III.

APPROACHING CAROLINA.

The book of moonlight is not written yet,
Nor half begun, but, when it is, leave room
For Crispin, fagot in the lunar fire,
Who, in the hubbub of his pilgrimage
Through sweating changes, never can forget

That wakefulness, or meditating sleep,
In which the sulky strophes willingly
Bear up, in time, the somnolent, deep songs.
Leave room, therefore, in that unwritten book
For the legendary moonlight that once burned
In Crispin's mind above a continent.
America was always north to him,
A northern west or western north, but north,
And thereby polar, polar-purple, chilled
And lank, rising and slumping from a sea
Of hardy foam, receding flatly, spread
In endless ledges, glittering, submerged
And cold in a boreal mistiness of the moon.
The spring came there in clinking pannicles
Of half-dissolving frost, the summer came,
If ever, whisked and wet, not ripening
Before the winter's vacancy returned.
The myrtle, if the myrtle ever bloomed,
Was like a glacial pink upon the air,
The green palmettoes in crepuscular ice
Clipped frigidly blue-black meridians,
Morose chiaroscuro, gauntly drawn.
[A feverish conception that derived
From early writs and marginal heraldry.

The poet, seeking the true poem, seeks,
As Crispin seeks, the simplifying fact,
The common truth. Crispin, however, sees]
How many poems he denies himself
In his observant progress, lesser things
Than the relentless contact he desires,
How many sea-masks he ignores, what sounds
He closes from his tempering ear, what thoughts,
Like jades affecting the sequestered bride,
He banishes, what descants he foregoes.
Perhaps the Arctic moonlight really gave
The liaison, the blissful liaison,
Between himself and his environment,
Which was, and is, chief motive, first delight,

For him, and not for him alone. It seemed
Illusive, faint, more mist than moon, perverse,
Wrong as a divagation to Pekin,
[One more frustration, beautiful, perhaps,
To beauty's exorcist, who postulates]
The vulgar as his theme, his hymn and flight,
A passionately niggling nightingale.
Moonlight is an evasion, or, if not,
A minor meeting, facile, delicate,
[Chanson evoking vague, inaudible words.
Crispin is avid for the strenuous strokes
That clang from a directer touch, the clear
Vibration rising from a daylight bell,
Minutely traceable to the latest reach.
Imagination soon exhausts itself
In artifice too tenuous to sustain
The vaporous moth upon its fickle wings.]
Crispin conceives his Odyssey to be
An up and down in these two elements,
A fluctuating between sun and moon,
A sally into gold and scarlet forms,
As on this voyage, out of goblinry,
And then retirement like a sinking down
[To sleep, among its violet feints and rest]
And turning back to the indulgences
That in the moonlight have their habitude.
But let these backward lapses, if they will,
Grind their seductions on him, Crispin knows
It is a flourishing tropic he requires
For his refreshment, an abundant zone,
Prickly and obdurate, dense, harmonious
Yet with a harmony not rarefied
Nor fined for the inhibited instruments
Of over-civil stops. And thus he tossed*

* *tossed.* The use of the past tense in this five-line passage (note
"saw" at the close) is unusual in this version. It serves to mark a
retrospective pause amid these tossings, before the hero, in the next
passage, goes forward boldly on his quest for the "fecund minimum."

Between a Carolina of old time,
A little juvenile, an ancient whim,
And the visible, circumspect presentment drawn
From what he saw across his vessel's prow.

He comes. The poetic hero without palms
Or jugglery, without regalia.
And as he comes he sees that it is spring,
A time abhorrent to the nihilist
Or searcher for the fecund minimum.
The moonlight fiction vanishes and spring,
Although contending featly in its veils,
Irised in dew and early fragrancies
Is gemmy marionnette* to him that seeks
A sinewy nakedness. A river bears
The vessel inward. Crispin tilts his nose
To inhale the rancid rosin, burly smells
Of dampened lumber, emanations blown
From warehouse doors, the gustiness of ropes,
Decays of sacks, and all the arrant stinks
That help him round his rude aesthetic out.
He savors rankness like a sensualist.
He notes the marshy ground around the dock,
The crawling railroad spur, the rotten fence,
[That makes enclosure, a periphery
Of bales, machines and tools and tanks and men,
Directing whistles, puffing engines, cranes,
Provocative paraphernalia to his mind.
A short way off the city starts to climb,
At first in alleys which the lilacs line,
Abruptly, then, to the cobbled merchant streets,
The shops of chandlers, tailors, bakers, cooks,
The Coca Cola-bars, the barber-poles,
The Strand and Harold Lloyd, the lawyers' row,
The Citizens' Bank, two tea rooms, and a church.
Crispin is happy in this metropole.

* *marionette.* Stevens' spelling, or his typist's.

If the lilacs give the alleys a young air
Of sentiment, the alleys in exchange
Make gifts of no less worthy ironies.
If poems are transmutations of plain shops,
By aid of starlight, distance, wind, war, death,
Are not these doldrums poems in themselves,*
These trophies of wind and war? At just what point
Do barber-poles become burlesque or cease
To be? Are bakers what the poets will,
Supernal artisans or muffin men,
Or do they have, on poets' minds, more influence
Than poets know? Are they one moment flour,
Another pearl? The Citizens' Bank becomes
Palladian and then the Citizens' Bank
Again. The flimsiest tea room fluctuates
Through crystal changes. Even Harold Lloyd
Proposes antic Harlequin. The bars infect
The sensitive. Crispin revitalized
Makes these researches faithfully, a wide]
Curriculum for the marvelous sophomore.
They purify. They make him see how much
Of what he sees he never sees at all.
He grips more closely the essential prose
As being, in a world so falsified,
The one integrity for him, the one
Discovery still possible to make,
To which all poems are incident, unless
That prose should wear a poem's guise at last.

IV.

THE IDEA OF A COLONY.

Nota: His soil is man's intelligence.

* *doldrums.* The carbon copy shows that Stevens first wrote "spoils
of starlight" here: "Are not these spoils of starlight poems in them-
selves"—a hypermetric line that nevertheless seems to make better
sense.

That's better. That's worth crossing seas to find.
Crispin in one laconic phrase lays bare
His cloudy drift and plans a colony.
Exit the mental moonlight, exit lex,
Rex and principium, exit the whole
Shebang. Exeunt omnes. Here is prose
More exquisite than any tumbling verse,
A still new continent in which to dwell.
What was the purpose of his pilgrimage,
Whatever shape it took in Crispin's mind,
If not, when all is said, to drive away
The shadow of his fellows from the skies,
And, from their stale intelligence released,
To make a new intelligence prevail.
[Hence his despite of Mexican sonneteers,
Evoking lauras in the thunderstorms.]
Hence the reverberations in the words
Of his first central hymns.* [Hence his intent
Analysis of barber-poles and shops,]
Invaluable trivia, tests of the strength,
Of his aesthetic, his philosophy,
The more invidious, the more desired.
The florist asking aid from cabbages,
The rich man going bare, the paladin
Afraid, the blind man as astronomer,
The appointed power unwielded from disdain.

His western voyage ends and it begins.
The torment of fastidious thought abates,
Another, still more bellicose, comes on.
[Crispin delineates his progeny:
A race of natives in a primitive land,
But primitive because it is more true
To its begetting than its patriarch,
A race obedient to its origins

* *his first central hymns.* Note that in the original version these hymns are not "the celebrants / Of rankest trivia"; they seem instead to be distinguished from the experiments with "trivia."

And from the obstinate scrutiny of its land,
And in its land's own wit and mood and mask,
Evolving the conjectural resonance
Of voice, the flying youthfulness of form,
Of a spirit to be singer of the song
That Crispin formulates but cannot sing.
It comes to that. This late discoverer
Discovers for himself what idler men
And less ambitious sires have dawdled with.]
He, therefore, writes his prolegomena
And, being full of the caprice, inscribes
Commingled souvenirs and prophecies.
He makes a singular collation. Thus:
The natives of the rain are rainy men.
Although they paint effulgent, azure lakes,
And April hillsides wooded white and pink,
Their azure has a cloudy edge, their white
And pink, the water bright that dogwood bears.
And in their music showering sounds intone.
[This is as certain as their cherry-ripe
Pips in the fruit-men in the month of May.
Virgins on Volcan del Fuego wear
That Volcan in their bosoms as they wear
Its nibs upon their fingers. They adorn
Their weavings with its irridescent threads.*
They shut its fury in each bangle-blaze.]
On what strange froth does the gross Indian dote
What Eden sapling gum, what honeyed gore,
What pulpy dram distilled of innocence,
That streaking gold should speak in him
Or bask within his images and words?
If these rude instances impeach themselves
By force of rudeness, [let the burgher say
If he is burgher by his will. Burgher,
He is, by will, but not his own. He dwells
A part of wilful dwellings that impose

---

* *irridescent.* Stevens' spelling, or his typist's.

Alike his morning and his evening prayer.
His town exhales its mother breath for him
And this he breathes, a candid bellows-boy,
According to canon.] Let the principle
Be plain. For application Crispin strives,
Abhorring Turk as Esquimau, the lute
As the marimba, the magnolia as rose.

Upon these premises Crispin propounds
And propagates. His colony extends
[From the big-rimmed snow-star over Canada,]*
To the dusk of a whistling south below the south,
A comprehensive island hemisphere.
[And here he plants his colonists.] The man
In Mississippi, waking among pines,
Shall be pine-spokesman. The responsive man,
Planting his pristine cores in Florida,
Shall prick thereof, not on the psaltery,
But on the banjo's categorical gut,
Tuck tuck, while the flamingos flap his bays.
Sepulchral señors, bibbing pale mescal,
Oblivious to the Aztec almanacs,
Shall make the intricate Sierra scan
[In polysyllabled vernacular.]
The dark Brazilian in his red café,
Musing immaculate, pampean dits,
Shall scrawl a vigilant anthology,
[Not based on Camoëns, but flushed and full,
For surfeit in his leaner, lusting years,
For something to make answer when he calls]
And be to him his lucent paramour.
These are the broadest instances. Crispin,
Progenitor of such extensive scope,
Is not indifferent to smart detail.
The melon shall have apposite ritual,

* *From the big-rimmed snow-star over Canada.* It seems a pity that
Stevens removed this line, which lends greater force to the line, "A
comprehensive island hemisphere."

Performed in verd apparel, and the peach,
When its black branches germinate, belle day,
Shall have an incantation, and again,
When piled on salvers its aroma steeps
The summer, it shall have a sacrament
And celebration. Shrewd novitiates
Shall be the clerks of our experience.

These bland excursions into time to come,
Related in romance to backward flights,
However prodigal, however proud,
Contain in their afflatus the reproach
That first drove Crispin to his wandering.
He could not be content with counterfeit,
With masquerade of thought, with hapless words
That must belie the racking masquerade,
With fictive flourishes that preordained
His passions' permit, hang of coat, degree
Of buttons, measure of his salt. Such trash
Might help the blind, not him, serenely sly.
It irked beyond his patience. Hence it was,
Preferring text to gloss, he humbly served
Grotesque apprenticeship to chance event,
A clown, perhaps, but an aspiring clown.
There is a monotonous babbling in our dreams
That makes them our dependent heirs, the heirs
Of dreamers buried in our sleep, and not
The oncoming fantasies of better birth.
The apprentice knows these dreamers. If he dreams
Their dreams, he does it in a gingerly way.
All dreams are vexing. Let them be expunged.
But let the rabbit run, the cock declaim.
[His colony may not arrive. The site
Exists. So much is sure. And what is sure
In our abundance is his seignory.
His journal, at the best, concerns himself,
Nudging and noting, wary to divulge
Without digression, so that when he comes

To search himself, in the familiar glass
To which the lordliest traveler returns,
Crispin may take the tableau cheerfully.]
Trinket pasticcio, flaunting skyey sheets,
With Crispin as the tiptoe cozener?
No, no: veracious page on page, exact.
[As Crispin in his attic shapes the book
That will contain him, he requires this end:
The book shall discourse of himself alone,
Of what he was, and why, and of his place,
And of its fitful pomp and parentage.
Thereafter he may stalk in other spheres.]

Wallace Stevens

PETER A. BRAZEAU

"A COLLECT OF PHILOSOPHY": THE DIFFICULTY OF FINDING WHAT WOULD SUFFICE

ALTHOUGH MOST OF WALLACE STEVENS' WORK SUR-
vives only in final form, "A Collect of Philosophy," his 1951
University of Chicago lecture on the poetry of philosophy,
exists both in its complete form, published in *Opus Post-
humous*, and as a work in progress. As Stevens was finishing
this essay in the fall of 1951, he received a timely query about
his manuscripts from Yale's Norman Pearson and agreed to
send the work in hand.[1] The result was nothing less than a
record of the essay's evolution from original manuscript to
final typescript. The following passages from the three manu-
script drafts of the third section, published here for the first
time, are the major variations that distinguish the work in
process from the final version. They offer a rare chance to
look over Stevens' shoulder, as it were, and observe him
working through the most difficult phase of this manuscript,
finding what would suffice to bring the essay to a satisfactory
close. A few comments will serve to suggest how such a view
enriches our understanding not only of the conclusion but
also of the essay as a whole.

Stevens began the lecture after preliminary readings and
correspondence with philosopher-acquaintances in the late
summer of 1951. The correspondence helps to explain why,
as the manuscript shows, Stevens had far less difficulty in
bringing the first two sections of this three-part essay to final
form. In these sections, in which he defines the poetry of
philosophy by negation and example, Stevens was in such
control of his ideas and their development at the outset that
only a single draft was necessary.[2] In part, this assurance was

the result of expanding on ideas already thought through in the letters and of following the sequence of ideas as set out in these letters.[3] Thus, composing the first two-thirds of the lecture was primarily an act of the mind expressing what it already knew it wanted to say.

Composition of the final section, however, became a different, more dramatic process, an act of the mind only gradually finding what would suffice. To read the first draft in the light of the final version is to see just how blurry Stevens' view actually was, however clear he thought it was, at the time he began, "Let us see, now, what deductions can be made from all this material" (OP, 196). At the very least, this original draft offers some classic Stevens observations— for example, his remarks on the changing imagination, the days as seasons, the automatism of the creative act—which were eliminated as he discovered his focus in the second version. More to the point of the essay's development, however, this first draft reveals that Stevens initially completed his conclusion without gaining a view of what later became the conclusion's central point: "my chief deduction: that poetry is supreme over philosophy . . ." (L, 729). Indeed, in the momentum of his argument on the inherent poetry of philosophy, he ended on a very different note. Anyone who had heard his Mount Holyoke lecture, "The Figure of the Youth as Virile Poet" (1943), in which he restricted the philosopher to "the gaunt world of the reason" and reserved to the poet the "radiant and productive atmosphere" of the imagination (NA, 58), would have been surprised to hear Stevens conclude here that "the delicacy and power of the philosopher's mind, the freedom of his imagination and the extraordinary scope of his sensibility" would make it "impossible to say whether he [the perfected poet] would emerge from the philosophers or from among the poets themselves."

In fact, no one was more surprised by this first attempt than Stevens himself, once he gained some distance from it. The result was the radically revised second draft, substantially the Opus Posthumous text. To read this draft in the light of its predecessor is to understand why, after completing this stage of the essay, he remarked to Barbara Church on October 2, 1951, "I was quite excited about it when I finished it" (L, 729). This draft has the character of a breakthrough. Stevens recognized the central point of his material—"the question of supremacy as between philosophy and poetry" (OP, 200)—enabling him to give it much greater focus. In his Mount Holyoke lecture seven years earlier, Stevens had been an extreme apologist in answering this question. Here he was far more benign, admitting that the philosopher was a creature of imagination, as well as the poet. Nevertheless, there is in the finale of this draft more than a little of the old-style apologist, which was later excised. While Stevens admits that philosophers' "ideas are often triumphs of the imagination" (OP, 200), he climaxes the passage with a view of the imagination in which poetry is triumphant, as he presents imagination as a resplendent peacock in a procession. In this gorgeous ceremony, which is quintessential Stevens, the imagination is presented exclusively on the poet's terms (defined earlier in the essay). The imagination is brought forth by the "poet's brilliant excess in accomplishment" (OP, 185). If Stevens can no longer exclude philosophers from this radiant region of the imagination, the celebration he concocts makes clear who rules there. Given the flush of the rhetoric, it is not surprising that Stevens was exhilarated when he finished this draft.

As the rhetoric cooled, however, so did Stevens' confidence in the results. In the letter to Mrs. Church telling of his initial excitement, he confided his current dismay with the lecture: "When I go back to it, it seems slight; and my chief deduction: that poetry is supreme over philosophy because we owe the idea of God to poetry and not to philosophy doesn't seem particularly to matter. Nothing seems particularly to matter nowadays" (L, 729). Thinking he had done all he could, Stevens, as the Yale material indicates, had the manuscript typed as his final version. He was clearly disheartened by his efforts. To read the manuscript in progress, however, is to see that his dissatisfaction was centered not on the breakthrough itself but on his inability to find the climax that would embody this chief deduction, since he subsequently revised only the finale.

Within a week, the final solution came—in the mail. The current issue of *Les Nouvelles Littéraires*, a paper he had subscribed to only a few months earlier, arrived with André George's note on the writings of physicist Max Planck. Though his essay was already typed, Stevens was stimulated to write a new ending, replacing the figure of the peacock with that of Planck. The final manuscript excerpt is a passage from his summary of George's note that was pared from the final remarks. To see his conclusion on Planck in the light of his earlier endings is to understand why Stevens had found what he needed. Through Planck he arrived at his ultimate deduction about the superiority of poetry: "my best point: the disclosure of modern man as one to be measured . . . by the idea of the greatness of poetry" (L, 734-35). This did not negate the breakthrough he had made in his second draft, that poetry is superior to philosophy because it is responsible for the idea of God. Rather, this ending extends it. Stevens had finally found a way to make poetry "matter nowadays," by seeing the greatness of poetry in modern man's "willingness to believe beyond belief" (OP, 202). It was the very modernity of the figure of Planck that made him so attractive, for now Stevens felt he was doing what he had found so precious in Jean Paulhan: he was "a man looking at the present" (OP, 195). The superiority of poetry is embodied not merely in a rhetorical space, but in the modern world. He had found what would suffice.

WALLACE STEVENS

THREE MANUSCRIPT ENDINGS FOR "A COLLECT OF PHILOSOPHY"

*Let us see, now, what deductions can be made from all this material.**

First Manuscript Version

A GOOD DEAL OF IT IS NO LONGER PART OF OUR THOUGHT. Nowadays, the soul and Leibniz' swarms of spirits and Schopenhauer's manifestations of will seem to be nonsense. These things may have perpetuated themselves in other guises, as, for example, the soul, which is an everlasting concept and lives to-day as the self, in spite of the niggling as to what the self consists of or is. There is, then, the same rise and fall of images in philosophy that there is in poetry. In the genealogy of representation there is the same eminent antiquity that there is in any other genealogy, at one end of the line, and the same restless, impatient, undisciplined fidgetting, at the other end. The conceptions of ancient thought may have passed out of belief. But we recognize them as forefathers and somewhat incredible kin. Immobile, they move within us. At one moment, we are in the presence of Socrates, in the chamber in which he was shortly to die and we listen to him as he expounds his ideas concerning immortality. At

* The italicized sentence is from the final version of the text in *Opus Posthumous*. It represents the point in the manuscript after which the original draft passage occurred. The italicized sentences at the beginnings of the second and third versions are from the final text. The final italicized sentence represents the point at which the third draft passage picks up with the final version of the text. —Peter A. Brazeau

another, we are looking over the shoulder of Jean Paulhan, in Paris, as he writes a letter in which he speaks of

"la confiance que le poète fait naturellement—et nous invite à faire—au monde."

A beautiful phrase, that: confiance au monde; and one that might well be the device of any poet today. It is obvious that there is a life and death of philosophy just as there is a life and death of poetry and that, as it lives, it changes direction, depth, color, character with the same certainty with which it lives. One is, therefore, tempted to ask, particularly at a moment when one is able to look backward, as the present moment, and has a view, both distant and near, of the course of its life, whether this is not merely a panorama in which one is able to observe the operation of the principle that the imagination never delights twice in the same thing. This is a fundamental principle in poetry. The principle may be more broadly stated, as follows: the imagination never returns or the imagination delights less in the same thing.

I am not about to say that the panorama at which we are looking is a panorama of the imagination. It is enough to say that it is one that looks like a panorama of the imagination. Possibly any view of an abandoned world, in the chiaroscuro of its faded geography, looks like a panorama of the imagination. There are differences, which are fundamental. But there are resemblances which are no less fundamental. The poet, in moments of exceptional concentration sometimes experiences an automatism in which the poem writes itself. It seems as if the imagination realized its intention, however obscure its intention may have been, with an instantaneous directness. The obscurity of the intentions of the imagination, (the source of poetic urgings,), and the accomplishing of the imagination's will by miraculous shortenings of mental process cannot be very different, in poets, from the obscurity of the intentions of the reason, (if that really is the source of philosophic urgings), and the accomplishing of the reason's will by miraculous accelerations, in philosophers. Surely one does not aim at insight by way of the reason. It will be observed that in the very act of contrasting the imagination of the poet with the reason of the poet I have tried not so much to state a distinction as to approach an identity. I am not trying to suggest that in the hermitage of the mind these two are one.

They are very close together. It is from the closeness that it comes about that it is often the case that the concepts of philosophy are poetic and, for that matter, that the concepts of poetry are philosophic. I said a moment ago that the imagination never delights twice in the same thing. One reason for this is that once the imagination has realized itself, or realized its intention, in a particular, it is not possible for it to do the same thing again in the same particular. The obscurity, once overcome, is overcome forever. One often wonders about the ultimate consequence of this law. We have seen that one of the consequences is that panorama of things that we have forsaken, which you will remember. What will be the ultimate consequence of this law to the idea of god, if the idea of god is a poetic idea, or even, indifferently, if it is a philosophic idea? Whatever its fate as a poetic or philosophic idea, it remains a natural idea with the immense support of religion beneath it. I assume that it is not necessary to define a natural idea, in spite of the fact that, if it happened to be an idea that would occur to an aboriginal, he might, after all, turn out to be a poet or a philosopher or both. One of the consequences of this law is that the themes of philosophy, like the themes of poetry, are not constant. It seems strange to apply a principle of the imagination to philosophy and yet this is a natural incident in any bringing of the two together. The ungeheueres à priori of Husserl may have some relevance to this. It seems all the more likely, under the influence of the feeling one so often has that philosophers often project their ends before they reach them. Everything proves what we want to prove under the beckonings of à priori. What difference is there between the imagination realizing its intention and the reason finding a reason for what is irrational? These things deserve saying because the mind is not the same thing as the text-books of the mind. People used to say that the year consisted of four seasons. Then they began to notice that there was a season between winter and spring and a season after summer, when summer had gone and before autumn had come, and, little by little, they reached a point where there was only one season, which was the year, or three hundred and sixty-five seasons, as they chose. One either amalgamates distinctions or, for true exactness, spreads them out. The more one spreads them out, the more one amalgamates them. Poetry and philosophy are not the same thing. There are many differences between them. When these differences become innumerable, it will be impossible to tell them apart. The whole scheme of the world as will occured [sic] to Schopenhauer in an instant, from the parts of his body to the parts of his soul. The time he spent afterward in the explication of that instant is another matter. The idea of the Hegelian state, one of the masterpieces of idealism, came into Hegel's mind effortlessly and as a whole and as a line of poetry comes into the mind of a poet.

Let me say again that though they are close together, so close that we often lose a sense of difference, so close that the conceptions of the philosopher often appear to be indistinguishable from the conceptions of the poet, yet they are not one. If they were one, if Plato, the poet, had returned generation after generation, with an ever-enlarging knowledge of life and death, with an imagination constantly keeping-up and constantly aware and with a reason more and more sensitive to the expeditings that come to it, we should not have heard of such a gaucherie as the *Monadology* nor have regarded a trouvaille like the *World As Will* as a serious work. If one is to be a poet one has to have in mind an image of the perfected poet, which I have just attempted to give and one has to be able to look back on so many works of so many philosophers and regret that, in addition to being philosophers, they were not also poets or, as I ought to say, better poets. I know that there are many kinds of poetry and that there are many people, very many, who would find the image that I have presented a disagreeable one. To be clear, I do not think that philosophy and poetry are convertible terms. But I do think that the delicacy and power of the philosopher's mind, the freedom of his imagination and the extraordinary scope of his sensibility are things that the poet shares freely with him to such an extent that in my looking-forward to the emerging of a perfected poet, it would be impossible to say whether he would emerge from the philosophers or from among the poets themselves. It is a common-place to say that their fields are different. But if philosophy and poetry are close, it follows that their fields are close. It is not as if it could be said that the poet is an artist and the philosopher is not, for Plato is universally recognized as an artist. On the other hand, if the poet is an artist, he may be expected to act in respect to the philosopher's field as an artist. It might be said that on that level where everything is a good, this bringing together would be a good. This is all that is suggested. Besides, the poet would retain everything that he has now and his activity would remain a matter of choice. One would like to resist the abhorrence that people feel in respect to philosophy in poetry, without admitting that this might accentuate the abhorrence that philosophers feel for poetry in philosophy, since poetry has always been a phase of philosophy.

I should like to come to an end by repeating Jean Paulhan's saying about the relation between poets and our confidence in the world. So many words other than confidence might have been used—words of understanding, words of reconciliation, of enchantment, even of forgetfulness. But none of them would have penetrated to our needs more surely than the word confidence. If giving confidence is the métier of the poet, it is even more certainly the métier of the philosopher. The poet may say that his role is to give pleasure and the philosopher may say that his is to find the truth. The poet about whom I have theorized will do both. It may be that his poetry will be the only valid metaphysics in that time to come when the physicists have, at last, found a language for their intuitions and when science, in restoring reality, will have left nothing else.

SECOND MANUSCRIPT VERSION

In his [Pascal's] words about the sphere of which the center is everywhere and the circumference nowhere, which I quoted a moment ago, we have an instance of words in which traces of the reason and traces of the imagination are mingled together. But since, as a poet, I hope that I have revealed something of the greatness of poetry and possibly some reason to believe in its superiority over its most ancient rival, let me indulge myself in a bit of final rhetoric, which, in spite of itself, will be acceptable, if you accept at all what I have been saying. There comes into the mind a procession of a great crowd of men, a little bent over as if they were scholars. They are holding on, by ceremonial ropes, to a kind of floor in the air, which they are conducting, or better, attending in its progress. As is natural to an aerial floor, in rhetoric, it is made of ivory. On it, and at its center, there is a blue peacock, blue and green and all the denser modulations of these colors, with gold and silver fans, which it turns to and fro as if to exhibit the brilliance of its mere presence and thereby to command. On the peacock's head, there is a diamond crown, like a coxcomb of darting light and darting fire. As this image of the imagination passes us, we are impressed by the manner of its attendant persons, silent and obedient, as if they were grateful for some expectation of their labor, of which they seem to feel sure.

THIRD MANUSCRIPT VERSION

He [Planck] was, of course, the patriarch of all modern physicists. André George published a note on these last writings of this great scholar in Les Nouvelles Littéraires, which I summarize to the extent that it is in point. He says that during his long life Planck had practiced the same philosophic and scientific credo: first, the lofty principles of duty and of moral conscience which his compatriot Emmanuel Kant had set up as universal maxims in the XVIIIth century; and second, the belief in a science of rigorous laws, the ideal reflection of events imperiously connected by a chain of effects and causes, a physics solidly determinist, of a tested classicism. On the quantic scale, the rigid determinism of classic science is dispelled, physics is able to say with certainty what phenomena are susceptible of observation, it calculates the measure of their respective probabilities, but it is not able to predict which of these phenomena is going to pass from the possible to the real, to the observable.

He says that today a new classicism is in course of establishing itself. Nature offers us on a grand scale a determinist aspect, thanks to the play of big figures, of statistical illusions. But on the atomic scale, at the level of elementary phenomena, an indeterminism, fundamental and, it must be added, well-defined, reigns alone. I quote what he says:

. . . *The last pages of the thesis are quite curious.*

A. WALTON LITZ

PARTICLES OF ORDER:
THE UNPUBLISHED *ADAGIA*

On écrit de telles choses pour transmettre aux
autres la théorie de l'univers qu'on porte en soi.
Ernest Renan, *Souvenirs d'enfance
et de jeunesse*[1]

ON FEBRUARY 21, 1906, AT THE AGE OF TWENTY-SIX,
Wallace Stevens copied a passage from Matthew Arnold's
Notebooks into his journal and then commented on his own
love for maxims and aphorisms.

> Have just finished Leopardi's "Pensieri" (translated by
> P. Maxwell—a scholarly major-general). They are para-
> graphs on human nature, like Schopenhauer's psychologi-
> cal observations, Paschals [*sic*] "Pensées," [La] Roche-
> foucauld's "Maximes" etc. How true they all are! I should
> like to have a library of such things. (*L*, 88)

Ultimately Stevens did acquire such a library. Among his
personal books that have survived, there are more than thirty
collections of aphorisms, proverbs, or pithy journal entries.[2]
Many of these were purchased in the 1930s and 1940s, when
Stevens was refashioning his poetic aims and had an almost
obsessive interest in recording his daily pensées. The range
of the volumes is quite astonishing. Standard collections of
sayings in English—*Proverbs and Family Mottoes, A Treas-
ury of English Aphorisms, The 100 Best Epigrams*—are sup-
plemented by less familiar volumes on the proverbial wisdom
of France, Italy, Morocco, China, Japan, and India.[3] Journals
and notebooks are also well represented, including those of
Arnold, Charles Baudelaire, Henry James, Marcel Proust,
Rainer Maria Rilke, and Georges Braque. The *Maxims* of
La Rochefoucauld are present in both French and English.

Other volumes testify to Stevens' fascination with the history of proverbial and aphoristic writing: from rare book dealers he obtained copies of Francis Quarles' *Divine Fancies Digested Into Epigrammes, Meditations, and Observations* (London, 1641), John Ray's *Collection of English Proverbs* (Cambridge, 1670), and the gathering of *Maxims, Characters, and Reflections* made by Fulke and Frances Greville (London, 1757). Taken as a whole, the collections of proverbs and aphorisms formed a significant part of Stevens' working library, and obviously reflect a major aspect of his poetic imagination. Few writers of any time or place can have given so much concentrated attention to the gnomic saying, both as private ritual and public utterance. Sometime after 1932, prompted by his lifelong interest in Goethe, Stevens read Frederick W. Felkin's centenary study, *Goethe: A Century After*, and copied this tribute into his first ADAGIA notebook: "From Goethe proverbs poured incessantly."[4] The same could be said of Wallace Stevens.

Early in the 1930s, as part of the general freshening of his poetic life that followed the long silence of 1924-1930, Stevens began to keep a notebook of aphorisms under the title ADAGIA. At much the same time he started to record memorable quotations in a commonplace book entitled SUR PLUSIEURS BEAUX SUJECTS [*sic*], often without comment, at other times with a personal gloss. Both enterprises eventually required second notebooks, AGADIA II and SUR PLUSIEURS BEAUX SUJECTS II (for a more detailed description see the following Note on the Text). The earliest pages of SUR PLUSIEURS BEAUX SUJECTS I, which can be dated ca. 1932-1935 from the quotations contain several isolated adages that Samuel French Morse printed at the end of his selection in *Opus Posthumous*. Presumably Stevens began by entering his own aphorisms in the first commonplace book, as well as interesting quotations, and then decided around 1934 to keep a separate notebook of *adagia*. The first ADAGIA notebook was filled by the mid-1940s, and Stevens turned to ADAGIA II, where he used only nine of twelve pages. A third, untitled notebook containing "Poetic Exercises of 1948" rounds out the record of Stevens' aphorisms.

When Samuel French Morse compiled *Opus Posthumous* he made an ample selection from the ADAGIA notebooks but omitted many entries and altered the format or sequence of others. The apparatus at the end of this essay, when used in conjunction with *Opus Posthumous*, will enable the reader to reconstruct the complete text of the ADAGIA notebooks. Although the entries omitted by Morse are sometimes weaker versions of other aphorisms, the complete text restores many unique sayings; but I believe that its chief value lies in its chronological record of Stevens' endless meditation on poetry and life. The entries of the 1930s (roughly *OP*, 157-62), many of which were submitted for publication in 1940 under the title *Materia Poetica*, serve as a gloss on the poems of that time. They remind one of the aphoristic stanzas in "Like Decorations in a Nigger Cemetery" or "The Man with the Blue Guitar," and were obviously part of Stevens' great effort—at first tentative, then more confident—to isolate points of order, moments of composed thought, in the midst of his complicated and often confused search for a theory of poetry that might become a theory of life. Helen Vendler has commented on the "quality of epigram" in "Like Decorations in a Nigger Cemetery," where the individual poems have the appearance of "jottings, *adagia*, epitaphs, the daily *pensées* of the inspector of gravestones."[5] Similarly, the taut couplets of "The Man with the Blue Guitar" often have the pithy quality of a proverb or saying, and show how Stevens used the method of the *adagia* to free himself from the loose and overly explicit rhetoric of *Owl's Clover*.

Stevens' willingness to publish some of the aphorisms in 1940 may be taken as a sign of his new-found confidence that he had won through to a tenable aesthetic, a confidence reflected everywhere in the "theoretic" poems of *Parts of a World*. As we read on in the *adagia* of the 1940s, the entries resonate with the growing power and assurance of the poetry of those years. The opening lines of "Asides on the Oboe" (1940),

> The prologues are over. It is a question, now,
> Of final belief. So, say that final belief
> Must be in a fiction. It is time to choose.
>
> (*CP*, 250)

have their prose counterpart in an ADAGIA entry, probably of the same year:

> The final belief is to believe in a fiction, which you know to be a fiction, there being nothing else. The exquisite truth is to know that it is a fiction and that you believe in it willingly. (163.3)

Entries such as "War is the periodical failure of politics" (164.13) remind us of the historical moment and of Stevens' preoccupation with the role of the hero (whether soldier or poet) in a time of war. "The death of one god is the death of all" (165.4) was incorporated directly into *Notes toward a Supreme Fiction* (1942), while "Poetry must resist the intelligence almost successfully" (171.9) was altered only slightly to make the opening line of "Man Carrying Thing" (1946). As we scan the *adagia* of the 1940s the leading themes of Stevens' life and art unfold before us: his interest in genealogy and a usable past, his search for a satisfying "esthetique," and his attempts to redefine the "romantic" for our time. Like the essays of *The Necessary Angel*, which they parallel, the *adagia* of the 1940s provide marginalia for the great long poems of that decade.

The *adagia* were the end result of a lifelong passion for aphoristic statements and gnomic utterances. The early letters and journal passages are filled with maxims and epigrams, which often take their place in catalogues of names, titles, colors, and sense impressions. Stevens' love for the single impression or effect, the right turn of mind or phrase, is evident in this description of the notes for his journal from a May 1909 letter to his fiancée, Elsie Moll:

> Scraps of paper covered with scribbling—Chinese antiquities, names of colors, in lists like rainbows, jottings of things to think about, like the difference, for example,

between the *expression* on men's faces and on women's, extracts, like this glorious one from Shakespeare: "What a piece of work is man! how noble in reason! how infinite in faculty!" and so on; epigrams, like, "The greatest pleasure is to do a good action by stealth, and have it found out by accident"—(could any true thing be more amusing?)—lists of Japanese eras in history, the names of Saints: Ambrose, Gregory, Augustine, Jerome; the three words, "monkeys, deer, peacocks" in the corner of a page; and this (from the French): "The torment of the man of thought is to aspire toward Beauty, without ever having any fixed and definite standard of Beauty"; the names of books I should like to read, and the names of writers about whom I should like to know something. (L, 143)

Many of Stevens' jottings are fragmentary and impressionistic, the record of "sensations" (in 1928 Stevens remarked that "Thirteen Ways of Looking at a Blackbird" was "not meant to be a collection of epigrams or of ideas, but of sensations" [L, 251]). Throughout his life Stevens collected such "sensations"—*données*, striking phrases, possible titles for poems. During the years of writing the *Harmonium* poems he grouped these *trouvailles* under the headings "Schemata" or "Memorias Antiguas";[6] in the 1930s and 1940s similar items were gathered in a notebook under the deliberately miscellaneous title FROM PIECES OF PAPER. This notebook of one-line entries contains imagistic moments of feeling ("The pine trees shudder in the shade"), signals of private experience ("A child playing with a ball"), lines that were to enter the poetry ("The mind is the great poem of winter," the opening of "Man and Bottle"), and titles both used ("Arrival at the Waldorf") and unused ("Mountain Disappearing in Twilight"). But even in these fragmentary *données* we sense the need for order, for abstraction, which is satisfied in the more formal *adagia*. "We live in a constellation / Of patches and of pitches, / Not in a single world," Stevens acknowledged in his late poem "July Mountain" (OP, 114-15), but we are always seeking moments of order in this "always incipient cosmos / The way, when we climb a mountain, / Vermont throws itself together." Stevens was both a modern skeptic who believed that we live in the margins or the space between the lines, knowing only disparate sensations, and a highly traditional writer who longed to find a central text, to give his intimations and sensations the authority of received truth. Poetry must be abstract, speaking of kinds and species, the forms of general nature; but it must also change, remaining faithful to the ever-fresh particulars of experience. In this unceasing dialectic between pure extremes, which the poem can approach but never fully embody, the *adagia* play a crucial role. Like Paul Valéry's "analects," they consist of "an abstract subject matter treated with the directness and simplicity of a memorandum made for private use."[7]

Stevens' poetry, from beginning to end, is filled with memorable aphorisms around which the tentative arguments revolve: "Death is the mother of beauty," "Poetry is the supreme fiction," "The death of one god is the death of all." The functions of aphorism in the poetry have been analyzed by Beverly Coyle, and although the following summary passage does not do justice to the subtlety of her thought, it deserves quotation:

Aphorisms have an affinity with the fragmentlike nature of experience. We experience ideas and even sensations in pieces. These pieces are neither all alike nor all unlike; instead, their relationship varies along a continuum between similarity and opposition. The tendency to experience life as fragments is, on the one hand, a *centripetal* tendency akin to aphoristic expression, in that in each case one momentarily pulls experience into a self-contained unit. For Stevens, however, such moments invariably give rise to other, different moments of the same sort and to a continuous interaction among them. This tendency to experience life as a complex series of interacting congeries leads Stevens to refuse final commitment to any one group of fragments, like or unlike. The result of the tendency is *centrifugal*, an encompassing of the plenitude of experience in all its contradictory fullness. Thus, whereas ordinarily one thinks of aphoristic expression as restricting the flux of experience, in Stevens' case it became the means of participating in that flux with a maximum of consciousness.[8]

Elsewhere in her essay Beverly Coyle rightly emphasizes the root meaning of aphorism, "to mark off a boundary or horizon," since Stevens' aphorisms are carefully designed to give a sense of finality, of a completed thought. But the feeling of completeness is only temporary, to be broken or modified by the next perception. This delicate balance between certainty and possibility, between abstraction and change, was recognized by Stevens in his early journal: "When you first feel the truth of, say, an epigram, you feel like making it a rule of conduct. But this one is displaced by that, and thus things go on in their accustomed way" (L, 91). In their formal design, the *adagia* combine the wit and finality of the epigram (something precise and "inscribed") with the general truth of the proverb: "There must be something of the peasant in every poet" (168.11). Each of the *adagia* persuades us momentarily by its air of received wisdom and by its structural completeness, but taken together they express the open and speculative quality of the poet's mind.

The habits of mind that underlay Stevens' interest in aphorisms are neatly revealed in a letter to Elsie Moll of 1909:

Last night I thought of you, too, and longed to have you with me. I had spent the afternoon and evening at the Astor Library looking through the books of Paul Elmer More, one of the most discriminating, learned and soundest critics of the day. He has a very marked tendency to consider all things philosophically, and that, of course, gives his views both scope and permanence. I quote a thing quoted by him—in Latin for the sound and sight of it:

> O vitae Philosophia dux! O virtutum indagatrix
> expultrixque vitiorum!
>
> Oh, Philosophy, thou guide of Life! Oh, thou that search-
> est out virtues, and expellest vices! — That struck me as
> such an admirable inscription for the façade of a library—
> or of one of those temples, bound to be built some day,
> when people will seek in a place not specially dedicated
> to religion, those principles of moral conduct that should
> guide us in every-day life—as distinct, say, from the pecu-
> liar life of Sundays. — My mind is rather full of such
> things to-day, and so resembles the mood that fastened
> me, a year or more ago, so intently on Matthew Arnold—
> and maxims! — But each for himself, in that respect; and
> I do not, therefore, make a point of what may not interest
> you. — To think occasionally of such things gives me a
> comforting sense of balance and makes me feel like the
> Brahmin on his mountain-slope who in the midst of
> his contemplations—surveyed distant cities—and then
> plunged in thought again. (L, 133)

Here the philosophic weight of the quotation from Cicero is
balanced against its sensory value, "the sound and sight of
it,"[9] just as the common sense of a maxim is balanced
against our personal and often eccentric concerns. The Brah-
min on the mountain slope who marked the horizon of
common experience and "then plunged in thought again" is
the type of the poet who tries to move in equilibrium be-
tween object and subject, the general and the particular.
Like the mountain of truth in "Credences of Summer"—a
mountain "half way green and then, / The other immeasur-
able half, such rock / As placid air becomes" (CP, 375)—
Stevens' aphorisms are part distillation of common expe-
rience and part solipsistic musings. It should not be surpris-
ing, then, that the adagia have reminded readers of Erasmus
and La Rochefoucauld, as well as Valéry and Georges
Braque. In their compounding of the public and the private,
the traditional and the modern, the adagia reflect in minia-

ture the complicated impulses of Wallace Stevens' poetic life.

A Note on the Text

Most of Stevens' aphorisms are to be found in two exercise books, labeled ADAGIA I and ADAGIA II. The first notebook contains twenty-four numbered pages, all filled. The twelve pages of the second notebook are unnumbered, and Stevens used only nine of them. The ADAGIA I notebook is stitched and has a light gray cover; it is similar in appearance to the two notebooks that Stevens titled SUR PLUSIEURS BEAUX SUJECTS [sic] I and II. The ADAGIA II notebook is stapled with a blue cover and resembles the two untitled notebooks that contain some of the late aphorisms (one of the untitled notebooks contains three pages of entries, the other has a single entry). The thirty-nine aphorisms that Stevens published as *Materia Poetica* were mostly culled from the ADAGIA I notebook; they appeared in the magazine *View* in September 1940 (*adagia* I–XXII) and October 1942 (XXIII–XXXIX). The typescript of all thirty-nine aphorisms was sent to *View* sometime after May 9, 1940; on that day Stevens wrote to the editor of *View* that he "could gather together a group of dicta about poetry under the heading of *Materia Poetica*, say fifteen or twenty of them, each a single sentence" (unpublished letter at University of Texas Library). A carbon of the *Materia Poetica* typescript survives in the Stevens archives at the Huntington Library.

The aim of the following transcriptions is to present the *adagia* in chronological order, amplifying and amending the entries in *Opus Posthumous*. Numerical references indicate the page in *Opus Posthumous* on which each proverb appears and its position on that page: e.g., 157.3 means page 157, third entry. Where the format or wording of the manuscript differs from that in *Opus Posthumous*, the manuscript form of the proverb is printed. Entries omitted from *Opus*

Posthumous are identified by parenthetical letters; e.g., 157.3(a) and 157.3(b) indicate that these aphorisms occur in the manuscript notebook immediately after the one printed in *Opus Posthumous* as 157.3.

When the entries in the *Materia Poetica* typescript are identical with those in the manuscript, a cross-reference by roman numeral is given. When a proverb in the *Materia Poetica* text differs from that in the manuscript, it is printed in full.

The editor and publisher of *Opus Posthumous* regularized Stevens' punctuation. When the differences are slight, no correction has been made. However, differences in punctuation or format that seem significant have been indicated by printing the full entry in its original form. Wherever possible, I have reproduced the format and punctuation, as well as the text, of the manuscript entries. However, following the model of the *Materia Poetica* typescript, all entries are ended with a full stop, although Stevens often omitted this in the manuscripts.

The source for one entry, 179.10 ("The imagination is the liberty of the mind and hence the liberty of reality"), has not been located in the manuscripts.

Grateful acknowledgment is made to the Huntington Library, San Marino, California, for permission to quote from the manuscripts of Wallace Stevens.

Adagia from SUR PLUSIEURS BEAUX SUJECTS I

[*These pensées are scattered through the first fifteen pages of Stevens' commonplace book. Most can be dated with some precision, since Stevens often noted the dates of publication for the quotations that surround them. They appear in* Opus Posthumous *as the last of the* Adagia, *pp. 179-80.*]

Success as the result of industry is a peasant ideal. [1932]

Success is to be happy with the wise. [1932]

Suppose any man whose spirit has survived had consulted his contemporaries as to what to do, or what to think, or what music to write, and so on. [1933]

In the long run the truth does not matter. [1933-1934]

It should be said of poetry that it is essentially romantic as if one were recognizing the truth about poetry for the first time. Although the romantic is referred to, most often, in a pejorative sense, this sense attaches, or should attach, not to the romantic in general but to some phase of the romantic that has become stale. Just as there is always a romantic that is potent, so there is always a romantic that is impotent. [1934]

Poetry creates a fictitious existence on an exquisite plane. This definition must vary as the plane varies, an exquisite plane being merely illustrative. [1936]

ADAGIA I
[*Opus Posthumous*, pp. 157-72]

157.3(a)   L'art d'être heureuse.

157.3(b)   Goethe's *General-beichte* was written of another who "spake three thousand proverbs, and his songs were a thousand and five. From Goethe proverbs poured incessantly."
Goethe: Felkin O Univ P. 1932.

[*This entry is adapted from the opening lines of Frederick W. Felkin's* Goethe: A Century After *(London: Oxford University Press, 1932). The full passage reads: "In one of Goethe's poems called 'The General Con-*

A. WALTON LITZ

fession' (General-beichte) *certain penitents are required to take a vow that they will wean themselves from half-measures and live resolutely in the Whole, the Good, the Beautiful. This motto sums up the striving of perhaps the largest life that a man ever lived—a life whose aim was Fruit, whose means Activity. It was written of another who drank of the stream of life deeply and with understanding that he spake of trees, from the cedar which is in Lebanon to the hyssop which springeth out of the wall; also he spake three thousand proverbs, and his songs were a thousand and five. From Goethe proverbs poured incessantly, and these not merely happy generalizations, but the aphorisms of a practical philosopher; in natural science he was continually making investigations and constructing hypotheses; in lyric song he was supreme —at least, in the opinion of Heine, no indulgent critic, and one whose praise outweighs that of a whole world beside."*]

157.7(a) The public of the poet. The public of the organist is the church in which he improvises.

157.8 *Materia Poetica* I.

158.7 It is life that we are trying to get at in poetry.

It is life that one is trying to get at in poetry. [*Materia Poetica* II]

158.10 The poet confers his identity on the reader. He cannot do this if he intrudes personally. [*Materia Poetica* III]

158.11 *Materia Poetica* IV.

159.3 Collecting poetry from one's experience as one goes along is not the same thing as merely writing poetry. [*Materia Poetica* V]

159.4   *Materia Poetica* VI.

159.6   *Materia Poetica* VII.

159.7   *Materia Poetica* VIII.

159.10   Usage is everything. (Les idées sont desti-
nées à être deformées à l'usage. Georges
Braque, Verve, No. 2). [*Materia Poetica* IX]

[*In the manuscript notebook, the citation
from Braque ("Les idées sont destinées à
être déformées à l'usage. Reconnaitre ce fait
est une preuve de désintéressement. Georges
Braque Verve No. 2") is a later addition, in
the right-hand margin, to the original prov-
erb, "Usage is everything." Verve No. 2 ap-
peared in early 1938.*]

160.3   *Materia Poetica* XI.

160.4   *Materia Poetica* X.

160.5   *Materia Poetica* XII.

160.6   Poetry may be an aspect of melancholia. At
least, in melancholy, it is one of the "aultres
choses solatieuses." [*Materia Poetica* XIII.
"Et aultres choses solatieuses" is an entry on
p. 2 of the* FROM PIECES OF PAPER *notebook.*]

160.7   The poet must come, at his worst, as the
miraculous beast and, at his best, as the mi-
raculous man. [*Materia Poetica* XIV]

160.7(a)   (Poet,) feed my lambs. [Also *Materia Poe-
tica* XV]

160.8   *Materia Poetica* XVI.

160.10   *Materia Poetica* XVII.

160.11   *Materia Poetica* XVIII.

160.12   *Materia Poetica* XIX.

161.2   *Materia Poetica* XX.

161.2(a)   There are two opposites: the poetry of rhetoric and the poetry of experience.

161.3   *Materia Poetica* XXI.

161.4   *Materia Poetica* XXII.

161.6   *Materia Poetica* XXIII.

161.9   Each of us has a sensibility range beyond which nothing exists. In each this is different. [*Materia Poetica* XXIV]

161.10   In poetry, you must love the words, the ideas and images and rhythms with all your capacity to love anything at all.

            In poetry, you must love the words, the ideas, the images and the rhythms with all your capacity, to love anything at all. [*Materia Poetica* XXV]

162.2   *Materia Poetica* XXVI.

162.3   Things seen are things as seen. Absolute real.

162.3(a)   Not all objects are equal.

162.5   *Materia Poetica* XXVII.

162.6   *Materia Poetica* XXVIII.

162.7   *Materia Poetica* XXIX.

162.9(a)   A new future is good business.

162.9(b)   Poetry is a form of melancholia.

162.11(a)   Poetry is not a personal matter.

162.12   Poetry is a means of redemption.
            Consider

I

That the whole world is material for poetry.

II

That there is not a specifically poetic material.

[*Both* Opus Posthumous *and* Materia Poetica (XXX) *omit "Poetry is a means of redemption." In the manuscript notebook it appears that "Consider . . ." was added at a later time, and Stevens may have thought of it as a separate entry.*]

162.13   *Materia Poetica* XXXI.

162.14   *Materia Poetica* XXXII.

[*No manuscript source has been located for the remaining entries in* Materia Poetica, *which comprise the last page of the 1940 typescript.*]

The essential fault of surrealism is that it invents without discovering. To make a clam play an accordion is to invent not to discover. The observation of the unconscious, so far as it can be observed, should reveal things of which we have previously been unconscious, not the familiar things of which we have been conscious plus imagination. [*Materia Poetica* XXXIII; see 177.5]

The imagination does not add to reality. [XXXIV]

The great well of poetry is not other poetry but prose: reality. However it requires a poet to perceive the poetry in reality. [XXXV]

At the moments when one's terror of life should be greatest (when one is young or old) one is usually insensible to it. Some such thing is true of the most profoundly poetic moments. This is the origin of sentimentality, which is a failure of feeling. [XXXVI; cf. 162.15]

Poetry is reality and thought or feeling. [XXXVII]

If one believes in poetry then questions of principle become vital questions. In any case, if there is nothing except reality and art, the mere statement of that fact discloses the significance of art. [XXXVIII]

The dichotomy is not between realists and artists. There must be few pure realists and few pure artists. We are hybrids absorbed in hybrid literature. [XXXIX]

163.4-5
I
All of our ideas come from the natural world: Trees = umbrellas.

II
There is nothing so offensive to a man of intellectual principle as unprincipled thinking.

163.9(a)   That part of the truth of the world that has its origin in the feelings.

163.11(a)   Poetry is the expression of the experience of poetry. Values other than those merely of the eye and ear.

[*These sentences may be two separate aphorisms: the first is at the bottom of one notebook page, the next at the top of the following page.*]

163.11(b)   seelensfriede durch dichtung.
[*Presumably* seelenfriede durch dichtung:

"spiritual harmony through poetry." In an unpublished letter of October 6, 1940, Henry Church wrote to Stevens: "And why shouldn't one bring about a Seelensfriede durch Dichtung. Poetry should diffuse to all channels even into Insurance & Bicarbonate." Stevens picked up the phrase in his letter to Church of October 15, 1940 (L, 377). "See-lensfriede durch Dichtung" is an entry on p. 8 of the FROM PIECES OF PAPER *notebook.]*

164.8 It is the explanations of things that we make to ourselves that disclose our character:

The subjects of one's poems are the symbols of one's self or of one of one's selves.

165.12 A poet looks at the world somewhat as a man looks at a woman.

166.3(a) La vie est plus belle que les idées.

167.6(a) Hermit of poetry.

167.7(a) Meine Seele muss Prachtung haben.
[Prachtung *appears to be Stevens' coinage. A translation would be, "My soul must have splendor."]*

167.8 The most beautiful (the only beautiful) (beautiful is an inadequate and temporizing improvisation) thing in the world is, of course, the world itself. This is so not only logically but categorically.

167.8(a) I believe in the image.

167.10(a) The satisfactions of nature.

167.11(a) The poet is a stronger life.

168.1 The great conquest is the conquest of reality. It is not to present life, in a moment, as it might have been.

168.6(a)   Poetry is metaphor.

168.9   In dramatic poetry the imagination attaches itself to a heightened reality. Degrees or planes of reality.

170.3(a)   A living poetry that deals with everything or none.

170.3(b)   To touch with the imagination in respect to reality.

170.3(c)   The world reduced to one thing.

170.5(a)   It is manner that becomes stale.

171.5   Since man made the world, the inevitable god is the beggar.

171.9   ["*almost*" *is an interlinear addition.*]

                              se   compose   de

171.12   Life is a composite of the propositions about it.

172.5(a)   The imagination is not the only co-relation of reality. Science etc.

172.9   [*The last entry in the* ADAGIA I *notebook, inserted in the margin.*]

ADAGIA II
[*Opus Posthumous*, pp. 172-78]

173.12   The poet is a god or The young poet is a god. The old poet is a tramp.

173.13   If the mind is the most terrible force in the world, it is, also, the only force that defends us against terror.   (or)

                The mind is the most terrible force in the

world principally in this that it is the only force that can defend us against itself. The modern world is based on this pensée.

174.9   [*The word "gaiety" in this aphorism is an afterthought, inserted interlinearly as an alternate to "joy."*]

175.1   If the answer is frivolous, the question was frivolous.

175.5   To be at the end of fact is not to be at the beginning of the imagination but it is to be at the end of both.

175.12   The mind is not equal to the demands of oratory, poetry etc.

176.4   Poetry is great only as it exploits great ideas or what is often the same thing great feelings.

177.1   A poem should stimulate the sense of living and of being alive.

177.5   [*Not in the manuscript notebook. Materia Poetica XXXIII.*]

177.8   To "subtilize experience" = to apprehend the complexity of the world, to perceive the intricacy of appearance.

177.11-12   [*"Originality is an escape from repetition" is a marginal gloss added later to the aphorism "Poetry is a renovation of experience."*]

178.1   [*This aphorism was glossed later, in the right-hand margin: "Christianity is an exhausted culture."*]

178.12   [*The last entry in the* ADAGIA II *notebook.*]

UNTITLED NOTEBOOK
[selections in *Opus Posthumous*, pp. 178-79]

Gaiety in poetry is a precious characteristic but it should be
a characteristic of the diction.

Poetic Exercises of 1948

Das Leben Als Glockenspiel. The world is a clock
The fire-flies are in the air, above the tree-tops,
On the night of June twelfth
In spite of a month of vicious weather.
It will thunder in July.
There is a continuing explosion of chimes.

Reality is a cliché
From which we escape by metaphor
It is only au pays de la métaphore
Qu'on est poète.

The degrees of metaphor
The absolute object slightly turned
Is a metaphor of the object.

Some objects are less susceptible to metaphor than others.
The whole world is less susceptible to metaphor than a
tea-cup is.

There is no such thing as a metaphor of a metaphor. One
does not progress through metaphors. Thus reality is the
indispensable element of each metaphor. When I say that
man is a god it is very easy to see that if I say also that a god
is something else, god has become reality.

Illegible events.

Poetry seeks out the relation of men to facts.

The imagination is man's power over nature. Query

Imagination is the only genius. Query

Relation of the German to his Forest.

How to change real objects without the aid of metaphor.
By feeling, style etc.

Poetry as manifestation of the relationship that man creates
between himself & reality.

The momentum of the mind is all toward abstraction.

Approchons-nous de Poussin peu à peu. A. Gide

The imagination of the blind man cannot be the extension
of an externality he has never seen. (Berkeley)

Imagination *per se*. Berkeley
Imagination as amusement & pleasure

The serious pursuit of pleasure & the pleasure worthy of
serious pursuit.

The effect of the imagination on the works of artists is a
different subject from that in which I am interested.
In art its effect is the production of qualities: as strength
(Pater, Michael Angelo) and its value is a question of the
value of those qualities. In life it produces things and its
value is a question of the value of those things as, for
example, the value of works of art.

UNTITLED NOTEBOOK

There are two arch-types of poets, of whom it is possible to
take Homer as an illustration of the narrative type and Plato,
regardless of the consideration that he did not write in
verse, as an illustration of the reflective type.

WALLACE STEVENS

A SELECTION OF STEVENS' LETTERS TO WILSON E. TAYLOR
(WITH A LETTER FROM STEVENS TO R. DORSEY WATKINS)

September 3, 1941

Dear Taylor:

I enclose a check for $3.00 for the Gregorovius book. It may be that this will not reach me for a day or two. I shall send you stamps to cover the postage when I return HARMONIUM to you, shortly.

Many thanks. I had not realized that the Brick Row Shop was still in existence. It started in New Haven with the same idea that the early missionaries had in distributing the Bible among the Indians. And, like the early missionaries, it came to nothing in New Haven.

Very truly yours,

October 1, 1941

Dear Taylor:

Here is another little job for you:
The best book on Persia is said to be a book by James Morier, called HAJJI BABA. I should like to get a copy of it, unless it should prove to be appallingly expensive. It has been reprinted in the Everyman Books and also in the World's Classics. I don't want any such trash; I want a nice old copy.

If you take this up with the Brick Row people, they may want to send to England for it. That is unnecessary; I can send to England myself.

Yours,

PERSONAL

January 6, 1942

Mr. W. E. Taylor
¢ Hartford Accident & Indemnity Co.
110 William St., New York

Dear Sir:

I suppose the explanation for the price of the gloves is that there are a lot of people in New York who know how desirable it is to change money into things during a period of possible inflation.

Last night I read the latest number of APOLLO, which contains reports of auction sales in England. As you probably know, the recesses of Wales are being ransacked now-a-days for books, paintings, etc. Apollo reports that at one sale in Wales there were no less than three thousand people present at each sale and that the prices were "highly satisfactory."

The Hispanic Society, which has its headquarters at something like Broadway and 155th Street, has just published Vol. 1, No. 1 of NOTES HISPANIC. I should like a copy of this. Copies may come in different forms: that is to say bound or unbound. If so, I want the best copy available, except that I don't want a de luxe copy. I shouldn't at all mind having this before the end of the week: see the final paragraph of this letter.

The Morgan Library, which you ought to know more about, is having a special exhibition illustrating The British Tradition. A catalogue has been prepared with an introduction by Professor Chew. I pine for a copy of the damned thing.

This is that final paragraph: Bribe one of your boys to get on a subway and go up to the Hispanic Society, pick up that catalogue; return to the Morgan Library, pick up that catalogue; bring them down to you, so that, after putting on your white silk gloves, you can take a look at them and then send them up to me. You will have to telephone both places to find out how much the things cost and at what time the boy could get in, etc. This is a job for an errand boy; I will pay his subway and 50¢ plus the cost of the catalogues, taxes, etc., etc., if you will tell me how much it all amounts to.

Very truly yours,

PERSONAL

February 6, 1942

Dear Taylor:

Many thanks for the catalogue. Catalogues are to me what honeycombs are to a bear.

I was down to New York on Wednesday, but had no time for fiddle-faddle.

Yours,

PERSONAL

February 14, 1942

Mr. W. E. Taylor
NEW YORK OFFICE

Dear Taylor:

I suppose you will wonder whether you are working for me or for the Company. Here is something that I cannot do for myself:

In my day, when lawyers were permitted to practice, it all took place at the appellate Division, and I suppose that in-quiry will have to be made of the Clerk of the Appellate Division, First Department. This used to be at 25th Street and Madison Avenue, but I don't know where it is now. I am going to apply for admission to the Bar in Connecticut. The first step is to make sure that I am still on the rolls in New York. Some years ago there was talk about weeding out from the lists lawyers who had not actively practiced there and, of course, I haven't actively practiced there for more than 25 years, but I have never forfeited my civil rights, have never done anything that even looked like moral turpitude, etc., etc. Am I o.k.?

Yours very truly,

November 18, 1942

Dear Taylor:

After you spoke to me, I took a look at the TIMES. There is apparently a catalogue of the Cezanne pictures at the Rosenberg Gallery; I should like to have a copy. I notice that ART NEWS has its finger in this pie. If the catalogue is merely a special number of ART NEWS (which I don't like), I don't want it, but there is probably a special number of that publication and the catalogue. If there is one catalogue more expensive than the other, I want the most expensive, which probably doesn't mean much, but does mean illustrations.

Among the lenders is Jakob Goldschmidt. The mere fact that a picture is owned by this man is a token of its quality. I have never seen any of Goldschmidt's pictures that were not superb. He was a banker in Berlin, I believe, and a friend of Mussolini's. Ordinarily, it wouldn't have been possible for him to take his pictures out of the country at the time when he did, but Mussolini interceded for him. He is living, I believe, in Cambridge at the present time.

Yours,

R. Dorsey Watkins, Esq.   January 19, 1943
¢ Piper, Watkins & Avirett
Baltimore Trust Bldg.
Baltimore, Md.

Dear Mr. Watkins:

Wilson Taylor has sent me the copy of the memorandum on Miss Turnbull which you were kind enough to prepare.

This is exactly what I wanted. It is impossible to examine Miss Turnbull's Plotinus without becoming exceedingly interested in Miss Turnbull herself. The truth is that I like the book more for Miss Turnbull than I do for Plotinus. I am going to insert your memorandum in my copy of that book. Plotinus himself is one of the hacks of philosophy classrooms, but if ever a woman was capable of filling a dead subject with a blaze of life, it is Miss Turnbull.

I look forward to her Seneca. I don't know whether you yourself are interested in this sort of thing. People in the 18th century used to have Seneca lying round the house. I suppose a man who wanted to look correct picked up a copy when the neighbors called. But I expect that Miss Turnbull would make a living creature of him.

Thanks for your kindness.

Very truly yours,
Wallace Stevens

April 17, 1944

Mr. Wilson E. Taylor
720 California St.
San Francisco, Cal.

Dear Taylor:

Thanks for yours of April 11th. I hope you got a few of these things for yourself if only to find out how good they are. I am particularly concerned about such things for next winter and I should like to make it clear in the case of the cherries and pears that what I am thinking of primarily is cherries and pears for next winter. If you know of anyone who does an equally good job, it doesn't make any difference where they come from. The apricots and prunes that are now on the way are all that I need this spring.

You will find a check for $3.25 (to balance) enclosed. I sent you a check for $25.00 a few days ago. You appear to be the only friend of mine that has a dollar to his name. I rather enjoy the change.

Of course you remember Mrs. Roney. She sold her house on the mountain and bought another down on the river at Saugerties. Then she started to improve the new house and, what with the terrific trimming she got, wound up in a state of collapse. I am going to meet her in New York next Tuesday, April 25th, to talk over fresh plans and shall try to bring her to a boil with the aid of a couple of cocktails. When she felt that she was in danger of passing out she sent me everything she had relating to my lines and I have all this bound up in two volumes that could knock your eye out. But every now and then I think of somebody that she forgot, particularly the Barcalows. These are the people that I am going to see her about. At least one Barcalow went to San Francisco and prospered, but I think that he spelled his name Barkeloo, or some such thing. Then there is a branch in the neighborhood of Los Angeles, possibly Pasadena. Is there a genealogical society in San Francisco? If there is, one of these days see if there is anything indexed on the Barcalows, with every possible variation of spelling, including Buckalew? All the Bucks County Barcalows, having little or no money, with lots of good looks, took their genealogy for granted, but those on the Coast having prospered are as likely as not to have employed somebody to tell them what's what.

Very truly yours,

August 15, 1944

Dear Taylor:

I imagine that Mrs. Batchelder sold her business with the orchard, and that what she used to sell her successor will sell. I hope so because her prunes were the only real equals of old Dr. Barker's. Be careful to get this year's crop. As a matter of fact, all of these things, except possibly the pears, ought to be available already. The drying process in that climate takes only a few days. Dried cherries are very difficult to get. You will probably have to get them in the country, yourself. If there is any way of arranging to have them put up in one-pound packages, like the apricots—everything except the prunes, don't hesitate to pay a little to have that done. I am enclosing $50 so that you won't have to use your own money. Finally, on this subject, I suppose by now you have discovered Goldberg-Bowen, the big grocery shop in San Francisco. They used to put up a mountain grove prune which was distinct. It was put up in a Redwood box, but there was nothing glacé about them. I don't want these unless it is completely impossible to get something like Mrs. Batchelder's prunes; if it is completely impossible, then I should just as lief have these.

About the book: A man has to use as much sense in placing a book as in placing anything else: that is to say, he must send it in good shape to a publisher that he thinks is likely to be interested in it. You haven't told me what sort of a book your friend has written. If it is a history of Fresno, he might as well keep it. I tried to tell Judge Powell what he ought to do with his book; he did everything but. First he tried his friends in Atlanta, all of whom had friends in New York, etc.; then he tried publishers' agents in New York. About the time when he was thoroughly discouraged, only because there was nothing else left for him to do, he went where I told him to go in the first place. They took his book and made great fuss over it, and the old man has been pleased with himself ever since. All there is to say about it is that he finally sent it to the right place. Probably your friend has written a novel. In that case, the question immediately after the question relating to some one likely to be interested is the question in respect to the publisher by whom he would like to be published. Harcourt-Brace are very decent people. Personally, I like Knopf, although, since I only publish poetry, the business end of it is slight. Simon Shuster are great money makers, but, personally, I wouldn't allow them to publish anything of mine, even if they wanted to and, since they have written me several times, I assume that they would be willing if I had anything in which they were interested. They are vulgar advertisers and they keep a very fair share of what they make, or so I am told. Harper is much interested in new people. All your man has to do is to write, say to Harcourt-Brace and say that he has a manuscript, describing it, and ask whether they would be interested in seeing it; if so, that is all there is to it.

About the Barkeloos: I haven't been able to get a single page out of Mrs. Roney during the present year, although I have paid her something like $700. She has sent me an incomplete section on the DeSille line, which I read and then returned to her because it was incomplete. But that is all I have seen during 1944. I have not heard from her since the middle of June and do not intend to make any inquiries until about October 1st. Mrs. Roney has lived alone for so long that she is inclined to magnify things that relate to herself. She cannot see her own experience in relation to the experience of other people. She sold her house, as I have probably told you, and then got a shock when she ran into the income tax following the transaction. Then she bought another house, which she started to remodel. The workmen gave her a terrible ride and at that left everything incomplete, as a result of which she collapsed. She went away for a while and then I met her in New York to make fresh plans. This was on May 1st. She seemed to be getting back to routine, but early in the summer she went to visit friends in Woodstock and since then I have not heard from her, very largely, I suppose, because I have been reluctant to write to her. In her last letter she spoke of having a blood pressure of 80 and seemed to be frightened to death. As a matter of fact, a blood pressure of 80, while definitely low, is perfectly normal to thousands of people. Mrs. Roney has probably been sitting in the undertaker's front parlor, fanning herself, afraid to move, for the last several months.

Very truly yours,

Enc.

October 30, 1944

Dear Taylor:

Thanks for your note of October 23d.

The cellar is slowly filling up with things that, if the war was going wrong (it isn't), and if the Nazis and the Nips were to come, all I should have to do would be to draw down the shades.

People in warmer climates think of us in the climate of Connecticut as beginning to draw back from frosts. The truth is that my wife and I spent yesterday in the garden, putting in new roses. Left to herself, she gets in about two a day; yesterday she got eight in. This gives you some idea of the extent to which I carried the water, removed clay, lugged up fertilizer, threw rocks over the back fence, and so on. This has been the mildest kind of an autumn.

Happy days.

Very truly yours,

PERSONAL

September 25, 1945

Mr. W. E. Taylor
Hartford Accident and Indemnity Co.
Hartford Building
San Francisco, Cal.

Dear Taylor:

It is really a little early to be ordering prunes for the winter, but I am sending you $50.00 for which I should like to have four 5-pound boxes and twenty-five pounds of apricots. This is about as much as I am likely to use during the course of the winter and, in fact, now that you have introduced me to Bee Ritchie and I have had stoned prunes, it may even be too much. Believe it or not, a box of the Ritchie prunes arrived in Hartford yesterday and I had some of them for breakfast this morning. Moreover, I made a deposit with these people. It seems that they dip their prunes in chocolate and sometime next month I expect to receive a load of those.

The reason I am sending you $50.00 is that you may see some other things that you think I ought to have, especially fine pears, peaches or cherries. One gets fed up on too much of the same thing. So far as the prunes are concerned, I should rather have them packed in 1-pound bags than in 5-pound boxes, but don't go to any trouble about that: I am merely expressing a preference.

We are going through a very dull period here in the office. We have always had this period at this season of the year, but the present period commenced long ago and looks as if it would go on for some time to come because, of course, we have been writing no contract business. Here we are with three-quarters of the year over and the fact is that we have a minus loss ratio in surety as distinct from fidelity, or almost a minus, if not quite. This gives me plenty of time for genealogy, the early history of Indiana, poetry, thoughts on prunes, etc.

Don't send back any of the money that I am sending you. During the course of the winter you may see some odds and ends: preventives against malnutrition and general all round builder-uppers.

Yours very truly,

March 9, 1949

Mr. W. E. Taylor
SAN FRANCISCO BRANCH OFFICE

Re: Bond #2317048—Cl. 125383—Denison & Stone
Favor: U. S. Dept. of Interior

Dear Sir:

I.

Will you ask the cashier of the San Francisco Office what he does about reporting your expenses or, if he does nothing, whether there is anyone else that does anything. I don't like to ask you to add another single operation to the many that you have to take care of at the present time. This sort of thing ought to be reported on the bordereaux. I never really noticed that your expenses were not being reported until lately. Then I noticed it only because they must be running into money: $2,000.00 or $3,000.00 a year, I should imagine.

II.

Perhaps I ought to write to you separately on this, but a letter is a letter. I have had it in mind for some time to suggest that you take on an assistant. A week or so ago we had a young man in the office from Cambridge. He does not graduate from the Harvard Law School until next June. He is a very likeable fellow: gives every sign of being someone with whom we should all like to work. He has had no experience. The Surety Claim Department needs some new young men because, as things are, we are not able to move people around from one place to another. The man that I am thinking of comes from near-by and might want to return here, although he seemed to be particularly interested in the Coast. It seems to me that you would find it desirable to have someone to do some of your traveling for you or, if you preferred to travel, to handle office details and keep things up to date, make routine reports, take care of salvage, etc. While the activity in your office has been exceptional, it has been exceptional for so long now that we should both stop to think about it and to provide for it. All of us here realize how much you have to do and for my own part I think that you have more to do than you can do and at the same time enjoy doing it. What do you think about this?

Yours very truly,

WS F

Mr. W. E. Taylor   *August 11, 1954*
SAN FRANCISCO BRANCH OFFICE

Dear Taylor:

Your letter of July 23 telling me about your Hawaiian trip not only gave pleasure to me but to a number of other people to whom I showed it, including my wife. I thought it might stimulate her interest in Hawaii. But she is so interested in the landscape in the rear of 118 Westerly Terrace, Hartford, that the letter made no difference. Yesterday and the day before she spent the whole day reading catalogues of day lilies (Hemerocallis). She has not the least doubt in the world that that sort of thing pays. We have had any number of hybrids. But she is a cruel taskmaster, so that we have thrown away any number of them. Those that remain are superb. During the early part of the summer we built a terrace, not close up to the house and in the shade for the purpose of drinking cocktails there, but in the very middle of the garden for the purpose of sitting there and looking around. If the sun is too hot, we put out Hollywood umbrellas.

We have not been away this summer and do not intend to go. For my own part, I never have any desire to go away in the early part of the summer. In the middle of the summer, the point at which we are now, it is too hot to go anywhere. But as summer begins to come to an end and some people begin to come home, I begin to think of country places in the Virgin Islands, or a Spumoni-colored villa in Bermuda. I have been thinking about some such thing ever since I came into the office. The great beauty about Bermuda is that it is civilized—every part of it. The great trouble with places like the Virgin Islands and West Indies is that civilization stops at the first curbstone. I read in last night's paper about a boy in Mexico who had been caught killing men for the purpose of going through their pockets. He confessed to having killed ten. You can have my share of Mexico.

Perhaps the origin of all this excitement is that a niece of mine who lives in Los Angeles is going to spend a little vacation soon at Mission beach near San Diego. She is going to stop at what she calls a fabulous motel called Bahia, or some such thing. Have you ever heard of it? I have an aristocratic prejudice against motels, even a moral prejudice. But it seems to me that a couple of million dollars must have been invested in things of this kind on the turnpike near Hartford and that quite a number of them are just as good in every respect as swell hotels. It is true that they don't have any grounds around them and most of them expect you to go to some neighbor or to Howard Johnson's for your meals. But, taken as places to stop and sleep, they are extraordinary, not to speak of the fact that they enable traveling salesmen actually to pay $3.00 or $4.00 for a night but to charge $8.00 or $9.00 on their expense accounts. I think this last feature probably has a great deal to do with their popularity.

I have no big news. You know, of course, that Mr. Rutherford was married again. He is back in the office but I believe he expects to go away shortly for a holiday. The Company as a whole seems to be progressing marvelously and this lends a generally cheerful air to the place because everybody is expecting a bonus and even though they should be disappointed, as I am sure they will be, they will immediately start hoping all over again when the time, next winter, has come and gone. I don't suppose it really matters because under the present economic regime it makes very little difference how much you get you are always broke just the same, or just about broke. I wish I could say that I knew someone, male or female, large or small, energetic or lazy, that was really making important progress year after year. But I don't. Life has become a sort of treadmill: there is always enough but there is never more.

Adios,

October 6, 1954

Mr. W. E. Taylor
SAN FRANCISCO BRANCH OFFICE

Dear Taylor:

Thanks for your birthday message. Working for the Hartford is just as effective in keeping one young as it is in keeping one poor. And things balance because I enjoy feeling young. We are all well and I am still able to write poetry which is a great thing.

Sincerely yours,

WS F

WILSON E. TAYLOR

OF A REMEMBERED TIME

AS WALLACE STEVENS ONCE WROTE, "ONLY THE RICH remember the past," and I count myself rich in the wealth of memories that have resulted from the twenty-five years during which I enjoyed his friendship, both by personal contact and by correspondence. Those years were the most stimulating and rewarding period that one could experience. Still, I accepted the opportunity to write this essay with some trepidation. Could my contribution, I asked myself, do justice to those memories? What I have to say comes from one whose feelings toward Wallace Stevens were a mixture of admiration, respect, friendship, and a deep and abiding affection— feelings that emphasize the painful insufficiency of words.

Stevens was truly a diamond of many facets, and it was my privilege to see him and to know him in many of his spheres of interest and activity. As John Malcolm Brinnin has said (in an article in the Spring 1945 issue of *Voices*, which was dedicated to Stevens), paraphrasing one of the poet's well-known titles, "there are at least thirteen ways of looking at Wallace Stevens."

In the course of becoming aware of Stevens' importance as a poet, many people are curious first about his ability to have combined successfully two diverse roles: lawyer-businessman and poet. Certainly the students I met with in May 1973, when I conducted a seminar on my acquaintanceship with Stevens for the Department of Modern Literature at Stanford University, revealed such curiosity. It was a most gratifying experience for me; I was delighted to see the interest that those young people were taking in the poet's work. Although the seminar lasted only one hour, I was detained another hour by a group of students who lingered because of their desire to talk with someone who had known Stevens personally. Of the many questions that arose during the seminar and after, one particularly interested me: "How did Stevens' life as a corporation executive influence his work as a poet?" My answer was that, while Stevens' interests were many and varied, his one and all-consuming interest was his poetry and other literary achievements, and his life as a corporation executive was merely a means to an end. It provided him and his family a very comfortable home life and permitted him to exercise his literary talents and aspirations with complete freedom from the financial worries that are so frequently a part of the lives of so many artists. This conclusion of mine is substantiated by a line from his beloved *Adagia*: "I have no life except in poetry. No doubt that would be true if my whole life was free for poetry" (*OP*, 175). Thus I think it can safely be said that the main influence his corporate life had on his artistic life was that the corporate life took too much of his time—time that he would have loved to have spent in creative writing. This thought is advanced without in any way depreciating his value or his loyalty to the company that he served most faithfully for over thirty years.

Stevens' entire life was governed by the very highest of ideals, and these ideals naturally prevailed in his corporate life and in his management of his department. In my long association with him I observed that in the performance of his duties he set and adhered to standards that I have seldom seen equaled and that I know will never be excelled. While he was ever zealous in protecting the rights of the company, he at the same time tempered his position with whatever leniency the circumstances suggested. These combined traits of justice and mercy contributed in large measure to the phenomenal growth that the company enjoyed during the period he served it.

Just what were his responsibilities? His home office duties as lawyer (and only as a lawyer) were pretty much the same as mine here on the West Coast. Suretyship is a field of practice that is completely unknown to the average lawyer.[1] Consequently, Stevens, in placing a case in the hands of some attorney, would have to guide him in the substantive legal aspects of the case. The specific procedural aspects, of course, the local attorney would know, while Stevens, in most instances, would know absolutely nothing. But in addition to having these strictly legal duties, he, as an executive of the company, presided over his department, which consisted of five attorneys and some clerical staff, along with the customary secretaries. Beyond directing the operation of this department, with its varying demands, he supervised the men in the field offices.

There were five field offices handling surety matters: the New York office had two men, while the Atlanta, Pittsburgh, Chicago, and San Francisco offices each had one. All of these men reported to Stevens and were in varying degrees autonomous. As an instance: Stevens had a visit one day from a gentleman here on the Coast who was not satisfied with the treatment he had received from me. When this man asked Stevens who had the final say here on matters such as his, the reply was a Stevens classic: "Taylor has, but we have the right to overrule him." A typical Stevens retort and, of course, the last thing that his visitor wanted to hear.

No, his duties as a corporation vice-president did not stand in the way of his refreshing wit. It was an unusual letter from him that did not contain a metaphor or an allegory that was as appropriate as it was humorous. In one instance that comes to mind, the company had sustained a loss of many thousands of dollars. The field office where the loss occurred had recovered from the person causing the loss the sum of five dollars. Stevens, in acknowledging this, said that he now knew how the hippopotamus felt when someone threw him a handful of raspberries.

Whatever the circumstances at a given moment required, Stevens possessed a remarkable quickness, adaptability, and wit. Seated with him at directors' meetings of one of the companies in the Hartford Group, I was aware that he presided with all the dignity and strength appropriate to his role. Yet his humor frequently punctured the seriousness of these meetings. One such incident occurred shortly after the United States went off the gold standard. This, of course, brought an abrupt end to the long-established custom of giving a gold piece to each director attending the meeting. But Wallace Stevens was not to be thwarted by an edict from the White House. At the conclusion of the meeting he presented each director with a gold coin—a chocolate impression of a coin, wrapped in gold-colored foil. To this day these coins are available at well-stocked candy counters.

I recall, too, a rather amusing incident that took place in a somewhat less formal setting. Stevens was to have a conference one day at the office of a Harvard classmate who was the senior partner in one of New York's old and distinguished law firms. There were just four of us present: Stevens, his classmate, myself, and a young lawyer, probably just admitted to the bar, who was representing the other party to the controversy. The young lawyer expounded at great length on the problem involved and the law that was applicable. Both Stevens and his Harvard classmate listened attentively, but when the end finally came, Stevens spoke up: "Well, I guess we country lawyers don't know as much about those things as you big city lawyers do." It is impossible to describe the devastating effect of that last remark. Stevens' classmate could hardly conceal his amusement, and the young fellow was rightfully astonished at its implications.

Anyone was apt to bear the brunt of his sense of humor. For many years his loyal and devoted secretary was Mrs. Baldwin, a dignified and staid New England lady, the kind to whom slang was as foreign as day is to night. She had a son at Stanford during World War II and made a trip to the Pacific Coast to visit him. While she was in San Francisco, my secretary took her to lunch, and later she came to my house for dinner, after which I drove her to the campus to visit her son. Upon her return to Hartford she related all this to Mr. Stevens, whereupon he proceeded to dictate a letter to me for her to type:

Mrs. Baldwin is back and, while she is quite tanned and

looks younger, she is still very New Englandish. She has expressed herself with the utmost discretion and yet, from things that she has said, I gather that you must have been drinking sequoia sap. She says that you haven't grown any smaller, but that is just the New England way of saying "O, boy!"

I have always had a mental picture of Mrs. Baldwin cringing upon being the subject of this deviation from cultivated speech.

Stevens was sometimes the delight and sometimes the despair of some of the younger people with whom he shared his corporate life. I recall one time when I was in Hartford, we were seated in his office after lunch when a most charming young miss, probably of high school age, who was working for the summer appeared at the door of his office with a handful of checks to be signed. Stevens motioned to her to come in. She laid the checks before him, and he started the process of signing each one. Without looking up, without disturbing the rhythm of signing, and without any preliminary remarks he said: "This is that girl I was telling you about at lunch today, Taylor." The child was embarrassed beyond words and, of course, pictured herself as having been thoroughly discussed and critically analyzed by each of us at lunch. While the incident was amusing, one could not help but feel for the young lady. To completely allay any lingering suspicions to the contrary, let me assure all readers that the young lady was not discussed by us at lunch.

We all know that Wallace Stevens had a keen mind, but what is not so well known is that he sometimes used this talent to produce a barb, which, if it happened to hit home, could sting. One such instance was a letter he wrote containing one of his classic metaphors. It illustrates how sharp his tongue could be, if the occasion, in his mind, justified it. Stevens had taken a particular dislike to some lawyer in Philadelphia, and in one of his letters he referred to this fellow as having a smile that was like the silver plate on a coffin.

Although Stevens was adept at relieving the pressures of the business world, those pressures were real. It is quite unlikely that many readers of this chapter have, or ever will, experience the hazards and the precariousness of corporate employment. While it has a great deal to commend it, at the same time there are moments of apprehension. Wallace Stevens was not completely immune to these hazards, and when one reads "The Poem That Took the Place of a Mountain" and considers that it was composed during some rather drastic changes in the company that affected him, the poem comes remarkably close to being a brief autobiography.

Essentially, however, Stevens was guarded when it came to his personal life. About those things that he considered private, there was to be no discussion unless he brought up the subject himself. Such a subject was the fact that Mrs. Stevens' profile was on the dimes that were in circulation from 1916 until our silver coins became debased with copper. It is now generally known that Mrs. Stevens was on both the dimes and the fifty-cent pieces, but I knew Wallace Stevens for over thirteen years before he ever mentioned this subject to me.

Only occasionally would he bring up the subject of his poetry. One such instance involved the title to a new volume that was soon to be published. The contents of the new work had been compiled and, except for the title, everything was in readiness. Two titles were being considered: *Parts of a World* and *The Man, That's All One Knows*. When Mrs. Stevens asked him whether "Knows" was to be spelled "Nose" he decided that the title had better be *Parts of a World*.

One day during the early part of our friendship, when I had just purchased my copy of *Harmonium*, I asked him whether he would autograph it for me if I sent it to him. He replied, "Isn't your copy of *Harmonium* autographed?" I assured him that it was not, whereupon he said that I should treasure it as the only unautographed copy of *Harmonium* in existence. He did indeed autograph it, with the inscription "As the reason destroys, the poet must create."

Another deeply personal subject with him was religion. During the years that I knew him, I cannot recall ever discussing this subject with him. Nevertheless, I observed many manifestations of the depth of his religious feeling. One is an entry in his cherished *Adagia*: "The mind that in heaven created the earth and the mind that on earth created heaven were, as it happened, one" (*OP*, 176). Two of his Christmas letters to me also contributed to this belief on my part. Wallace Stevens deplored the way that the commercial aspects of Christmas have so nearly obliterated the true meaning of the holiday season. In one of his letters he expressed this by opening with "Blessed be the Holy name of Santa Claus." In another letter he wished my wife and daughter "fewer dishes to wash and long prayers in warm rooms."

A further and very strong indication of the depth of his religious feeling occurred one evening in June 1938 when I was in Hartford. Stevens had arranged for a dinner that evening, to be held at a place in the country not far from Hartford. All the men in his department were invited, as well as one or two from other offices in the company. With a few preliminary drinks, singing began, and when the general and somewhat limited repertoire became exhausted, one of the fellows started "Onward Christian Soldiers." Stevens immediately held up his hand and shook his head in decided disapproval. "Onward Christian Soldiers" was not to be sung under these circumstances and, in this instance, did not get beyond the three title words.

Stevens did not conceal his deep interest in his genealogy. Many of his letters to me relate to his association during the late 1930s and early 1940s with a Mrs. Roney. Born in Reading, Pennsylvania, of Dutch ancestry, he desired to belong to the Holland Society, a genealogical organization in the New York area, founded in 1885. Membership is extremely difficult to attain. A prospective member must show an unbroken line of Dutch ancestry on the male side, back to, or prior to, 1675. Mrs. Roney was supposed to be an expert at tracing ancestry, and Stevens, I know, paid her many hundreds of dollars to trace his ancestry to qualify him for membership in the society. But Mrs. Roney went to her just rewards without establishing Stevens' ancestry to meet the requirements of the society. It was a matter of keen disappointment to him that he could not become a member. On November 16, 1944, just about two weeks after Roosevelt had been elected to the presidency for the fourth time, Stevens wrote me:

> Mrs. Roney died suddenly on election day. It seems a strange thing to think, but it is quite possible that, as the returns indicated the overwhelming victory of Roosevelt, Mrs. Roney, who regarded him as the arch-enemy of the past, may well have crawled upstairs and taken an overdose of sleeping powder. That is my guess of about what happened, but I don't know. The last time I saw her, she looked the wrath of God; nothing really happened to her that ought to have made all this difference. She probably lost a good deal of money, but she could very well have said to herself that she was busted and then have gone to New York and started all over again. Nevertheless, this is a crude way of muffing a real tragedy. She was, after all, a lonely woman who regarded herself as the subject of a vicious fate.

What is worth noting here, of course, is the way Stevens' sympathy for the woman breaks through at the end. His wit did not preclude sensitivity to the suffering of others.

One of the chief impressions I have of this unusual man is of his intense desire to experience the many possibilities that life has to offer. The closing of his wonderful letter to me of June 23, 1948, probably best reflects the insatiability of this desire:

> What I want more than anything else in music, painting and poetry, in life and in belief is the thrill that I experienced once in all the things that no longer thrill me at all. I am like a man in a grocery store that is sick and tired of raisins and oyster crackers and who nevertheless is overwhelmed by appetite.

Some might detect a note of melancholy in these lines. On the contrary, they clearly show his constant and profound joy in living. As his friend Alfred Kreymborg said, "He wrote purely for the pleasure of writing, as he lived for the pleasure of living."

At times his pleasure could take the form of sheer gustatory delight. It is no secret to readers of his *Letters* that he was a connoisseur of a rich variety of delicacies for the palate. I was surely aware of this fact. In the town in New Jersey where I lived before moving to the West Coast there was a Danish baker by the name of Alfred Monde. As a boy he had been apprenticed in a Danish *conditori*, and upon coming to America he began the active practice of his art. The comestibles that he produced were beyond description, and the holiday season always saw specialties, which in some instances were made from dough prepared the previous August. It was in December of 1940, just about the time that Germany moved into Denmark, that I sent Stevens a box of these Danish delectables. On January 13, 1941, he wrote me:

> I suppose Denmark was a push-over on account of the pastry they eat there. In any event, I am just chock-full of the stuff you sent me. That man in Plainfield is some pastrician! . . . I feel confident that I am surrounded by people who are based on squash pie and pumpkin pie. In this inimical atmosphere the less one says about chocolate whipped cream the better.

Such tastes would have been disastrous for a completely sedentary person, but Stevens was of course a great walker.

While I know that he enjoyed the relative quiet and calm life that Hartford gave, I also know how he thoroughly enjoyed the faster pace, the comparative excitement, and the vast montage of people that only New York can offer. One of his chief pleasures in coming to New York was to indulge in his love of walking. Many times I met him at the Commodore Hotel, where he generally stayed, and we would walk for probably two hours before we finally reached our destination for dinner. He once remarked to me that walking in

New York was so unlike walking in Hartford. In Hartford, he said, if you went out for a walk of a summer's evening, sooner or later you would hear someone say, "There goes that man again."

But his walking was not confined to New York. His home was in West Hartford, and it was his habit to walk to the office in the morning and to walk back to his home in the late afternoon. In fact, I have it on no less an authority than his secretary that it was during the solitude of these morning walks that much of his poetry was composed.

Aside from football at the college level, he had no interest in what we today loosely refer to as sports. After I left the East for San Francisco, he once asked me whether I ever went to football games. He said that I should, for it would keep me in touch with young people. This thought was probably best expressed by him in his letter to me of November 21, 1949. Stevens and two of his friends at the office went to the Harvard-Yale game at New Haven, which he described as "a very dismal occasion." But then he said:

> The only bright spot for me was a very charming couple that sat in the next row but one in front of me. She kept her head on his shoulder throughout the game and every now and then he would turn towards her and they would stay that way for minutes at a time—oh boy.

Obviously, he appreciated exquisite feelings wherever he found them.

I knew him also as a man of letters—a true and intense intellectual. His interest in the arts was catholic and, in paintings, was centered on the works of Cezanne. In March 1938 I wrote Stevens about an exhibit of Cezanne's art, and in that letter I spoke of his watercolors in terms that did violence to Stevens' appraisal of them. He replied to this letter on March 31, 1938:

> Thanks very much about the Cezannes. I think you will find that you get a catalogue when you pay for admission.
> I hope to get down next week and, if I am, I expect to see the monstrosities for myself.

When I stop to think that Cezanne has been the source of all painting of any interest during the last 20 years, say, it becomes pretty clear that there is something wrong about calling the damned things monstrosities. It is the way he composes, as one might say to a bar tender.

But along with his high regard for Cezanne and that artist's contribution to the school of impressionism, he also devoted time and admiration to the schools of modernism and, to some extent, realism. Shortly before the outbreak of World War II we spent an afternoon in the Metropolitan Museum of Art enjoying an exhibit of interiors by Walter Gay. The entire exhibit was on its way to the Louvre.

An afternoon spent with Stevens in New York might embrace visits to the various galleries in the 57th Street area, or an afternoon at the Metropolitan Museum of Art or at the Museum of Modern Art. An evening might include a concert of chamber music or an entire program of Stravinsky. Although Beethoven was his favorite composer ("Beethoven is my meat," he said in a letter to me of June 23, 1948), he always seemed to enjoy the works of more modern composers. And his aesthetic interests extended to other areas. I have been with him at furniture exhibits at the Parke Bernet Galleries. The New York Flower Show always attracted him, and for several consecutive years I attended that display with him (his absorbing delight in flowers is both delicately and amusingly conveyed in his letters to me of August 20, 1947, and June 23, 1948; see L, 564, 603). In his case it is not a cliché to say that aesthetic variety was the spice of life. For me, it was a privilege to share in his rich variety of tastes.

I am sure that I shall never know anyone who enjoyed the New York World's Fair of 1939-1940 as much as Wallace Stevens did. Time and time again we would go there in the afternoon, walk for a few hours, and always end up in the French Pavilion, where, after taking in some of its exhibits and a vermouth-cassis or two for our jaded appetites, we would have dinner. This was his favorite building in the fair, and he spent many hours there among the works of art and the other exhibits. One thing in particular caught his fancy, and one day toward the end of the second year of the fair he phoned me from Hartford to see whether I could go with him to the fair that evening. He explained that he had an appointment with the manager of the French Pavilion to see a stained-glass window that he was interested in purchasing.

Stevens, I am sure, realized that the window was standing well within the building and away from any daylight illumination. What I am sure he did not realize was that its location was not the only reason for its being artificially lighted. I recall its scene as a deep forest with lush undergrowth and with a deer standing in the foreground. However, when the pavilion manager opened the door in the rear, showing the reverse side of the scene, one saw jagged pieces of glass of completely random lengths and shapes. The artist had simply taken huge chunks of colored glass that had been smashed indiscriminately and pieced them together, forming the pastoral scene that one saw from the front. Thus it took light bulbs varying in intensity from 25 watts to probably 500 watts to produce the properly balanced color scene that one saw from the front. Stevens' surprise at what he had just seen was equaled by his amusement when the pavilion manager told him that there were two prospective purchasers for the window. One was Wallace Stevens and the other was International Business Machines Corporation.

Stevens' love for the fair endured far beyond its closing in the autumn of 1940. The following spring we exchanged letters on the subject of a picture of the French Pavilion. He was at this point living with many fond memories of the pavilion, its works of art, its dining facilities, its menus, and its view of the fireworks and fountain display that were nightly features. He wrote me early in April of 1941, asking whether I could locate a suitable picture of the French Pavilion. On this subject, two of his letters follow. In one dated April 19, 1941, he said:

> Of the two pictures of the French Pavilion I like the one with the board walk and the people, which I shall call

A; The other one, B, is spoiled by the fact that the chairs are on the tables in the restaurant, which is a hell of a place for chairs.

The letter then discusses two other places that might have better pictures of the pavilion. One of these places did indeed have a suitable picture, which produced the following letter, dated April 29, 1941:

This photograph is about right. In the foreground and a little to the left there are two females; one of them appears to be holding a copy of GONE WITH THE WIND, and the other really looks as if she was gone with the wind. . . . You may recognize them; they look like visitors from Plainfield. . . . If you could get this same photograph with better looking girls in it, it would be perfect. Look at those two over to the right: as perfect a pair of kitchen heavyweights as I have ever seen!

What I believe I will do is this: I will take a copy of picture A which I mentioned in my letter of April 19th, and I will take this new picture without having it enlarged. . . .

There are some good points about this picture; that looks like a very nice girl in shorts under the maple tree. Apparently the thing was taken at about 1:30 on a cloudless afternoon. There are no shadows: it looks like a photograph of the new world that is said to be coming into existence, in which everything is bright and cheerful, except the people in it.

Despite the jaundiced nature of the final phrase, Stevens was concerned about the health of the world and its people, and he devoutly felt that poetry should have a supreme function in any new world of value that might "be coming into existence."

Surely Stevens' poetry will be a source of meaning and pleasure for future generations. A timely article in *American Scholar* put into sharp focus for me how essential the printing process and books are to preserving knowledge so that it survives the death of the individual or of a generation. Thinking about that article in relation to Stevens has brought to mind an evening when I had dinner with Mr. and Mrs. Stevens in New York. During the course of the evening's conversation he expressed some concern as to what, if anything, he was contributing to society that would be remembered after his death. Mrs. Stevens reminded him of his poetry and cited it as a sure manifestation of his immortality. The event I have just described took place after Stevens had written:

> Beauty is momentary in the mind—
> The fitful tracing of a portal;
> But in the flesh it is immortal.
> The body dies; the body's beauty lives.

Stevens the man is gone, but the beauty of his mind will live in the body of his poems, thanks to the process of printing, of making books.

HOLLY STEVENS

HOLIDAYS IN REALITY

ON SUMMER DAYS WHEN I WAS SMALL, MY MOTHER and I used to sit in the sun on the west side of the house where we lived at 735 Farmington Avenue, in West Hartford, near our front door (which was really the side door to the house). One of my earliest memories is of being there and watching her brush and comb her long blonde hair in the sunshine: it resembled strands of pure gold. She combed and brushed for a long time, parting her hair over and over again, applying hair tonic at each part, which added to the glistening effect: "The hair of my blonde / Is dazzling."

It was in that side yard that my father set up a small playground when I was a little older. There was a slide and a seesaw, but I don't remember using the seesaw often, perhaps because there were few other children of my size in the neighborhood. What I liked best was the swing, especially when my father pushed me up so high that I almost flew; as he pushed he recited Robert Louis Stevenson's verse, "How do you like to go up in a swing," and soon I had memorized it too.

But my first swing was in the playground in Elizabeth Park, where we went every weekend. It was only a short walk away, half a block down Farmington Avenue, then a long block on Walbridge Road to Fern Street, and then another block or less, depending on which entrance to the park we took. My favorite entrance was through the stableyard, where the horses that were used for grounds maintenance were kept; my father carried sugar lumps in his pocket and taught me to hold my palm flat so that the horse's tongue could sweep over it and carry the sugar away. We also fed the ducks in the pond, who were so tame that they would take a piece of bread directly from your fingers; I remember being more afraid of their beaks than of the horses' teeth.

There was a bridge over a narrow section of the pond, with stone walls in a gentle curve on either side. My father would lift me up so I could walk on the wall, holding his hand and feeling very tall, for my head was on a level with his. In winter there was skating on the pond, and children went back and forth under the bridge, where the ice was apt to be thin. I don't remember my father doing that, but he was a very good skater and everyone admired his "figure eights."

We often walked in the rose garden, under the arches to the central "summer house," whether the roses were blooming or not. Across the road was the rock garden, and near it a less well-kept area, where lilacs and a grove of holly trees grew. Sometimes we picnicked there, as I imagine my parents had done before I was born, for it was where I got my name. My father's choice had been "Sylvia" or "Sybil," I forget which, and my mother hadn't liked the alliteration; she told me they settled on "Holly" because the tree had attractive berries, but also prickly leaves, which lent it a standoffish quality.

On the western edge of the park, beyond the playground, there was a sloping hillside, with large trees along the road at the top and woods at the bottom. Daffodils grew here in great profusion, and it was where we had our picnics in the spring, my father carrying the hamper, which was quite a proper one with china plates and real silverware, though the cups or glasses we drank out of were made of celluloid.

In the greenhouses, in addition to the flowers and plants, there were small ponds where goldfish swam; in the pond outside there were goldfish and catfish as well as ducks. Coming from the cold outdoors in winter to the tropical glassed-in heat, we would try to recognize the fish that had swum in a larger world the previous summer; my father had a name for one of them, but I have forgotten it. But not the world that the park was for us and where, many years later when I had a child of my own, I would sometimes walk with my father on Sunday mornings.

In 1929, when I was five years old, we went to Atlantic City on vacation, the first time I remember being away from home for any length of time. We stayed at a very large hotel that had wings stretching toward the sea from a main building, which faced the boardwalk. To reach the sea, you had to go through the basement of one of the wings and then through a sort of tunnel under the boardwalk, which led to a narrow wooden walk that crossed the sand to the water's edge. I don't remember that we did this very often; my mother didn't like the sea and couldn't swim. She even objected to the sound of the waves that came into the room we shared at night, while I was enchanted by it. She told me that my father had almost let her drown once, and that was why she was afraid of the water. On the other hand, I have heard stories in Reading of my father saving the life of a drowning swimmer; he gave up the sport only when his doctor told him that it was bad for his ear, which was becoming deaf.

My father's room was long corridors away from ours, either in the opposite wing or at the back of the hotel. I remember hobbling there after turning my ankle, and it seemed miles; my reward was that he carried me back. We ate saltwater taffy and took long walks on the boardwalk; sometimes we rode in the rolling chairs.

The next year we went to Pocono Manor, high in the mountains of Pennsylvania. I remember tripping on a porch step at the hotel; it was another time my father carried me. My mother liked the place (I didn't know then that she had been there previously, long before I was born) and was happy to be there; she had friends who were also staying there and played golf with them occasionally. I remember walking on the golf course with my father, though I remember a path through woods better; it led to a lake where I took my first swimming lessons.

During the summer of 1931 my mother and I were enrolled in the Institute of Euthenics at Vassar College, where my father joined us on weekends. Then, instead of returning to Hartford, we went on to a camp in the Adirondacks because there was an epidemic of some sort in Connecticut. I don't remember where the camp was, but I think it was called "Gardner-Dewing"; there were accommodations for parents as well as for children, and the emphasis was on arts and crafts. My favorite activities were a game called "Statues" and dancing on the grass; my mother's interest became weaving, and that was the craft we brought home with us. When we moved to Westerly Terrace in 1932 we both had looms set up in the sunroom, and a teacher came in periodically to show my mother how to change the threading to produce different effects; I still have samples of our work, in pillow covers and bureau runners. The looms disappeared long ago, but after my mother died in 1963, I found a large supply of thread that had been saved. I don't remember what my father did while at the camp, but he had often taken me fishing when we were at Vassar and perhaps did so at camp also.

Then, for several years, we did not take summer vacations, though my father went to Florida in the winter. One of the acquaintances he made there was Peter Schutt, who was manager of the Casa Marina in Key West. In the summer of 1939 Schutt was managing the Holly Inn at Christmas Cove in Maine; whether it was because he was there or simply because the opportunity for a vacation arose, we went to Maine. Christmas Cove is not far from Damariscotta, at the end of a finger of land a few miles west of another finger that ends at Pemaquid Point. The inn was a large, rambling place made of wood and painted white; I learned later that it was the third inn built on the same site, replacing predecessors that had burned down, as this one also did a little later. As I recall, it was on a slight rise, looking over the sea toward Boothbay Harbor, which was invisible in the distance even when it wasn't foggy. Close to the water was a saltwater pool, the icy stream piped so rapidly over a rocky bluff that it had no chance to warm up en route. It seems to me that there was no beach or direct access to the cove for swimming, but there must have been a pier or dock, because one could go on boating excursions to various points of interest. Coming back from one of these we were marooned in fog for a long time before the captain found his way; I remember my father telling stories and jokes to divert our attention from the possible danger.

One of the excursions we took, on a sunny day, was to Monhegan Island. I don't remember that we landed, but certainly we circled it by boat. The most vivid sense I've ever had of color I experienced there, where the water at the foot of the cliffs shaded from deep blue, almost black, through lighter shades into a pale turquoise: it was truly aquamarine. For years anything with that blue-green miraculous hue—a dress, a vase, a painting with that color in it—was something I longed for. Some twenty years later I went back to the island and stood on the cliffs looking down at the sea; from that vantage point it had lost some of its magic, but the color was still there.

Among our fellow guests was a young English couple on their honeymoon. Peter Oldham (if I remember his name correctly) was an officer in the Royal Air Force; I often wonder whether he survived World War II, and whether he and his wife are still together. They spent a lot of time by the pool, and my father often joined them for long conversations, which undoubtedly included discussion of the situation in Europe.

It was the summer that my father wrote "An exercise in viewing the world" in his poem, "Variations on a Summer Day." As he commented to Hi Simons:

> The ordinary, everyday search of the romantic mind is rewarded perhaps rather too lightly by the satisfaction that it finds in what it calls reality. But if one happened to be playing checkers somewhere under the Maginot Line, subject to a call at any moment to do some job that might be one's last job, one would spend a good deal of time thinking in order to make the situation seem reasonable, inevitable and free from question.
>
> I suppose that, in the last analysis, my own main objective is to do that kind of thinking. On the other hand, ["Variations on a Summer Day"], from which every bit of anything of that sort has been excluded, also has its justifi-

cations. In a world permanently enigmatical, to hear and see agreeable things involves something more than mere imagism. One might do it deliberately and in that particular poem I did it deliberately. (L, 346)

Some of the references in the poem bring back visual images to me: "light blue air over dark blue sea," "Star over Monhegan," "timothy at Pemaquid"; but my image for "spruce trees" is the young RAF officer:

> Everywhere the spruce trees bury soldiers:
> Hugh March, a sergeant, a redcoat, killed,
> With his men, beyond the barbican.
> Everywhere spruce trees bury spruce trees.

And isn't the "barbican" the Maginot Line? "It was not yet the hour to be dauntlessly leaping."

The onset of war and the inevitability of the United States being drawn into it contributed to my father's decision to take my mother and me with him when he went to Florida the following winter. I did not want to go; it was the height of the high school social season (I was then a junior), and I had a "crush" on a young man. But I was given no choice in the matter.

We flew from Hartford to Jacksonville, making several stops on the way; Eleanor Roosevelt was a fellow passenger between Washington, D.C., and Atlanta, and was much more attractive than any of us had imagined from her photographs. Even my mother commented on this, although she was airsick throughout the trip and didn't notice much else. We stayed in Palm Beach for a while and, among brief visits, paid one to St. Augustine; but most of the vacation was spent in Key West at the Casa Marina.

It was there that I met Robert Frost, who came along one day as I was idly batting a tennis ball against a wall. We started talking and I must have told him how lonely I was and how much I would rather have been at home. Here in Florida, where I'd thought it possible for exotic things to happen, I was either treated as a child or ignored. With some sympathy and, as I recall, a wicked glint in his eye, we conspired together: one evening soon afterwards, without consulting my parents, Robert Frost took me to my first cocktail party. I was allowed to stand in a corner with a glass of ginger ale and watch people smoking and drinking and moving about gaily from one conversational group to another. I may even have been introduced to one or two of the other guests, but at the time that wasn't important. The newness and headiness of the experience were what counted, for at home my parents almost never entertained, and there was no such thing as a "cocktail hour" if they did; nor did they ever sit down together for a drink before dinner. At last, an "exotic" experience, and I don't think my father ever found out about it, for I was back at the hotel in good time (and condition) for dinner. I was amazed years later, when I took my son to hear Frost read at Wesleyan University shortly before his death, that he remembered the occasion well and had delighted in "putting one over" on Wallace Stevens.

I'm not sure where I'd first heard the term "cocktail party," but I saw something similar with my father in Florida—from a distance. One of our regular walks in Key West was to the Coast Guard tower, which we would then climb. In 1940 the foliage was neither as high nor as dense as I found it to be on my second visit there in the early 1970s; earlier the top of the tower was an excellent point from which to look down on Ernest Hemingway's house and swimming pool. Most of the time there was only one person there, a woman, alone, sunbathing; but one day there was an enormous crowd in and around the pool, many with glasses in hand, and I remember my father remarking, "Hemingway's back in town."

The other celebrity I remember was the union leader John L. Lewis, who was also at the Casa Marina. In those days one of my hobbies was photography, and I became so excited at the chance to take his picture (with those great, bushy eyebrows) coming through the doorway from the hotel to the loggia that I forgot to wind the film; the result was a double exposure of Lewis and Stevens.

My father's friend from high school days, Ned (Edwin de Turck) Bechtel, and his wife were also guests at the hotel that winter. I believe it had been some time since they had seen each other, and they were glad to have a chance to "catch up." Judge Arthur Powell and his wife were also there. I think it was the first time my mother had met them, although the judge and my father had been visiting Florida together for years; I think the women liked each other as well. But I don't remember ever seeing the Powells again, though the Bechtels both became good friends, in part because Louise was a Vassar graduate, and my father had decided that Vassar was where I should go to college. For me that winter vacation was the beginning of my transition from child to adult; for my father there was reunion, but also a final "Farewell to Florida."

We never spent another vacation together, though I encountered Peter Schutt and his family once more, in the summer of 1941, when I was allowed to take a vacation alone at the Bethel Inn in Maine, which he was managing. Over the years we had visited other places: Washington, D.C.; Natural Bridge, Williamsburg, Monticello, the campus of the University of Virginia, and somewhere near the Skyline Drive, in Virginia; Boston, Lexington, and Concord (but not Cambridge), Massachusetts; Reading, Lititz, Hershey (but not Philadelphia), Pennsylvania. I'm sure there were others, but I am more surprised by the omissions than that I don't remember more places or when we were there.

Beginning when I was six or seven, we paid countless visits to New York on weekends, for shopping and theater. By the late 1930s I could tick off all the plays listed in the front of *The New Yorker*, including musical comedies, and some we saw twice. By then I also knew the floor plan of the Hotel New Weston, at East 50th Street and Madison Avenue, by heart; "our" favorite accommodations were on the floor below the Vassar Club, a two-bedroom suite with a large living room, which, before we arrived, was provided with bouquets of flowers and bowls of fruit, as well as a good supply of Poland water (we never drank tap water as I was growing up; even at home fresh spring water was delivered regularly).

Toward the end of my father's life he said that he was uncomfortable whenever he slept away from home. When I first began to be included in the weekends in New York I was taught to call the New Weston "home" while we were there. The other places to which I gave the same name were in Atlantic City, the Poconos, Poughkeepsie, the Adirondacks, Christmas Cove, and Key West. All except Atlantic City have been "celebrated" by my father: the mountains, Maine, and Florida in poems, and Vassar in a series of sketches he titled "Viewing Vassar Voraciously," which is now in the Stevens Archive at the Huntington Library.

But there was one other place that was "home" for my father, not a "home away from home," but an extension (as a garden is) of the place where one lays one's head at night. Even when we moved to Westerly Terrace, Elizabeth Park was nearby, within easy walking distance, and my father spent some time there almost every day. It provided a perennial vacation at hand; where he could meet old friends, or make new ones; where he could revisit familiar spots but always find something new; where ideas could come and breed and grow; where the poet could enjoy a needed solitude or bring his family. It was a place for "the finding of a satisfaction, and may / Be of a man skating, . . . a woman / Combing. . . ."

PETER A. BRAZEAU

A TRIP IN A BALLOON:
A SKETCH OF STEVENS' LATER
YEARS IN NEW YORK

IN 1949 WALLACE STEVENS DESCRIBED WHAT HIS FRE-
quent visits to New York meant to this Connecticut poet-
executive: "Hartford is the best place in the world for me
to be in day after day but I do occasionally like a trip in a
balloon" (L, 630). Although he felt at times that his New
York visits were "delusions, in the sense that I go there to
get away from my limitations . . . and find myself stepping
into another set of limitations," more often Manhattan was
an invigorating and necessary part of his Hartford life.[1] Ste-
vens left New York to join the Hartford Accident and In-
demnity Company in 1916. That Manhattan was only a few
hours away by train or car was one reason Hartford was an
acceptable home to Stevens for nearly forty years: New York
offered an important outlet for Stevens the man-about-town,
the connoisseur, and the public man of letters. A selection
from the recollections of friends who shared Wallace Ste-
vens' New York allows us to hitch a ride on that balloon.

In New York, Stevens enjoyed being the man-about-town,
a role in which he was not often seen in Hartford. "I was
part of the fun-and-frolic side of Wallace Stevens' life," Mar-
garet Powers recalls.[2] A most vivacious lady, she and her hus-
band James, Stevens' assistant in Hartford for a time, were
close friends of the poet for more than twenty-five years. She
remembers how much Stevens enjoyed the lighter side of
Manhattan in the 1930s and 1940s, treating his young friends
to occasional nights on the town. The recently married Pow-
erses were living in Greenwich Village in 1929 when Stevens
came to be introduced to Mrs. Powers:

Jim was in the shower when the guests arrived, and I had
to meet Wallace Stevens all by myself. He was always on
time. . . . There I was, this little girl absolutely in awe of
this man, scared green. He realized the situation . . . so
what did that darling person do but just have me rolling
on the floor telling me about somebody's funeral. It
sounds blasphemous, but he made it so funny. . . . When
he [Jim] came out, I was just madly in love with Wallace
Stevens. . . .

We went out to dinner and the theater, or something.
He was always finding new places for us to go to. He loved
the theater . . . musicals and so forth. . . . A year or so later,
in the summertime he took us to "The Third Little
Show." . . . It was . . . all top comedians.[3] We sat always
in the third row, not balcony the way the Powerses would
do it. . . . He just loved the theater. . . . He was always
taking us to things like that. He knew all the comedians
and appreciated their humor, oh, boy, yes. He liked the
music, too.

One such night on the town culminated in Stevens' morn-
ing-after poem, "A Fish-Scale Sunrise," in which he ad-
dresses the Powerses. Mrs. Powers remembers that evening
in 1933 vividly:

Jim and Wallace . . . had been together all afternoon, and
I met them about 6 or so. . . . And then we started out.
We went to a couple of speak-easies, then this place
where he got the singer to play "La Paloma": that's where
we had our dinner. When we got through there, it was
about 11:30 or 12, and then we went to the Waldorf Roof,
which had just opened,[4] and did the dancing—first time
he had ever danced, so we danced. And he loved it. He
was doggone good; he had a wonderful sense of rhythm.
. . . He seemed to enjoy it thoroughly, and that was a new
experience for him. . . . He insisted on ordering pickled
herrings. Now that comes from reading German, I sup-
pose. We tried it, but he loved them. . . . It was an impet-
uous evening. . . . I think we just meant to meet and have

cocktails, but we went on and on and on. . . . I think he
felt quite close to Jim and me that evening. He kissed me
—the only time in his life—he wasn't that type. . . . I un-
derstood the evening and what it meant to all of us, but
. . . I can't when he put it in poetry.

A Fish-Scale Sunrise
Melodious skeletons, for all of last night's music
Today is today and the dancing is done.

Dew lies on the instruments of straw that you were
    playing,
The ruts in your empty road are red.

You Jim and you Margaret and you singer of La Paloma,
The cocks are crowing and crowing loud,

And although my mind perceives the force behind the
    moment,
The mind is smaller than the eye.

The sun rises green and blue in the fields and in the
    heavens.
The clouds foretell a swampy rain.[5]

When we glimpse the background of such a casual phrase as
"the dancing is done," it is interesting to see the understated
way in which Stevens might, at times, translate personal
experience into poetry.

Anthony Sigmans, a close business friend of Stevens for
over twenty years, first met Stevens on such a night club tour.
Though it was an evening on the town with a twist of busi-
ness, here again is the Stevens who enjoyed the night spots
and Big Band atmosphere of New York in the 1930s.

It was in 1934 that I first made his acquaintance, and it
came about in an odd sort of way. At the time, I was
employed by Glens Falls Indemnity Company. . . . My
work was similar to that of Mr. Stevens. . . . We had a
brief phone conversation, and it was agreed that I would
meet him at the Commodore Hotel on a day certain and

to come up to his room immediately on arrival. The hour was about 6 o'clock. I knocked at his door, and what I saw was a towering figure over six feet tall, weighing 250 or more pounds. To say the least, I felt insignificant. . . . Mr. Stevens greeted me cordially and immediately inquired if I had [had] dinner. And with that, he commented he had just consumed several pounds of Pennsylvania Dutch sausage, one of his favorites, and consequently did not have much of an appetite. He suggested that we see the town, which was something new to me. . . . Nothing was said at the time concerning the purpose of the visit. We left the hotel and got in one cab after another, visiting night spots and having drinks. He never failed upon entering a club to tip the orchestra leader and have the orchestra play "Have You Ever Seen a Dream Girl Walking" [sic], which was popular at the time and one of his favorites. During the course of the evening, nothing whatever was said concerning business or the purpose of my meeting him. . . . Toward midnight, I told Mr. Stevens I could drink no more and that my drinking habits were conservative. Seemingly pleased, he immediately urged me to start drinking coffee, commenting he would have another drink or two. At this juncture, I made it a point to inquire what he wanted to see me for. He bluntly replied that he wanted to offer me a position.

Sigmans offers an interesting interpretation of that night on the town as Stevens' subtle test of a prospective assistant: "the company was known for its alcoholics. He had one or two men in the department there that were alcoholics in a sense, and I think he wanted to make damn sure that I was not an alcoholic when he took me on this tour." Despite Stevens' particular motive in avoiding any mention of the business behind the evening's pleasure, it was characteristic of him to resist talking business when enjoying himself with his insurance colleagues. During his weekly lunches at his businessman's club "he refused to talk shop," Sigmans and others emphasize.

Wilson Taylor, a colleague who was also a close friend and confidant of Stevens in New York, recalls the frequent visits to the city made by Stevens the connoisseur of art and antiques.

> If he was going to be down there on a Saturday, very frequently I would meet him, and we'd go to various of the small galleries. One day, we met and were having lunch, and I brought up the subject of the exhibit of Walter Gay at the Metropolitan. "Oh, yeah," he said, "we must go see that today." He had planned that. . . . He used to read *The New Yorker* a lot, and he'd get those current exhibits. . . . I don't think he ever came down that he didn't read *The New Yorker* on the way.[6]

Visiting Manhattan exhibitions, of course, was a longstanding practice that Stevens began almost as soon as he moved to New York after leaving Harvard.[7]

Taylor notes that for Stevens the connoisseur, some of the Manhattan cityscape he enjoyed stretched "from 42nd Street north to the Carlyle Hotel, and in between there were bistros and there were art galleries; this, that, and the other. This is mostly on the East Side . . . up and down Madison Avenue." Mrs. Powers recalls:

> We used to walk up and down Madison Avenue at night where all the antique shops were, lighted and beautifully so. Then he'd point out these *objects d'art* . . . particularly Oriental art. He knew a great deal about it. He was dippy about Oriental rugs. . . . Then, of course, he knew modern French painting. . . . It was just fascinating to be with him.

Colleagues at the Hartford's home office mention that Stevens frequently received catalogues there; when he was not able to go to New York, he would use his subordinates as he might Leonard C. van Geyzel in Ceylon or Mrs. Lucy Monroe Calhoun in China to satisfy his tastes for such delicacies as jasmine tea. This was one of the perquisites of his position as vice-president that he took full advantage of. "He used to send me down the catalogue on [the] Parke-Bernet

Galleries. . . . He'd want a painting, or he'd want a book, or he'd want something else," John O'Loughlin, Stevens' close associate from the mid-1920s on, recalls. "He'd send me the check . . . and say this is the maximum you can bid for it. So I'd go up there, and once in awhile I'd pick it up."

Just as he hoped the paintings sent by the Vidals from Paris would be of quality and a bargain, so in his New York dealings he was a careful buyer. Taylor smilingly recounts a trip with Stevens to certain Manhattan "auction rooms. He was looking for a sofa, and this girl was showing him this handsome sofa. . . . She said, 'That's a good-looking sofa for $200.' And Stevens' reply was, 'You don't know how good $200 looks.' " Sigmans, who occasionally took weekend trips with Stevens or drove him to New York adds, however, that "He was not mercenary. Money did not mean a great deal to him except to buy what he wanted." Indeed, Taylor notes both Stevens' willingness to pay for antiques he wanted and his comfortable circumstances during the Depression. Stevens' years at the Hartford had given him a financial security far different from those lean years as a young man in New York recorded in his journal. Taylor remembers:

> He called me Monday morning, said he'd been down Saturday, and at this particular [shop that had been closed] . . . he saw this lamp. He recognized it as a choice piece of pottery, porcelain I guess it was, and some kind of a fancy silk shade on it. He wanted to know if I could get up there that day and see if I could buy it for him. So I went up, and the price on this little old table lamp . . . was $200. That was a lot of money in the thirties. "Oh, good God," he said, but he sent $200 down. He said, "Make them pack it well, and they'll have to pay the cost of shipping." . . . He was very comfortable during the Depression; it was about '34 that he was made vice-president.

As an important executive in the Hartford Accident and Indemnity hierarchy, of course, business responsibilities also brought him to New York occasionally. As Sigmans remarks, "Once or twice a month he'd be out [of Hartford on busi-

ness] . . . particularly down to New York," adding that "he'd
go to New York once or twice a month even if he didn't have
any business." These business trips might involve surety
claim matters, which it was his principal task at the company
to oversee. Again, he might be at meetings of a surety asso-
ciation or at directors' meetings of the Hartford Live Stock
Insurance Company, a company subsidiary. O'Loughlin, a
devoted friend, recalls Stevens' abrupt manner when he
would arrive in New York on business: "He'd come in the
office . . . walk right by you, say hello and goodbye and keep
right on going, walk right out. He never stayed, never wanted
to sit down. . . . You had to understand him." This abrupt-
ness was, apparently, typical of Stevens' business manner in
the home office as well. O'Loughlin continues: "When they
[his superiors] called him in, he'd . . . recite his piece, and
pick himself up, and get out. There were no if's, and's, or
but's." Not all of his colleagues were so tolerant of his ways
as were such friends as O'Loughlin.

In New York, this abruptness may also have been
prompted by a desire to accomplish his business with time
to spare so that he could be more than a business executive
in the city. In a 1954 letter to Barbara Church, for example,
Stevens mentioned that "as always on the third Thursday of
March" he was to be in New York and hoped "to see the
Indian things at both the Metropolitan and the Modern
Museum" (L, 824-25). Such annual trips were necessary be-
cause of his responsibilities in the Hartford Live Stock Com-
pany, of which he was a director from 1916 to 1920 and from
1937 to 1955. This was one of Stevens' few other official
responsibilities within the Hartford beyond handling bond
claims. The Hartford Live Stock was licensed in New York,
so certain meetings had to be held there annually. Because
the company was almost wholly owned by the Hartford Fire
Insurance Company, the directors simply functioned as "a
legal board that was without any great responsibility," recalls
Stevens' fellow director, Arthur Polley. He adds that Stevens
"always went down because he conducted the meeting."[8]

Making plans to meet with Mrs. Church after the 1949

director's meeting, Stevens remarked ruefully that one such "annual third Thursday in March . . . [was] the same day on which I saw Mr. Church for the last time, coming up town too late for us to have lunch together."[9] Lunches, as such, were an important part of Stevens' later life, not only in New York but in Hartford as well. From the recollections of those who knew him, it is clear that luncheons were among his few social outlets, since the Stevenses rarely entertained at home. In Hartford, of course, such lunches were usually in the log-cabined setting of the Hartford Canoe Club with his "boys" from the office or emissaries from the literary world, such as Richard Eberhart or Seymour Lawrence. In New York, the settings were more polished, reflecting Stevens' taste for both exclusivity and haute cuisine. John Sauer, Stevens' nephew by marriage, details one such luncheon when Stevens "wanted to chat with me . . . about . . . backing up some of his [genealogical] research" in the 1940s. He remembers, with a chuckle, the horror with which Stevens reacted to his suggestion that they meet for lunch at the serviceable businessman's hotel where he was staying. "Good Lord, no!" Instead, Stevens selected a restaurant

way up in the East 70s, or something like that, a very fine little French restaurant. . . . He was very jovial, and yet he was very proper and very prim. . . . He just rattled off a lunch in French. . . . We talked about whatever he wanted me to research. . . . A good bit of the conversation . . . at the table was [about music]. . . . He told me how fond he was of good music, that he had quite a collection of records. Well, I told him that I had some good records, too, like the Philadelphia Orchestra and what I considered some light operatic music or what not. "Oh good Lord, John, I'm not speaking of that!" It was all on this heavy stuff, so we did talk about the records. That was a good part of the conversation, and he was very proud of his record collection; it must have been quite something. . . . He said it thoroughly relaxed him. [Stevens added] Elsie didn't appreciate the music. Elsie was a good cook, "That's

why I've got this obese look about me"—very conscious
of his big belly, very conscious of it. He said that Elsie
couldn't appreciate things that he does: "She's a damned
good cook and a faithful wife." . . . When we wound up
lunch . . . he said, "Well, let's stop in here at my favorite
delicatessen, and I'll buy you a piece of cheese to take
back to your brood."

As his letters and the memories of friends indicate, New
York was a place where Stevens could satisfy his well-defined
palate. The goal of the long walks in the city, so much a part
of the recollections of those who knew Stevens in New York,
might well be some tasty treat. John Gilmore, an associate,
recalls:

> He was a lover of raisin buns; on numerous occasions [he]
> would walk miles in New York City to this bakery to get
> them. . . . I met him on one occasion; I happened to be
> at a meeting. I bumped into him in the old Commodore
> Hotel. He said, "Red, let's take a walk." I don't recall the
> name of the bakery but it was miles away from the Com-
> modore Hotel. I suggested we take a cab back home. He
> said, "No, walking is good for you; look at me, I'm a
> healthy man."

He often frequented special shops to select items to carry
back and savor in Hartford. After O'Loughlin had been reas-
signed to the home office, he notes that when Stevens arrived
at the Hartford depot after a day in the city, "Maybe he'd
call me up and say, 'Look, I've got some fruit down here
I've got to take home. Will you drive down?' " Interestingly,
O'Loughlin, like many close business friends who carted
items back to Stevens' home, got only "as far as the door . . .
[I] never got inside the house" on Westerly Terrace.

At his luncheon with John Sauer, Stevens enlisted his
nephew's help in his consuming research in the 1940s into
his family background. This was a period during which,
while he was tracing his ancestry, he was also coming to
know the family that was left to him, especially the children

of his brother John and sister Elizabeth. Jane MacFarland Wilson, Elizabeth's only child, was one of the nieces who kept in closest contact with Uncle Wallace after she met him for the first time at the funeral of his brother John in 1940. She remembers a most pleasant day with him, for example, in the mid-1940s, again involving the posh lunches that meant so much to him. "Wallace and I planned to meet in New York. . . . He took me to lunch at the Waldorf Astoria, and then he took me to see 'Bloomer Girl.' He loved it and I loved it. . . . This was probably relaxation for him, and he knew I enjoyed it."

At times, Stevens' New York lunches might have a more distinctly literary flavor. One of those friendships between Stevens and young, admiring scholars that marked his last years began with such an invitation. In the late 1940s Bernard Heringman, then a graduate student at Columbia University, recalls:

> When I was working on my master's, I wrote him a letter importuning him in effect, but as politely as I could, wondering if I could come and talk to him in Hartford to ask questions. He wrote back a very polite but very cold rejection. . . . After it [the M.A. thesis on Stevens] was done . . . I sent him a copy. . . . He read it, and liked it very much, and invited me to have lunch with him the next time he was in New York, when he would give it back to me.

Heringman sketches the courteous Stevens, "gracious without being at all condescending." He could be as thoughtful as he was abrupt. When they met for lunch, Stevens

> acted as if I were as rich and courtly and so on as he, and he wondered if the Passy would be good enough. He allowed it wasn't so good as it used to be, but there weren't too many talkative women. . . . It was a very pleasant lunch. . . . He had a real grace. He asked me if I'd like a drink first. He was taking me to lunch; I couldn't have possibly afforded that sort of a lunch. . . . I said, "Well,

certainly, if I can share one with you?" So he ordered one
for himself, too. . . . I learned sometime later in the con-
versation the same day that his doctor had told him not to
drink until dinnertime. In other words, he had a drink
. . . broke his doctor's orders in order to put me at ease.
. . . [He] later mentioned it perfectly accidentally. . . .
That touched me.

During the long lunch that ensued, Stevens, so often curt
when quizzed about his work, showed his willingness to dis-
cuss his poetry with one whom he felt might be among that
select group of readers he valued, those "very few readers
who pick up the feelings that one puts into one's poems"
(L, 436):

He was a little cautious with me at first, but apparently I
had the right questions or the right manner or something,
and he immediately took to me, as I could gather. We
never became at all personally friendly; I mean there was
a great reserve about him. But for him, he was very inti-
mate, I would suppose, and friendly, engaging, willing to
talk about whatever we talked about. It seemed to me not
right to make it a strictly interview luncheon, so . . . I
didn't prepare a list of questions: I had some preparatory
notes, but nothing much.

A few excerpts from Heringman's recollections of the discus-
sion of poetry, based on notes made soon after the lunch, in-
dicate the range of Stevens' conversation about his work.

[He] wants to do a hymn to Johannes Zeller, not his
mother's father but an earlier ancestor . . . who came over
in the second wave of German immigration . . . for reli-
gious reasons. . . . I asked about the name "John Rocket":
an arbitrary name . . . "MacCullough" also an arbitrary
name, he said. . . . I asked about "Major Man." [His]
answer: "Nearest thing to God there is." I asked about the
possibility of "Peter Quince" being in quartet structure.
No, but he was thinking in terms of musical movements,
a sort of libretto, he said.

Though Stevens was quite willing to clarify elements of his poetry to this young scholar, Heringman recalls a "rough quotation" of Stevens on the question of his poetic obscurity:

> Stevens says his "poems aren't obscure. He writes something he sees or has seen or known, clearly. The main thing is to have it right for yourself. Nobody else ever sees it exactly the same way anyway, but you put it down as it is to you, and it's clear, and sharp, and simple. . . . You fail sometimes." He gives an example I couldn't remember to locate accurately. I think it was from "Examination of the Hero in a Time of War" . . . where he didn't get it clear to himself.

Heringman provides a helpful view of Stevens' tone when the conversation turned to the more philosophic level typical of Stevens' discussions of poetry in the essays that were collected in *The Necessary Angel*, which was published a few years after this luncheon.

> Poetry for poetry's sake; we referred to that concept. He said it depends on what you mean by poetry. Approximate quote: "The poet supplies the whole spiritual life; the idea of God is a poetic idea. Poetry is everything on that side." . . . He was really very modest and very humble in manner. . . . He didn't talk oracularly. He said this in a offhand way. . . . He did not speak with a capital P, Profoundly. . . . That's partly what I liked about him.

While admiring Stevens' poetry, Heringman also shared Stevens' interest in things French, in music, and in painting, though not always Stevens' enthusiasms. He recalls the poet's interest in Bruckner at that lunch as he urged Heringman to listen to a particular recording of the Seventh Symphony. When Stevens mentioned that he had recently received two paintings by Eric Detthow, Heringman noted "he raves about them quietly."[10] Stevens added that Detthow was "Swedish, French School, contemporary, cheap." Obviously pleased with this young man, whom he met on other occa-

sions in New York, Stevens finally felt comfortable in invit-
ing him to Hartford in 1952.

It is a cliché of Stevens criticism that, while he may have
discussed his poetry with a scholar or fellow poet, he did not
share his poetic endeavors with his insurance colleagues at
the Hartford. This is more myth than fact. Although Stevens
did not do so with a great many associates, Wilson Taylor
is one of a number of colleagues with whom he talked of his
poetry. Taylor recalls discussions with Stevens in New York,
noting an important qualification: "Sometimes we'd talk
about his poetry. Things like that were things that he would
have to bring up. If he brought them up, we might spend an
hour or two talking about them. If I brought them up, why
nothing further was said." Taylor describes a humorous inci-
dent at a New York restaurant that suggests how Stevens
might arrive at his fascinating titles:

> We were at dinner one night at the Carlyle [Hotel], and
> Stevens looked up at the waiter. "My God, it's Bruno
> Richard Hauptmann [the Lindbergh kidnapper]!" He just
> looked exactly like him. So he laughed . . . and he said,
> "Two Egyptians being served by a Nazi." And then he
> said, "Gee, that's a good title for a poem; I must write that
> down," so he pulled out a little card.

A study of Stevens' continuing literary relationships in
New York after his move to Hartford is beyond the scope of
this sketch of Stevens' later forays there. In his last years,
however, Stevens' trips to Manhattan occasionally involved
him in the role of the public man of letters. Though always
dubious about his ability in this role, he read and lectured
in New York more often than in any other place, appearing
at Columbia, the Metropolitan Museum, the YMHA, and
the Museum of Modern Art, for example. Though willing to
be the public man of letters in New York at times, he stead-
fastly refused to appear in this capacity in Hartford, as
Charles Cunningham, then curator of Hartford's famous art
museum, the Wadsworth Atheneum, learned in the early

1950s. Hearing of Stevens' lecture at the Museum of Modern Art, Cunningham invited him to do the same at the Atheneum. Stevens declined, saying that in Hartford he was known as an insurance executive.

After delivering the Museum of Modern Art lecture, Stevens remarked, "A certain amount of reading is a useful experience" (L, 705). John Malcolm Brinnin, then director of the YMHA Poetry Center, recreates one such New York appearance that allowed him this opportunity in 1951:

> After he had refused one invitation, I made another, which he accepted with the proviso that there be no reception or any other social gathering in connection with his appearance. He came with Holly and we met in the Green Room of the Poetry Center. He wore evening clothes and looked rather grand. When we were alone, he turned to me: "You know," he said, "on an occasion like this the voice is the actor." I said to myself—fine, he understands that a reading is a performance. Then he went onstage and read for nearly two hours in the strictest monotone anyone had ever heard. The audience walked out in droves; they couldn't hear him or, if they did, found what he read absolutely without dramatic interest. A girl I knew left quite early. When I had a chance to ask her why, she said: "He looked like *my father*." They had come to see Wallace Stevens the romantic poet and found themselves looking at a business executive. Those who loved him, of course, stayed until the end. But, as an evening's entertainment, it just didn't work. On the recording [taped at the reading] there's much more interest: whatever mental force directing what he's saying comes through.

Samuel French Morse was, of course, such a lover of Stevens' poetry, and interestingly, one of the few young men Stevens sought out in his last years. The elder poet seems to have regarded this younger poet-scholar-friend as one of those who would help to "get it straight one day." In the audience for Stevens' 1954 YMHA reading, he speaks for the minority of those who remember Stevens' readings more positively. While acknowledging that Stevens "was not a good reader . . . [as] he read the poems, I learned something about the way certain lines went together and a little bit about his sense of stress and organization. You had to get this from watching, watching and listening."

Morse had driven him to New York on the day of the YMHA reading and remembers the pleasure Stevens took not only in New York itself but in the rustic drive down the Merritt Parkway.[11]

> He loved the landscape going down; he talked about things that he saw going by. . . . He liked the hills, and the feeling that he has in that little piece on Connecticut that he did for the Voice of America and "A Mythology Reflects Its Region," that kind of feeling was there. He gossiped a little bit about some writers. I remember his asserting again that E. E. Cummings had behaved better than anybody else during the war. It wasn't anything malicious at all, but perhaps a little skeptical about the accomplishments of some of our . . . poets. . . . Again, he could be generous.

One of Stevens' last visits to New York involved a pleasant lunch with Barbara Church on March 17, 1955. It was appropriate that this should have been among his last visits, since his meetings with the cultivated Churches were among the highlights of his trips to New York in the 1940s and 1950s. The ambience at their gatherings, as described by Kurt Roesch, a painter and professor at Sarah Lawrence who was part of the Church circle, hints at the pleasures that Stevens enjoyed at these Park Avenue gatherings.

> They had a French cook: the food was marvelous, the champagne was good. . . . There were these really remarkably good pictures: good Juan Gris, good Picasso. . . . They were pictures which were not only the best, but they were livable. . . . [Barbara Church] was not a person who would admire fringes, not on carpets or anything. She had imagination, sympathies.

There one might not only be in the company of painters, poets, gallery owners, and museum directors but also encounter "a Russian émigré [who] was once the head of the secret police under the tsar" or "Russian princesses, very, very simple, Mother Russia, you know: very nice, and round, and plump, and warm." Roesch adds that Stevens would be at both the larger parties that overflowed into the hall and the smaller gatherings, though usually leaving early to return to Hartford.

A small Church gathering was often held on St. Patrick's Day. At one such lunch, this Pennsylvania Dutch-New England poet was made an honorary Irishman by the group. It was a fitting title for Stevens, some of whose best late poems were prompted by his imaginings of Ireland. James Johnson Sweeney recalls:

> I think I did tease him about writing on a subject [Ireland] he was not immediately in touch with. Why didn't he come to Ireland and join us there? . . . I think he said that he was not interested in the representational . . . [but] the idea it gave him, which was more important than the real landscape . . . that he had a feeling through [Thomas] McGreevy and his idea of Ireland which would be diminished if he had seen the real thing.

Such an Irish celebration was among Stevens' final pleasant moments in New York. "Last Thursday's lunch was the most cheerful kind of lunch and I enjoyed it immensely," he wrote to Mrs. Church on March 21, 1955 (L, 876). A week later he made his first visit to the Hartford physician who was to treat him during his terminal illness. Earlier that month Stevens had begun to register the effects of the cancer that ended his life five months after that New York fête. The balloon had landed.

GEORGE S. LENSING

WALLACE STEVENS IN ENGLAND

THIRTY YEARS SEPARATED THE PUBLICATION OF WAL-lace Stevens' *Harmonium* (1923) and the first publication in England of a volume by him. A selection made by Stevens himself for Faber & Faber's *Selected Poems* (1953) marked the first authorized and representative collection of the American poet's work in that country. Until then, Stevens' poems were familiar only to a small circle of English readers through a few anthologies and magazines. An attempt to publish a book-length selection in the 1940s had been aborted by a series of charges and countercharges between two competing English firms and their appeals and claims to publishing rights from Stevens' American publisher, Alfred A. Knopf Inc. In exasperation and some fear of injuring his standing with Knopf, Stevens called a halt to the project in 1946. Seven years later, however, only weeks before the publication of the Faber volume, a totally unauthorized collection published by the Fortune Press, one of the competing firms in the earlier imbroglio, suddenly appeared in England. Legal action initiated against that firm by Knopf led to the confiscation of undistributed copies.

The various individuals involved in this publication drama include, in addition to Stevens: Nicholas Moore, poet and son of the Cambridge philosopher George Edward Moore, who offered to make a selection of poems by Stevens for the Fortune Press in 1944; and Tambimuttu, a Ceylonese who was an important publisher, editor, and early champion of T. S. Eliot. Faber's interest in Stevens had been endorsed by directors Peter du Sautoy and Eliot himself, in part through the beseechings of Marianne Moore. Miss Moore also had a hand in the final selection of Stevens' poems for Faber &

Faber. Alfred Knopf, along with Herbert Weinstock and William Koshland of the Knopf publishing house, was actively involved in the various negotiations from America. A literary agent acting for Knopf in England at that time, Laurence Pollinger, of Pearn, Pollinger & Higham, was also a party in the episode.

The sequence of complications that blocked the publication of a Stevens volume in England before the early 1950s is extraordinary in itself; it also clarifies an historical note in the poet's publishing career. In addition, a revealing view of Stevens' own conception of himself as a poet and his ambition to enlarge the number of his readers abroad is also disclosed through his publication history in England. The high value he placed on his association with his American publisher is perhaps the key factor in his own role in the long episode. Not until just prior to his death did he have the satisfaction of seeing his work seriously estimated by a general English audience.

Stevens' introduction to English readers antedates *Harmonium*, but the initial publication cannot have been totally pleasing to him. Early in 1920 John Gould Fletcher, in a letter to the editor of the *London Mercury*, had singled out Stevens, along with Conrad Aiken, Carl Sandburg, Alfred Kreymborg, and Maxwell Bodenheim, as one of the young American poets who had shown "signs of genius, each in an entirely different and quite individual way."[1] In the *Chapbook* of a few months later in the same year, Fletcher presented a sample of Stevens' verse, along with poems from a number of younger American poets and an introductory essay by himself. Stevens was represented by a four-stanza version of "Sunday Morning." In his commentary, Fletcher found "Sunday Morning" "deliberately cryptic," although he classified it as "another *Portrait of a Lady* better and more memorable than T. S. Eliot's."[2] Harriet Monroe's famous five-stanza abbreviation of the eight-stanza "Sunday Morning" had already appeared in her magazine *Poetry* five years earlier, and the selector for the *Chapbook* (Fletcher or

editor Harold Munro?) used that version, but exercised fur-
ther editorial liberties. Already cut by three stanzas in
Poetry, the poem was now cut by one more.³ The *Chapbook*
numbered the stanzas I, II, III, and V, simply inserting
"(One stanza omitted)" between III and V. Only with the
publication of *Harmonium* three years later was the much-
shredded poem restored to its original order and length.

Stevens' first previously unpublished poem to appear in
England, "Mandolin and Liqueurs," also appeared in the
Chapbook in April 1923. About a year earlier, Conrad Aiken
wrote to Stevens soliciting his permission to include five pre-
viously published poems ("Peter Quince at the Clavier," the
five-stanza version of "Sunday Morning," "Le Monocle de
Mon Oncle," "Thirteen Ways of Looking at a Blackbird,"
and "Domination of Black") in an anthology to be pub-
lished in England. Aiken's remarkable keenness in selecting
these major *Harmonium* poems before their collection in
that volume is a tribute to his independent critical alertness.
His anthology, *Modern American Poets*, was published by
Martin Secker of London in 1922.⁴

Stevens' poems appeared irregularly in English magazines
throughout the 1930s and 1940s. All were directly or indi-
rectly solicited by the editors. "Farewell to Florida," for ex-
ample, first appeared in *Contemporary Poetry and Prose* in
1936, following a request from Roger Roughton. In 1937
Julian Symons, an early and enduring champion of Stevens
in England, published two of the poems that were even-
tually to be absorbed into *The Man with the Blue Guitar*
(V and XXVI). His *Twentieth Century Verse* also pub-
lished "Connoisseur of Chaos" in 1938. When Cyril Con-
nolly wrote to Stevens in April 1947 asking for a poem to
be published in a special number of *Horizon* on the arts in
America, Stevens sent him "The Owl in the Sarcophagus,"
which appeared in *Horizon* later that year. Nicholas Moore,
a key figure in the ensuing publishing events, was coeditor
and copublisher of a magazine called *Seven* in the late 1930s
and early 1940s. Stevens sent him three poems during this
period: "The Blue Buildings in the Summer Air," "Thunder

by the Musician," and "Yellow Afternoon." Apparently the writing of the long poem *Owl's Clover* was stimulated by an invitation from Richard Church of J. M. Dent in London. In his correspondence of 1935, Stevens indicated that Church was collecting a "series of long poems" for publication and wanted one from him (*L*, 279). There is no evidence that the poem was ever sent to or used by Church, however.[5]

Besides the magazines and Aiken's early anthology, a few poems by Stevens began to appear in various British collections, but these never numbered more than a handful, often the same ones reappearing. Among the more widely accessible of these anthologies was *The Oxford Book of American Verse*, which was published in 1950 and contained twenty-five Stevens poems. B. Rajan's *Modern American Poetry*, published in London also in 1950, collected four poems by Stevens, including "Credences of Summer," and an essay by Louis Martz entitled "The World of Wallace Stevens." As a result of scattered publications such as these, poems by Stevens gradually found acceptance and respect in England, but the admirers remained small in number. The poet David Gascoyne, for example, wrote to Stevens in 1944, asking that copies of several of his American volumes be sent over, and Stevens quickly accommodated him. In 1951 another English poet, Charles Tomlinson, also posted laudatory remarks to Stevens and included an essay on "Credences of Summer," to which Stevens responded affirmatively.

Two of the anthologies containing poems by Stevens that appeared in England in the early 1940s signaled Nicholas Moore's deepening interest in the poet. Having earlier published the poems by Stevens in *Seven*, Moore requested additional ones for a collection to be issued in 1942 by the Fortune Press, entitled *The Fortune Anthology*. Stevens arranged for him to use "Asides on the Oboe" and "Mrs. Alfred Uruguay," both of which had appeared earlier in American magazines. In the notes on the contributors, Stevens is identified as "an elder American poet, well-known there, but not here."[6]

A year later, in August 1943, Moore again requested some poems for still another anthology that he was coediting, the *Atlantic Anthology*, which was also to be published by Fortune Press. Ever wary of copyright complications, Stevens suggested that Moore consult his recently issued *Notes toward a Supreme Fiction*. The Cummington Press had published the volume during the previous year, and the poet controlled the copyright himself. Moore, having been licensed by Stevens, selected cantos from the longer poem almost randomly, choosing finally eight from the thirty-one that comprise the complete poem. Again, Stevens was introduced as a poet with "a considerable reputation in America, but . . . comparatively little known in England."[7] It was to remedy just that defect that the Fortune Press wrote to Stevens on March 20, 1944, offering to publish a volume of his verse in England, the poems to be selected by Nicholas Moore.

As early as 1927, three years after its founding by Reginald A. Caton, its publisher, Stevens had written the Fortune Press requesting a list of its publications. By 1944 he had seen his poems arranged by Nicholas Moore and published in *The Fortune Anthology*. Plans for the second anthology selection were underway. Moore himself had also published poems by Stevens in *Seven*, and Stevens' personal library contained inscribed volumes of poetry by Moore. The poet was also acquainted with Moore's parents, and in his correspondence with Moore, fondly recalled occasional meetings with G. E. Moore and his wife in America. Consequently, when the March 1944 letter from the Fortune Press arrived offering to publish a volume of his work selected by Moore, Stevens had no reason to accept the news in any way other than with delight: "No doubt I owe this suggestion to your interest and kindness, for which I am sincerely grateful," he wrote to Moore on May 9. In the second paragraph of the letter, Stevens introduced the question of copyright and his own obligations to Knopf:

It so happens that Mr. Knopf, who has published my

books in this country, has a contract with me under which the permission would have to come from him. Let me say at once that my relations with Mr. Knopf have always been everything that I could possibly want them to be and that I feel that I am under obligations to him. But, in view of this arrangement, it is necessary for me to send the letter of The Fortune Press to Mr. Knopf; he will write directly to The Fortune Press. It would do no good for me to attempt to do so because I could agree to nothing.[8]

In his next letter to Stevens, Moore acknowledged that he had himself suggested to Caton that Fortune Press issue a volume by the American poet. The prospect of an early publication seemed favorable. Before the end of the summer, however, Stevens received another letter from a London publisher, a man who identified himself as Tambimuttu, editor of the influential *Poetry London*. Tambimuttu also proposed the publication of a volume of Stevens' poems and indicated a longstanding attempt on his part to purchase the British rights, although Stevens himself had no knowledge of such negotiations. A subsidiary of Nicholson & Watson Ltd., but controlled editorially by Tambimuttu, *Poetry London* had been appearing since 1939. The name itself was used to indicate both the firm and the magazine. As a publishing house, the subsidiary had brought out volumes by Kathleen Raine, David Gascoyne, and translations of Hölderlin by Michael Hamburger. The firm likewise had close ties with Nicholas Moore, publishing his volume of poems, *The Glass Tower* (1944), as well as an anthology of short fiction edited by him. Moreover, Tambimuttu's *Poetry London* was preparing to republish a poem by Stevens with an exegesis by Moore, "A Difficult Poem: The Woman That Had More Babies than That." It was in part Nicholas Moore's divided loyalty between the Fortune Press and the firm of Poetry London that helped to erect the barriers that were to prevent the publication of a volume by Stevens in England during the 1940s.

When he received Tambimuttu's letter, Stevens sent a complete copy of it to Knopf, adding, "what I want to say in substance amounts to this, that I am very much interested in seeing something of this sort done and should, of course, be willing to waive payment of any sort."⁹ Alfred Knopf's response to Stevens on September 21 made clear the distribution of publishing rights:

> In May of this year, at your request, we wrote the Fortune Press, Ltd. in London about your poems. In June they replied explaining on how small a scale they operated. In July we countered with the suggestion of a fee of ten pounds for an edition of one thousand copies.
>
> Meanwhile, in September '43, a London agent wrote about Tambimuttu's interest in your book. We replied to this letter and sent copies of the books, but up to July '44 neither letter nor books had been received on the other side.
>
> Then a few days ago we had a letter from the Fortune Press accepting our offer and last week an agreement was sent them.
>
> Thus, as matters stand, I do not see that we can do anything for Mr. Tambimuttu and I return his letter of August 10th to you herewith. . . .¹⁰

The precise nature of the dealings between Knopf's London agent at that time, Laurence Pollinger, and the Tambimuttu firm before July 1944 is unclear. Tambimuttu took the position that he had a prior claim upon the British publication rights, while Knopf and his agents found no justification for such a claim. The impact of Knopf's letter, however, did not disturb Stevens. Without reservation, he accepted Knopf's arrangement and responded to Tambimuttu on September 23 accordingly: "Since Mr. Knopf controls my things in England, I am very much afraid that this eliminates you."¹¹ The controversy might very well have been averted at this point, as the Fortune Press, having signed the agreement with Knopf, proceeded with its own publication plans.

Tambimuttu, however, was not easily appeased. In an October letter to Stevens he proposed a compromise. Moore would go ahead with a small selection for the Fortune Press, but this would be followed with three more extensive selections for Poetry London. The letter concludes with Tambimuttu's promise to consult with Pollinger. Continuing to keep Knopf fully informed, Stevens forwarded Tambimuttu's letter on to his New York publisher.

Stevens' own association with Knopf since the publication of *Harmonium* had always been professionally cordial. Nonetheless, Stevens had arranged to have a number of volumes published by small independent presses on the grounds that these presses were not commercial rivals of Knopf, and the latter always had the option of reissuing them for the wider market. The Alcestis Press, for example, had published Stevens' second volume, *Ideas of Order*, in 1935, followed by *Owl's Clover* the next year. The Cummington Press had also published 273 copies of *Notes toward a Supreme Fiction* in 1942, with a second limited edition the following year. As early as 1935, however, Knopf had tried to discourage Stevens' independent publishing adventures, though he never absolutely forbade them. It is clear that the poet was aware of potential strains with Knopf over the British rights, and he went out of his way to avoid them. Even so, he was also eager to exercise his own influence to expedite publication. To Tambimuttu, Stevens then wrote: "I hope that you and Mr. Pollinger will be able to come to an agreement."[12]

For the next seven months Stevens' correspondence with the London publishers came to a halt. In the interim, he had negotiated both with the Cummington Press to publish *Esthétique du Mal* in a limited edition and with Knopf to reissue *The Man with the Blue Guitar*. On July 10, 1945, however, Nicholas Moore wrote to Stevens a long and angry letter. In it he made clear his own disenchantment with the Fortune Press, his personal animosity toward Laurence Pollinger, and his loyalty to Tambimuttu and Poetry London, whose staff he was joining. The letter proposed an altogether new publishing strategy. The Fortune Press would be forgotten, while Poetry London would publish three separate volumes of poems by Wallace Stevens: *Parts of a World*; a volume of fifty other poems, selected by Moore, the list of titles enclosed in the letter; and a book of more recent poems, including *Notes toward a Supreme Fiction* and *Esthétique du Mal*. In the first two cases, permission from Knopf would have to be secured, but a second letter from Moore to Stevens complained of Knopf's annoyance with him and with Poetry London arising from his own *volte-face*.

Having received the second letter before the first, Stevens responded to Moore: "Mr. Knopf, who is ordinarily an amiable sort of person, seems to be a little on edge about Tambimuttu. Just what this is all about I do not know."[13] When the earlier letter arrived and Stevens began to perceive the rivalries and bickering at large, he can only have regarded the episode with dismay and no little incredulity. He did not, however, despair. Obviously believing that publication rights might yet be arranged with Knopf, Stevens found Moore's alternate plan for publication plausible. In an important letter to Moore, dated July 25, 1945, Stevens joined forces with Moore, Tambimuttu, and Poetry London:

> I like the plan outlined by you. PARTS OF A WORLD is, in my own judgment, my best book and I am glad to hear that you are going to publish it first and, apparently, in its entirety. The ESTHETIQUE is a small collection of related poems, which ought to run to not more than about 20 or perhaps 25 pages. It will contain illustrations of a sort. It happened to be just the right size for The Cummington Press.
>
> Mr. Knopf has no status as yet respecting NOTES TOWARD A SUPREME FICTION; the same thing is true as to the ESTHETIQUE. Both of these books were published by The Cummington Press, which does not have nearly the acute sense of property that Mr. Knopf seems to have. However, I owe a good deal more to Mr. Knopf than I do to The Cummington Press, so I want to leave that subject alone.[14]

A copy of this letter was sent to Harry Duncan of the Cummington Press, who soon endorsed the plan of allowing publication of *Notes toward a Supreme Fiction* and *Esthétique*

du Mal as Poetry London's projected third volume. Depart-
ing from his customary practice of keeping Knopf fully ap-
prised of his own actions, however, Stevens did not forward
a copy of this letter to his New York publisher.

A few months later, on November 1, Knopf's increasing
annoyance with Poetry London, as well as with Stevens' con-
tinuing association with the Cummington Press, came to a
head. To Stevens he wrote:

> I hope that some day you will visit me here in my office.
> When you do, I will show you the file of correspondence
> and cables that we have collected in connection with For-
> tune Press, Nicholas Moore, and Wallace Stevens. This
> has been so time-consuming, expensive, and exasperating
> that I think we ought to assign back to you any British
> rights, excluding Canada, which our contracts with you
> ever gave us, leaving you free to make your own arrange-
> ments over there as you would seem to be doing in any
> case. For example, I hear that Mr. Moore has arranged
> with you and the Cummington Press to publish next year
> in one volume your "latest two books." But I have not
> heard of this from you. In view of our long, and certainly
> not unpleasant, publishing relationship, I think we should
> be taken rather more fully into your confidence. After all,
> there could never be any money involved for anyone in
> connection with placing your books in England, and we
> only represented you as a matter of friendly service. But in
> thirty years of publishing, I give you my word I have never
> run into such a mess all around as arose, or so it seems to
> me, from these English people discovering that they could
> deal with you and with us at one and the same time.[15]

Determined to make his peace with Knopf, Stevens replied
immediately: "I know nothing about what is going on in
England and know of nothing that would justify you or any-
body else in saying that I have been dealing directly. Any
letters that I have received from publishers over there have
been sent to you and the writers have been referred to you."
The poet then went on to quote to Knopf the tripartite pub-

lishing plan of Nicholas Moore and Poetry London and cited
directly from the July 10 letter wherein Moore promised to
arrange publication rights with Pollinger. He continued, "I
wrote in reply: 'I like the plan outlined by you.' Mr. Moore
has not written to me since, nor have I written to him."[16]
Not leaving the matter to the mails alone, Stevens followed
the letter with a personal visit from Hartford to New York
in order to meet with Knopf, but he failed to get in to see
his publisher. At about the same time, Oscar Williams had
written to Stevens requesting "So-And-So Reclining on Her
Couch" for his A Little Treasury of Modern Poetry. Stevens'
November 20 reply hinted at his continuing anxiety over
Knopf's displeasure: "I am glad that you have applied to
Knopf because I rather think that he regards the idea of
using uncollected poems in anthologies as irregular. Nat-
urally, I want to keep my relations with Knopf topside up."[17]
    Knopf then sent to Stevens a lengthy memorandum sum-
marizing the sequence of his communications with his agent
in London and the two English firms. Its most pertinent dis-
closures account for some of the entanglements. Six months
before Stevens received the first letter from the Fortune
Press proposing publication of a volume, Tambimuttu had
indeed approached Pollinger, expressing an interest in releas-
ing such a volume from Poetry London. Books (Stevens' vol-
umes, one assumes) were requested by him and, according
to Knopf, dispatched. Tambimuttu later claimed never to
have received them. In September 1944, a year after Tambi-
muttu's initial overtures to Pollinger, the Fortune Press ac-
cepted an offer to purchase Stevens' publishing rights for a
volume, although a final contract was not completed until
the following year. By November 1944, Pollinger reported to
Knopf, a falling out between Nicholas Moore and the owner
of the Fortune Press had occurred. A testy letter from Regi-
nald Caton to Pollinger followed in January 1945, in which
the publisher made clear his resolve to sacrifice under no
circumstances his signed agreement with Knopf to publish
the Stevens volume. These events understandably irritated

Knopf and, as it turned out, eventually dashed Stevens' own hopes for a publication in England.

On February 20, 1946, twenty-three months to the day after receiving his first letter from the Fortune Press, Stevens wrote to Moore withdrawing his endorsement of the plan. Foremost in his own thinking was the preservation of good feelings with Knopf, who was proceeding to publish *Transport to Summer*:

> Things in England have not been straightened out, and it would probably make it all the more difficult to straighten them out eventually if I were now to publish a book there. I am free to do so as far as Mr. Knopf's rights are concerned, but, in view of what has happened and of the possible effect of streightening [*sic*] things out in England eventually, and of the very good chance that he would take offense, I think I shall not go any farther with this. A poet must have a publisher and is fortunate to have a decent one after his first book or two. It is not the easiest thing in the world to persuade a publisher to publish one's sixth or seventh book. Knopf is as good a publisher as there is in this country and I value my connection with him. I think you will understand all this and I hope that you will think that I am doing the right thing. While I am doing it for my own welfare, nevertheless I think it is the right thing to do from any point of view. It is not necessary to say how much I regret having put you to so much trouble. I am grateful to you.[18]

A few weeks later, to his friend Henry Church, Stevens spoke of the British publication as "something that I have wanted very much to bring about," but he had withdrawn his approval "because of a possible conflict with Knopf."[19]

Where precisely to lay the blame for this outcome in 1946 is not apparent. Nicholas Moore's personal alienation from the Fortune Press after his agreement with them and his subsequent alliance with Tambimuttu and Poetry London were in part responsible. All the parties involved, including

Stevens, Knopf, and Poetry London, persisted in the belief that Moore should be retained to make the selection of poems for the volume. (Stevens remained on friendly terms with Moore; in October 1949, responding to a request from Moore, the poet sent him "Angel Surrounded by Paysans," which first appeared in *Poetry London*.) The Fortune Press itself stubbornly but legally refused to give up its claim to publish, in spite of Moore's desertion and overtures from Knopf. By first refusing to make the selection of poems, Stevens sacrificed control of the venture, even as he greeted all publication proposals with epistolary encouragement. Communication, mostly by letter, with so many parties, and over such distances in wartime, led to minor misunderstandings that took on exaggerated importance. Such appears to have been the case with Stevens' letter to Moore of July 25, 1945, in which he endorsed the plan of Moore and Tambimuttu to publish three volumes, a letter that Knopf learned of only later, to his chagrin, and one that Poetry London took as a green light from America.

As a coda to the two-year struggle for publication, the Fortune Press tried once again in October 1946 to interest Stevens in selecting poems himself for a volume, Nicholas Moore having removed himself from consideration. Advertisement for the volume had led to subscriptions, the letter informed Stevens, and there was need for a speedy resolution. Stevens sent the letter on to Knopf, but with a disclaimer: "I think that if anything comes of it the selection should be made by someone in England. Taste in the two countries is quite different. Anyhow, I should not be willing to make the selection."[20] Nothing came of it for the next five years.

Efforts toward publication in England of a volume by Stevens were resumed in the fall of 1951, this time with Faber & Faber, Ltd. Free this time from recrimination and delay, arrangements were quickly and easily concluded on October 11. When Herbert Weinstock, a senior editor at Knopf, wrote to Stevens in October announcing the plan, he conveyed the wishes of Faber that Stevens himself make the selection of poems. Though not unequivocal in his reluctance, Stevens still demurred: "I think that it would be a mistake for any one over here to make the selection."[21]

T. S. Eliot, then a director of Faber & Faber, later recounted his own role in the publication of a Stevens volume: "I had taken for granted that some other firm had published his work [in England], and wondered at their incompetence in taking so little trouble to make the fact known: it was one of my fellow directors [Peter du Sautoy] who first called my attention to the fact that Stevens, although his name and some of his poems were very well known to the élite who really know, had had no book to himself."[22] Eliot, responding to Stevens' unwillingness, proposed the name of Marianne Moore as the one to make the selection for Faber. A close friend of Stevens, Miss Moore had in fact been urging Peter du Sautoy to publish Stevens' work, though her importuning on Stevens' behalf apparently came after an agreement had been reached. Du Sautoy recalls that the suggestion to publish Stevens was his: "I think it would be true to say that the publication of Wallace Stevens's works by Faber and Faber resulted from my initiative, though T. S. Eliot was always consulted and fully approved."[23] Stevens at first agreed to the suggestion that Marianne Moore make the selection for Faber, but when he learned that Knopf would not be able to provide remuneration for her efforts, he agreed finally to make the selection himself.

The poet's role as self-editor, one he would exercise again when the *Collected Poems* was published three years later, was limited by the publishers' stipulation that the volume consist of 160 pages. In sending the list to Weinstock, Stevens insisted that it was "representative," but not "a list of things that are what 'the author wishes to preserve' " (*L*, 732). Poems were chosen from all of Stevens' volumes, including the long poems "The Man with the Blue Guitar" and "Notes toward a Supreme Fiction" in entirety. *Harmonium* was the volume most widely represented, with thirty-four poems, though most of these were relatively brief lyrics. *Ideas of Order*, on the other hand, was represented by only four poems, and *Parts of a World*, once regarded by Stevens as his most distinguished collection, by five. In addition to "Notes toward a Supreme Fiction," *Transport to Summer* was also represented by "Credences of Summer" and six other shorter poems. A shorter version of "An Ordinary Evening in New Haven" was included, along with four other poems from *The Auroras of Autumn*. The title poem from that volume, however, was included only as an alternate and was not among the contents of the final determination.

Although Marianne Moore did not make the selection of poems, she took a keen interest in the project and persuaded Stevens and Peter du Sautoy to include "Final Soliloquy of the Interior Paramour," a poem that had recently appeared in the *Hudson Review* but not in any other collection. Miss Moore exercised one other *sub rosa* role for Stevens when she inquired of Faber & Faber the terms of tax exemption for Stevens on the publication of the volume abroad. (She reported back to him early in 1952 that the matter was to be treated directly with the publishers.)

Unknown both to Stevens and his London publishers, Reginald Caton of the Fortune Press was simultaneously proceeding with his own publication of a *Selected Poems*. Peter du Sautoy learned of its completion from an announcement in the *Times Literary Supplement* on December 26. Stevens heard of it only when his friend John Sweeney sent a review by Austin Clarke, which had appeared in the *Irish Times* on February 14, 1953. Stevens' astonishment must have been at least as great as Clarke's:

> Now, at the age of seventy-four, Wallace Stevens has achieved the minor success of having two selections from his poems published in London at the same time. Curiously enough, no explanation of this double celebration is given to us by either publisher. "Selected Poems," published by Messrs. Faber, is well set out and the book is pleasant to look at. "Selected Poems," issued by the Fortune Press, is closer set and contains more poems, page for page; the choice was made by Mr. Dennis Williamson and he has written an agreeable foreword.[24]

Dennis Williamson, himself a poet who had recently come down from Oxford, had just published *The Modern Genilon and Other Poems* through Caton's firm the previous July.[25] In introducing the Fortune Press' *Selected Poems*, he begins by acknowledging that Stevens, "one of the most skilled and stimulating of American poets, is generally known in this country only by a few 'anthology pieces.'" He makes clear his personal preference for *Harmonium*, and indeed, thirty-five of the total eighty poems selected by him are from that volume. Though *Parts of a World* demonstrates a greater social awareness on Stevens' part, Williamson allows, he also discerns a "less finished technique."[26] The longest poem in the collection is "The Comedian as the Letter C"; none of the later longer poems reproduced in the Faber selection is included.

Upon receiving Sweeney's letter with the review from the *Irish Times*, Stevens wrote at once to Herbert Weinstock requesting further information. Weinstock's reply brought news of the resolution: "To our consternation we later heard that Fortune Press, despite the cancellation of the contract, was proceeding to publish. . . . When simple suasion failed, we had a firm of barristers take the matter in hand. . . . The barristers had some trouble locating the proprietor [Reginald Caton]. At last, he agreed to withdraw the book and destroy all copies of it except a few that had already gone out to reviewers."[27]

What had happened? The contract between Knopf and the Fortune Press, which had been concluded in 1945, was later cancelled by Knopf. Peter du Sautoy recalls that "there had been a contract between Knopf and the Fortune Press for such a volume but the time limit for its publication had expired, so Knopf were fully entitled to make an agreement with us [Faber & Faber]."[28] In fact, the contract had expired on December 31, 1946. Even as late as February 1951, Knopf had extended a final six-month grace period to Caton. With no publication forthcoming from the Fortune Press, negotiations with Faber commenced in August of that year. Had Caton heard of the proposed Faber volume and rushed into print his own collection six weeks in advance of the other?

Did he somehow believe that he still enjoyed a valid contract with Knopf? Charles Skilton, the current proprietor of the Fortune Press, is unsure: "[Caton] ran the business entirely as a one-man show—very industriously but highly eccentrically—and most of the history of it died with him."[29] Weinstock's letter to Stevens indicates that Caton at first resisted "simple suasion," but on January 17 he informed Knopf's attorneys in London that the sale of the volume was being abandoned. By February 5 he had agreed to destroy all remaining copies, though a few had already been dispatched to reviewers like Austin Clarke.

Reaction in England to the legitimate *Selected Poems* was laudatory. John Wain, for example, composed an admiring review, "The Freshness of Ourselves," for the BBC Third Programme, which was broadcast on March 29, 1953, along with a reading of some of the poems. Stephen Spender, writing in *Encounter*, proclaimed Stevens "one of the half-dozen great representatives" of American poetry.[30] For Donald Davie, Stevens was "a poet to be mentioned in the same breath as Eliot and Yeats and Pound. . . . He is a great poet indeed."[31] Two longer reviews, however, dealt with issues that were to restrict the appeal of Stevens in the first years after his publication in England. The anonymous reviewer in the *Times Literary Supplement*, for example, acclaimed Stevens as "the best poet writing in America, and one of the best now writing in English." Half of the review, however, chided the poet for deliberate obscurity: "the average man is going to find that—charmingly stated or not—confusion differs from order, and that these poems, if full of meaning, leave much of their meaning merely noted."[32] For Bernard Bergonzi, Stevens' constant concern with a "poetic epistemology" isolated his work from more conventional themes and left it "lonely and depopulated." He concluded that Stevens' poetry "represents a life-time of magnificent achievement. But it is, alas, essentially a barren magnificence (which is not to imply that younger poets cannot learn much from Stevens about the art of poetry)."[33] A similar limitation bothered William Empson: "One can't help wishing he had found more to say, if only because he could evidently say it."[34]

Charges of obscurity and dispassion were of course not limited to his British readers, but these purported handicaps had more than a little to do with the slowness with which Stevens' poetry caught on in England. Julian Symons, writing a year after the Faber publication, contended that Stevens was simply not widely read: "It remains true, however, that Stevens is held in no such esteem here as that accorded to T. S. Eliot and Ezra Pound; it is doubtful if he has even the small band of devoted admirers possessed by John Crowe Ransom and Conrad Aiken."[35] Of the 1,000 copies of the first edition of *Selected Poems*, 820 were sold in the first year, and fewer than 150 copies were sold annually during the next ten years.

More than anything else, it was the loyalty of Faber & Faber to the publication of his work that assured Stevens' ultimate success in England. A second printing of *Selected Poems* in 1954 was followed by an English edition of *The Collected Poems of Wallace Stevens* in 1955. Since Stevens' death, Faber has issued editions of *Opus Posthumous* (1959), *The Necessary Angel* (1960), and *Letters of Wallace Stevens* (1967). It was, however, the third printing of *Selected Poems* in 1965 in a paperback edition that truly launched Stevens' popularity in England. Peter du Sautoy, now chairman of Faber & Faber, reports that sales "really took off when the paperback appeared."[36] That growing interest was partly spurred by the 1960 publication of Frank Kermode's pioneering critical study, *Wallace Stevens*, in the Writers and Critics series.

In the last weeks of his life Stevens suddenly resumed correspondence with one of the figures from the earlier publishing controversy. Tambimuttu, the editor of *Poetry London* who in the mid-1940s had vied with the Fortune Press in bringing out a Stevens collection, was resuming the publication of his magazine, to be renamed *Poetry London–New York*, and wanted a poem from Stevens. There was certainly no lingering hard feelings on Stevens' part ("Greetings and welcome—just as if I owned the place"),[37] but surgery for cancer prevented him from sending a poem. Tambimuttu, ever resourceful and persistent, invited himself to Hartford for a personal meeting, but, writing from the Avery Convalescent Hospital a couple of months before his death, Stevens politely discouraged it.

At the time of his death, Stevens' reputation in America was secure. He had the further satisfaction of witnessing a widening reputation in England. For example, Alan Pryce-Jones had written in 1954, requesting poems for the *Times Literary Supplement.* Stevens responded with two of his final poems: "Presence of an External Master of Knowledge" and "A Child Asleep in Its Own Life." More significant, not only had *Selected Poems* received a second printing, but the Faber edition of *The Collected Poems* had been announced. It was to appear two months after Stevens' death. T. S. Eliot, writing about a year before Stevens' death, perhaps best described the poet's new-found success in England:

> Now, his reputation is beginning to spread to the people who don't know. There is no compliment on my own work that gives me more pleasure than that of the man who says, "I didn't know anything about this chap, but I picked up a volume of his the other day—and I found I *liked* it!" I have heard that said lately several times, about the book of Wallace Stevens.[38]

RICHARD ELLMANN

HOW WALLACE STEVENS SAW HIMSELF

IN HIS *PRINCIPLES OF PSYCHOLOGY*, WILLIAM JAMES recalls from the Martinus Scriblerus papers that Sir John Cutler owned a pair of black worsted stockings; these his maid had darned so often with silk that they became at last a pair of silk stockings. If they had been endowed with consciousness throughout the darning, they would at the end have thought of themselves as still a pair of worsted stockings, even though not a thread of the original material was left.[1] The self is equally subject to change, bound chiefly by memory to its earlier stages, and always very difficult to define. David Hume points out that nothing in one's experience quite answers to the word "I," and William James finds the self to be "only a loosely construed thing."[2]

Yet that there is, as Wallace Stevens said in "Le Monocle de Mon Oncle," "a substance in us that prevails" is an assumption that can hardly be renounced. It may well be that biographers are wrong to assume, as they generally do, that their subjects have essences or characters that flow liquidly in childhood and jell in youth, and perhaps petrify in old age. There may be almost as much discontinuity as continuity. The child may father a man who scarcely resembles him, in defiance of Freudian theory, which holds that the character is formed by the age of five, or of cultural rituals, which defer the moment until the onset of puberty. Existential biographers like Jean-Paul Sartre prefer to see the self as faced with a series of dramatic choices, none of which presupposes those that follow, while a writer like

Michel Leiris in *L'Age d'homme* sees the self as by nature fitted and forced to pass through a series of mythical identifications.

With most lives, documentation is sparse for the years of childhood, so not much can be said about them anyway. Writers do, it is true, often speak of their early years in autobiographies, but they see childhood chiefly in terms of the elements that proved fit to survive. Those elements that were sloughed off, and why, they rarely remember, or at least rarely confide to us. What a biographer would like to do is to enter the cloud of unknowing that precedes knowledge, of indecision the precedes choice. If only we could return to those fits and starts, vaguenesses and blurs, small humiliations and anguishes and small efforts to cope with them, we might recover the atmosphere in which a being seeks and measures its place among other beings. Long before anything occurs that could qualify as an event, there must be preliminary stirrings. Events are only residues. If we could, we would go back behind history to prehistory, searching for primitive tools and weapons, even though the pygmies who used them have long since disappeared into the giants who took their places.

As a biographical subject, hardly anyone offers more difficulties than Wallace Stevens. He was born four years after Robert Frost, whom he does not resemble, and well before Pound and Eliot, who do not resemble him. His life presents, like that of Shakespeare and those of most literary men, an image of attentive boisterousness in youth and boisterous discrimination in age. Not much is known about his life in either period, and perhaps not much is to be known. He had, for example, a great appetite for travel, but like the young Parisian in Joris Karl Huysmans' *A Rebours*, who reveled in the prospect of a trip to England, then suddenly anticipated its discomforts and remained in Paris instead, Stevens mostly stayed home. He resembled also his Crispin, whom he described in prose as "an every-day man who lives a life without the slightest adventure except that he lives it in a poetic atmosphere as we all do" (*L*, 778). From nine to five each day he applied himself to insurance dossiers at the Hartford

Indemnity and Insurance Corporation, an occupation he shared with Charles Ives and Franz Kafka, though they worked for rival concerns. "At night," he said, "I strut my individual state once more" (L, 121). Stevens prided himself on the disconnection of his two careers. Has there been since Shakespeare a poet who made himself so impenetrable? Hartford might be Stratford for all we know of it from him. If Stevens called his friend William Carlos Williams anti-poetic, he was himself anti-autobiographical. Instead of the urge to confess or at least to confide, which, happily for biographers, most of their subjects evince, Stevens displays a counterurge to conceal and fall silent.

Notoriously uncomfortable with his fellow poets, he chose as his boon companions men who were anything but memoir writers by temperament. They vindicated his appraisal by leaving no records. Other friends, including some of his principal correspondents, he never or rarely met, and they remained Mr. and Mrs. Such incidents as are reported remain of uncertain reliability, such as Witter Bynner's statement that Stevens left Harvard under a cloud, possibly because of his mock-rape of a waitress,[3] or of uncertain significance, such as Ernest Hemingway's slugging Stevens and giving him a black eye.[4] It might have been expected that his letters to his wife, especially during their five-year courtship, would reveal the inner Stevens, but, tender and considerate as the letters are, they thwart the biographer's longing for lapses of decorum. Holly Stevens, the poet's daughter, reports that her mother disliked seeing Wallace Stevens' books because they contained poems that she regarded as having been written solely to her. But the poems she so regarded seem scarcely private at all.

That such a man should have kept a journal might appear a contradiction, especially since he titled the journal, "The Book of Doubts and Fears." Yet intimacies are exactly what it does not contain. Perhaps there were some at one time, since passages have been excised, though whether by Stevens or by his wife is uncertain. But a reference backward to one such excised passage indicates that even there he did not give up all reserve. His entry of March 28, 1900, says, "I find that in the early part of this book I have written that I could never be a great poet except in mute feeling" (*SP*, 39). (The entry referred to is not to be found.) He then, at the age of twenty-one, challenges this self-estimation that dated from his nineteenth year as "silly and immature." (Yet a certain muteness in feeling went with his lifelong articulateness.) Another characteristic statement comes from 1900: "Personality must be kept secret before the world" (*L*, 44). He would later, in "The Figure of the Youth as Virile Poet," find authority for his view in Aristotle: " 'The poet should say very little *in propria persona.*' " Still, while disavowing direct egotism, he insists there that "without indirect egotism there can be no poetry. There can be no poetry without the personality of the poet . . ." (*NA*, 45-46). His letters are equally at cross-purposes on the subject: "one struggles to suppress the merely personal," he told Harvey Breit (*L*, 413), but, at the same time, the personal is the "origin" of poetry (*L*, 526). Similarly, he confessed that he read little verse by other poets for fear of echoing them (*L*, 575), yet he declared more proudly, "While, of course, I come down from the past, the past is my own and not something marked Coleridge, Wordsworth, etc. I know of no one who has been particularly important to me. My reality-imagination complex is entirely my own even though I see it in others" (*L*, 792). In fact, no contemporary poet seems less derivative.

Stevens' projections of himself in his verse are mostly ironical; he would not have described himself, as Yeats did, as "one who ruffled in a manly pose / For all his timid heart."[5] In a letter Stevens spoke of his friend Thomas Mc-Greevy as "an inhabitant of the world of names" (*L*, 738), perhaps because he thought of his own world as essentially a nameless one. ("Our Stars Come from Ireland," in which McGreevy is named, was an exception, a tribute to a name from a consciousness that automatically excluded such identification.) Stevens preferred to use names like Peter Quince or Crispin or Jocundus or Mrs. Alfred Uruguay. When, as in "The Idea of Order at Key West," he did use an actual

name, Ramon Fernandez, he immediately disclaimed any re-
lation between the critic named Ramon Fernandez and the
character in the poem. There are, nonetheless, occasional ref-
erences in his later verse to Freud, Nietzsche, Claude, Whit-
man, or to places like New Haven, and these are all quite
startling in context, like the sudden incursions of an arctic
explorer into Africa.

If, then, we look to Stevens to find early stirrings of his
character, suppression of personal circumstances and feelings
is clearly an attribute, even if an unhelpful one. In a letter
written to Elsie Moll two years before his marriage to her in
1910, he speaks of having written for an hour in his journal,
only to emphasize that he has left out a great deal: "it did
not seem desireable to disclose so much of my own spirit," he
says, then hastens to add, "I cannot pretend to any mystery"
(L, 112). There must have been enough mystery to warrant
reticence. Not to disclose his own spirit is a curious motto
for a poet in any age, but especially if the poet is a lyrical
one and writes in the age of Yeats, Pound, and Eliot, whose
works he knew well. None of these was confessional in the
present-day mode, but each told us overtly a good deal more
about himself than Stevens did.

The delineation of Stevens' idea of himself is then some-
thing he purposely impeded. Still, the difficulty may serve
as a spur to explore his "mind's native land," to use a phrase
of Mallarmé. In the absence of much in the way of external
incident, there are still hints, almost enough to enable us to
map that native land, establish some of its contours, surmise
its weather conditions, and perhaps speculate on the erup-
tions that brought it into being. Harold Bloom denies that
Stevens "ever underwent an intense crisis of an intellectual
variety,"[6] but it is just that area that I propose to trace.
Stevens' early materials are scarce and were written before the
work of Freud fostered systematized scrutiny by writers of
their own thoughts and images. They reveal in the young
poet, besides the craving for secrecy I have mentioned, an
unquenchable energy of contemplation. He is fond of the
quality of "force," as, in later life, he would also become fond

of the quality of "centrality." Since Frost was to dismiss Stevens as a bric-a-brac poet, it is notable that Stevens did not care for effeteness, even in 1900, when effeteness was in vogue. In that year he remarked of another poet, "His verses occasionally have much beauty—though never any great degree of force—other than pathetic" (L, 46), and commented in his journal, "How much more vigorous was the *thought* of the old fellows than is that of any modern man" (L, 46). The title he gave to one of his later poems, "Poetry Is a Destructive Force," embodies the same view. He complains surprisingly even of Hans Arp, that whatever its emotional intensity, Arp's work "lacks force" (L, 628). His letters speak frequently of poetry as "fury" and "violence" (L, 350), as "momentary violences" (L, 249), and even more purposefully, as "letting myself go" (L, 264).

Stevens no doubt manifested his youthful energy in many ways, but one way was in natural description. In 1897 Garrett Stevens remarked to his sixteen-year-old son on "your power of painting pictures in words" (L, 14), as if this had been well established already, and he even noted, not just jocularly, "eccentricities in your genius" (L, 16), as if this power in language had already shown itself to be phenomenal.

Garrett Stevens offers considerable assistance in deciphering what Wallace Stevens was like. The relations of the two were affectionate, and in Stevens' childhood, close. Later Stevens came to regard his father as having been the practical one, and his mother the imaginative one (SP, 8). But this view of them is not borne out by the letters that Stevens kept. His mother's letters—those that survive, at least—are routinely maternal, but his father's are the letters of a man interested in literature. That Stevens should characterize his father simply as practical implies a powerful and uneasy urge on his part to dissociate himself from the parent stem. Garrett Stevens wrote sketches, stories, and poems for a Reading newspaper from 1906 until his death in 1911, and the poems, whatever their defects, exhibit a propensity, of which his son was legatee, to introduce phrases in foreign languages. By

profession a lawyer and businessman, Garrett Stevens was
not so practical as to avoid a nervous breakdown about 1901.
Stevens was aware that in some ways he had imitated his
father. As he said, "I decided to be a lawyer the same way
I decided to be a Presbyterian; the same way I decided to be
a Democrat. My father was a lawyer, a Presbyterian and a
Democrat."[7] Unwittingly, Stevens disclosed deeper affinities.
"[H]e was one of the most uncommunicative of men" (L,
458), he wrote of his father in 1943, as if he were describing
someone very different from himself. And again, "The greater
part of his life was spent at his office; he wanted quiet and,
in the quiet, to create a life of his own" (L, 454). He forgot
having acknowledged not long before about himself, "People
say that I live in a world of my own . . ." (L, 352). He de-
scribes life in his father's house in Reading: "At home, our
house was rather a curious place, with all of us in different
parts of it, reading" (L, 391). And his daughter Holly Ste-
vens has indicated that Wallace Stevens' house in Hartford
was inhabited in much the same way.

Garrett Stevens' letters posed questions that his son ac-
cepted as crucial ones. The father had the same pleasure in
packaging wisdom into apothegms, and one of the most be-
guiling is, "A little romance is essential to ecstasy" (L, 14).
I suspect he wrote this in part as an admonition to his son,
who was cynically mocking away romance altogether in the
same fashion that Mrs. Alfred Uruguay would wipe away
moonlight like mud. Wallace Stevens conceded that "poetry
is essentially romantic" but insisted that the romantic he
sought would eliminate "what people speak of as the roman-
tic" (L, 277).

Garrett Stevens liked to go into the library of his house on
a Sunday afternoon and settle down with a long novel. His
library also included many books of poetry, and he appears
to have set the pattern for the discussion of books in the
family. In an early letter to Wallace, he praises the New
England writers, not for their profundity, which would be
the expected thing, but for their "suavity" (L, 14). In the
same way, he commends the taste for elegance among what

he inelegantly calls the "Bostonese" (*L*, 14). This emphasis upon the high gloss of literature, upon dapperness as a mental quality and even a moral one, caught the attention of his son and seems latent in Wallace Stevens' project of confecting "the final elegance," which he announced as a goal in "Notes toward a Supreme Fiction."

I have mentioned Garrett Stevens' linguistic virtuosity. This appears quite strikingly not only in his poems but also in a letter he wrote facetiously congratulating his son on election to the Harvard literary society, the Signet:

> Just what the election to the *Signet signifies* I have no *sign.* It is *significant* that your letter is a *signal* to *sign* another check that you may *sigh* no more. I suppose you thus win the privilege to wear a seal ring or a badge with the picture of a *Cygnet* on it—to distinguish you from commoner geese, or it may be you can con*sign* all studies de*signed* to cause re*signation,* to some as*signed* port where they will trouble you no more. (*L*, 26)

This fancy fooling is directly anticipatory of Stevens' "The Comedian as the Letter C." In that poem, he confessed long after, he had disported outrageously with the *x*, *ts*, and *z* sounds of the letter *c*, as in the line, "Exchequering from piebald fiscs unkeyed" (*CP*, 43). Garrett Stevens' little game was still being played, if on a grander scale, after his death.

But the father's influence extended also to the discovery of topics. So far as can be determined—and of course the evidence is skimpier than one would wish—he not only joined the great internal debate of Wallace Stevens about the intercourse of the mind with reality, he also initiated it. In a letter of September 27, 1897, he writes his eighteen-year-old son: "When we try to picture what we see, the purely imaginary is transcended, like listening in the dark we seem to really hear what we are listening for—but describing real objects one can draw straight or curved lines and the thing may be mathematically demonstrated—but who does not prefer the sunlight—and the shadow reflected" (*L*, 14). The

expression is somewhat tortured, but Garrett Stevens is pro-
posing, astonishingly, that when we try to say what we see,
we do so through our imagination, and yet that we transcend
that imagination because of the strong pressure of reality.
It is the same, he says, when the sense involved is hearing:
listening in the dark, we conjure up and yet really hear the
sounds we imaginatively crave. ("That music is intensest
which proclaims / The near, . . ." his son writes in "To the
One of Fictive Music" [CP, 88].) Finally, he contrasts the
abstract patterns into which imagination can turn real ob-
jects with the greater attractions of those objects in real
sunlight and shadow. After all of which his letter gruffly
concludes: "Point in all this screed—Paint truth but not al-
ways in drab clothes" (L, 14).[8] This is only half of the point,
the other half being: Ground the imagination in the real.
Between these two poles moves his son's verse. In his poem,
"The Common Life," Wallace Stevens contrasts the reality
of man and woman with "A black line beside a white line"
(CP, 221) as, in "The Rock," he wryly describes a meeting
of two lovers as "A theorem proposed between the two"
(CP, 525). Or, to take another example, his poem "So-And-
So Reclining on Her Couch" allows the imagination to turn
the actual woman into projections A, B, and C, but then ac-
cords the unprojected, living model a virtue that these fine
inventions cannot claim:

> The arrangement contains the desire of
> The artist. But one confides in what has no
> Concealed creator. One walks easily
>
> The unpainted shore, accepts the world
> As anything but sculpture. Good-bye,
> Mrs. Pappadopoulos, and thanks.[9]
>
> (CP, 296)

In another exchange between father and son a month and
a half later, Garrett Stevens writes: "You have discovered I
suppose, that the sun is not a ball of fire sending light and
Heat—like a stove—but that radiation and reflection is the

mystery—and that the higher up we get—and nearer to the sun the colder it gets . . ." (L, 16). This is bad physics but good metaphysics, and as metaphor it recurs in Stevens' verse —as in "Credences of Summer," "Trace the gold sun. . . . Look at it in its essential barrenness" (CP, 373), or in "The Sun This March," where he says, "Cold is our element . . ." (CP, 134).[10] The conception of the sun as surrounded by cold, a tropic conjoined to an arctic, is one that Stevens refined with enthusiasm.

His father had obscurely yet subtly glimpsed the kind of writer his son might become, an artist suave and elegant, a quizzer of both the imagination and the real, sensible of the seductions of both truth and delight. He saw him also as like himself, given over to reflection more than to action, to rumination more than to confession. Inklings of such characteristics, and others, in Wallace Stevens can be found in rare places. For example, by the time he reached high school he was demonstrating his remarkable appetite for sights and sounds and his expressive dexterity. His school friend Edwin de Turck Bechtel offers a few particulars. Bechtel is quoted by his widow as saying that " 'at high school Wallace was a whimsical, unpredictable young enthusiast, who lampooned Dido's tear-stained adventures in the cave, or wrote enigmatic couplets to gazelles' " (SP, 11). The recollections sound accurate. They indicate that Stevens' earliest poems involved some jollying of traditional romantic situations and some mustering of picturesque creatures. Bechtel's memory appears to be confirmed by later poems that revamp the original conceptions. In "Le Monocle de Mon Oncle," for example, another woman—tear-stained as Dido, and saluted with regal conjurations ("'Mother of heaven, regina of the clouds, / O sceptre of the sun, crown of the moon'" [CP, 13])—is reproached for her gloom, which is motivated in this case by the departure not of her Virgilian lover but of her own youth, and for her gullibility to the false romanticism of pious hereafters. As for the "enigmatic couplets to gazelles," these may well anticipate the enigmatic couplets addressed later to "Bantams in Pine-Woods." Bechtel saw

Stevens as at once enthusiast and mocker, the poet who would offer his Crispin one integration after another, in each of which "an ancient Crispin was dissolved" (CP, 29).

Bechtel's testimony is corroborated in Stevens' correspondence. By the time he began his journal at the age of nineteen, Stevens thought of himself as a poet, not so much by choice as by necessity. I suspect that he began to write out of ebullience and self-mockery and out of a disquietude over the coexistence of both qualities in his mind. In the to-and-fro of being magnified and minimized, the world might be lost; thus Stevens wrote, he said, "to relate myself to the world" (L, 306). Accordingly, he wrote poetry as if he had to, as he said of himself in contrast to another poet (L, 876). He needed poetry as "one of the sanctions of life" (L, 600). The first of Stevens' letters that survives, sent to his mother when he was fifteen, indicates that he had some conception as I have said of his mixture of self-canceling qualities. Stevens had been dispatched for a holiday to the Ephrata Mountain Springs Summer Resort, some fifteen miles from Reading. At first he wrote to complain:

> My Dear Mother—
> I write this letter in depressed spirits. I have decided to come home. Ephrata as a summer resort is still extant [but] as a pleasure resort is dead, very dead, indeed, or has my cynicism embittered me. I can get along first rate but one feels the difference from home and Ephrata. (L, 5)

The word "cynicism" is unexpected here. His allusion to it is at once so casual and so distinct that we may suppose it to have been a quality that he had long noted in himself, and one with which his mother was already familiar. Such a conclusion is borne out by his journal for July 31, 1899. Here is the best evidence for Stevens' intellectual crisis. One must imagine the layers of reticence that had to be cut through before he wrote these lines:

> Somehow what I do seems to increase in its artificiality. Those cynical years when I was about twelve subdued

natural and easy flow of feelings. I still scoff too much, analyze too much and see, perhaps, too many sides of a thing—but not always the true sides. For instance I have been here at Wily's almost a month, yet never noticed the pathos of their condition. The memory of one day's visit brought tears to Livingood's eyes. I am too cold for that. (*L*, 31)

Perhaps no one could compete with anyone named Livingood, but Stevens is severe with himself. Here his cynicism does not stand alone, as in the letter from Ephrata; it is part of a cluster of derogatory words that includes artificiality, many-sidedness carried to excess, and coldness. These are all qualities of which Stevens' critics have accused him, but what seems important is that at the age of twenty he charged himself with them.

What he meant by cynicism is presumably what Bechtel meant by mockery. It is clarified by one of Stevens' rare reminiscences about his childhood. "When I was a boy," he wrote Hi Simons in 1940, "I used to think that things progressed by contrasts, that there was a law of contrasts" (*L*, 368). The alternation, as of cynicism with enthusiasm, which in retrospect he recognized as characteristic, was at first a private habit to be reproved, as his use of the unpleasant word "cynicism" confirms; it became—and this was the way the crisis was resolved—a response to a law that applied to things generally. He would say later, "North and South are an intrinsic couple" (*CP*, 392), and in "The Glass of Water" an object is "merely a state, / One of many, between two poles" (*CP*, 197). He appears to be thinking indulgently of the same seesaw when he says of Crispin, "Thus he conceived his voyaging to be / An up and down between two elements, / A fluctuating between sun and moon" (*CP*, 35).[11] So his cynicism, originally a source of guilt, was gradually transformed into just a pole of thought—a necessary one—as he proceeded through crisis into self-justifying maturity.

I am not suggesting that he accomplished this transition

without paying a toll of anxiety. With Stevens, anxiety had the effect of making him aggressive in defense of qualities for which he had originally felt remorse. In the journal I have quoted he refers to his many-sidedness as perhaps excessive. The word "many-sided" was not in itself pejorative; in fact, the term was customarily applied in the nineteenth century to Goethe, who himself liked to use it, though in *Wilhelm Meister* he said the quality was useful only if it was the prelude to single-sidedness.[12] (G. H. Lewes, and J. S. Mill after him, gave it as Goethe's special quality, and since Stevens was studying Goethe at this time, he may well have come across it in Lewes' biography.) At first, however, Stevens allied it with his tendencies toward cynicism and artificiality and feared that the many sides he saw were not the right ones. Since he rarely admits in his journal to being bothered about anything, he was presumably bothered a good deal. Perhaps, like Yeats, he felt that he was on the path of the chameleon, and being, as he said later, at that time "all imagination" (L, 320), he felt drawn in too many directions, toward too many "jocular procreations of the dark" (L, 364). Only gradually did he find "the courage to be himself, which is, I suppose, the first necessity of any artist" (L, 537).

I cannot fix the date when Stevens' remorse over many-sidedness and cynicism became an affirmation of them. His anxiety over the subject is clear in 1901; that it was followed by much mulling over and finally quelled is suggested by a letter from his father to him in November 1907, when his father replied, obviously to some expression of confidence by Wallace, "I am glad you feel strong and self reliant."[13] It does not seem that Stevens ever achieved untrammeled assurance, but he had tenacity and boldness. For expression he needed to rely on his own psychic history rather than to accept what others had accumulated. The events that fostered this impulse were probably the First World War, which with its bareness questioned his profuseness, and the Armory Show of 1913, which endorsed multiple perspectives on experienced objects. By 1917 he was celebrating the

Argus-eyed observer in that baker's dozen of many-sidedness, "Thirteen Ways of Looking at a Blackbird";[14] a year later he wrote his wife, "I have always been of two minds about Tennessee"; and in 1919 the two-mindedness emerged, as Holly Stevens suggests, in "Anecdote of the Jar" (SP, 151). Here pleasure in the vegetable profusion of Tennessee is cynically countered by suspicion of its artistic unkemptness, while delight in the jar's perfection is tinged with cynical regret at its un-Tennesseean aridity. Stevens' friend Bechtel would have recognized both minds.

Stevens not only looked outward to see different aspects, he also looked inward and found the same phenomenon. What in his journal in 1899 he had considered artificiality now began to seem altogether natural. For he had come to William James' conclusion, which he had perhaps heard or read at Harvard, that every self is many selves. A letter written to Elsie Moll in that period of consolidation of 1906-1907 that his father had commended declares, "After all I'm not one thing or another, but this thing today, and that, tomorrow" (L, 94). He sets out the matter more amply in his journal for April 27, 1906:

There are no end of gnomes that *might* influence people—but do not. When you first feel the truth of, say, an epigram, you feel like making it a rule of conduct. But this one is displaced by that, and thus things go on in their accustomed way. There is one pleasure in this volatile morality: the day you believe in chastity, poverty and obedience, you are charmed to discover what a monk you have always been—the monk is suddenly revealed like a spirit in a wood; the day you turn Ibsenist, you confess that, after all, you always were an Ibsenist, without knowing it. So you come to believe in yourself, and in your new creed. There is a perfect rout of characters in every man—and every man is like an actor's trunk, full of strange creatures, new + old. But an actor and his trunk are two different things. (L, 91)

The metaphors propose that we don't take on roles delib-
erately, as actors do, but simply express seriatim the latent
possibilities or selves in our nature without premeditation.
So he could write in 1935: "To my way of thinking, there is
not the slightest affectation in anything that I do" (*L*, 287).
This declaration finds a gloss in a three-line poem that he
sent to Harriet Monroe in 1920:

> *Poupée de Poupées*
> She was not the child of religion or of science
> Created by a god as by earth.
> She was the creature of her own minds.[15]

Many-sidedness, instead of being a sign of weakness, is here
the controlling principle. It became in fact Stevens' poetic
enterprise.

But he still had to cope with the other quality for which
he berates himself in his journal of July 31, 1899: coldness.
Coldness is a subject to which he frequently returns. In his
journal for the next day, August 1, 1899, he proposes to over-
come this quality in a sonnet, for which he presents this
romantic plan: "Frost in a meadow. Is there no bird to sing
despite this? No song of Love to outquench the thought of
Death?" (*L*, 31). But gradually Stevens began to think of a
kind of song that would affirm rather than deny coldness or
frost. In fact, there is a persistent lowering of the tempera-
ture in his mind's native land. He did not abjure Livingood's
capacity for pity, but other perspectives, he came to see,
might also have their uses and would save him from that
"slushiness" against which Ezra Pound was later to inveigh.
So, two years after he expressed such disquietude about his
own coldness, Stevens began to preen himself on not yielding
so readily to warmth:

> To illustrate the change that has come over me I may
> mention that last night I saw from an elevated train a
> group of girls making flowers in a dirty factory near
> Bleecker-st. I hardly gave it a thought. Last summer the

pathos of it would have bathed me in tears. (*L*, 53 [Journal for March 12, 1901])

It is as if he were saying farewell to Florida, and treating cold as a part of experience to be valued as highly as warmth. He does not exclude the pathos, but in a palpable hit at Livingood he overcomes it "by building his city in snow" (*CP*, 158). As he wrote to Richard Wilbur, "The greater part of the imaginative life of people is both created and enjoyed in polar circumstances" (*L*, 740). And in his very last poem, "As You Leave the Room," he remarks, "Now, here, the snow I had forgotten becomes / Part of a major reality. . . ." (Another version of this poem, "First Warmth," speaks of "the warmth I had forgotten.")[16] By this time Stevens might well feel that he had given equal play to both temperatures.[17] Perhaps the locus classicus for this defense of polar weather is "The Snow Man," where Stevens insists that only with "a mind of winter" can one regard the frost and the snow properly. The wind's misery has to be mentioned, just as the pathos of the factory girls had to be taken into account, but the mind must be cold to understand snow.[18] Stevens may have been brought to this revised attitude in part because he read in G. H. Lewes' biography of Goethe that coldness was a major component of the Goethean personality.[19] In any case, freezing temperatures played a large part in self-scrutiny. Yet the problem does not end there. Misery remains, and the snowman's solidity is most fragile. There are sounds he cannot hear but that question his absolute authority.

This defense of coldness leads toward "The Emperor of Ice-Cream." Some twenty years ago, I offered the view that the emperor in this poem could not be death, as had been conjectured, nor could he be life, but that he must be being, which includes death and life and the imagination that plays over both.[20] A letter afterwards printed in Stevens' *Letters* (p. 341) obligingly confirmed this interpretation. What needs to be added is that the defense of the emperor of ice cream is part of that defense of coldness, which Stevens came to see as integral in his perspective. The succulence of ice cream can only exist in a frame of cold. Hence the quality of coldness over which he had once experienced remorse no longer seemed a defect. He became suspicious of poets, like Robert Frost (in spite of the latter's name), who kept offering up humanity in their work as though warmth were the only key to the world.

I suspect that Stevens felt increasingly that his recognition of cold, with its attendant and implicit images of death, nakedness, nothing, and saying no, was part of his original contribution to poetry. A letter from him to Harriet Monroe apologizes for having talked "gossip about death" (April 8, 1918, L, 206), to the dismay of Miss Monroe and other guests; evidently his at once obsessed and dispassionate consideration of the subject had given them pain. As more than the annalist of plums, he recognized an obligation to envisage plumlessness as well. " 'I have said no / To everything, in order to get at myself,' " says Mrs. Alfred Uruguay (CP, 249). Stevens saw more fully now the correctness of his father's insistence that the sun was surrounded by cold. The women in "Sunday Morning" and "Le Monocle de Mon Oncle" who talk of death and nothingness are not wrong, only one-sided; plenitude depends upon famine, as density upon blankness. The "littering leaves" of "Sunday Morning" connect with the "leaflessness" of "An Ordinary Evening in New Haven." Poetry, being "a destructive force," must recognize not only things of this world but also their absence. The urge to strip bare is as basic as the urge to bedeck. Affluence is joined to poverty (OP, xvii) as Oxidia to Olympia. So in his play Carlos among the Candles, Stevens shows the poet lighting twelve candles in turn—a Promethean gesture—and then extinguishing them in turn, like cold yielding to abundance yielding to cold. He would speak later of a cycle from romanticism to realism to fatalism to indifferentism (L, 354) in a restatement of the same idea. For Stevens, reality contains and entails its own negation, just as the imagination contains and entails its own negation. As he says in "Notes toward a Supreme Fiction": "it was not a choice /

Between excluding things. . . . He chose to include the things
/ That in each other are included . . ." (*CP*, 403). Hence
he searches for "a poetry divested of poetry" (*L*, 631).

Stevens resolved his personal crisis by affirming what he
had once anguished over, but some of the anguish remained.
That is why his characterizations of himself or of his poetic
personae seem to render them precarious, whether they are
called snowman or uncle, Peter Quince or Crispin. Not only
are there many selves, but self hovers on the edge of self-
annihilation, and while death is for Stevens, as for Rilke,
"also part of the process," misery and despair are not encom-
passed altogether successfully by noble axiomata about being.
If these components I have mentioned were essential to
Stevens' view of himself and of his poetry, then his intellec-
tual crisis of the early years of this century can have been
only partially resolved. A residue of raging unhappiness clung
stubbornly to even the most comprehensive poetic ordering
of the world.

For an account of Stevens' dilemmas, a poem like "Thir-
teen Ways of Looking at a Blackbird" may convey as much
as his journal and letters. To many readers this poem is a
jumble of impressions or meditations. But I suggest that this
seeming discreteness masks an underlying, reticent related-
ness, and that the poem came into being as a series of vi-
gnettes of his mental history. If so, it would be a covert auto-
biography, written, appropriately, when Stevens was getting
on toward forty. It dates, in fact, from the same year, 1917,
as his play *Bowl, Cat, and Broomstick*, which purports to
describe a love poet, a seventeenth-century Frenchwoman,
and to do so offers an obviously inadequate sketch of her
life, portrays her hair, eyes, and chin, and quotes from her
verse. At the end her essence remains as unrecoverable as
before. No biographical pigeonhole will contain the fugitive
flutterings of that delicate being.[21]

"Thirteen Ways of Looking at a Blackbird" similarly im-
plies its own insufficiency as memoir. But Stevens makes the
attempt nonetheless. The poem connects with another poem
written in the same year and also for a time arranged in

thirteen parts. This was "Lettres d'un Soldat," which orig-
inally was a chronological sequence based upon actual entries
in the journal of a French soldier. The individual "letters"
do not follow closely on one another, any more than do the
thirteen ways; but Stevens begins with the soldier's resigna-
tion to his soldier's lot and ends with his disgust at digging
his comrades' graves. While no close analogy can be drawn,
"Lettres d'un Soldat" discloses Stevens' dejection over the
war and helps to explain why (as he told his Italian trans-
lator) the last part of "Thirteen Ways" should have been
devoted to "despair."

In the "Thirteen Ways," however, Stevens works more
closely with the passages of spirit he had experienced in his
own life. The poem begins and ends with a snow scene, but
the tone in the first is quite different from that in the last,
and the blackbird's eye, initial sign of animation among
inanimatenesses, emerges like an infant consciousness. The
effect is similar to that in Stevens' "A Discovery of Thought,"
where he sees, "in an infancy of blue snow," "The cricket of
summer forming itself out of ice."[22] From this moment when
consciousness, like the poem, is born, Stevens voyages
through the history of his self-identification. He could do
this in only one way, not by narrating external events, which
were always for him of doubtful solidity, but by naming
those prior elements of consciousness that he had discovered,
brooded upon, and to some extent reconstituted. The uneasi-
ness that he continued to feel about the phases of his intel-
lectual crisis kept him from accepting any single formulation
as authoritative.

Accordingly, the first thing he mentions is that habit of
many-sidedness that at first had caused him so much distress.
He recalls it in stanza II lightly and even self-mockingly, as
befits a memoirist who puts no stock in memoirs:

> I was of three minds,
> Like a tree
> In which there are three blackbirds.
>
> (CP, 92)

Nature offers its modest warrant, by the multiplicity of black-birds, for the multiplicity of the observer's minds. In the third stanza the world is a pantomime in which the black-bird, like—it may be—a child reconciled to Ephrata Mountain Springs Summer Resort, is willingly whirled. When love comes in youth, with its implicit change of climate, there is no fear that it will drown out the poetic mind, for the creative consciousness harmonizes with love as the blackbird with a man and woman in love. Its song is in fact a celebration, and is welcomed as one.

These nuptial intimations lead, however, to thoughts of death, which in Stevens are never far apart from those of love. If this autobiography were an external chronicle, the deaths of his father and mother in 1911 and 1912, not long after his marriage, would be referred to, but in this internal voyage there is no place for exact allusions. In several of his early poems Stevens insists that love derives its savor from perishability, that without death, love could not exist. Now the sudden intrusion of icicles upon the long glass—the window that suggests warm, civilized life—reminds one not only of winter but also of a cold beyond that of winter, an ultimate cold. The blackbird, as it moves across the ice, seems to denote some indecipherable first principle, as if it were the mark of creation across chaos.

Then follows the reproof of the "thin men of Haddam." In *Harmonium* the principal reproofs are addressed to women—to "A High-Toned Old Christian Woman," to the dishevelled companion in "Le Monocle de Mon Oncle," and to the distraught companion in "Sunday Morning." These three are admonished by the poet for much the same failing, that they insist upon finding the actual world to be "nothing" and upon seeking surcease for that nothing in heaven. The urgency and frequency with which the subject is pursued in these poems may well signal a recurrent effort by Stevens to cope with his wife's gloom. But in the seventh way of looking at a blackbird he makes his target the thin men of Haddam, who also fall into the heresies of rejecting the beauty of this world as if it were nothing and of attending only to the heavenly esoteric. He insists that the vital, simple, basic imagination, which in "The Rock" (CP, 528) he calls "the main of things, the mind," and for which the blackbird in nature mostly stands model, is involved in everything, both the visible reality and the highest art. Even when the mind enters, as in stanza IX, into regions beyond its compassing, it delimits and marks them as, in "The Idea of Order at Key West," the maker's words order the chaos of the sea. Poetasters, whom in stanza X he describes as "the bawds of euphony," cannot deny, must indeed admit this essential vitality.

Yet the imagination, like being, embraces death with life, and in those unaware of its dual character, can still provoke terror, however much they try to shelter behind reality-proof glass. Having misconstrued appearances, they misconceive implications. That imaginative life has a less benevolent aspect is, however, conceded and recorded in the last two sections. Stanza XII indicates, Stevens said, "the compulsion frequently back of the things that we do" (L, 340). His explanation confirms that the blackbird, while retaining its place in nature, stands for human qualities. The mind is subject, at least sporadically, to blind forces it cannot direct. The final section, the luckless thirteenth, pictures the immobilization of the creative consciousness in a nature in which time is askew—"It was evening all afternoon"—like a poet in his prime brooding on death (CP, 95). The snow, which in the first section had offered a handsome white backdrop, is now disagreeable, the world is dark. Do what it will, the mind, like the blackbird, must at moments amalgamate with cold, which is death's climate. No imaginative recovery of the world, such as in happier moments Stevens devised, could lead to continuous warmth. "But time will not relent" (CP, 96). Yet the blackbird, still animate even if inert, seems to testify that despair, with its motionlessness, is as much a part of the pantomime as the earlier euphoric whirling. In this recognition the poem finds a place to stop, for one cycle is over, and yet all the elements necessary for a new cycle are already gathered. The eye of the blackbird will move again.

The individual life is a parable of all life. Hence "Twenty men crossing a bridge, / Into a village," as he wrote the following year in "Metaphors of a Magnifico," are also "one man / Crossing a single bridge into a village" (CP, 19). With his thirteen phases of the blackbird Wallace Stevens had attempted something like Yeats' description of consciousness in terms of phases of the moon. (His earliest mature lyrics were called "Phases" [OP, 3], as if the discovery of this world had liberated him.) In Stevens' verse the oscillation between cold and warmth is like Yeats' gyres alternating between primary and antithetical. As did Yeats, Stevens presented a mode of apprehending reality that is also a reflection of the inner mechanism of that reality. The process by which worsted becomes silk is then not simply a record of evolution, it is a definition of consciousness. The progressive recognition of those elements that constitute being is the only true model for autobiography.

If this account of Stevens' conception of himself is valid, then the familiar separation of life and work, on which biography often rests, is inapplicable to him. The intellectual crisis shadowed forth in his letters and journal and in his poems antedates any such bifurcation. Stevens is as much concerned with his possible limitations as mortal man as with his possible limitations as immortal poet. Perfection of the work as opposed to perfection of the life is not, whatever Yeats' poem says, a genuine choice, for the opposites interpenetrate. The images that Stevens had formed of his internal being, of its needs and gratifications, its appetites, its shortcomings, its extenuations, are prior to major acts, whether of life or of literature, and yet determinant upon them. How he saw himself, how he valued and then revalued what he saw, provided the impetus to write that poetry in which he was both actor and spectator. In this sense he was right to consider that his poetry was personal. He was right to identify himself not with Shakespeare, whom he described as "a nonentity about which cluster a great many supreme plays and poems," but with Goethe, who was "a nucleus for his productions" (L, 22). Stevens could say, in "Thirteen Ways" and in his work generally, as Goethe said, that his poems are fragments of the grand confession of his life.

HELEN VENDLER

STEVENS AND KEATS'
"TO AUTUMN"

THROUGHOUT HIS LONG LIFE AS A POET, STEVENS RE-
turned again and again to Keats' ode "To Autumn." The
history of those returns provides a classic example of how
literary materials can be reworked by a modern artist. We
are accustomed to this process in modern art, especially in
painting and sculpture; E. H. Gombrich has pointed out, in
Art and Illusion, how artists reproduce, not what they see,
but rather some amalgam of that and an antecedent pictorial
schema already in their minds. For Stevens, Keats' ode of-
fered an antecedent model that proved irresistible, and I
believe that Stevens hovered over the ode repeatedly in his
musings. He became, to my way of thinking, the best reader
of the ode, the most subtle interpreter of its rich meanings.
Our understanding of some latent significance in the older
poem broadens when the ode is seen refracted through Ste-
vens' lines. At the same time, we may perceive in Stevens'
departures from the ode implicit critiques of its stance.

We may recall Stevens' definition of poetry as an art em-
bracing two different "poetries": the poetry of the idea and
the poetry of the words. My own work on Stevens has hith-
erto been chiefly a commentary on the poetry of the words,
but here I must turn to the poetry of the idea. Stevens
helpfully remarked that the idea of God is a poetic idea; it
seems from his poetry that he considered the idea of a sea-
sonal cycle a poetic idea as well, since it embodies the nat-
ural counterpart to the poetic "exhilarations of changes," the
motive for metaphor:

You like it under the trees in autumn,
Because everything is half dead. . . .

In the same way, you were happy in spring,
With the half colors of quarter-things. . . .

                                        (CP, 288)

The seasonal idea, though immemorially present in lyric, seems to have been mediated to Stevens through Keats, no doubt through the sonnet on the human seasons as well as through the odes.

In commenting on a received aesthetic form, an artist can take various paths. He may make certain implicit "meanings" explicit; he may carry certain possibilities to further lengths; he may choose a detail, center down on it, and make it into an entire composition; he may alter the perspective from which the form is viewed; or he may view the phenomenon at a different moment in time. We are familiar with these strategies in painting, in the expansion and critique of classical forms practiced by all subsequent schools, but most noticeably for us, perhaps, in the dramatic and radical experimentation with classic forms in our own century. Stevens is modern as Cezanne is modern; he keeps the inherited shapes, is classic in his own disposition of materials, is rarely bizarre, and stays within the central tradition of Western art. Stevens' "copies" never forget their great originals; but in following Stevens' experiments with the materials of the autumn ode, we may see how a modern originality gradually declares itself while deliberately recalling, even into old age, the earlier master's prototype.

The presence of Keats' ode within a great many of Stevens' poems is self-evident. I wish to begin here with the single most derivative moment in Stevens, the end of "Sunday Morning"; then I shall sketch briefly the fashion in which Stevens, in my judgment, read the autumn ode. After that, I shall turn to Stevens' two "panels" to the autumn ode, "Credences of Summer" and "The Auroras of Autumn"; and finally, I shall suggest the outer limits of Stevens' response to and adaptation of Keats' ode. It is impossible to enumerate

here the lesser appearances of fragments of the ode through-
out Stevens' work; anyone familiar with the poetry will rec-
ognize in Stevens Keats' fruits, autumnal female presence,
cottage (transmuted to an American cabin), cornfields
(changed to American hayfields), wind, muted or unmelo-
dious birds, stubble plains (reduced to bare stalks or thin
grass), clouds, and bees. Our recognition of such echoes is
usually intermittent; but to read through Stevens' poetry
with "To Autumn" in mind is to be suffused by the lights
that Stevens saw presiding over the trash can at the end of
the world, that resting place of tradition:

> Above that urn two lights
> Commingle, not like the commingling of sun and moon
> At dawn, nor of summer-light and winter-light
> In an autumn afternoon, but two immense
> Reflections, whirling apart and wide away.
>
> (OP, 50)

The closing of "Sunday Morning" is a rewritten version of
the close of Keats' ode; such risktaking in a young poet ar-
gues a deep engagement with the earlier poem. The resem-
blances are obvious and have been often remarked.[1] Both
poets use successive clauses of animal presence (gnats, lambs,
crickets, redbreast, and swallows in Keats; deer, quail, and
pigeons in Stevens); both poems close with birds in the sky
(gathering swallows in Keats; flocks of pigeons in Stevens)[2]
and with the sense of sound (a whistling bird in each); and
Keats' soft-dying day becomes Stevens' evening. However,
Stevens' stance, unlike that of Keats, is the homiletic and
doctrinal one inherited from religious poetry and so dear to
American poets. It is true that Stevens, as a modern poet,
offers a choice of doctrines to his reader: we live, it would
seem, either (1) in chaos or (2) in a system of mutual
dependency, or (3) in a condition of solitude, which may
itself be seen as (3a) lonely ("unsponsored") or (3b) liber-
ated ("free"), but which is in any case inescapable. The
passage allowing doctrinal choices is followed by the passage
on deer, quail, berries, and pigeons (these wilderness forms

replace Keats' domestic ones), in which the doctrinal options are both alluded to and, in the end, left undecided. The quail utter "spontaneous" cries, and their adjective hearkens back phonemically to our "unsponsored" state; the pigeons fly in an "isolation" that etymologically resembles our "island" solitude; the "chaos" of the sun recalls orthographically the "casual" flocks of pigeons. In the end, as the pigeons inscribe their transient motions in the air, their calligraphy is read as elusively ambiguous by the poet seeking significance, and doctrinal choice dissolves in mystery. But while metaphysical certainty remains unattainable, the truth of existence is clear. The final motion, whether or not definable as one of chaos, dependency, solitude, freedom, or unsponsoredness, is "downward to darkness." In such an ending, *be* is final of *seem*, and death is the only certainty uninvaded by metaphysical doubt. Whereas Keats rests in the polyphony of the creatures in their autumnal choir, Stevens (though his adoption of Keats' principal trope, enumeration, shows him to be not insensible to the plenitude around him in the scene) makes his landscape depend for its significance on what it can explicitly suggest about the truth of the human condition.

With the example of Keats' beautiful implicit meanings before us, we may tend to recoil from what seems crudity in Stevens, as he speckles the visible scene with invisible queries —chaos? dependency? solitude? unsponsoredness? freedom? isolation? casualness? ambiguity? We may also resent the coercion of cadence, which forces the innocent landscape to enact a Stevensian entropy:

> And,
>   in the isolation of the sky,
>   At evening,
>   casual flocks of pigeons
>   make
> Ambiguous undulations as they sink,
>   Downward to darkness,
>   on extended
>   wings.

Stevens' final clause is lightly imitative of Keats' passage on the gnats among the river sallows,

Keats' imitation of randomness is changed by Stevens into an imitation of decline. But Keats, of course, went on to forbid himself such naive stylistic equivalences:

> And full-grown lambs loud bleat from hilly bourn;
>   Hedge-crickets sing; and now with treble soft
> The red-breast whistles from a garden-croft;
>   And gathering swallows twitter in the skies.

These clauses are the source for Stevens' earlier ones ("Deer walk upon our mountains," etc.), but we see that what Stevens has done is to reverse the rhetorical order of Keats. Keats writes a long clause about the gnats, then follows it with shorter ones, dwindling to "hedge-crickets sing," then broadens out to end his poem. Stevens writes short clauses followed by a final long one. There results a gain in climactic force and explicit pathos, but a loss in stoicism and discretion of statement. Keats' pathos (at its most plangent in the small gnats who mourn in a wailful choir, helpless in the light wind, less insistent but still audible in the bleating lambs, but largely absent in the whistle and twitter of the closing lines) reaches us with steadily diminishing force, in inverse relation to Keats' recognition of the independent worth of autumnal music, without reference to any dying fall. Stevens' pathos, on the other hand, is most evident in the closing lines. In short, Stevens has adopted Keats' manner—the population of animals, the types of clauses, the diction, even the sunset landscape—without at all embracing Keats' essential stylistic argument against nostalgia. Nor has he imitated Keats' reticent diction and chaste rhetoric; instead, he writes with an increasing opulence of rhetorical music and imposes explicit metaphysical dimensions on the landscape.

Nevertheless, the imitation, however inferior to its source, argues that Keats' ode had penetrated Stevens' consciousness and imagination absolutely and was already provoking him to see the world in its light, even if he found the world insufficient without attendant metaphysics. Keats' ode continued to provide Stevens with material to the very end of his life. In the *Adagia*, Stevens asks the question that the ode, among other works, must have prompted: "How has the human spirit ever survived the terrific literature with which it has had to contend?" (*OP*, 168).

If on the total evidence of Stevens' poetry we ask how he read "To Autumn," we can sketch out, for the moment neglecting all chronology, elements of his understanding of the ode. He thought, at first, that Keats was being evasive in the stasis of the first stanza, that he was avoiding the most repellent detail of natural process: death. (Stevens was, in taking this severe view, misinterpreting Keats, whose subject was not natural process but rather human intervention in natural process—harvest, rather than death.) In both "Le Monocle de Mon Oncle" and "Sunday Morning" Stevens insists that everything "comes rotting back to ground" and that "This luscious and impeccable fruit of life / Falls, it appears, of its own weight to earth," and he writes what seem to be taunts directed at the changeless ripeness of Keats' first stanza:

> Is there no change of death in paradise?
> Does ripe fruit never fall? Or do the boughs
> Hang always heavy in that perfect sky?

Allowing the fruit to follow its natural trajectory, Stevens lets autumn not only "swell the gourd" but strain it beyond its own capacity to swell until it becomes distorted in shape and its skin becomes streaked and rayed:

It comes, it blooms, it bears its fruit and dies.

. . . .

Two golden gourds distended on our vines,
Into the autumn weather, splashed with frost,
Distorted by hale fatness, turned grotesque.
We hang like warty squashes, streaked and rayed,
The laughing sky will see the two of us
Washed into rinds by rotting winter rains.

(CP, 16)

In spite of this "realist" critique of Keats' benign autumn, Stevens' poetry here is still Keatsian: no new style of language has arisen to support the new harshness of position. And the unfairness of the critique is of a piece with the "realist" position. Stevens comes much closer to the true Keatsian stance in a later poem, "On the Road Home," where plenitude is seen to stem not so much from any group of items in the landscape as from the rejection of doctrine in favor of perception, from the measuring of the world not by thought but by eye:

It was when I said,
"There is no such thing as the truth,"
That the grapes seemed fatter. . . .

. . . .

It was at that time, that the silence was largest
And longest, the night was roundest,
The fragrance of the autumn warmest,
Closest and strongest.

(CP, 203-4)

Whatever the objections that could be urged against the final formulation here, it is in its near tautology and solemn playfulness recognizably Stevensian and not Keatsian in language; even when metaphysically in agreement with Keats, the later Stevens speaks in his own voice.

When Stevens writes, in "The Rock," his final retraction

of the "realist" view expressed in "Le Monocle," he alludes to his own dictum from the early poem—"It comes, it blooms, it bears its fruit and dies"—but he quietly corrects himself by omitting the death. The leaves that cover the rock, standing for the poem as icon, "bud and bloom and bear their fruit without change." This is not written in agreement with Keats, who allowed his fruit to change, if not through death, at least through harvest. But neither is it written to correct him. Rather, it is written to give credence to the plenty of the world as it is preserved in the mind, always Stevens' chosen territory. The leaves

> bloom as a man loves, as he lives in love.
> They bear their fruit so that the year is known,
>
> As if its understanding was brown skin,
> The honey in its pulp, the final found,
> The plenty of the year and of the world.
>
> (CP, 527)

Here, precisely because he is speaking of internal, not external, fruition, Stevens is able to leave the fruit on the tree, the honey in the hive, without irritably reaching out to force them to fall and rot or to be harvested.

No previous source in poetry seems to me so rich for Stevens as the second stanza of "To Autumn." Keats' goddess of autumn, nearer to us than pagan goddesses because, unlike them, she labors in the fields and is herself threshed by the winnowing wind, varies in her manifestations from careless girl to burdened gleaner to patient watcher, erotic in her abandon to the fume of poppies, intimate of light in her bosom friendship with the maturing sun, worn by her vigil over the last oozings. She reappears in innumerable guises in Stevens' work, but is more often than not maternal: "The mother's face, / The purpose of the poem, fills the room" ("Auroras of Autumn"). I believe that her maternal nature was suggested by Keats' ode (which itself borrows from Shakespeare's image of "the teeming autumn, big with rich increase, / Bearing the wanton burden of the prime,

/ Like widow'd wombs after their lord's decease" [Sonnet XCVII]). Keats' season is an earth goddess whose union with the sun makes her bear fruit; the sun, his part in procreation done, departs from the poem as the harvest begins, and the season ages from the careless figure on the granary floor to the watcher over the last drops of the crushed apples. Finally, when she becomes the "soft-dying day," she is mourned by creatures deliberately infantine, as even full-grown sheep are represented as bleating lambs: these creatures are filial forms, children grieving for the death of the mother. Stevens, I believe, recognized these implications and brought them into explicitness.

The most beautiful modern commentary on Keats' invention of a humanized goddess of the ripe fields is Stevens' "The Woman in Sunshine":

> It is only that this warmth and movement are like
> The warmth and movement of a woman.
>
> It is not that there is any image in the air
> Nor the beginning nor end of a form:
>
> It is empty. But a woman in threadless gold
> Burns us with brushings of her dress
>
> And a dissociated abundance of being,
> More definite for what she is—
>
> Because she is disembodied,
> Bearing the odors of the summer fields,
>
> Confessing the taciturn and yet indifferent,
> Invisibly clear, the only love.
>
> (CP, 445)

The "poetry of the idea" here comes from Keats, the "poetry of the words" from Stevens. The iconic image, surrounded by words like "empty," "dissociated," "disembodied," "taciturn," "indifferent," and "invisibly clear," is wholly Stevensian, as is the rhetoric of "it is only," "it is not," and "it is empty." Stevens has taken a detail from his source and has enlarged it to fill a new and more modern space. This goddess takes various forms in Stevens, most of them beneficent. When Stevens is most depressed, "mother nature" (as she is named, along with Stevens' matching invention, "father nature," in "Lulu Morose") turns either actively malevolent (curdling the kind cow's milk with lightning in "Lulu Morose") or, worse, devouring but indifferent (as in "Madame La Fleurie," where mother and father nature are conflated into one androgynous mother who feeds on her son, "a bearded queen, wicked in her dead light"). But such "corrections" of Keats' goddess are infrequent in Stevens. Rather, Stevens tends to expand Keats' figure until she becomes one of "The pure perfections of parental space, / . . . the beings of the mind / In the light-bound space of the mind . . ." (CP, 436). Though he acknowledges fully the fictive nature of the goddess, Stevens can move insensibly into speaking of her as if she were real, as if she were in fact all there is of reality. This he learned from Keats' fully formed and fully imagined relation to the autumn goddess, whom Keats begins by celebrating in tones of worship and ends by consoling in the accents of intimacy: "Think not of them, thou hast thy music too."

Keats' third stanza gave Stevens his crickets, his bare spaces, and all his autumn refrains of thinning music. But, more centrally, it invited him to participate in its debate on the value of a diminished music and in its speculation on the relation of that music to the ampler choirs of spring. Stevens recognized, I think, that Keats' ode is spoken by one whose poetic impetus arises from a recoil at the stubble plains; the method of the ode is to adopt a reparatory fantasy whereby the barren plains are "repopulated" with fruit, flowers, wheat, and a providential goddess. But Keats subsides, at the end, into the barrenness that had first stimulated his compensatory imagination, and he leaves in the fields nothing but his poem—that autumnal thin music—where there had briefly been a feast for sight and touch.

Nostalgia, so gently put aside by Keats when his goddess sighs for the songs of spring, is more vindictively suppressed by Stevens in one of the more astonishing poetic descendants of the ode. "Think not of them," says Keats to that part of himself that has looked longingly backward to the nightingales' spring songs.[3] Stevens begins his corresponding late passage in "Puella Parvula" by telling us that "Every thread of summer is at last unwoven." It is the "season of memory, / When the leaves fall like things mournful of the past. . . ." But over the dissolving wind, "the mighty imagination triumphs," saying to nostalgia not Keats' kind words but rather,

> Keep quiet in the heart, O wild bitch. O mind
> Gone wild, be what he tells you to be: *Puella.*
> Write *pax* across the window pane. And then
>
> Be still. The *summarium in excelsis* begins. . . .
> (CP, 456)

The taming of mind to the season is common to Keats and Stevens, but Stevens' regret, the regret of the man who rarely had the satisfactions of summer, is more bitter. What is left from romance is "the rotted rose," and Stevens must squeeze "the reddest fragrance from the stump / Of summer." The violence of the modern supervenes on the romantic *nachschein.*

These, as Stevens would say, are only instances. For Stevens' grandest meditation on "To Autumn" we must look to two of his long poems. "Credences of Summer" centers on the moment when "the hay, / Baked through long days, is piled in mows," the moment before the stubble plains. "The Auroras of Autumn" centers on the approach of "boreal night" after "the season changes." The light wind of Keats' soft-dying day modulates into a fiercer form: "A cold wind chills the beach." The stubble plains at the end of "The Auroras" are metaphorically ignited to form the flares of the aurora borealis, "these lights / Like a blaze of summer straw, in winter's nick." In between "Credences" and "Auroras," radiating back to the one and forward to the other, stands Keats' ode.

The boldness of "Credences of Summer" lies in its suggestion that the perception of Keats' bees—that "warm days will never cease"—is no self-deception to be patronized, however wistfully, by the poet, but rather one of the authentic human states of being:

> fill the foliage with arrested peace,
> Joy of such permanence, right ignorance
> Of change still possible. . . .
>
> The utmost must be good and is
> And is our fortune and honey hived in the trees.
>
> (CP, 373, 374)

And yet Stevens knows that the song of "summer in the common fields" is sung by singers not themselves partaking of that summer, just as Keats' ode of fruition and repose is sung by one gazing at the stubble fields. Stevens' singers are "far in the woods":

> Far in the woods they sang their unreal songs,
> Secure. It was difficult to sing in face
> Of the object. The singers had to avert themselves
> Or else avert the object. Deep in the woods
> They sang of summer in the common fields.
>
> They sang desiring an object that was near,
> In face of which desire no longer moved,
> Nor made of itself that which it could not find. . . .
>
> (CP, 376)

In spite of this admission that the singers sing out of desire rather than out of satisfaction, the poem begins, as Keats' does, with the benevolent fiction that the singers are in the midst of the landscape they celebrate:

> young broods
> Are in the grass, the roses are heavy with a weight
> Of fragrance and the mind lays by its trouble.
>
> (CP, 372)

This is the moment of the marriage of earth and sky, the

time of conspiracy between the sky god, the sun, and the earth goddess, the queen, to produce the young broods: this is "green's apogee / And happiest folk-land, mostly marriage-hymns." Keats had begun his ode with the symbolic marriage of earth and air, but had sketched it with the lightest of suggestions. In Stevens, the family constellation appears and reappears as he draws Keats out to iconic completion:

> these fathers standing round,
> These mothers touching, speaking, being near,
> These lovers waiting in the soft dry grass.
>
> (CP, 372)

The queen is "the charitable majesty of her whole kin" and "the bristling soldier" is "a filial form and one / Of the land's children, easily born. . . ." Like the earthly paradise where flowers and fruits coexist, this paradise contains harmoniously all stages of human existence—the young broods, lovers, fathers and mothers, and an old man—but its chief emblem is "The youth, the vital son, the heroic power," the filial form whom age cannot touch. Yet, after the admission that "a mind exists, aware of division," the heroic attempt to maintain the privileged moment falters, and Stevens' more grotesque stubble fields make their appearance, with a presiding form resembling Keat's redbreast. There is even a recollection of Keats' river sallows:

> Fly low, cock bright, and stop on a bean pole. Let
> Your brown breast redden, while you wait for warmth.
> With one eye watch the willow, motionless.
> The gardener's cat is dead, the gardener gone
> And last year's garden grows salacious weeds.
>
> (CP, 377)

Even Keats' twice-repeated "soft" appears in this canto ("Soft, civil bird," and "not / So soft"). For the agricultural laborer-goddess and her creatures Stevens substitutes the gardener and his cat, deriving the gardener perhaps from Keats' "gardener Fancy" in the "Ode to Psyche." Stevens' way of solving the encroachments of decay on his scene of happiness is to attribute to his singers, even though they are only the creations of "an inhuman author," a will of their own, as though the author is himself mastered by the rise of desire in the hearts of his characters:

> the characters speak because they want
> To speak, the fat, the roseate characters,
> Free, for a moment, from malice and sudden cry,
> Complete in a completed scene, speaking
> Their parts as in a youthful happiness.
>
> (CP, 378)

These characters who speak of their own free will resemble Keats' creatures, who, in spite of the season's sadness, sing their own music. It is clear from Stevens' ending that "malice and sudden cry" are likely to be the ordinary states of the characters of the inhuman author, and that the miraculous lifting, for a moment, of their usual oppressive state allows them not youthful happiness, but a state resembling it. Seen in this way, "Credences of Summer" becomes, like "To Autumn," a backward-glancing poem, as its author, for a moment liberated from misery, looks for the perfect metaphor for the feeling he experiences in that moment and decides that youthful happiness (after spring's infuriations are over, after one's mortifying, adolescent, foolish selves are slaughtered) is the vehicle he needs. It is only in retrospect that we see the hovering of a divided mental state at the end of the second stanza:

> This is the last day of a certain year
> Beyond which there is nothing left of time.
> It comes to this and the imagination's life.
>
> (CP, 372)

"This"—the perfect day—staves off for a while the full realization of the other: the imagination's life. But by the end of the poem, with its meditation on the observant mind, imagination is in the ascendant, and the rich day has decayed into the salacious garden. The war in the poem between the warmth of Keatsian language and the chill of metaphysical analysis means that Stevens does not have in this poem a language that would embrace both the physical pine and the metaphysical pine. The presentation of summer cannot co-exist in tone or diction with the anatomy of summer, and the anatomy, skirted and then suppressed in Keats in favor of self-forgetfulness, is given full play by Stevens. If the bees are given full credence, so is the undeceiving questioning of the aloof mind, and Stevens' poem, unable to maintain a Keatsian harmony, divides sharply in consequence of its "mind, aware of division."

If "Credences of Summer" goes both backward from Keats and further with his questioning (thereby losing the precarious Keatsian balance), "The Auroras of Autumn" fastens on the question "Where are the songs of Spring?" and makes a poetics of it. Keats stops in autumn to imagine spring and rebukes himself for his nostalgia, which implies a criticism of the season in which he finds himself. "Think not of them," he says of the spring songs. Stevens, in contrast, decides to think deliberately about them. What does it mean—for life, for poetry—that we cannot rest in the present, in any present? It means that the desire for change is more deep-rooted than the pleasure of any permanence, no matter how luxurious:

> Is there an imagination that sits enthroned
> As grim as it is benevolent, the just
> And the unjust, which in the midst of summer stops
>
> To imagine winter?
>
> (CP, 417)

Every making of the mind moves to find "What must unmake it and, at last, what can." After being "fattened as on a decorous honeycomb," "We lay sticky with sleep," like Keats' bees. Stevens is Keatsian in accepting the fact of change; he is also Keatsian in his elegiac strain, substituting a Keatsian "farewell" for the even more Keatsian "adieu":

> Farewell to an idea . . . A cabin stands,
> Deserted, on a beach.[4]
>
> (CP, 412)

Stevens is Keatsian, too, in making the goddess who presides over the dissolution of the season a maternal figure who says neither farewell nor adieu but (as to children) good-night, good-night:

> Farewell to an idea . . . The mother's face,
> The purpose of the poem, fills the room.
>
> .   .   .   .
>
> She gives transparence. But she has grown old.
> The necklace is a carving not a kiss.[5]
>
> (CP, 413)

Stevens offers a critique of Keats by leaping over Keats' set piece of sunset and twilight bird song and taking his poem beyond the death of the mother, after sunset, into boreal night.[6] The birds, instead of going downward to darkness or gathering into a Keatsian flock, are set wildly flying:

> The theatre is filled with flying birds.
> Wild wedges, as of a volcano's smoke. . . .
>
> (CP, 416)

Across his sky Stevens displays his auroras, his earthly equivalent to the serpent-god sloughing skins at the opening of the poem, both symbols of change. The auroras are both beautiful and intimidating; they leave us in the state of Keats' gnats and bleating lambs, "A shivering residue, chilled and foregone." The auroras change "idly, the way / A season changes color to no end, / Except the lavishing of itself in change." All natural changes are equal; there is no entropy in nature; all events are simply songs of "the innocent mother." The specter of the spheres, like the inhuman author of "Credences of Summer," contrives a balance to contrive a whole. The new poetic wishes not only to relish everything equally (in itself a Keatsian idea), but also to relish everything at once, to imagine winter in summer and summer in winter, to meditate

The full of fortune and the full of fate,
As if he lived all lives, that he might know,

In hall harridan, not hushful paradise,
To a haggling of wind and weather, by these lights
Like a blaze of summer straw, in winter's nick.
(CP, 420-21)

This finale of "The Auroras" is an implicit boast. Everything, however, is intrinsically less expressible than something: the close is less beautiful than the vision of the aurora itself. In this respect, Stevens is Keatsian, substituting one form of landscape—the later auroras—for another: the romantic sunset.

It is time to glance back at a poem that arises from the same Keatsian injunction that prompted "The Auroras"— "Think not of them"—and that is in fact an extended think- ing-and-not-thinking. I mean of course "The Snow Man," which might as well be called "The Man Standing in the Stubble Plains." Snow, like harvest, eliminates vegetation; and Stevens, like Keats, faces the question of how to praise a world from which the summer growth has disappeared. Keats' "light wind" blowing over the bare fields is intensified, al- ways, in Stevens into a *wind* of *winter* (and Stevens relishes the phonemic echo). Oddly enough, beheld with a mind of winter, the world does not appear bare: the boughs of the pine trees are crusted with snow, the junipers are shagged with ice, the spruces are rough in the distant glitter of the January sun. It is only with the introduction of the wind, and misery, and the noticing of the few remaining leaves on the deciduous trees that the world becomes "the same bare place." The regarder and beholder, who saw such a rich world, becomes a listener who, nothing himself, "beholds / Nothing that is not there and the nothing that is" (CP, 10). The turn from beholding to listening is of course borrowed from Keats' ode, and it coincides, as it does in Keats, with a pained turning from plenitude to absence. But Keats finds a new plenitude—that of the ear—to substitute for the visual

absence. Stevens, finding it impossible to sustain the pleni-
tude perceivable by a mind of winter—that plenitude of
encrustation, shagginess, and rough snow-glitter—reverses
Keats and finds bareness in listening. He turns, therefore,
from the Keatsian trope of plenitude, enumeration, which
he had employed in his listing of pines, junipers, and spruce
trees, and uses instead a trope of reductiveness, becoming
a modernist of minimal art. He hears, in a deadly repetition
of the same few words,

> *the sound of the wind*
> *the sound of* a few leaves
> *the sound of the* land
>   full of the *same wind*
>   that is blowing in the *same* bare place
>   for the *listener,* who *listens* in the snow
>   and, *nothing* himself, beholds
>   *nothing that is* not there
>   and the *nothing that is.*

Another fairly early attempt at "thinking with the season"
occurs in "Anatomy of Monotony." If, says Stevens, we must
have the pathetic fallacy, let us have it on nature's terms, not
our own. Since the earth "bore us as a part of all the things /
It breeds," it follows that "Our nature is her nature":

>   Hence it comes,
>   Since by our nature we grow old, earth grows
>   The same. We parallel the mother's death.
>   (*CP,* 107-8)

But the earth has a wider vision than our narrow personal
pathos:

>   She walks an autumn ampler than the wind
>   Cries up for us and colder than the frost
>   Pricks in our spirits at the summer's end,
>   And over the bare spaces of our skies
>   She sees a barer sky that does not bend.
>   (*CP,* 108)

This widening of perspective is borrowed from Keats too, though it applies Keats' technique (broadening from the cottage and its kitchen garden and orchard to the cornfields and outbuildings, and finally extending to the horizon, the boundary hill and hedges, the river, and the horizon) only to the bare spaces of Keats' final stanza. In reading Stevens it seems as if each aspect of the autumn ode called out to him to be reinterpreted, reused, recreated into a poem.

Much later, in "World without Peculiarity," Stevens "rewrites" "Anatomy of Monotony," achieving at last, however briefly, the power to think with the season. What is most human is now no longer (in Stevens' hard saying) sadness, pathos, nostalgia—that projection of ourselves into and onto other things that fail, die, or wane—but rather solitary existence as a natural object. Stevens may be remembering, in his extraordinary central stanza, Whitman's line about "the justified mother of men":

> What good is it that the earth is justified,
> That it is complete, that it is an end,
> That in itself it is enough?
>
> It is the earth itself that is humanity . . .
> He is the inhuman son and she,
> She is the fateful mother, whom he does not know.
>
> She is the day. . . .
>
> (CP, 453-54)

Here there are no verbal echoes of Keats; yet this seems to me a poem that could not have been thought of except by someone who had incorporated into his imagination that sense of life and nature voiced in the autumn ode.

Just as Stevens' "Woman in Sunshine" removes the mythological solidity from Keats' goddess in the fields and reminds us that she is a fictive construct, so "Less and Less Human, O Savage Spirit" wishes for a god both silent in movement and quiet in dwelling, "saying things," if he must, as light and color and shape "say things," a god who "will not hear us when we speak." This god, unable to say "Where are the

songs of Spring?" is at once more earthly and more disem-
bodied than Keats' goddess, pressing further toward the fictive
and the inanimate at once. Always in Stevens there is a new
precipitate from the Keatsian solution, because mind and
sense cannot coexist in equilibrium. No writer, in Stevens'
view, could avoid asking the fatal question about the songs of
spring. In Stevens' second-order reflection on the inevitability
of questions, in "The Ultimate Poem Is Abstract," Keats (or
a poet like him) is treated ironically and called "the lecturer
/ On This Beautiful World Of Ours." He "hems the planet
rose and haws it ripe, / And red, and right." But his hem-
ming and hawing into roses and rosehips and red haws can-
not last:

> One goes on asking questions. That, then, is one
> Of the categories. So said, this placid space
>
> Is changed. It is not so blue as we thought. To be blue,
> There must be no questions.
>
> . . . .
>
> It would be enough
> If we were ever, just once, at the middle, fixed
> In This Beautiful World Of Ours and not as now,
>
> Helplessly at the edge, enough to be
> Complete, because at the middle, if only in sense,
> And in that enormous sense, merely enjoy.
>
> (CP, 429-30)

Such a poem is a rewriting, at a second-order level, of the
Keats ode; it recounts in an abstract way Keats' attempt to
remain "at the middle" of the beautiful world, praising its
generosity to all the senses, its plenitude of being. The inva-
sion of Keats' enjoyment by questioning, an *event* in the ode,
becomes then a *topic* for Stevens. In other poems Stevens
comments on each stage of the Keatsian process—how one
sees first the earth "as inamorata," but then sees her "without
distance . . . and naked or in rags, / Shrunk in the poverty of
being close." She has been a celestial presence among labor-

ers, an angel surrounded by paysans, an "archaic form" evok-
ing "an archaic space," but then her appurtenances fade
(the moon "is a tricorn / Waved in pale adieu") and "she
is exhausted and a little old" ("Things of August" [CP, 494-
96]).

It seems to me, as I have said before in writing about Ste-
vens, that the late poetry of receptivity and inception, com-
ing after the poetry of age and exhaustion, is nothing short of
miraculous. Here Stevens follows Keats' "Human Seasons"
beyond the winter of gross misfeature, finding "The cricket
of summer forming itself out of ice," "not autumn's prodigal
returned, / But an antipodal, far-fetched creature . . ." ("A
Discovery of Thought" [OP, 95-96]). As he listens to winter
sounds, he hears "the crickets' chords, / Babbling, each one,
the uniqueness of its sound," and decides to do without the
archaic forms:

> There was no fury in transcendant forms.
> But his actual candle blazed with artifice.
> ("A Quiet Normal Life" [CP, 523])

In "Looking across the Fields and Watching the Birds Fly"
he forgoes "the masculine myths we used to make" in favor
of "A transparency through which the swallow weaves, /
Without any form or any sense of form," and he decides that
our thinking is nothing but our preestablished harmony with
the grand motions of nature:

> We think, then, as the sun shines or does not.
> We think as wind skitters on a pond in a field. . . .
>
> .   .   .   .
>
> The spirit comes from the body of the world. . . .
>
> The mannerism of nature caught in a glass
> And there become a spirit's mannerism,
> A glass aswarm with things going as far as they can.
> (CP, 518-19)

This sublime self-transformation into a modern version of an

Aeolian harp immolates the mind. If we pose questions, it is because the earth poses them. There is no longer any need to say "Think not of them": everything is permitted, because everything is a natural motion.

Stevens' last tribute to Keats' stubble plains is his transmutation of Keats' bareness into "The Plain Sense of Things." This poem presses Keats' *donnée* to its ultimate point: there is no goddess, not even a dying one; there is no memorial gleam cast through rosy clouds; there is no music; there are no touching filial forms. The surrogate animal for the human is not the laden honeybee but the inquisitive pond rat:

> After the leaves have fallen, we return
> To a plain sense of things. It is as if
> We had come to an end of the imagination,
> Inanimate in an inert savoir.
>
> . . . .
>
> Yet the absence of the imagination had
> Itself to be imagined. The great pond,
> The plain sense of it, without reflections, leaves,
> Mud, water like dirty glass, expressing silence
>
> Of a sort, silence of a rat come out to see,
> The great pond and its waste of the lilies, all this
> Had to be imagined as an inevitable knowledge,
> Required, as a necessity requires.
>
> (*CP*, 502-3)

The ode "To Autumn" represents for Keats a retraction of the "Ode to Psyche." In the earlier ode Keats had hoped that the imagination could be fully reparatory for an external absence; piece by piece, he constructs his interior fane to compensate, warmly and luxuriously, for the earthly temple that the goddess lacks. By the time he wrote "To Autumn," he had lost not the impulse (his impulse on seeing stubble plains is to go home and write a stanza loaded and blessed with fruit and to invent a harvest goddess), but the ability to close with "a bright torch, and a casement ope at night, / To let the warm Love in!" The "absence of fantasia" in the

bare fields might have tempted Stevens earlier to a compen-
satory opulence of reconstruction (as when Crispin popu-
lated his cabin with four daughters with curls in "The Co-
median as the Letter C"), but now he finds a discipline in
poverty. The comedian had boasted that he would find "A
new reality in parrot-squawks," but the old Stevens finds that
"new reality" at last in another detail borrowed from Keats
and expanded into its own poem, the detail of an unmusical
bird cry. In "Not Ideas about the Thing but the Thing It-
self" the "wailful choir" of the ode gives way to an imagined
choir of aubade, as Stevens draws the ode forward from its
sunset into a new sunrise:

> At the earliest ending of winter,
> In March, a scrawny cry from outside
> Seemed like a sound in his mind.
>
> . . . .
>
> That scrawny cry—it was
> A chorister whose c preceded the choir.
> It was part of the colossal sun,
>
> Surrounded by its choral rings,
> Still far away. It was like
> A new knowledge of reality.
>
> (CP, 534)

There is no "new reality," only a "new knowledge of real-
ity." The "marvellous sophomore" had boasted "Here was
the veritable ding an sich, at last." But his boast was pre-
mature. Stevens did not find "the thing itself" until very late,
and then on a scale Keatsian in its humility. Although "Not
Ideas" is Stevens' most beautiful late reflection on both his
own beginnings (as the comedian as the letter c becomes the
chorister whose c preceded the choir) and on Keats' ode and
its minimal music, I close not with this last successful medi-
tation but rather with a poem that in its own relative failure
shows Stevens' stubborn ambition, even at the expense of
violent dislocation of form, to have plenitude and poverty at

once, to possess Keats' central divine figure opulently whole
and surrounded by her filial forms, while at the same time
asserting the necessary obsolescence of her form and of the
literature about her. She remains, he says, for all her inevi-
table vanishing, "The Hermitage at the Centre":

> The leaves on the macadam make a noise—
>   How soft the grass on which the desired
>   Reclines in the temperature of heaven—
>
> Like tales that were told the day before yesterday—
>   Sleek in a natural nakedness,
>   She attends the tintinnabula—
>
> And the wind sways like a great thing tottering—
>   Of birds called up by more than the sun,
>   Birds of more wit, that substitute—
>
> Which suddenly is all dissolved and gone—
>   Their intelligible twittering
>   For unintelligible thought.
>
> And yet this end and this beginning are one,
>   And one last look at the ducks is a look
>   At lucent children round her in a ring.
>
>   (CP, 505-6)

Stevens' response to Keats' ode was so long-lived that this
brief sketch can be nothing more than a reminder of Keats'
persistence in Stevens' mind and verse. The central problems
of the ode—process, termination, interruption of ripeness,
the human seasons, the beauty of the minimal, the function
of nostalgia, the relation between sense and thought—be-
come central to Stevens' poetry as well. His attempts to go
"beyond" Keats in various ways—to take the human seasons
further, into winter, into boreal apocalypse, into inception,
to find new imagery of his own while retaining Keats' crick-
ets and bees and birds and sun and fields, to create his own
archaic forms in the landscape—define in their evolution
Stevens' own emerging originality. Though he retains a clas-

sical structure to his verse, his diction and rhetoric become ever less visibly romantic, as a plain sense of things and an absence of fantasia supervene. Everywhere we hear Stevens meditating on Keats, whose fashion of beholding without comment must have seemed to Stevens uniquely modern. Stevens sensed that the poem of presentation is the poem of earth: just to behold, just to be beheld; what is there here but weather. These are the assumptions that Stevens found and grasped for himself in the most untranscendental of the great romantic odes.

ISABEL G. MACCAFFREY

THE WAYS OF TRUTH IN
"LE MONOCLE DE MON ONCLE"

HARMONIUM IS ONE OF THE MONUMENTS OF THE modernist movement in America, however much it has come to seem, in our hindsight, relatively nonradical in its experimentalism. Some of Stevens' experiments sprang from his short-lived interest in imagism.[1] Others, more prophetic of the innovations that were to characterize his late poetry, reveal an early interest in discontinuous, even disjunctive forms as shattered mirrors of certain preoccupations in the modern consciousness. Helen Vendler's judgment that "the poetry of disconnection is Stevens' most adequate form" is an insight that could be illustrated many times over from the poetry of *Harmonium* to *The Rock*.[2] Of the two most famous poems in *Harmonium*, "Sunday Morning" and "Le Monocle de Mon Oncle," the former is much less radical in its abandonment of the civilities of discourse. It is in fact discursive, a dialogue in which certain propositions are argued by shadowy participants, proceeding at a steady pace that admits few interstitial gaps. The spaces between stanzas have not yet become eloquent with inexplicit meanings.

If "Sunday Morning" is "the only truly great 'traditional' poem that Stevens wrote,"[3] "Le Monocle" has impressed most readers as a genuinely original work. Its dispossession by "influence" authenticates its claim to modernism:

This great poem abrupts into Stevens' poetic world with such energy and polished perfection that its origins must remain partly in mystery. Like "Sunday Morning," it towers over the poems which precede and follow it; but unlike "Sunday Morning" it does not fit easily into the tradition of English poetry.[4]

One of Stevens' famous adages can take us close to the heart of "this great and obscure" work[5]: "Every poem is a poem within a poem: the poem of the idea within the poem of the words" (OP, 174). This formula is unsatisfactory insofar as it suggests that "the poem of the idea" can somehow be arrived at without the help of "the words." But it indicates that Stevens himself was aware of a peculiar relationship in his most characteristic poetry between medium and message, language and referent. We can say that the rhetoric and the subject in "Le Monocle" and a large number of later poems, including "Notes toward a Supreme Fiction," approach each other by meanders rather than forthrights, or that sometimes they seem not to approach at all, but rather to shout at each other across an abyss of noise, raising echoes and alarming hoo-has from the icy elysées en route.

It is not strange, therefore, that attempts to identify the subject of "Le Monocle de Mon Oncle" have been more than usually tentative. The title is only the beginning of the poem's elusive inarticulateness. It is "a poem about language and love," says Litz.[6] Yes, indeed. But the key terms contain multiple possibilities of meaning and are problematically related to one another. We may well be tempted to resort, with Frank Kermode, to the Cerberus principle: "with such verses it is true that one needs to quiet the housedog of the mind with any meat so that the poem may do its work."[7] Yet Stevens does provide us with a few clues as to how his poem should be read, notably in the opening stanza, which he divides into two parts, the second commenting upon the first —perhaps to encourage the reader to take over a commentator's role in later stanzas.

After the mock-heroic invocation, spoken "aloud" in quotation marks, the speaker turns to contemplate his own motives, that is, the sources of "magnificent measure":

> And so I mocked her in magnificent measure.
> Or was it that I mocked myself alone?
> I wish that I might be a thinking stone.
> The sea of spuming thought foists up again
> The radiant bubble that she was. And then

> A deep up-pouring from some saltier well
> Within me, bursts its watery syllable.

"The sea of spuming thought" characterizes the action, namely, the incessant alterations of the organism that eventuate in what we call "thought"—a kind of spume that is the vocalized evidence of depths below. "I wish that I might be a thinking stone" is a cry for stillness, for an end to the eternal restless change that is the measure of living. But to think and to be a stone are incompatibles, as Aquinas knew. So we sink deeper into the well of the unconscious, into an extraordinarily visceral sequence of appeals to voiceless sensation. Imagination "foists up" the memory of what "she was," an image out of the drowned past that floats for an instant to the mind's surface to be contemplated. "Foist" is the perfect verb for the intrusiveness and fraudulence of memory, palming off its irresistible bygones upon the unwilling consciousness, which can no more inhibit their formation than the ocean can prevent a bubble rising to *its* surface. But the bubble is only a "watery syllable" in the interior world; and indeed, all syllables have watery origins, as the stanza makes clear. The "deep up-pouring" is a rush of sensation and emotion, of flooding awareness, as the springs of feeling open unexpectedly. They are salty with the taste of sex, of blood, of the sea that is within us as well as all around us. The movement is regressive,[8] for the salty well is, above all, a source, and by the end of the stanza Stevens has gotten to the bottom of the splendid mockery of the initial sentence.

He later said that "the Mother of Heaven was merely somebody to swear by" (*L*, 251), the point being that all this gorgeous rhetoric, while not exactly meaningless, is misleadingly expressive; its true referents lie in the interior world, at the feeling source. The pompous phrases move associatively, from the Queen of Heaven to "regina of the clouds," and then to her heavenly paraphernalia—sun and moon, scepter and crown. It is easy to piece together an explication of these epithets in terms of Stevens' sun/moon imagery elsewhere, to say that the heroine of "Le Monocle" unites male reality with female imagination, or to invoke literary analogues, such as Britomart's dream at the Temple of Isis in *The Faerie Queene*—another concordant image, where the dreamer sees the statue's transfiguration of costume from a "Moone-like Mitre to a Crowne of gold" (v.vii.13). Such an exercise would be otiose, for Stevens' lines merely let us hear the imagination babbling out loud in the way it always has, turning over the watery syllables on its tongue to articulate its salty sensations.

A more exact Spenserian parallel, and one that does shed some light on the subject of "Le Monocle," is the vision evoked by Colin Clout's music on Mount Acidale in Book VI. The maiden at the center of the concentric garlands of dancers is as anonymous as Stevens' lady—simply "she that in the midst of them did stand," and by so standing, caused the pattern to form:

> But that faire one,
> That in the midst was placed paravaunt,
> Was she to whom that shepheard pypt alone;
> That made him pipe so merrily, as never none.
>
> (VI.x.15)

While Frank Kermode quite properly identifies the object of Stevens' address as the Interior Paramour, there is nothing to prevent her also being an actual paramour, for the Muse has many avatars. Hence the arguments about whether these lines refer to a "real" or an "ideal" woman usually miss the point, and Spenser's stanzas show why this is so: the laws of psychic necessity require that feeling always be immediate and concrete in its attachment to objects, and only feeling is potent enough to generate the construction of cloud-capped towers or reginas who preside there. Imagination draws its strength from the viscera, feeds upon who-knows-what nameless orts of emotion. It is almost impossible not to stumble over alimentary and sexual metaphors in trying to verbalize imaginative process. The embrace of poet and Muse rationalizes events that transpire at a subverbal level, and Stevens' poem is an attempt to intimate, if not completely to articulate, the nature of these events. "A deep up-pouring from some saltier well" gives rise to the high talk of the apostrophe; the woman addressed is "somebody" to whom emotion is attached and therefore the cause, in all senses of the term, that the poem comes into being. "That made him pipe so merrily."

The opening pomposities of "Le Monocle" are thus deflated by a visit to their oceanic origins in "The Creations of Sound":

> We do not say ourselves like that in poems.
> We say ourselves in syllables that rise
> From the floor, rising in speech we do not speak.
>   (CP, 311)

It is always the speech we do not speak that Stevens is striving to articulate; hence the snares spread in the nets of discontinuous form that the poet weaves:

> Tell X that speech is not dirty silence
> Clarified. It is silence made still dirtier.
>   (CP, 311)

To make the silence dirty, thick with the syllables we do not speak, Stevens contrives a rhetoric of intermittences, of false starts and misleading clues, of centerless labyrinths, hollow resonances, eloquent silence, visionary blankness. Many of these tricks are evident in "Le Monocle," and so is one of the consequences of employing them: a willingness on the part of the poet to appear foolish, precious, dandified, superficial. Stevens creates surfaces behind which essential meanings can emerge and gambol, meanings too shy to be observed directly and lying, as Wordsworth said, "far hidden from the reach of words." The large assurances, positive gestures, confident assertions are attention-getting devices by the sleight-of-hand man, so that we shall be distracted from the urge to paraphrase long enough for significances to form unobserved.[9] The result is not only a perverse use of language in the interests of silence, but also a persistent duplicity of voice. Parallels can be found in Wordsworth, some of whose assumptions about language were shared by Stevens. The swervings and changes of tack in *The Prelude* have been often remarked, and "Resolution and Independence" is another poem in which a dithering, or flat, or loftily inconsequential surface makes a protective shell for the delicacies of self-accusation, self-doubt, condolence, and consolation that are Wordsworth's real subjects.

Style in such poems moves away from the mimetic to a kind of anti- or counterexpressionism. An ostensible speaker is permitted to maunder, "expressing" his perceptions or feelings or thoughts in a manner that is visibly inadequate, bombastic, bland, or self-deceiving. Meanwhile, by devious means (such as the impervious though taciturn integrity of Wordsworth's Leech-gatherer) these verbal gestures are shown up for what they are and replaced by a "meaning" that, while never completely articulate, can be apprehended behind the words. The first stanza of "Le Monocle de Mon Oncle" exposes this strategy with special clearness while at the same time introducing us to the most important of the poem's unspoken premises. Its most general form has been stated by Hugh Kenner: "language . . . can mime the wordless world only by a kind of coincidence."[10] Magical theories of language, to which most poets subscribe at one time or another, assert that coincidence is a version of fate, that the poet uses language in a way that will bring out the hidden logic of its affinities with "the wordless world." Stevens resisted magic on principle, and almost consistently; in "Le Monocle" he created a poem that accepts Kenner's principle and its consequences for poetry, but without resorting to occult explanations. It is possible, then, to reconstruct a skeletal system of assumptions that lie behind this poem and of which the actual stanzas on the page are the symptoms; but it is hard to feel that in doing this we have found a "subject" in any traditional sense.[11]

The reconstruction would proceed as follows. Poetry's most important subjects belong to "the wordless world," the world of Eros, who, alas (or perhaps fortunately), is dumb.

This world generates language and the need to use it, but it does not speak directly to us. So Stevens' poem invites us, and the speaker, to verbalize experience, yet perpetually repudiates or mocks the result, as the "I" mocks his own magnificent measure in stanza I. "Love and language," to be sure: love is the source of language, and also its destroyer. A discontinuous form is the inevitable vehicle for this theme; its interstitial white spaces can become dirty silences, and its perpetual new beginnings can palliate, if not cure, the bad faith of poets who would claim too much for their fictive music.

The hostility between poetry and its subjects, between language and experience, manifests itself in two ways, both unacceptable to a serious poet. On one hand, it produces a self-nourishing but irrelevant rhetoric, as in Stevens' first stanza; on the other hand, awareness that words "in giving form and order to emotion also kill the true feeling" may produce the poet's ultimate despair: silence.[12] This is not a new predicament. Philip Sidney, repudiating traditional rhetorics in the first sonnet of *Astrophil and Stella*, followed his Muse's advice and looked into his heart. But it led him, at the climax of the sequence, to poetically unwelcome conclusions:

> Come then my Muse, shew thou height of delight
> In well raised notes, my pen the best it may
> Shall paint out joy, though but in blacke and white.
> Cease eager Muse, peace pen, for my sake stay,
>   I give you here my hand for truth of this,
>   Wise silence is best musicke unto blisse.
>
> (Sonnet LXX)

"Well raised notes" or "wise silence"—does the poet's choice reduce to these forbidding alternatives? Innovating poets have always denied it. So we find Wordsworth brilliantly defending the fiction-making power of imagination in its role as mediator between unexpressed feeling and an uncommunicating world. At issue is the meaning of the Leech-gatherer, a "reality" that must somehow be shown to be linked with obscure sources of emotion in the poem's speaker. In his revision, Wordsworth added a stanza that, through two similes ("As a huge stone is sometimes seen to lie . . ."), creates this link. The maker of the fiction justifies his conceits as an instance of imagination's legitimate function: "In these images, the conferring, the abstracting, and the modifying powers of the Imagination, immediately and mediately acting, are all brought into conjunction."[13]

In thus acting to unite the world without and the world within, imagination is taking a liberty. It is putting words between experience (the speaker's feelings) and uninvented images (the mysterious presence of the old man). These words, the similes in Wordsworth's ninth stanza, have no immediate referents in the poem but are "conferred" upon, "abstracted" from, and "modify" the given raw materials. Stevens defined imaginative liberty of this kind as "an intervention" (NA, 128). Many stanzas in "Le Monocle de Mon Oncle" are instances of intervention, the creation of fables or parables like Wordsworth's stone and sea-beast that will exemplify the proper function of a healthy and self-chastising imagination. But Stevens' demonstrations complicate Wordsworth's. His distrust of imagination's megalomania went deeper; Wordsworth, after all, had spoken approvingly of its "indestructible dominion." Stevens was bothered by the notion that "Things as they are have been destroyed" ("The Man with the Blue Guitar" [CP, 173]) in modern art by an imagination conceiving of itself as indestructible; hence his choice of discontinuous forms, which permit him to wipe out successive attempts at articulation and begin again. He was also less confident than Wordsworth that language could *ever* render the plain sense of things. Thus in "Le Monocle" and other major poems of his middle period there is nothing to correspond to the factuality of "Resolution and Independence," which surround stanza IX and allow us to see how "mediation" occurs.

Instead, there are dirty silences and enigmatic self-mockery, as in stanza II of "Le Monocle":

A red bird flies across the golden floor.
It is a red bird that seeks out his choir
Among the choirs of wind and wet and wing.
A torrent will fall from him when he finds.
Shall I uncrumple this much-crumpled thing?
I am a man of fortune greeting heirs;
For it has come that thus I greet the spring.
These choirs of welcome choir for me farewell.
No spring can follow past meridian.
Yet you persist with anecdotal bliss
To make believe a starry *connaissance*.

The first four lines represent imagination's effort to introduce the third major term of the poem's "subject": it is "about" not only love and language, but also death, about the fact that Eros and Thanatos must embrace, and imagination must find words for their love affair. The words that speak of a red bird and a golden floor are nonreferential within the poem's world, like Wordsworth's stone and sea-beast, but more like the latter. Stones, after all, are "sometimes seen to lie" on eminences; imagination, in noting the fact, is behaving mimetically, at least to begin with. "A sea-beast crawled forth" onto a shelf of rock is much more rarely seen—is seen, perhaps, by imagination's eye alone when it requires a link between inorganic and organic being to complete the mediational circuit. But Wordsworth, in his later explanation, uncrumples his invention much more fully than Stevens allows the speaker of "Le Monocle" to do. The later poet refuses at this stage to make the fiction-devising power seem natural and inevitable; rather, he presents us with an extreme case, enigmatic and tantalizing, of imagination at its hermetic games.

The uncrumpled "meanings" that follow line four do not satisfy as explications. They have some reference to the dark brilliance of the initial images, but in trying to work out the relationship, we are frustrated. The effect is to make the parable of the red bird more opaque, mysteriously significant, and mute when parable gives way to ineffectual paraphrase:

"I am a man of fortune greeting heirs"; "No spring can fol-
low past meridian." Stevens employs "statements" like these
to undermine the adequacy of statements and so, at last, to
convince us of the need for parabolic utterance, the dark
conceits that mediate between the "wordless world" and that
articulateness that is the mark of consciousness.

Having rebuked high talk in stanza i and commonsense
explication in stanza ii, Stevens proceeds in eight of the
remaining stanzas to propose additional parables that will
close in upon and gradually circumscribe the poem within
the poem, which concerns in part, of course, the problem of
meaning itself. It is a fact, however deplorable, that mean-
ings entail some sort of articulation. In his essay "The Ef-
fects of Analogy," Stevens defends, even celebrates, the use
of words to articulate "the objects of . . . passions,"

> the objects before which [poets] come and speak, with
> intense choosing, words that we remember and make our
> own. Their words have made a world that transcends the
> world and a life livable in that transcendence. It is a tran-
> scendence achieved by means of the minor effects of figura-
> tions and the major effects of the poet's sense of the world
> and of the motive music of his poems and it is the imag-
> inative dynamism of all these analogies together. (NA, 130)

The "sense of the world" given body in "Le Monocle" is
Stevens' awareness of the transient fragility of every human
moment and every human contrivance, including the contriv-
ances of poetry. They are "trivial" and evanescent, but nec-
essary: "This parable, in sense, amounts to this"; "This trivial
trope reveals a way of truth." Dissolving his parables at the
end of every stanza, Stevens resumes after the white space
the incessant effort to speak "The speech of truth in its true
solitude" ("Things of August" [CP, 490]).

"The imaginative dynamism" of multiple analogies, as it
emerges from this poem, requires attentiveness to Stevens'
"figurations" as they attract and repel one another. The final
quatrain of stanza iii is one of the poem's most obscure
patches; Kermode admits that the "last two lines are among

the most beautiful in Stevens, and I do not know what they mean."[14] The poet himself explained them "as meaning simply that the speaker was speaking to a woman whose hair was still down" (L, 251). But the questions posed by this speaker are not answered:

> Alas! Have all the barbers lived in vain
> That not one curl in nature has survived?
> Why, without pity on these studious ghosts,
> Do you come dripping in your hair from sleep?

The study of "inscrutable hair in an inscrutable world" ("The Comedian as the Letter C" [CP, 27]) is questioned: "Is it for nothing, then. . . ?" Yes and no. Hair, in China, Japan, and eighteenth-century England, has been twined into a metaphor for various deep significances: the philosophy of old men, "the end of love" in both senses of the word "end." "The mountainous coiffures" that expressed their makers' sense of meaning have perished. But the urge to educe meanings, and to devise forms for them—"all-speaking braids" or poems—does not perish. The dying of things, Stevens wrote three years before, goes on like "A wave, interminably flowing" ("Peter Quince at the Clavier" [CP, 92]); and yet Venus arises again from the sea every time a woman enters a lover's consciousness, "dripping" in her hair, to motivate his poems.

The watery imagery of this line harks back to the salty well of stanza I and anticipates the lily pool of stanza XI and its "odious" frog music. Deep in the belly's dark, love has its source; but what human beings do with it once it is born is the main focus of interest:

>   I pursued,
>   And still pursue, the origin and course
>   Of love. . . .

The course of love brings decay and loss; it also brings high talk. And it brings "Doleful heroics, pinching gestures forth / From madness or delight. . . ." These rhetorical gestures are efforts to express the nature of love (or, indeed, any human emotion), which alters from minute to minute:

> But in our amours amorists discern
> Such fluctuations that their scrivening
> Is breathless to attend each quirky turn.
> When amorists grow bald, then amours shrink
> Into the compass and curriculum
> Of introspective exiles, lecturing.
> It is a theme for Hyacinth alone.

But Hyacinth is aphasic. Experience can only be captured—in contemplation or in art—after the fact, by men of forty, introspective exiles, dull scholars, and dark rabbis. The predicament is not altogether remote from Wordsworth's struggles in the "Immortality Ode" to find in the lucid contemplation of mortality compensation for the loss of childhood's intensity.

> O joy! that in our embers
> Is something that doth live,
> That nature yet remembers
> What was so fugitive!

Stevens' subjects in "Le Monocle"—love, death and change, poetry—often come close to Wordsworth's in the "Ode," and an offhand description he gave of his own poem could refer to either.[15] Protesting against his correspondent's "much too close" reading, he insists that "I had in mind simply a man fairly well along in life, looking back and talking in a more or less personal way about life" (L, 251). The retrospective point of view establishes each poem as an instance of what both poets are talking about: the fact that an unbridgeable gap yawns between experience and the articulation of experience. The intensities of childhood or first love—"fiery boys" and "sweet-smelling virgins"—contrasted with the sobrieties of middle age, manifest this troublesome disjunction: the distance between words and things, reality and its reflection in art, the deep sources of poems and poems themselves, all surface and bravura.

These paradoxes are pursued by both Wordsworth and Stevens through two principal techniques: disjunctive stanzaic forms and the self-conscious use of taciturn myths or mythical images. Wordsworth's preference for the continuous form of blank verse gives way in the "Ode" to the irregular stanzas of the revived Pindaric, whose disjunctiveness is underlined when we recall the poem's slow gestation. Stevens' unrhymed stanzas are less irregular but even more ostentatiously unrelated to one another; and as in Wordsworth's poem, their separateness is insisted upon by Roman numerals. Wordsworth invokes the May mornings of conventional pastoral in stanzas III, IV, and X; in stanza V he has recourse to the less predictable Platonic myth of recollection, and in VII and VIII, to his own version of childhood's primitive and potent imaginative life, which offended Coleridge and many later readers. The poet's language, especially in section VIII, is indeed extravagant; one might surmise (remembering the Leech-gatherer and the mythic status conferred upon other unlikely personages) that Wordsworth half intended the claims made here to sound outrageous, to produce a reaction disproportionate to their literal sense. Certainly Stevens intends *his* outrageousness, for instance in stanzas VII, X, and XI of "Le Monocle." Both poems also display alterations of tone that suggest the limits of the writer's control over his material.

The point of such deliberate violations of decorum would be to deal with the inadequacy of fiction by flaunting and exaggerating it, to affirm the necessity of myths, images, all poetic inventions, at the moment of declaring and illustrating their foolish insufficiency. Both the "Ode" and "Le Monocle" are modern poems in Stevens' sense, poems in the act of finding what will suffice. Since total sufficiency is impossible, it can be most closely approximated by insisting that no invention really suffices.

> Most venerable heart, the lustiest conceit
> Is not too lusty for your broadening.

It is, in fact, never lusty enough. But, after all, he must try
again:

> The fops of fancy in their poems leave
> Memorabilia of the mystic spouts,
> Spontaneously watering their gritty soils.
> I am a yeoman, as such fellows go.
> I know no magic trees, no balmy boughs,
> No silver-ruddy, gold-vermilion fruits.
> But, after all, I know a tree that bears
> A semblance to the thing I have in mind.
> It stands gigantic, with a certain tip
> To which all birds come sometime in their time.
> But when they go that tip still tips the tree.

The tree of this stanza anticipates Yeats' great-rooted blos-
somer as an emblem for the life principle that is eterne in
mutability. It gathers the implications of three other stanzas:
"this luscious and impeccable fruit of life" (IV); the golden
gourds that are also warty squashes (VIII); the eternal bloom
of the imagined damsel and the evanescent honey of earth
(VII). Stevens' exploration of the origin, course, and curious
fate of love in these conceits comes to a focus in the non-
magic tree, which bears none of the silver and golden apples
yearned for by Yeats' Wandering Aengus. This tree bears
instead a semblance. The fops of fancy give way to the
yeoman-poet, Peter Quince the carpenter, nailing together
his flimsy frames of meaning. Stevens' description of the tree
contains an imaginative precision within the images. The
delicate tip, a perch for a successive stream of birds that
never ends, is a careful analogy for "a substance that pre-
vails," which Stevens attempted to capture again in "Martial
Cadenza":

> The present close, the present realized,
> Not the symbol but that for which the symbol stands,
> The vivid thing in the air that never changes,
> Though the air change. Only this evening I saw it again,

At the beginning of winter, and I walked and talked
Again, and lived and was again, and breathed again
And moved again and flashed again, time flashed again.

                                        (CP, 238)

This stanza describes an antiepiphany: the recognition that
the meaning of our lives lies in their ongoingness. The mo-
ment "out of time," the instant of mystical insight treasured
by writers of all ages, and especially vivid in Yeats and Eliot,
is here reintegrated with temporality, located in a season "at
the beginning of winter." This experience "was like sudden
time in a world without time." "The present" is realized as
part of a continuum; the changeless thing never manifests
itself to us except in change. In stanza x of "Le Monocle"
Stevens balances the notion of enduring stillness ("that tip
still tips the tree") with temporality ("all birds come some-
time in their *time*"). The birds that repeatedly serve this
poet as indicators of life in time are here the means of
knowing that the tree and its tip exist.

Stanza x is central to Stevens' defense of fictions in "Le
Monocle"; it brings together explicitly the idea of change
and the imagination's need to confront and come to terms
with it. Behind the poem's title is a modern version of
Blake's prayer: "May God us keep / From single vision and
Newton's sleep!" In the self mockery of his one-eyed persona,
Stevens calls into question the single vision of the self-deceiv-
ing fancy,[16] but the successive fables offered in these brilliant
stanzas are also a rebuke to the Newtonian sleep of those
who will not dream of baboons and periwinkles. Stanza x
opens on an ambiguous note but soon deepens into the se-
rious and beautiful "semblance" of the yeoman-poet. And
even the "fops of fancy" are not unequivocally dismissed.
"Memorabilia of the mystic spouts" fails to conjure up any
visual image that is not absurd, but it is consistent with the
notion of a hidden watery source of imagination, which Ste-
vens relates throughout the poem to spontaneity and change.
"The verve of earth" has been linked with "the intensity of

love" (v), and these spontaneous intensities are in turn linked with intimations of mortality: "inklings of your bond to all that dust." The "poem of the idea" in "Le Monocle" concerns the deep affinities between love and death (and, therefore, the earth that is the source and end of love) and the reluctant submission of a healthy imagination to death, if it is to devise the great poem of earth.

> This luscious and impeccable fruit of life
> Falls, it appears, of its own weight to earth.
> When you were Eve, its acrid juice was sweet,
> Untasted, in its heavenly, orchard air.

These lines condense the meaning of stanza VI of "Sunday Morning" and present us with a twentieth-century version of the Fortunate Fall. The apple falls inevitably from "heavenly orchard air" to earth because it has weight and substance; its fall and Eve's tasting are associated, as in the original myth. But in a post-Newtonian context both events take on the inexorability of natural law, and in the next quatrain Stevens diagrams this law for us in the most basic of all geometries:

> An apple serves as well as any skull
> To be the book in which to read a round,
> And is as excellent, in that it is composed
> Of what, like skulls, comes rotting back to ground.

The delicate sound patterns of "Le Monocle" rarely assert themselves as noticeably as this; the rhyme imitates the finality of the cyclical process. Hamlet, reading a round in Yorick's skull, proves that "imagination [may] trace the noble dust of Alexander" through an ecological cycle:

> as thus: Alexander died, Alexander was buried, Alexander returneth into dust; the dust is earth; of earth we make loam; and why of that loam, whereto he was converted, might they not stop a beer barrel?   (v.i)

Stevens, with like severity and facetiousness, reads in apples and skulls an unsentimental "way of truth": "An ancient aspect touching a new mind." The idyll of stanza IV becomes the surreal grotesquerie of stanza VIII, the lovers

> Two golden gourds distended on our vines,
> Into the autumn weather, splashed with frost,
> Distorted by hale fatness, turned grotesque.

"This trivial trope reveals a way of truth." The truth-revealing tropes of this poem all concern the natural cycle, life bearing and death dealing, and our dependence upon it as the world in which we have our happiness, or not at all: "Yet you persist with anecdotal bliss / To make believe a starry *connaissance*." Make-believe is the product of an imagination that has failed to root itself in the deep rhythms of nature and acknowledge our "bond to all that dust." Its "anecdotal bliss" fixes on isolated moments and draws from them intimations of a heavenly wisdom that might make sense of our lives. That the hand of providence writes its hieroglyphs in the sky is a belief that many have found comforting, but Stevens throughout his life was to deny it. Although acknowledging the seductiveness of such make-believe in some enchanting lines of stanza VII, he insists that transcendental imaginings remain in the region of *if* and *may*: "Suppose these couriers brought amid their train / A damsel heightened by eternal bloom." Eternal bloom is repeatedly denied. *Suppose* has no consequence.

This is the difficult confession hammered home in the dull scholar's Hamlet-like meditation upon Eros and Thanatos in the following stanza. "A damsel heightened by eternal bloom" is an invention of fancy, imagination in its wish-fulfilling mood. "Suppose. . . ." But meanwhile there is the "ancient aspect" of actual love: "It comes, it blooms, it bears its fruit and dies." The "way of truth" that cures the ground and chastens fables insists that "our bloom is gone." So much for "eternal bloom." In these adjacent stanzas, therefore, Stevens offers his dominant, interlaced subjects in dynamic but inexplicit relationship. Imagination, the mediating and expressive power, can deal with its major theme, love, in two ways. It can perpetuate radiant bubbles, the remembered glory of time past, in fictions that make-believe the heavenly origin of beloved damsels: "The mules that angels ride . . ." and so forth. Yet, there is a darker awareness that counters the starry *connaissance*, bursts the bubble. This "deep up-pouring from some saltier well" knows that love's origin lies deep, not high, in those depths from which the beloved arises "dripping in your hair from sleep." The responsible imagination of the yeoman-poet recognizes that starry fables are for fiery boys and sweet-smelling virgins unaware of their mortality and addresses itself to the difficult task of charting "the origin and course / Of love" over an entire life span. The point is that this task too requires trivial tropes, requires the oblique and self-annihilating activity of fiction making.

The last of Stevens' anecdotal meditations, before he winds up "Le Monocle" in stanza XII, speaks, tropically, of mature love. It begins with a commentary in the conditional mood. "If sex were all, then every trembling hand / Could make us squeak, like dolls, the wished-for words." It is a stanza that has given much trouble to readers,[17] but may give less if we recognize that in it the poet knots together the strands of his imagining on the subjects of language, love, and organic mortality, and that the image of the last four lines is another version of the basic spatial model that undergirds the poem.

To say "If sex were all" is to say that it is not all. "That first, foremost law" does not dictate the words of poems like "Le Monocle de Mon Oncle." Rather, love does that—"madness or delight"—causing us to "shout / Doleful heroics" like the opening phrases of the poem. Stevens knows, of course, that sex and love are both rooted in the watery unconscious world "down there," where the frogs boom:

> Last night, we sat beside a pool of pink,
> Clippered with lilies scudding the bright chromes,
> Keen to the point of starlight, while a frog
> Boomed from his very belly odious chords.

This trivial trope reiterates the principle of relationship between opaque, visceral depths and dazzling verbal surfaces that is both the subject and the methodology of the poem. The "odious chords" arise from the same region as the "deep up-pouring" of stanza I, and the newborn Venus ascending from the world of sleep in stanza III. "Odious chords" affront imagination, which desires always to convert animal noises to articulate language and sense-making fables that will suffice for our mixed being. Lilies and starlight belong to conventional love language, and Stevens' style in these three lines is as mannered as it is in any passage in the poem. And yet, every depth has a surface, every spasm of madness or delight aspires to articulateness. "Fate" has decreed a double allegiance in us, to the dark emotions in the belly and to "the wished-for words." Stevens' image of surface and depth, like the Freudian model that lies behind it, makes us see these two motives as basically continuous, however often they may conflict in practice. Stanza XI, unexpectedly, offers a biological explanation for imagining, which allows for mutuality of effect between the emotions yearning for words and their visceral origins. "If sex were all," odious chords would be enough. But we are not stirred by "every trembling hand," only by a particular hand at a particular moment of a temporal "curriculum." The hand belongs to the "she" who brings words into being and is endowed with her love-attracting power by the feeling and imagining being in the grip of the "foremost law" of his being.

The philosophic roots of Stevens' poem lie close to those expressed in Spenser's Garden of Adonis.

> That substance is eterne, and bideth so;
> Newhen the life decayes and forme does fade,
> Doth it consume and into nothing goe,
> But chaunged is, and often altred to and froe.
>
> (III.vi.37)

"There is a substance in us that prevails." The speaker's awareness of himself as implicated in dying generations, his effort to come to terms with the indifferent substrate of his biological and temporal being, is the situation for which Stevens provides successive parabolic comments. He must discover how to speak accurately about an ever-changing world in which love, and every loved object, "both comes and goes at once." A saying of the truth about a fluent *mundo* can never be definitive; any lapidary claims it may make will betray the superficiality of its source, and it will end up on the dump. "The dump is full / Of images" that have lost their verve:

> Is it a philosopher's honeymoon, one finds
> On the dump? Is it to sit among mattresses of the dead,
> Bottles, pots, shoes and grass and murmur *aptest eve*:
> Is it to hear the blatter of grackles and say
> *Invisible priest*; is it to eject, to pull
> The day to pieces and cry *stanza my stone*?
>
> (CP, 203)

The aptest Eve is the one who becomes a warty squash in "Le Monocle." The stanzas of the poem do not profess to be stones; thinking stones, in particular, are dismissed at the beginning. The tropes are effective precisely *because* they are trivial, ephemeral, because they trace intensities and verves through their fluctuations with a breathless scrivening. Stevens' twelve stanzas show him to be a master of repetitions in the terms of his own later definition. The poem shows why repetition is necessary for faithful speech, and it awards its instances precisely the degrees of credence and skepticism that they deserve. They will grow more shrunken and distant from their origin as the years go by:

> When amorists grow bald, then amours shrink
> Into the compass and curriculum
> Of introspective exiles, lecturing.

As the "man fairly well along in life" is exiled from the fiery boy he once was, so the poet is exiled from the experiences that supply him with his materials:

> the hiding-places of man's power
> Open; I would approach them, but they close.
> (*The Prelude*, XII, 279-80)

The introspective exile continues, however, to lecture, to

read, and to write. He wields a compass that can trace, though now on a flat surface, the circles of skulls and apples. *Curriculum* is a dry word for the lecturer's paradigm, but it is also *curriculum vitae*, the necessary course of a life. In a late poem, Stevens associates it with the flowing "river of rivers":

> It is the third commonness with light and air,
> A curriculum, a vigor, a local abstraction . . .
> Call it, once more, a river, an unnamed flowing,
>
> Space-filled, reflecting the seasons. . . .
> ("The River of Rivers in Connecticut" [CP, 533])

Scrivenings are shrunken, flattened, and attenuated versions of "reality," but they can reflect the seasons of a human life if the scrivener will take chances, discard dead decorums, and resist the temptation to lapidary utterance and premature closure. Both Wordsworth and Stevens shocked their early readers, and both were accused of triviality and deliberate obfuscation. From the 1970s they look like heroes precisely because they admit the foolhardiness of what they do and are capable of allowing themselves to assume a fool's role in some of their poems.

Stevens' last persona in "Le Monocle" is the rose rabbi who in the final stanza reads yet another round, the eloquent figures traced by the birds, who in stanza x visited the gigantic tree of reality. Now they make a final sense of "a moving chaos that never ends" in a close that manages to evade finality. The poem's ultimate conceit perfectly adumbrates the poise of vision that rewards imaginative *ascesis*:

> A blue pigeon it is, that circles the blue sky,
> On sidelong wing, around and round and round.
> A white pigeon it is, that flutters to the ground,
> Grown tired of flight.

One hesitates to mangle the delicacy of implication in these lines. The "it is" of lines one and three is an early example of a stylistic device that later pervaded Stevens' poetry; and like the late examples, these *it*s have indefinite reference.

The blue and white pigeons are figures for whatever comes to life and makes its mark on the isolation of the sky—birds, human beings, loves, poems. The circles are related to the apples and skulls of stanza IV; all are books "in which to read a round." Stevens in his next volume celebrates "The Pleasures of Merely Circulating" and queries the "secret in skulls," concluding, "Yet that things go round and again go round / Has rather a classical sound" (CP, 150). He is after something more subtle than the classical notion of cycles. The classical sound is avoided in "Le Monocle" by breaking the "round and round" of the first two lines with the ravishing cadences of the next two. Nevertheless, this stanza has more end rhymes than any other in the poem: *round* rhymes with *ground* and *found*; *pursued* and *knew* is a near miss. So the classical sound is not altogether denied. Stevens is working for a conclusive cadence that will imitate the inconclusiveness of the "inner poem."

The blue pigeon circles; the white pigeon settles to a dying fall. Stevens is speaking of the ends of things, but so gently that repose seems as desirable as it is inevitable. The poet and the bird both grow tired of flight and return to rest in the ground of their being. But flight is natural to them, and they, or others like them, will fly again. The stanza's middle lines turn the speaker's irony upon himself again; his mincing machine mutilates what it devours. But in modulating from the presumptions of the dark rabbi to the hesitations of the rose one, Stevens achieves an eloquent seriousness.

> Like a rose rabbi, later, I pursued,
> And still pursue, the origin and course
> Of love, but until now I never knew
> That fluttering things have so distinct a shade.

The poem ends in the evanescent present moment of insight. As Wordsworth regards the meanest flower that blows, Stevens observes the fluttering thing that casts its intensely significant shadow. "Shade" carries many meanings; it touches lightly the territory of the "studious ghosts" in stanza III and the place where shades and ghosts live. Shadows and substance change places in the last line: "real" things flutter and distinctness belongs to shades. This is a commentary upon distinctness. We cannot know, or embody, or grasp anything more distinct than a shadow, and so the shadows that imagination conjures up are as enduring, and as fleeting, as the solemn temples, the great globe itself.

By concluding the great "Ode" with a reference to "thoughts that do often lie too deep for tears," Wordsworth confesses a final inarticulateness. Thoughts too deep for tears are also too deep for linguistic expression, and indeed, they remain unspecified. The poem ends, having approximated, as best it may, the poem within. Both the "Ode" and "Le Monocle de Mon Oncle" illustrate Stevens' proposition in "Man Carrying Thing," that "The poem must resist the intelligence / Almost successfully" (CP, 350); they also, to some extent, explain why.[18]

Poetry and its sources are connected only through "intimations," Wordsworth's stubbornly precise word for "what remains behind" in the poet's cabinet. Yet all men desire to know themselves and to speak of their knowing; the instinct to understand, to contemplate, to express, is almost as deeply rooted in *nature* as the primary experience itself. From these features of "our climate," Wordsworth deduced his theory of poetry and Stevens the propositions concealed behind "Le Monocle." The effort to understand, which for the language animal means the effort to speak, will continue as long as the human race continues; expression will invariably be inadequate to intuition, and therefore unsatisfying; "what will suffice" will forever elude us, but forever retain its power to re-enchant the imagination to yet another adventure.

STRANGE RELATION:
STEVENS' NONSENSE

STEVENS' BEST POEMS ARE THOSE THAT DRAW AND HOLD us by their surface. The charm and mystery of the sounds and turns of phrase, the drama of the leaps from one point of view to another, the subtlety and irony of the changing moods, the flickering of the language between refinement and coarseness—all these produce delight before we are aware of doctrine. For such elements, the nonsense syllables in the poems provide an enveloping air of freedom and comedy. The author apparently lets himself go, abandoning his voice to cheerful or satirical impulse. Yet when one examines them, these irrational sounds seem to embody remarkable aspects of the poet's meaning.

In his best poems, Stevens keeps several subjects going at once. "Depression before Spring" (CP, 63) shows how he does it. Here, on the level of common human experience, a man tired of winter looks for a sign of spring. On the level of a theory of the imagination, the poet in a barren season waits for inspiration that does not come. At the same time, in Stevens' myth of a romance between the mind and reality, an observer makes love to the world, but the world does not respond: it remains untouched by the imagination. In the course of this poem Stevens gives himself several forms. He appears first as a cock crowing and waiting for a hen that never appears. He is also a potential king who cannot claim his throne until an absent queen accepts him. He is at the same time a lover who fails to find his mistress.

The story of the poem comes out in several modes: third-person narrative, dramatic speech, and nonsense. To start with, the author speaks as a narrator telling a story: "The cock crows / But no queen rises." In line 3, the character's voice is heard directly. But instead of crowing, the character speaks, praising the beloved in mockery: "The hair of my blonde / Is dazzling. . . ." The speech ends in onomatopoetic ejaculations, "Ho! Ho!" suggesting the laughter of self-ridicule. Then the narrator returns and continues his story on the level of cock and hen: "But ki-ki-ri-ki / Brings no rou-cou. . . ." In the last lines Stevens climbs back to the meta-phor of royalty and the reference to the seasons: "But no queen comes / In slipper green"—the world in springtime being a princess wearing green slippers.

Why does Stevens draw these parallels, change his narra-tive point of view, and resort to onomatopoetic nonsense? I think he wishes to establish his esthetic theory on the basis of other realities, such as plant and animal life. So he sug-gests, for example, that the world awaits spring with the same inevitability that the cock's sexual instinct drives it to court a hen and that men give human, imaginative meaning to independent reality. The nonsense is the actual cry of the animal world making its poetry or song; the direct speech is that of a man expressing his love of the world; the narrative is that of a poet interpreting the action for us.

In this case the poet does not win his beloved. The imag-inative vision eludes him, and the failure is reflected in the bizarre simile he employs for the song of courtship: the blonde mistress, he says, dazzles one like "the spittle of cows / Threading the wind." Yet the coarseness and sunny bright-ness also imply a contact with true reality, not a "romantic" fantasy. Even while complaining of failure, therefore, the poet manages modestly to succeed.

The cock and his nonsense appear again in "Bantams in Pine-Woods" (CP, 75). Here, on the level of human inci-dent, a bantam meets the poet in the woods and, unable to conceive of persons who do not belong to its own species, challenges him as another bird, only bigger. "Fat! Fat!" he says to Stevens, who indeed had a bulky figure.

This poem is a dramatic monologue, and the similes are chosen to suit a bantam's imagination. So the poet becomes a cock, and his poems are "hoos." From the imaginative point of view the audible, moving bird is an esthetic focus for the wooded scene around it and "points" the tangs of the pine trees: the unique, changing animal establishes an esthetic order in the motionless world of plants. On the other hand, the poet works by giving general significance to the bird or any other particular, and his imagination strives to illuminate the world as the sun cannot. So he is charged with arrogance: "Damned universal cock, as if the sun / Was blackamoor to bear your blazing tail." Stevens tries to capture the scene in human speech, but employs onomatopoetic nonsense to suggest that the sounds of nature and the words of a poem have a similar function. He would like his own speech to be as true to experience, as spontaneous and expressive, as the call of a bird. He would also like to be tall in a poetic sense, gifted with a large mind, a spacious vision.

The problem of the poet is to dramatize not the behavior of the bantam but the difficulty of grasping and truly rendering the whole situation. The challenge is what the bantam alludes to when it says, "Your world is you. I am my world." It is the man's pretensions as a poet that make the bird ridicule him. As if to shame the human, the bird with its "Fat! Fat!" speaks naturally, effortlessly, and accurately for a world that is always beyond the poet's grasp.

Nonsense syllables seem often to have signified for Stevens the artless power of a natural sound to bring the individual and his world together. " 'Ohoyaho, / Ohoo,' " cry Bonnie and Josie as they celebrate "the marriage / Of flesh and air" ("Life Is Motion" [CP, 83]).[1] "Tum-ti-tum, / Ti-tum-tum-tum!" the ploughman sings in "Ploughing on Sunday" (CP, 20) as he drives into the soil, getting North America ready for spring. His musical rhythm suggests the deep, subrational quality of the pleasure he feels in being at home in the world, ploughing instead of praying. Sadly enough, this expressive ease must be denied to the conscious poet, who has to struggle deliberately with human speech. What "Fat! Fat!" accomplishes for "Bantams in Pine-Woods," the human artist can accomplish only by the careful, yet hardly successful (as Stevens saw it) design of that attractive poem.

In a much later poem, "On an Old Horn" (CP, 230), Stevens comments on what the bantam was doing.[2] This time we meet a bird with a ruddy belly, evidently a robin welcoming the spring. The poet wishes to suggest that what matters in human nature is the power to respond coherently and imaginatively to the world. Such a power establishes one's individual character and gives shape to a world that would otherwise be chaotic. If a bird had the power, it would possess the special value we attach to humanity. So Stevens conceives of a robin that can make figurative connections between men and birds, just as men make them between birds and men. To signalize its accomplishment, the robin utters its characteristic sounds, or blows a "trumpet." Such a creature would belong in a new place on the scale of being, perhaps as an incipient human with some rodent traits— "A baby with the tail of a rat?"

The poet proceeds to distinguish between odor and color, treating one as objective and the other as subjective. If the bird merely enjoyed the spring smells, he would act mechanically. If he responded to the colors, he would be imaginative (like a human poet celebrating a landscape); that is, he would express the kind of synthesis that alone keeps us from chaos: "a man, or more, against / Calamity. . . ."

In a brief second part the poet takes his turn and speaks in a human equivalent of the bird's song. Having reflected in the first part upon imaginative coherence, he will now convey his own spirit by imagining chaos. To do so, he conceives of the stars as moving not together but apart, "Flying like insects of fire in a cavern of night. . . ." Then, to mark his success, he too blows a horn by uttering some onomatopoetic nonsense syllables: "Pipperoo, pippera, pipperum." Like the bird, he identifies himself by the spontaneous, characteristic notes of his peculiar instrument.

"The rest is rot," says Stevens at the end of the poem; that is, what matters is that one should give voice to one's own view of the world, whether one be man or bird. By imitating a horn, he suggests the spontaneous quality of his sense of things—the natural feeling that underlies his meditations.

"On an Old Horn" is an unpleasantly self-indulgent poem in which Stevens lets theoretical considerations swamp his design. But it shows again how closely music, nonsense, and a feeling of intimacy with reality are joined in his work. Besides expressing a feeling, Stevens' nonsense can also point to some of his doctrines. In "The Ordinary Women" (CP, 10) he deals with his beloved polarity of reality and imagination. To commonplace minds, familiar things are tedious and strange things are interesting. As soon as such minds enter the realm of imagination, they look away at what lies elsewhere. They yearn to abandon the near for the remote, and when they reach that, they yearn for what now looks remote but was at hand a little while ago. The reason for their oscillations is that they lack imagination themselves. Unable to transform their surroundings creatively, they first diminish them and then exchange them capriciously for others. Being conventional, they cannot face the world without reducing it to formulae. Instead of sky and stars, they see old religious symbols: "beta b and gamma g." Erotic thoughts scare them; rather than seek a union between the self and the world, they think of a heavenly union, presumably with Christ. The musicians of their projections are gaunt or ghostly, reflecting the thin sensibilities of the "ordinary women." Having reduced the sights and sounds of the palace to inconsequence, the visitors leave.

Nonsense occurs three times in the poem. The loges of the palace mumble "zay-zay" when the women first arrive. These onomatopoetic syllables imitate the sound of the guitar and suggest the mystery of moonlight, the initial fascination of the new scene. When the women look at the nocturnal sky, they "read of marriage-bed," and the poet comments, "Ti-lill-o!" as if to mock their prudery. The guitarists keep playing, but rumble "a-day, a-day," as if to suggest that the women have tired of the erotic night of fantasy, and are eager for the release of daytime. At last the music, moonlight, and erotic feelings move them to speech. But instead of making poetry, they merely say goodbye to halls that have grown dim. Leaving dry guitars, they return to catarrhs, that is, coughs rather than eloquence.

The women may be timid impulses of the mind to handle the malady of the quotidian. They may anticipate the sister of Canon Aspirin in "Notes toward a Supreme Fiction" (CP, 401-2), who is associated with poverty and rejects dreams. It seems significant that the women do not utter nonsense but shy away from it. If nonsense syllables often express a union of the self with the world, the women have no right to use them. The precious vocabulary of the poem suggests the falseness of the women's "romantic" aspirations, and Stevens' style in the poem ridicules those aspirations, although it is precisely the vocabulary and the patterns of sound that make the whole thing irresistible.

The doctrinal argument comes to a finer point in "A High-Toned Old Christian Woman" (CP, 59). Like the "ordinary women" and Canon Aspirin's sister, this character has a fearful mind and narrows her imagination to correct, religious themes. She is in fact the muse of the religious imagination, widowed because her god is dead. The poet challenges her by pointing out that as a source of consoling ritual and myth the pagan gods served quite as well as the Christian. So he proposes a new source: not a self-denying, ascetic faith directed toward heaven, but self-indulgent joys centered on the earth. The old imagination produced the spiritual music of the spheres; the new may produce something more boisterous, a "jovial hullabaloo." (The epithet points to Jove rather than Christ.)

The poet calls his celebrants of earthly pleasure "disaffected flagellants," or lapsed Puritans, and he foresees that they may well be proud of their new forms of art: "Proud of such novelties of the sublime, / Such tink and tank and tunk-a-tunk-tunk. . . ." I think that the echo of *Trial by Jury* is fortuitous, and that the rhythm of the nonsense suggests banjos, the syncopated jazz and free verse of the early part of the century. It deliberately evokes secular and frivolous pleasures, in opposition to the serious, didactic art of Christian tradition. The poet has adapted the hymn-playing harmonium to worldly entertainments.

So we may give three general meanings to Stevens' nonsense. It can be the joyous sound of the self when directly in touch with reality, or the poet's laughter as he defies the old morality. But most significantly, it can be the voice of reality or of the natural world producing the spontaneous, adequate music that the poet would like to match.

It would be hard to overestimate the importance Stevens attached to this last principle. When *Harmonium* appeared, he closed the book with "To the Roaring Wind" (*CP*, 113). When a second edition was called for, he added more than a dozen poems, but arranged the new book so that it still ended with that finely tuned coda. He also paired it carefully with the preceding poem, "Tea" (*CP*, 112). The point of "Tea" is that somebody—an attractive young woman—has arranged the room around her so that it consoles the poet for the advent of autumn. The weather outdoors has disintegrated, but the weather indoors makes up for it: "Your lamplight fell / On shining pillows, / Of sea-shades and sky-shades. . . ." By her imaginative art the girl has given the poet the solace and refreshment—the "palm"—that a focused landscape would have supplied.

In "To the Roaring Wind" the poet suggests that he would like to do what the girl did. "What syllable are you seeking?" he asks the wind. Of course, he would like to find it. He wants to speak for the world as the world might speak for itself. The wind—*pneuma, spiritus*, ghost of religious enthusiasm and creative inspiration—has here become only the wind, voice of reality, independent of human feeling. This is what the poet means to emulate. He calls the wind "Vocalissimus," which sounds like onomatopoetic nonsense but could mean "most expressive." Because the wind speaks in the "distances of sleep," it echoes the opening poem of *Harmonium*, "Earthy Anecdote," in which bucks respond esthetically to the movements of a "firecat" until the spontaneously creative firecat sleeps. In "Earthy Anecdote" nature herself (presumably in the form of a brush fire) acts as an artist, suggesting Stevens' often-quoted words, "I want, as a man of the imagination, to write poetry with all the power of a monster equal in strength to that of the monster about whom I write" (L, 790). So in the last poem of the book Stevens would be about to wake up and start the cycle again, the cycle of trying to play nature's part and of finding that he is only a poet.

If we suspend consideration of nonsense and attend to this important theme, we shall find it exquisitely embodied in "Two Figures in Dense Violet Night" (CP, 85). Here the world takes the form of a young woman who scolds the poet for wooing her ineptly. She wishes him to celebrate her beauty in nocturnal (that is, imaginative) language: "Be the voice of night and Florida in my ear." It is a command that anticipates exhortations to come—"Be thou the voice" in "Mozart, 1935" (CP, 132), and "Bethou me" in "Notes toward a Supreme Fiction" (CP, 393). He is to speak as if she spoke for him:

> As the night conceives the sea-sounds in silence,
> And out of their droning sibilants makes
> A serenade.
>
> (CP, 86)

Of course, the poet imitates the sibilants of the waves—the self-made poetry of the sea—in these very lines. But then, at last, the proper language emerges, and the girl tells him to describe a moonlit vista composed by the eye of sleeping buzzards: it will contain stars, sky, palms, and moon, but no men. So the poet gives us, as she speaks, once more a landscape brought into focus not by a human mind but by a bird, standing for reality untouched by human distortion—"simple seeing, without reflection" (CP, 471), as he put it many years later. The reference to a hotel in the opening line is meaningful because Stevens thought of poetic reality as a place one visited like a hotel.[3]

With such doctrines in mind it becomes easy for one to appreciate the poet's preoccupation with musical instruments.[4] The "ordinary women" flit to and from guitars; the ploughman tells Remus to blow a horn. Crispin is a lutanist and a conductor; he plays the banjo, hears horns and trumpets, clarions and tambours, draws comparisons with bassoons and marimbas. In "Anecdote of Men by the Thousand" the poet names the mandoline as being the natural expression of certain places. In "A High-Toned Old Christian Woman" he refers to citherns and saxophones. There are lutes in "Sunday Morning" and gongs in "Cortège for Rosenbloom." Peter Quince plays the clavier; Susanna hears a cymbal, horns, and a noise like tambourines. And along with these instruments go many kinds of singers and singing.

The peculiar feature of music is that it seems both a human and a natural form of pleasing, significant sound. The same rhythms and tones we hear in the compositions of artful men are also produced by birds and the elements. In the latter, moreover, the cause is instinctive, unwilled, perfectly spontaneous. The sea and the robin cannot help making precisely the noises they create, and those sounds convey the essence of their makers. We know the cock by its crowing, the dove by its cooing. Now, as in prehistoric times, the song and the bird are inseparable. Their music has the inevitability that all human art aspires to. As a poet, Stevens wanted to find words that would convey his moods and meanings with such propriety and inevitability. It is in this sense that his poetry aspires to the condition of music, and it is for this reason that he named his first book *Harmonium*.

The connection between music and nonsense is direct enough. Music represents, for Stevens, the effect of adequate poetry, while nonsense is the verbal equivalent of music. In the deeply moving "Mozart, 1935" (*CP*, 131) the poet is asked to play the music of the present on the piano, "Its shoo-shoo-shoo, its ric-a-nic. . . ." The present is ugly and wintry, like the rhythms of popular dance tunes. But it is also a challenge to the creative powers of the poet-pianist. As he plays, a "body in rags" is carried downstairs—obviously the body of the noble past, the art that no longer seems appropriate. (This is the same corpse that appears in "The Emperor of Ice-Cream.")

However, the poet is also commanded to become the voice of these years of abysmal wretchedness, the mid-thirties:

> Be thou the voice,
> Not you. Be thou, be thou
> The voice of angry fear,
> The voice of this besieging pain.
>
> (CP, 132)

These are the words that were to be echoed by the sparrow in "Notes toward a Supreme Fiction," saying to the blade of grass, "Bethou me" (CP, 393), which I interpret as, "Give me the voice of your inmost, essential self." Thus, when the poet wishes to speak immediately for his times, he approaches the state of a musician and utters appropriate nonsense—nonsense that stands for appropriate music.

The inmost self is subrational and prelinguistic. It holds the feelings and tastes that move us to speech, not those that issue from speech. Stevens' nonsense syllables bypass the conscious, literary, reflective mind, as music does, to suggest the impulses that determine poetry from within and that link it to the reality enveloping and dominating us from without.

Such a linkage of nonsense syllables with music and the revelation of essence seems natural for Stevens. In "The Man with the Blue Guitar" he calls the truly imaginative, creative mind "man number one" (CP, 166), which may be a political metaphor referring to "premier." Stevens then speaks of getting at the essential nature of such a person and describes the task as performing a biopsy on the brain, or pinning it down the way one might nail a hawk across a barn door. He also compares the process with striking the correct note on a guitar and tuning the instrument perfectly: "To strike his living hi and ho, / To tick it, tock it, turn it true. . . ." Music, essence, and nonsense come together here. "Hi and ho" represent not the meaning of number one's words but the timbre of his liveliness,[5] the liveliness that gives rise to his characteristic speech. "To tick it, tock it" suggests picking the strings while turning the pegs. The whole series of metaphors suggests fierceness and high spirits, one from the cutting and impaling, the other from the music and nonsense. Finally, these attributes mingle in the playing of the guitar: "To bang it from a savage blue, / Jangling the metal of the strings. . . ."

Music too is an immediate expression of feeling, and poems written to be sung often have nonsense syllables for their refrain. It is also conventional for words in songs to be divided so that the separate syllables or vowels receive vocal elaboration while being reduced (apart from the music) to meaninglessness. Therefore, telling a poet to play the "hoo-hoo-hoo" of the present on a piano is the same as asking him to express the quintessential, prelinguistic character of the times in which he lives. So also to entitle a book *Harmonium* is to indicate that one is a modest artist, old-fashioned in sensibility, striving to give immediate expression to the life around one.

The purely musical possibilities of nonsense syllables make themselves heard in "Snow and Stars" (*CP*, 133). Again the poet is tired of winter and eager for spring; or he feels oppressed by the wretchedness of the 1930s and longs for an age more propitious to the imagination. Once more, he uses a bird as his spokesman. Generally, birds suggest poetry not only because they sing but also because they fly arbitrarily into view and away, to be seen in glimpses, like glimpses of ultimate reality. A colorful bird, such as a pheasant, brightens the mind with the effects of rich, imaginative poetry. A black bird, such as a grackle, darkens the mind like bleak poetry. In "Snow and Stars" the harsh sound of the grackles is appropriate to the bleak mood of the poet. The lines in which Stevens describes them are heavy with unpleasant sibilants. In contrast, the poem moves at the end to lines ripe with *l* sounds, for the approach of spring. Against this polarity the poet sets the opposition of nonsense syllables, "bing, high bing," and "ding, ding, dong."

The song the grackles sing occupies three of the four stanzas of the poem. It seems to play with the myth of Dis and Persephone. The devil is asked to take and wear earth's robe of winter—snow and winter stars—and in exchange to give the world the clothing of the early-leafing willow, harbinger of spring. The piercing sounds of "bing, high bing" evoke the festiveness of the overheated population of hell when receiving the cold robe. The anticlimactic sounds of "ding, ding, dong" evoke the dullness that will be buried in the "hill" (or hole) of the underworld when wintriness leaves the earth.

Stevens' little game does not yield an attractive poem. The heavy sound patterns and forced imagery coarsen a *donnée* that required subtle modulation if it was to draw many readers. I suspect that the poet kept this work as a pendant to the superior poem, "The Sun This March," which follows it. But as an experiment with rhymes, alliteration, assonance, and nonsense, it indicates how deliberately Stevens employed such devices.

If I am right, Stevens uses nonsense most effectively when it does not merely stand for the ineffable but also conveys precise suggestions of attitudes or feelings. It should seem casual and unpremeditated, like the subrational moods to which it points. But it should also bear a meaning sufficiently determined by the context. So long as contrasting points of view are associated with the nonsense, we can give it significant direction.

"Anything Is Beautiful if You Say It Is" (*CP*, 211) seems a good example of minimal differentiation. Here two similar figures utter similar nonsense syllables; yet the poet distinguishes between them. Both are indecent young women, one a concubine, the other a "demi-monde." They suggest shopworn views of the world, and "demi-monde" may be a pun. One of them is in a garden, the other, on a "mezzanine," suggesting the polarity of outdoors and indoors. Both sound displeased with life. The concubine says, "Phooey! Phoo!" and whispers, "Pfui." The demi-monde says, "Phooey" and "Hey-de-i-do!" These sounds had wide currency in the thirties. "Phooey" of course implies a blasé discontent with the state of the world. "Hey-de-i-do" is typical of the cheerful noises of contentment affected by jazz singers, especially crooners. So we have an outdoor figure and an indoor figure

expressing trite moods of discontent, with the latter quali-
fying her complaint by making the best of the situation.

In the middle section of the poem Stevens continues to
balance outdoors against indoors. He abandons the sweetness
of spring to the bees, then says that the chandeliers are neat
but glaring, and adds some parrots troubled by the cold.
People, animals, and things are all inexpressive, out of touch
with the present. It seems therefore that in spite of the
presence of spring, the poet's outdated, "beautiful" visions,
whether of interiors or of landscapes, leave him dissatisfied.

In the last part of the poem he offers the alternative to
such stale images: an intense contemplation of grim reality,
uniting things of nature with those of man. As if to signal
his satisfaction with this choice, he asks an appropriately
named servant to bring a suitable wine, a Teutonic, northern
one. At last the poem comes to coherent life:

> The Johannisberger, Hans.
> I love the metal grapes,
> The rusty, battered shapes
> Of the pears and of the cheese
>
> And the window's lemon light,
> The very will of the nerves,
> The crack across the pane,
> The dirt along the sill.

The design of the poem is subtly in keeping with the doc-
trine. The opening and middle sections sound disjointed and
trivial, to support the poet's rejection of the two attitudes.
Yet these contain the "beautiful" things of the title. It is in
the last section, when Stevens turns to immediate, ugly real-
ity and transforms it by his language, that the style grows
lucid and unified. The role of the tired nonsense is therefore
correct: it belongs with the heterogeneous, false half worlds,
not with the simple whole.

Among the subtlest uses of nonsense in Stevens' work is
the example of "Page from a Tale" (CP, 421). This rather
hard-worked parable picks up the themes of "Farewell to
Florida" (CP, 117), which is written in the same stanza

form and has the same elements of imagery. The peculiar
feature of "Page from a Tale" is the way Stevens relates non-
sense to meaningful speech. Toward the end of the poem he
speaks of the "miff-maff-muff of water," a typical, apparently
offhand use of onomatopoetic syllables. Only by a careful
response to the whole poem can one tell how deeply calcu-
lated the effect is. At first, the water makes no sound because
the sea is frozen. But Hans does hear the wind, which speaks
in German, presumably his native language. It says "so blau"
and "so lind" and "so lau" (so blue, so gentle, so mild)—
ironically soft cliché rhymes of romantic poetry and ironically
soft epithets for a winter wind.[6] From the thought of water
and wind Stevens goes on to make Hans recall the sounds
that the water might evoke if he could hear it, and these
emerge as some words from a poem in English, a poem in
which the speaker keeps hearing the sound of water. It is
Yeats' "Lake Isle of Innisfree." The thought of those words
leads to the image of a steamship caught in the ice; the Ger-
man words return, "so blau, so blau." Now big stars come
out, bringing "death" to the ship, which receives a southern
name, "Balayne," echoing the German words. The name
may mean "whale," perhaps to evoke Jonah and the theme
of resurrection. Certainly it refers to the ship in "Farewell to
Florida," which moved easily through free, southern waters.
So it represents a warm season of the mind, an early Yeatsian
imagination that the poet has discarded.

As Hans thinks of another line from Yeats' poem, lights
begin to move on the ship. He now knows that men will
come ashore at dawn, no doubt abandoning the doomed ves-
sel. Stevens says they will be afraid of the angels of those
skies:

> The finned flutterings and gaspings of the ice,
> As if whatever in water strove to speak
> Broke dialect in a break of memory.
>
> (CP, 422)

The memory breaking through is, I think, the communal,
archetypal memory of feelings that stay below the level of

language. This memory takes us back to ancestral impressions, first impressions, the primordial response to the world, without myth, symbolism, human associations.

Such a response produces in turn a new sun, which Stevens describes not as the chariot of Apollo but simply as a wheel. It also produces a new kind of moon, another wheel below the first. These suggest, I think, a new, wintry consciousness and a new, wintry imagination. "Weltering illuminations" appear, and out of them step at last the men from the foundered ship, whom Stevens calls "kin." If we glance at "Large Red Man Reading" (CP, 423), the poem that immediately follows "Page from a Tale," we shall meet similar figures: "ghosts that returned to earth" in order to hear the phrases of the poet. Or if we look back at "A Completely New Set of Objects" (CP, 352), we shall meet "shadows of friends" paddling canoes and bearing what seem to be archetypal images for the poet to use.[7]

The men leaving the ship carry electric lamps, or modern imaginations. They act, I think, like souls returning from the underworld in a dangerous, quasi-destructive resurrection. Stevens says they could "melt Arcturus to ingots dropping drops." In other words, these archetypal, ancestral minds underlying our own could, if revived (or modernized and electrified), strip the north star of its familiar associations and melt the ice of the wintry season by enabling men to confront the world directly. Stevens says their gestures could "spill night out" in the "miff-maff-muff" of water. In effect, therefore, they restore the nonsense syllables and remove the language of poems like Yeats'. We are back at the beginning, but with a difference. It is no longer nonsense that sounds like speech but nonsense that sounds like water.

If we want more explicit doctrine concerning nonsense, we may find it in some effortful passages of "Notes toward a Supreme Fiction" (CP, 380). Frank Doggett has drawn attention to the levels of nonsense in the third poem, where Stevens argues that the task of poetry is to restore freshness or "candor" to our perceptions. I take him to mean that a man's imagination enables him to throw off stale views of the world and to see things as if for the first time. Working down from conscious thought, the poem ultimately exhilarates our sensations.

To illustrate the theory, Stevens offers three examples, one human, one animal, and one inanimate. First, to indicate how men convey their sense of the world, he produces an astonishing metaphor, treating the imaginative self as an Arabian seer who comes into one's room at night chanting "hoobla-hoobla-hoobla-how" and throwing stars around the floor in an act of augury. The owllike sounds are perhaps an audible equivalent for a moonlit night, symbol of imagination. In effect, therefore, the poet has translated a visual experience into sound and identified it with an exotic human being.

The other examples are of a wood dove chanting "hoobla-hoo" and of the ocean, "the grossest iridescence," howling "hoo." Each level of sound thus matches a level of iridescence and of animation: Arabian, bird, water. We associate the personified moon with one kind of nonsense, the iridescence of the dove with a simpler kind, and the grossest iridescence of the ocean with the simplest. Presumably, the reader will for the moment enjoy a fresh idea of these phenomena, thanks to the magical connections the poet has arbitrarily established for them with varieties of "meaningless" syllables. It is significant that the poet associates the Arabian with the future, the dove with the past, and the ocean with the present. Only the human imagination knows of the future; the animal has some memory, but no foresight; the inanimate is ignorant of change. "Life's nonsense," says Stevens, "pierces us with strange relation."

JOHN HOLLANDER

THE SOUND OF THE MUSIC OF
MUSIC AND SOUND

THE WHOLE OF "THE WHOLE OF HARMONIUM" IS A musical trope, but it is a kind of master trope of such complexity that merely to catalogue its elements can be bewildering. Pianos, oboes, orchestras, mandolins, guitars, claviers, tambourines, and songs; the musics of Mozart and Brahms, and all the bird songs and other noises of nature; the sounds of language deconstructed into vocables; the visionary phonetics of transcendent tongues; music claimed for language as well as language claimed for music; music abstract and concrete; music simply or complexly figurative—from the clattering of bucks to a scrawny cry from outside, Stevens' poetry is suffused with systematic sound. To say that all this music—high, low, noisy, verbal—is metaphorical is surely not enough. And even to map those metaphors—the movement between "music" and "a music" in "Peter Quince at the Clavier," say, and the kinds of transition from section to section within the poem that are those of program music ("clavier" or no, the *poem* is playing Schumann)—is to deal with dense terrain. Figures of persons, things, or activities in Stevens are always full of shadows and echoes of other figures, and most importantly, figurations of previous tropes. It is almost as if the analogue of the process by which verbal wit can reanimate a cliché or dead metaphor (for example, by momentarily literalizing it) were the imagination's making figures of figures. When "the theatre was changed / To something else" ("Of Modern Poetry" [CP, 239]), then the truly poetic had to twang "a wiry string that gives / Sounds

passing through sudden rightnesses," not an old and pretti-
fied, but soundless, lyre. Nowhere is this more locally evident
in Stevens' verse than in his imagery and mythology of music
and of the traditionally figurative "music" of natural sound.

There is no manifesto about musical figures more powerful
or more direct than the beginning of "The Idea of Order at
Key West," where the voice of the singing spirit and the
"constant cry" of the sea are emphatically denied a relation
that their forerunners have had throughout the history of
our poetry. After an initial correction of what might be an
inevitable mistake in interpretation ("The sea was not a
mask. No more was she"; that is, neither is a mere per-sona
through which some hidden or higher voice is sounding)
there is another corrective adjustment:

> The song and water were not medleyed sound
> Even if what she sang was what she heard,
> Since what she sang was uttered word by word.
> It may be that in all her phrases stirred
> The grinding water and the gasping wind;
> But it was she and not the sea we heard.[1]
>
> (CP, 128-29)

The "medleyed sound" is no less than one of the oldest and
most powerful tropes of eloquence: that blending of human
music, whether vocal or instrumental, and natural sound
that I have elsewhere referred to as "the mingled measure."[2]
Drawing upon two conventions of literary pastoral—the echo-
ing of poetic song by nature and the catalogue of pleasant
sounds in the *locus amoenus* (the wind in the trees, the elo-
quence of moving water, bird song, etc.)—the figure under-
goes a romantic transformation, becoming the basis in all but
a few English poets for a new authentication of human mu-
sic as an instance of something transcendent (a status it had
lost when neoclassic rhetoric and rationalist cosmology had
disabled *harmonia mundi* for poetic purposes, and *musica
humana* had become the busy institutional churning of opera
house, salon and concert hall). The blending of contrived,
human music with the spontaneous noises of nature, the

blending of mere literal music with sounds that are only figuratively so, becomes a dominant romantic musical image. In English and American poetry, at least, the layered blendings of natural symphony and human singing and playing is the only poetic sound.

In the lines quoted above, Stevens is rejecting the possibility of using the old figure in any unfigured way. To have heard and reported on nothing but grinding of water and gasping of wind would have constituted modernist poetic journalism of a sort still, alas, too much with us. To have heard and celebrated a "medleyed sound" would have been humming slightly new, but not inappropriate, words to a very corny old tune. The wind and water music stirred "in all her phrases" (although of her text or melody we are, significantly, not told—such is the magic of verse) because it is her song that can "make" by being able to imbibe, digest, and transform literalness.

Perhaps we can see this more clearly by turning to some American romantic instances of the medley and its versions. William Cullen Bryant's "Summer Wind" comes heroically upon a scene of attentive silence (save for the "interrupted murmur of the bee" at his sweet and sexual work on "the sick flowers"): hills, "With all their growth of woods, silent and stern, / As if the scorching heat and dazzling light / Were but an element they loved." The poet awaits the coming of this heroic bridegroom, lying "where the thick turf, / Yet virgin from the kisses of the sun, / Retains some freshness." He woos the wind, and, after a preceding vision of natural declarations of fealty (the pine "bending his proud top," etc.),

> He comes;
> Lo, where the grassy meadow runs in waves!
> The deep distressful silence of the scene
> Breaks up with minglings of unnumbered sounds
> And universal motion. He is come,
> Shaking a shower of blossoms from the shrubs,
> And bearing on their fragrance; and he brings

> Music of birds, and rustling of young boughs,
> And sound of swaying branches, and the voice
> Of distant waterfalls. . . .

Save for the remarkably deployed context of marriage and its poetic consequences (the wind is causing landscape to sing her own epithalamium, but of his composition), the catalogue of polyphonic voices is quite traditional. It is of the sort dangerously travestied in Spenser's Bower of Bliss and taken up by Wordsworth's eighteenth-century predecessors.

Or we might adduce the contrasted inner and outer sound-scapes[3] in Whittier's "Snowbound," where "within our beds" the remembered sleepers heard

> The wind that round the gables roared
> With now and then a ruder shock,
> Which made our very bedsteads rock.
> We heard the loosened clapboards test,
> The board-nails snapping in the frost. . . .

But those sounds underwent transformation in visionary sleep:

> Faint and more faint the murmurs grew,
> Till in the summer-land of dreams
> They softened to the sound of streams,
> Low stir of leaves, and dip of oars,
> And lapsing waves on quiet shores.

Imaginatively transformed or no, these are not the syllables sought by a later poetic "Vocalissimus, / In the distances of sleep" ("To the Roaring Wind" [CP, 113]). Emerson teaches a similar lesson, but it has to be learned from him at several removes. In "Forerunners," the writer catches the scent of poetic flowers strewn by "happy guides," as "tone of silver instrument / Leaves on the wind melodious trace." The syntax of the last three words is Miltonic, the transition from a scent to an outdoor music is one of the commonplaces of the music of earthly paradises, and the complex image of "tracing" the sound of an already figurative (neoclassical and emblematic) instrument on the more imaginatively authentic wind is confirmed in the unusual reversal of the received metaphor. The musician wind usually plays upon the figurative strings of the trees, all of nature being, in this set of instances, an Aeolian harp. Emerson has taken care, in a parable about poetic predecessors, to adapt the precursory commonplace. (I think that Robert Frost followed Emerson along the "shining trails" of the landscape in this poem, and although the same voices may not have echoed in a "harp-like laughter" of unabashed bardic power as they did for Emerson, he did keep hearing a chuckle.)

Emerson is as insistent about transforming old images for poetry as he is about quickening poetry itself, which is why in "Bacchus" music must be mingled with wine, and why in "Merlin" all the socially contrived salon music must be transfigured:

> Thy trivial harp[4] will never please
> Or fill my craving ear;
> Its chords should ring as blows the breeze,
> Free, peremptory, clear.
> No jingling serenader's art
> Nor tinkle of piano strings. . . .

This is taken by subsequent American poetry to be a parable of form and a plea for the arrival of Whitman's free verse. But it should be read more deeply, less as a fable of scheme or formal surface than of trope, and the first line must refer, for any poet following Emerson, to "thy trivial '*harp*' " as well; use and mention, as it were, become procreatively confused. Merlin's powerful banging must mingle with more than the natural voices domesticated by centuries of earlier poetry. They must chime

> with the forest tone
> When boughs buffet boughs in the wood;
> Chiming with the gasp and moan
> Of the ice-imprisoned flood;
> With the pulse of many hearts;

> With the voice of orators;
> With the din of city arts;
> With the cannonade of wars;
> With the marches of the brave;
> And prayers of might from martyrs' cave.

This chorus is represented with the batterings of anaphora; it is the sound of the strings of the major harp of the cosmos, the figurative, figuring one of major poetry, rather than the trivial synechdoche, whether "lute" or "harp" or "lyre." It heralds the coming of Whitman, but by precept.

Emerson had realized, with Wordsworth and Coleridge, that "The oratorio has already lost its relation to the morning, to the sun + the earth,"[5] but he also knew that the received rhetoric that had echoed in his own earlier poetry, the artificial music attempting to regain such relations by mixing with natural sound, had lost its own imaginative force. "The Bell" of 1823, ringing across water in a key tuned originally by *Il Penseroso*, concludes:

> And soon thy music, sad death-bell,
> Shall shift its notes once more,
> And mix my requiem with the wind
> That sweeps my native shore.

But this is itself the music of the trivial harp, and in such descriptions of natural and human music as in "May Day" Emerson transcends such easy and mechanical mixtures.

The solemnizing of older sound imagery by taking it one step further into figuration seems to be a peculiarly American poetic activity. Thoreau shares in this in his elaborate prose odes to sound and its power (in the "Sounds" chapter in *Walden*) and in the amazing, extended series of transfigurations of the romantic mythology of the Aeolian harp in what he called "the undecayed oracle" of his "telegraph harp"— the inadvertent external music of the wind in the wires, whose internal state is agitated by the transformed sounds of electrical impulses—which extend through his journal entries of the early 1850s. He frequently imposes layer upon

layer of musical figure, often letting his represented sounds
yield tropes of light:

> All sounds, and more than all, silence, do fife and drum
> for us. The least creaking doth whet all our senses and
> emit a tremulous light, like the aurora borealis, over things.
> As polishing expresses the vein in marble and the grain in
> wood, so music brings out what of heroic lurks every-
> where.[6]

Emily Dickinson, with her wish that "the ear had not a
heart / So dangerously near," constantly performs quirky re-
visions and reinterpretations, whether of the musicians who
"wrestle everywhere" and the various unsatisfactory readings
of that noise of living consciousness itself, or of the profuse
strains of unpremeditated art in a singing bird that "was
different—'Twas Translation—Of all tunes I knew—and
more—."[7] And Walt Whitman's very mode of rewriting the
audition of transcendent music has itself become almost
canonical. For Whitman, as for few poets writing in English
in the nineteenth century, the oratorio and, particularly, the
opera maintained a multitude of glowing relations to the
morning, the sun, and the earth:

> Through the soft evening air enwinding all
> Rocks, woods, fort, cannon, pacing sentries, endless
>   wilds,
> In dulcet streams, in flutes' and cornets' notes,
> Electric, pensive, turbulent, artificial. . . .

This image from "Italian Music in Dakota" (ca. 1880) is
the sound of a regimental band playing operatic arrange-
ments and paraphrases of Bellini and Donizetti, artificial at
several removes,

> (Yet strangely fitting here, meanings unknown before,
> Subtler than ever, more harmony, as if born here, related
>   here,
> Not to the city's fresco'd rooms, not to the audience of
>   the opera house,

Sounds, echoes, wandering strains, as really here at home,
Sonnambula's innocent love, tries with *Norma's* anguish,
And thy ecstatic chorus, *Poliuto;*)
Ray'd in the limpid yellow slanting sundown,
Music, Italian music in Dakota.

This is not just opera in itself, of course, but opera echoed,
invoked, recalled, turned into a sublimely oom-pahed version
of all that it could ever mean.[8]

While Nature, sovereign of this gnarl'd realm
Lurking in hidden barbaric grim recesses,
Acknowledging rapport however far remov'd,
(As some old root or soil of earth its last-born flower
    or fruit,)
Listens well pleas'd.[9]

Whitman's natural choirs, then, can enlist all voices.
"Strange that a harp of thousand strings / Can keep in tune
so long," goes the text of one of William Billings' fuguing
tunes, and the "varied carols" of American sound maintain
in Whitman a *discordia concors*. A poem of 1861 consists
entirely of the figuratively revised natural concert:

I heard you solemn-sweet pipes of the organ as last
    Sunday morning I pass'd the church,
Winds of autumn, as I walk'd up the woods at dusk I
    heard your long-stretch'd sighs up above so mournful,
I heard the perfect Italian tenor singing at the opera,
    I heard the soprano in the midst of the quartet singing;
Heart of my love! you too I heard murmuring low
    through one of the wrists around my head,
Heard the pulse of you when all was still ringing little
    bells that night under my ear.

This is Whitman's "At a Solemn Music," and it adduces the
only available form of the music of the spheres in an other-
wise untuned world. It is carefully orchestrated; lines about
"war-suggesting trumpets" and a lady playing "delicious mu-
sic on the harp" were cut from an earlier version. The layer-

ings of upper and lower "parts," the movement toward total
musical authentification in the movement from the sounds
of church music to art to the ultimate metaphorical bells
calling him to an internalized worship of, and in, the body
are themselves a figure for musical scoring.[10]

Whitman's more elaborated symphonies of music, of the
noise of human occupation and sounds of discourse include,
on the one hand, minor, ad hoc occasional pieces like the
late "Interpolation Sounds" and, on the other, a major musi-
cal ode, "Proud Music of the Storm," his adaptation of the
tradition that extends from Dryden through its figurative
form in Collins to Wordsworth. The ode encompasses pass-
ing figures like those in "Song of Myself 18" ("With music
strong I come") and the full-fledged chorus of 26 ("Now I
will do nothing but listen"); but with that music always
round him, Whitman hears polyphonically, comprehends
the dramaturgy of independent part and vertical harmony
striving always for phenomenological priority:

> I hear not the volumes of sound merely, I am moved by
>   the exquisite meanings,
> I listen to the different voices winding in and out,
>   striving, contending with fiery vehemence to excell
>   each other in emotion;
> I do not think the performers know themselves—but
>   now I think I begin to know them.

"The performers" are almost the voices themselves, and the
act of knowing them is one of recognizing the uniqueness
and universality at once of the reinvigorated trope of musical
harmony for both inner and outer energies.[11]

But Whitman's imagery of music and sound can easily
harden into something brittle and empty: chant, in America,
reduces in a generation to cant. A further transfiguration of
the "exquisite meanings" of sound and noise that live in and
outside of discourse is necessary if poetry is to renew itself
by continually sloughing off its husk of rhetoric. "The music
brought us what it seemed / We had long desired," begins
one of the most Stevensian poems not written by Stevens,[12]

talking of the incapacitated older fictions, "but in a form /
So rarified there was no emptiness / Of sensation. . . ." Even
Whitmanic chorales of everything in life entering, *fugato*,
the scene of awareness can become what John Ashbery goes
on to characterize as "the toothless murmuring / Of ancient
willows, who kept their trouble / In a stage of music." The
willows almost have trivial harps hanging from them. So that

> The truth is that there comes a time
> When we can mourn no more over music
> That is so much motionless sound.
> There comes a time when the waltz
> Is no longer a mode of desire. . . .
> ("Sad Strains of a Gay Waltz" [CP, 121])

This is Stevens' version of the oratorio having lost its relation
to the morning, and he could have gone on revising almost
indefinitely—fugues unleashed from memory become tedi-
ously scampering beasts, and so forth. But his general poetic
project, to be the "harmonious skeptic . . . in a skeptical
music" that will be "motion and full of shadows," could not
merely catalogue the nostalgias of old flowers, nor rest con-
tent in hearing a not newly new replaying of the music of
the spheres:

> The heaving speech of air, a summer sound
> Repeated in a summer without end
> And sound alone.
> ("The Idea of Order at Key West" [CP, 129])

His project always carries him beyond these alternatives.
One of the asides one mutters on the oboe concerns the
obsolete fiction of the lyre somewhat loudly swept, and the
implication is that the oboe itself must be abandoned, not
broken like a pastoral pipe or hung on a tree, but loudly
junked: one must move on to the next thing. The ultimate
instrument upon which Hoon hums his hymns ("And my
ears made the blowing hymns they heard") may be a subtle
transformation of the most complex form of the romantic
seashell, which is shaped like both ear and mouth and which

adds to our own ear and speaks into it when we hold it up
for news of the sea's depth and vastness. But Hoon being
Hoon, every trace of this has been swallowed up. Throughout
Harmonium Stevens reveals a restlessness with available fig-
urations of sound, and any revision of them can become
anecdotal. The reading of the winter music in "The Snow
Man," the triumph of "Heavenly labials in a world of gut-
turals" in "The Plot Against the Giant," the epitome of all
serenade when in "Le Monocle de Mon Oncle" the frog
"Boomed from his very belly odious chords" (best quitted
with disdain)—these are all familiar modes of transforma-
tion of older tropes. The "spontaneous cries" of the quail at
the end of "Sunday Morning" echo the "unpremeditated
art" of a Shelleyan bird, even as the "casual flocks of pi-
geons" shadow the Keatsian swallows. And in the penulti-
mate stanze of that poem, the moment of unqualified sub-
limity allows for a pre-Whitmanian natural chorus:

> And in their chant shall enter, voice by voice,
> The windy lake where in their lord delights,
> The trees, like serafin, and echoing hills,
> That choir among themselves long afterward.
>   (*CP*, 70)

The hills, more than merely affirming (in metaphor) the
truth of a poetic outcry by echoing it, continue to resound
with echoes of their own echoing: we are gently and im-
plicitly reminded that the echoes outlast the primary voice,
and that those lasting echoes must themselves enter the
polyphony of the great imagined chanting.

We usually think of Stevens' musical metaphors as re-
working and reinventing the outworn and broken instru-
ments of the Sublime: the lyre, harp, and lute of neoclassic
diction; the Aeolian harp and singing seashell of earlier ro-
manticism, the virtuoso pianism or homely parlor upright of
its later phase; personal instruments, such as the guitar ("This
slave of Music" given by Shelley-Ariel to Jane-Miranda); and
the bird song, to which I shall return. There is, in fact,
hardly a scrap of traditional auditory mythology upon which

Stevens has not improvised. At the beginning of "Evening without Angels," the familiar Christianized version of the heavenly choir of *harmonia mundi* is queried as to its right to represent the eloquent significance of our surrounding element:

> Why seraphim like lutanists arranged
> Above the trees? And why the poet as
> Eternal *chef d'orchestre?*
>
>   Air is air,
> Its vacancy glitters round us everywhere.
> Its sounds are not angelic syllables
> But our unfashioned spirits realized
> More sharply in more furious selves.
>
>   (CP, 136-37)

The answer is that there *is* such a right, but that it must be exercised in a way so as not to abrogate itself. We are, after all, "Men that repeat antiquest sounds of air / In an accord of repetitions. . . ." (As so often in Stevens, the genitive phrase is ambiguous: the sounds are made *of* air and *about* it.) But the repetitions are not elements in a unison of redundancy and monotony: "If we repeat, it is because the wind / Encircling us, speaks always with our speech."

The voices of air are like other natural sounds in that we are in them, but there is no sentimentality here. It is noteworthy that Stevens seems largely uninterested in any diachronic myth of the origin of the language of air. It clearly transcends the empty prattle of moving water: the antiquest tropes of the stream's eloquence and the pool's reflectiveness. But the figure of noise as music is almost a *donnée*. The closest Stevens seems to come to accounting for its emergence is at a tender and privileged moment, when the actual imprinting of human meaning upon nature is treated visually:

> Now, of the music summoned by the birth
> That separates us from the wind and sea,
> Yet leaves us in them, until earth becomes,

By being so much of the things we are,
Gross effigy and simulacrum, none
Gives motion to perfection more serene
Than yours. . . .
    ("To the One of Fictive Music" [CP, 87])

That masquelike music called up by a transformed Lucina
is itself almost the music of wind and sea, yet something
from beyond them both. The voices of earth and air and
water alike become auditory simulacra at the same time. But
this is vastly different from the witty, precise myth of origina-
tion in Frost's "Never Again Would Birds' Song Be the
Same," wherein the birds, after hearing Eve's "daylong
voice," added to their own voices an "undersound"—her
"tone of meaning" but lacking "the words." It is always the
speech, and never the music, that the Frostean protagonist
is striving to hear and to decipher. "To hear is almost to
understand," says Santayana,[13] but Frost and Stevens would
make very different things of this observation. Frost will won-
der whether a natural noise is whispering a text, for sounds
are almost like visual hieroglyphic signs. He will produce
keener demarcations, ghostlier sounds; Stevens will be over-
whelmed with the music of our own listening.[14]

    This distinction is particularly noticeable with respect to
the two poets' respective kinds of attention to bird song.
Frost's sonnet about the ovenbird is exemplary: the poem
addresses itself to the philosophical bird whose song cele-
brates midpoints, whose inflections do not hymn but ques-
tion ("what to make of a diminished thing"). The cry of the
ovenbird is traditionally called "Teacher! teacher!" Stevens
hears birds singing "Preacher! preacher!" and turns away in
weary distaste; or, they say "Creature! creature!" calling him
to a mode of the erotic to which he will not dance. At best,
he will hear their songs as asserting their own exemplariness
("Feature! feature!"?). The "warblings early in the hilarious
trees / Of summer, the drunken mother" ("Meditations
Celestial & Terrestrial" [CP, 124]) do in fact undo him a bit.
"A passionately niggling nightingale," however, is the hymn

and flight of the vulgar ("The Comedian as the Letter C"
[CP, 35]), and it heads a catalogue of problematic songbirds
throughout Stevens' poetry.

"Autumn Refrain" is a sad and beautiful poem, and its
attempt to take up again the rejected nightingale of moon-
light from "The Comedian as the Letter C" is fraught with
the presence of silence. The silence, when it comes, is both
acoustical—the silence of not being able to hear anything—
and rhetorical—the silence of having nothing to utter.

> The skreak and skritter of evening gone
> And grackles gone and sorrow of the sun,
> The sorrows of sun, too, gone . . . the moon and moon,
> The yellow moon of words about the nightingale
> In measureless measures, not a bird for me
> But the name of a bird and the name of a nameless air
> I have never—shall never hear. And yet beneath
> The stillness of everything gone, and being still,
> Being and sitting still, something resides,
> Some skreaking and skrittering residuum,
> And grates these evasions of the nightingale
> Though I have never—shall never hear that bird.
> And the stillness is in the key, all of it is,
> The stillness is all in the key of that desolate sound.
>
> (CP, 160)

Harold Bloom has pointedly called this poem "a debate be-
tween the grackles and Keats," associating the "skreak and
skritter" here with the "blatter" of those same grackles in
"The Man on the Dump" and their other unpleasant appear-
ances.[15] The Keatsian nightingale may sum up a whole tradi-
tion for Stevens. There are in America neither larks nor
nightingales of the kind that have astonished English poets
for their invisible voices; there are only copies of the poems
about them. There are no sweetly singing English blackbirds
here, only grackles, named with a skreakingly assonantal
diminution of "blackbirds," worldly gutturals below the sing-
ing of more heavenly labials. But I wonder whether the
nightingale is not Milton's as much as it is Keats'; the for-
mer's first sonnet broods on the voice of the nightingale and

wonders what it could mean. Is it an emblem of love or of poetry? Virginal to the first, already significantly affianced to the second, the young poet complains to the bird that "thou from year to year hast sung too late / For my relief." For Stevens, it is not that the bird sings too late but that it is all too late in the year and in the day, and always will be. There will be no easily audited poetic bird for Stevens. The "skreaking and skrittering residuum" that lies below stillness is hardly a cosmic music, itself a residuum of the demythologized music of the spheres that for George Eliot lay "on the other side of silence." Even that residuum has been internalized. It "grates these evasions of the nightingale," but this statement, too, is rhetorically problematic: the typical Stevenson ambiguity lies in the "of—" phrase (archetypally, in "the malady of the quotidian," where the meanings "the malady that the quotidian condition entails," "the malady *called* the quotidian" and "the malady that *marks* it" are, significantly, not sorted out). Two evasions are grated, and their very identification is part of the poem's concern: the "measureless measures" of the old nightingales are themselves evasions, and, if used at too late a time, doubly so. But the world of grackles and the stillness that is *their* residuum are evasions in another sense. They are necessary ones, performed lest the first evasions that *are* the bird's song be unwittingly espoused in the belief that they are direct confrontations.

This is certainly, as Bloom suggests, the poem of a silent time, and it is forced back on its own meager musical resources.[16] The refrain here is not provided by any bird song or cricket chirp from without, nor is there any of the hum and bustle of harvesting or the slow, "hours by hours" drip of some sweet *Spätlese*. The refrains in the poem are generated by its own words, repeated elegiacally as refrainlike phrases, or, almost parodistically, as conjoined word—"the moon and moon." The anapestic cadence first heard in "but the name of a bird" itself becomes a prosodic refrain, closing the whole poem with its last occurrence, which underscores the second of two corollaries about "stillness is all." The nightingale in this poem is not only like the later, blattering grackles (in "The Man on the Dump"), like Milton's later, prophetic nightingale, an "invisible priest"; he is silent, he is absent. The key of the residual sound totally contains, but is not to be identified with, silence; "that desolate sound" may only be breathing, and to that degree it is not to be associated with utter poetic death.

A word about the word "refrain." As designating a repeated line or phrase or burden, it comes from a romance term for "breaking off" (as to return again); but the verb "to refrain" (from a late Latin sense of "bridling, holding back") haunts this instance of its homonym, for the skrittering repetitions in the poem are necessitated by something (a bird, a muse, a poet) that has refrained from singing. This double refraining is all that there is, a kind of low point at the bottom of a parabola. The problem is what to make of an emptied thing—a capacity for singing, a trope for that capacity—and the poem provides no answer.

It is indeed only the continuing body of Stevens' work that will provide it, although when he can return to natural choirs and choruses of birds it will be to at least a mildly ironic accompaniment. The various instruments of metaphor that will be able to sing sufficiently of their own turnings will yield "The luminous melody of proper sound." The antiphonal choirs of "ké ké" and "bethou me" in the sixth canto of "It Must Change" both undo the traditional work of polyphonic harmony: the first moves toward a monotony, a dead unison, the second through a quickening mockery, through a touch of reintegrated skyey harmony (but only in default: "There was such idiot minstrelsy in rain, / So many clappers going without bells, / That these bethous compose a heavenly gong" [CP, 394]). But the chorded *bethous*, too, will fall toward that ultimate entropy of image, when trope hardens into statue and even into idol.

"A tune is a kind of tautology, it is complete in itself; it satisfies itself," observed Wittgenstein in another context. Well and good; but what if it satisfies itself only? The danger of changing and changing only to achieve this ungenerous and ungenerating situation is inherent in the unending

process of variation in Stevens' "music." Whether this con-
cerns figurations of sound, or what they are synecdochic for
(the figurative life that has become more than *merely* figura-
tive), or the rhetorical music that seems to embody the
figurations—Stevens' restless ear is always able to agitate
what it is hearing, and his tunes, of whatever sort, never
rise to tautological purity. There is a hint of this problem
in the questioning of the pianism of B. in "Esthétique du
Mal":

> A transparence in which we heard music, made music,
> In which we heard transparent sounds, did he play
> All sorts of notes? Or did he play only one
> In an ecstasy of its associates,
> Variations in the tones of a single sound,
> The last, or sounds so single they seemed one?
>   (CP, 316)

There are monotonies of variation as well, and Stevens is
constantly revising his own mode of variation, backtracking
when necessary, denying significance of the wrong or easy
sort, emptying a sound of sense in order to refill it.

> Item: The wind is never rounding O
> And, imageless, it is itself the most,
> Mouthing its constant smatter throughout space.
>   ("Montrachet-le-Jardin" [CP, 263])

Stevens adduces the very problematic character of half-articu-
lation in the course of unfolding a more complex catalogue,
but the assertive value of, at least, the semiotically dirty,
mumbled smattering over the possibility of the O (itself half-
glossed by the preceding line's "an inaccessible, pure sound")
is still clear. (Frost, a schoolmasterly decipherer, would de-
vote himself to comprehending the smatter.)

One of the problems of Stevens' musical program is to
create that smatter throughout the depths of his poetic lan-
guage. It is not only in the realm of trope that the demarca-
tions become more ghostly, but also at the surface of scheme,
where the sounds are more keenly heard. His poetry contains

an encyclopedia of one kind of echo: that play of sound
sounding like sense in verse, that game of rhyme and asso-
nance and alliteration used as implicit copulas of predication,
that has occupied English verse since Shakespeare. Fre-
quently, these games will play upon logical confusions of use
and mention, a marriage of meta-object and meta-languages.
The protagonist of "Anglais Mort à Florence," for whom the
music of Brahms began to fail, remembers when it did not
and when he could feel and see the moon "In the pale
coherences of moon and mood" (*CP*, 149). These coher-
ences are themselves those of the assonance, and when Ste-
vens employs his famous arrays of purely onomatopoetic syl-
lables, he is doing something very like extracting the "ooo"
from the sentimental correspondences. The level of figurative
rhetorical music, the so-called music of poetry in the dimen-
sion that Pope explored in the famous passage about sound
and sense in the *Essay on Criticism*, misled many early critics
of Stevens into thinking of it as dandified nonsense, as high-
flown joking about elevation of voice. But he was as serious
about the music of his own verse as about anything external,
and this provides an additional layer of complexity for the
analysis of his images of music.

Stevens is always conceiving words

> As the night conceives the sea-sounds in silence,
> And out of their droning sibilants makes
> A serenade.
> ("Two Figures in Dense Violet Night" [*CP*, 86])

And he does so even as evening turns the sibilance of the
stressed syllables in the first of these lines into the proper
initial phoneme of "serenade." The very operation of seman-
tic punning on the word and its designatum is the operation
of poetic music. The phonetic and thematic kinds of music
come together elegantly and somewhat sadly in "Mozart,
1935":

> Poet, he seated at the piano.
> Play the present, its hoo-hoo-hoo,

> Its shoo-shoo-shoo, its ric-a-nic,
> Its envious cachinnation.

But the present throws stones on the roof of the poet practicing arpeggios, and as for

> That lucid souvenir of the past,
> The divertimento;
> That airy dream of the future,
> The unclouded concerto . . .
> The snow is falling.

The mingling of another voice from that of the pianist proper is required, although this is no romantic blending of piano and wind sighing in willows. The wind is the wintry follower of Shelley's autumnal voice, and the injunction to fuse wind and words move in the opposite direction to Shelley's. The poet-pianist is urged

> Be thou the voice,
> Not you. Be thou, be thou
> The voice of angry fear,
> The voice of this besieging pain.

> Be thou that wintry sound
> As of the great wind howling. . . .
>   (CP, 131-32)

As if it were not enough to be oneself (be the *voice*, not *you*), it is only after that other voice has been absorbed that "We may return to Mozart," amid the snow and the streets "full of cries." The properly prepared poet can now be urged to take his place at the properly prepared piano: "Be seated, thou." (The "be thou" here is, syntactically, still Shelley's; a next stage of rewriting this injunction will be to convert the phrase to a punning verb, as in the sixth canto of "It Must Change.") The poem itself has properly prepared music to serve as a metaphor for poetry in an aftertime (Mozart "was young, and we, we are old") by combining three kinds of poetic music: *musica instrumentalis* (or, literally, music, piano and orchestral, by, say, Mozart); *musica mun-*

dana, realized in its romantic form as natural noise of wind; and *musica loquacitatis,* the verbal music of Stevens' own poetic language. And even the older romantic fiction of blending or mingling the sounds is reworked, schematically, in the poem.

But this metaleptic process is at work in Stevens all the time, in so many areas of imagery.[17] Music used naively is like all manifestly available public mythologies; for the imagination, they are all like statues, immobile. Metaphors reached down from a shelf cannot descend, as do resonant tenors in their shining vehicles, to ransom us from deadly literalness. Stevens represents such tropes "whom none believe" as "A pagan in a varnished car" ("The Man with the Blue Guitar" [CP, 170]); in a figure as wittily self-descriptive as anything in Stevens, the "polished car" of the new star at the end of Milton's "Ode on the Morning of Christ's Nativity" has become tarnished for the imagination as it gets varnished for reuse. As with the metaphor of music for poetry, so with the "music" of nature. In Frost as well as in Stevens, we have seen a general transfiguration of the music of nature, but in Stevens there is an additional complexity. The very music, as it were, of that transfiguring, the sounds of the act of the mind—itself part of that natural music— must undergo renewal.

So that when we find in the late poems a return to what would have seemed withered figures of music as the vehicles for poetry, as the tenor of natural noise, it is not the result of any exhaustion. The lightly troped, almost Tennysonian choruses of bells in "To an Old Philosopher in Rome," the imitative soundscape of the defunctive music in "Madame La Fleurie" ("The black fugatos are strumming the blacknesses of black . . . / The thick strings stutter the finial gutturals" [CP, 507]), the dampened dove of "Song of Fixed Accord," are all surely instances of this renewal. "Things of August" is almost explicit about it:

> These locusts by day, these crickets by night
> Are the instruments on which to play

> Of an old and disused ambit of the soul
> Or of a new aspect, bright in discovery. . . .

And Stevens can conclude:

> Nothing is lost, loud locusts. No note fails.
> These sounds are long in the living of the ear.
> The honky-tonk out of the somnolent grasses
> Is a memorizing, a trying out, to keep.
>   (CP, 489)

And, most certainly, the unidentified bird's cry in "Not Ideas about the Thing but the Thing Itself" is part of that very ancient claiming of musical status for natural sound by the language of poetry. The "scrawny cry from outside" is no self-generated echo but comes truly from outside; no mere cockcrow heralding light, no ké-ké or bethouing from the coppice, but rather a voice more like the "frail, gaunt and small" appearance of a darkling thrush at Hardy's coppice gate. In thin lines of verse and by means of a scrawny pun (on the letter *c* and the musical pitch it names) its unqualified heralding is made clear:

> That scrawny cry—it was
> A chorister whose c preceded the choir.
> It was part of the colossal sun,
>
> Surrounded by its choral rings,
> Still far away. It was like
> A new knowledge of reality.
>   (CP, 534)

The initial consonant of *cry, chorister, choir, colossal, choral* (and *coral* and *coronal* as well) is the note to which all the choired words are tuned, a synecdoche of the ever-primal sun —no mere alarm-clock bird, the text of whose song is the light to which it awakens one. The music of that cry, extracted by the meanest and scruffiest of poetic arts, is nonetheless an affirmation of the continuing possibilities of a world of music and sound in which more is heard than meets the ear.

FRANK KERMODE

DWELLING POETICALLY IN
CONNECTICUT

THE LAST POETRY OF WALLACE STEVENS, WHICH MAY
be his greatest, seems not to have found the critic who can
speak for it. The present essay will not do so, for my purpose
is the marginal one of reflecting on various interests that we
know Stevens to have had in his last years, in the hope that
they may have some relevance to those venerable poems.
They are mostly poems of death, or of the achievement of a
posture in which to meet it correctly. Stevens was a correct
man. There was also a proper mise en scène for poetry; he
cared for the physical presentation of his and other people's
poems, as if their disclosures, even the most exalted, the clos-
est to a final truth, required the art of the typographer and
the gold, leather, and linen of the binder as accompaniments
to revelation. Propriety is not always satisfied by grays and
blacks; ideas, poems, and persons may need or deserve some
decorous slash of vivid color from the remoter parts of the
lexicon, some gaiety. Or, if they do not deserve it, they should
get it: "Merit in poets is as boring as merit in people" (Ada-
gia, OP, 157).

In these years Stevens was also interested in Friedrich
Hölderlin, who also knew that merit was not enough: "Full
of merit, yet poetically / Man dwells on the earth." And
because of Hölderlin he looked toward the poet's great ex-
plainer, the philosopher Martin Heidegger. Whether he ever
found Heidegger is an interesting question. Between them,
Hölderlin and Heidegger form a kind of model of that com-
posite poet, virile youth and old tramp, who seized on Ste-
vens' imagination. But Stevens himself was not very like

them. For him the poetical, the supererogatory grace might be a gaiety, "light or color, images," or a gilt top edge. Like Hölderlin, he thought of the poet as "the priest of the invisible"; but unlike him, he would choose a wild word with sane care and give his poems wry titles to make them self-ironical. Like Heidegger, he thought of poetry as a renovation of experience; unlike him, he thought that the truth in the end did not matter. And even as he grew old, Stevens was never the tramp, as he had never been the virile youth. The encounter of being with death was not far off, but there was time for these interests, the well-made typeface or rich binding, the Germans, mad and obscure.

As for the fine bindings and limited editions, Stevens came to like them more and more, and not only for his own poems. He wrote letters to printers and binders about the way books should be produced. He told his editor, Katharine Frazier, that he would rather rewrite lines in *Notes toward a Supreme Fiction* than have ugly turnovers in the printed copy (*L*, 407). Later he had bibliopegic correspondence with Victor Hammer, a Viennese who operated first the Anvil Press in Lexington, Kentucky, and then the Aurora Press at Wells College. In 1946 he bought Janet Lewis' *The Earth-Bound*, beautifully published by Mr. Hammer, and negotiated for a bookplate. On January 22, 1948, he wrote to Hammer ordering a copy of his limited edition (fifty-one copies only) of Hölderlin's *Poems 1796-1804*—"I read German well enough," he remarked—and he later thanked Hammer for the book in terms that bore entirely upon the beauty of the printing (*L*, 576, 681). He spoke not of Hölderlin's art but of Mr. Hammer's.

It was not unimportant to Stevens that Hammer was living in Kentucky. Reality changes, he observed, and "in every place and at every time the imagination makes its way by reason of it." He thought of this Viennese printer in Kentucky and reflected that "A man is not bothered by the reality to which he is accustomed, that is to say, in the midst of which he has been born. He may be very much disturbed by reality elsewhere, but even as to that it would be only a question of time" (L, 577). He wondered whether Hammer could procure him a drawing of a necessary angel by Fritz Kredel. Mr. Kredel was "to state in the form of a drawing his idea of the surroundings in which poor people would be at rest and happy." A few weeks later he explained why this was desirable, referring to his "Angel Surrounded by Paysans": "there must be in the world about us things that solace us quite as fully as any heavenly visitation could." The plan was given up; perhaps Kredel could not see that particular angel (L, 656, 661, 662-63).

Although he said nothing about the contents of Hammer's *Hölderlin*, Stevens was presumably interested in them. He had recently acquired a German edition of the *Gedichte*, published in 1949. This book is described in the catalogue of the Parke-Bernet sale of Stevens' books (March 1959) as a small folio, full niger morocco, gilt fillets on sides, gilt edges. "In a morocco-edged linen slipcase. . . . A SUMPTUOUS BOOK PRINTED WITH A SPECIALLY CUT TYPE-FACE AND PRINTED ON HAND-MADE PAPER." Angels visiting the poor were, for Stevens, none the worse for top-edge gilt, even though they might themselves claim to have no "wear of ore" and to "live without a tepid aureole." Still, he must have looked inside this splendid package. He was certainly reading *about* Hölderlin, for example, an essay by Bernard Groethuysen, which he read in May 1948. Four years later he discovered that "Heidegger, the Swiss philosopher," had written a little work on Hölderlin, and he asked his Paris bookseller, Paule Vidal, to find him a copy. He would prefer, he said, a French translation, "But I should rather have it even in German than not have it at all" (L, 758).

As it happens, his local bookseller could have provided him with the essay in English, for a translation of the *Erläuterung zu Hölderlins Dichtung* was included in a collection of essays by Heidegger, *Existence and Being*, in 1949. Perhaps its workaday appearance would not have suited Stevens in any case. He asked Mme Vidal for a copy from "some bookseller at Fribourg." Probably she did not find one, for when Stevens' Korean friend Peter H. Lee was in Freiburg in June 1954, Stevens wrote asking him about Heidegger in terms that do not suggest close acquaintance with his work: "If you attend any of his lectures, or even see him, tell me about him because it will help to make him real. At the moment he is a myth, like so many things in philosophy." At the end of September, still unsatisfied and still apparently under the impression that Heidegger was Swiss, he asked Lee whether the philosopher lectured in French or German (L, 839, 846). That letter was written two days before the publication of *Collected Poems*, three before Stevens' seventy-fifth birthday, and less than a year before his death. At that late date his knowledge of Heidegger seems scanty enough, more myth than reality. The only certain fact is that Stevens was mixing up the Swiss and German Freiburgs, which is why he used the French form of the name of the city and referred to Heidegger as Swiss. He can therefore have known nothing of the philosopher's brief tenure as the Nazi-appointed rector of Freiburg University. It is an odd mistake, if one reflects that Heidegger spent about as much time outside of Germany as Stevens did out of the United States.

Still, he must have heard talk of Heidegger and the Hölderlin essays (though he mentions only one). His belated career as a lecturer and reader at colleges and universities had made him acquainted with philosophers—people who did their probing deliberately, he said, and not fortuitously, like poets. But we can be sure that he did not know Heidegger, even in French, as he knew, for example, Emerson, Santayana, and William James. Heidegger's was a book he did not, as a reader, "become." Years before, a philosophy professor had asked him why he did not take on a "full-sized" philosopher, and, when asked by Stevens to name some, included C. S. Peirce on the list. In his relation of this episode to Theodore Weiss, Stevens added, "I have always been curious about Pierce [*sic*], but have been obliged to save my eyesight for THE QUARTERLY REVIEW, etc" (L, 476). Since his correspondent was the editor of *The Quarterly Review*, we must take this as banter, but all the same, he probably meant that he preferred being curious about Peirce to reading him.

Perhaps for his purposes a smattering of knowledge was more useful than an understanding. Some image of Heidegger in his peasant clothes, darkly speculating upon his hero and supreme poet, precursor of the angel most necessary when, after the failure of the gods, our poverty is most complete, suited Stevens better than a whole philosophy, however vatic in expression. Perhaps the notion of this venerable man as having thought exhaustively about death and poetry and about the moment of their final encounter was enough. Stevens would try by his accustomed channels to acquire the sage's book, but if it did not come, it would still be interesting to know how he looked and what language he spoke in his Freiburg lecture room, in the midst of his accustomed reality.

It is sometimes argued that Stevens' poems are suffused with the philosophy of others, indeed, that they are sometimes virtually paraphrases of such philosophies, so that the sense of, say, "The Bird with the Coppery, Keen Claws" must be sought in William James' *The Pluralistic Universe*.[1] However that may be, the focus here is on something else. Heidegger thinking about Hölderlin—his great poet of the Time Between the failure of God and the birth of a new age, and of the sense in which man dwells poetically on earth —was meditating on the essence of poetry, its disclosures of being and its relation with death, which completes and annihilates being. He was probing these matters as deliberately as his extraordinary pre-Socratic manner allowed, and the text he meditated was the text of a schizophrenic seer who also loved those philosophic origins and sought to subvert the civil languages that had supervened upon them. Perhaps, borrowing Housman's joke, one could say that Stevens was a better poet than Heidegger and a better philosopher than Hölderlin, and so found himself, in a manner, betwixt and between. But there he was in the accustomed reality of Connecticut, meditating these very problems, probing fortuitously, and commenting on his own text. The projects were related. It was a leaden time; when reality is death, the imagination can no longer press back against it. When you live in "*a world that does not move for the weight of its own heaviness*" (NA, 63), you may imagine how differently it might appear to a young virile poet, but in the end you must find out for your aging self how that weight is to be lifted, what fiction will transform death.

In "The Poet's Vocation," Hölderlin calls upon the angel of the day (*des Tages Engel*) to awaken the people, stupefied by their world, and enable them to help the poet by interpreting him. But even if he is denied that help, he goes on all the same

> And needs no weapon and no wile till
> God's being missed in the end will help him.[2]

Stevens was capable of a fair degree of rapture at the poetic possibilities opened up by the death of God; indeed, on this point he is less gnomic than his precursor. But like Hölderlin, he also felt the cold: "wozu Dichter in dürftiger Zeit?" (Ham., 250). What are poets for in the time of poverty? is a question he often asked in his own way. In his own way he also maintained, though his obscurities are not Hölderlin's, that "Voll Verdienst, doch dichterisch, wohnet der Mensch auf dieser Erde [full of merit (what would be a better translation?), yet poetically, man dwells on this earth]" (Ham., 600-601).[3] Does the approach of death make this a little difficult to see?

In his essay "Effects of Analogy" (1948), Stevens proposes: "Take the case of a man for whom reality is enough, as, at the end of his life, he returns to it like a man returning from Nowhere to his village and to everything there that is tangible and visible, which he has come to cherish and wants to be near. He sees without images. But is he not seeing a clarified reality of his own? Does he not dwell in an analogy?" (NA, 129). He thinks that the being-toward-death, as Heidegger would call it, finds its form in the roofs, woods, and fields of a particular accustomed reality. It is a theme not altogether remote from that of Hölderlin's "Homecoming" ("Heimkunft"). And it is central to Stevens. The place where the poet dwells, especially if it is his place of origin, will be his *mundo*, a clarified analogy of the earth he has lived in, the more so as death approaches. In the same essay he explains that a poet's sense of the world, his sense of place, will color his dealings with death. James Thomson has a melancholy sense of the world; his place was a city of dreadful night, and he writes "We yearn for speedy death in full fruition, / Dateless oblivion and divine repose." Whitman, on the other hand, speaks of a "free flight into the wordless, / Away from books, away from art, the day erased, the lesson done. . . ."[4] Stevens does not enlarge upon these disclosures. They are effects of analogy; death is understood analogously, the last reality has the color and the shapes of a clarified reality of one's own. In "Imagination as Value," delivered as he approached his seventieth birthday, Stevens spoke of Pascal as one who, for all his hatred of the imagination ("this superb power, the enemy of reason"), clung "in the very act of dying" to the faculty that, however "delusive," might still create "beauty, justice and happiness" (NA, 135-36). As Pascal needed it to comprehend his death, so the poet needs it, especially in a time when "the great poems of heaven and hell have been written and the great poem of the earth remains to be written" (NA, 142).

The point is Heideggerian; Stevens does not quote Heidegger here, one feels, only because he had not read him. Instead, he thinks of Santayana, whom he had known well at Harvard fifty years before. He thinks of him as one who gave the imagination a part in life similar to that which it plays in art. For the art of dying depends on our having dwelt poetically on earth. And so Santayana in old age "dwells in the head of the world, in the company of devoted women, in their convent, and in the company of familiar saints, whose presence does so much to make any convent an appropriate refuge for a generous and human philosopher. . . . there can be lives in which the value of the imagination is the same as its value in arts and letters and I exclude from consideration as part of that statement any thought of poverty or wealth, being a *bauer* or being a king, and so on, as irrelevant" (NA, 148). Reflecting on Santayana's death in a letter to Barbara Church (September 29, 1952), he thinks again of one who abandoned poetry for thought but made this imaginative gesture, the choice, for a long old age, of a Roman convent, of a kind of poverty (he "probably gave them all he had and asked them to keep him, body and soul" [L, 762]), of an image of oncoming death founded in the accustomed reality of prayer, liturgy, and the earthly city, which, being the heart of one world, may be the figure of another, the more so if, in dwelling poetically, we dwell in analogy. So the poem he might have written for Heidegger became a poem for Santayana.

"To an Old Philosopher in Rome" is about such dwelling, and about the moment when accustomed reality provides a language for death, invents it, as it invents its own angels, by analogy. The poem straddles the threshold, "the figures in the street / Become the figures of heaven. . . . The threshold, Rome, and that more merciful Rome / Beyond, the two alike in the make of the mind" (CP, 508). It is, one may say, a great poem, though perhaps not wholly characteristic of Stevens in the persistence with which it fills out its scenario of antitheses: "The extreme of the known in the presence of the extreme / Of the unknown"; the candle and the celestial possible of which it is the symbol, life as a flame tearing at a wick; grandeur found in "the afflatus of ruin," in the "Profound poetry of the poor and of the dead"; splendor in poverty, death in life. It is language accommodating itself to that which ends and fulfills being, an image of that "total grandeur." This is a grandeur made of nothing but the bed, the chair, the moving nuns, the bells, and newsboys of the *civitas terrena*; but it is total, and the only image of a grandeur still unknown.

Note also that it is *easy*: "How easily the blown banners change to wings." Somehow it has become easy to find heaven in poverty's speech. The ease is the "ease of mind" mentioned at the beginning of "Prologues to What Is Possible," where the rowers are sure of their way, and "The boat was built of stones that had lost their weight and being no longer heavy / Had left in them only a brilliance, of unaccustomed origin" (CP, 515). The voyager easily passes into the unfamiliar—into death—as if it were the known. I do not mean that for Stevens this step is always easy, only that there is a kind of comfortable grace in some of his accounts of the threshold, an absence of what might be called, after Heidegger, *care* (to say nothing of dread), a grace that arises from acquiescence in the casual boons of the world of poverty, even at the moment when suffering caused by the absence of the gods might be most acute.

Heidegger called Hölderlin the poet of the Time Between —between the departure and the return of the gods—the midnight of the world's night. Stevens is consciously a poet of the same time. His answer to Hölderlin's question, "wozu Dichter?" (which Heidegger took as the title of his astonishing lecture on the twentieth anniversary of the death of Rainer Maria Rilke), would not be, in essence, different from either the poet's or the philosopher's. He had long been trying to make poetry out of commonplaces, for instance, in *Owl's Clover* in the thirties, and in 1949 he said that in "An Ordinary Evening in New Haven" his interest was "to try to get as close to the ordinary, the commonplace and the ugly as it is possible for a poet to get. It is not a question of grim reality but of plain reality. The object is of course to purge oneself of anything false" (L, 636). At the end of that poem reality, plain reality, is given some of the imagery of death: "It may be a shade that traverses / A dust, a force that traverses a shade" (CP, 489). Those "edgings and inchings of final form," those statements tentatively closing in on the real, are in their way a figure for the imagination's edging and inching toward the comprehension of death. Hence, too, the idea of self-purgation; the moral and the poetic functions of imagination grow toward identity and in virtually the same way labor to include death in being. Death is a threshold, the commonplace on one side of it, its transcendent analogue on the other, as the Santayana poem at once asserts.

And that notion is much prefigured, for Stevens is a poet of thresholds: even summer is a threshold and, in "Credences of Summer," an image of death. At the end of "The Auroras of Autumn" the "scholar of one candle" opens his door and sees across the threshold "An Arctic effulgence flaring on the frame / Of everything he is. And he feels afraid" (CP, 417). Finally, the supreme poet understands, out of the partial fact that we are "An unhappy people in a happy world":

> In these unhappy he meditates a whole,
> The full of fortune and the full of fate,
> As if he lived all lives, that he might know,
>
> In hall harridan, not hushful paradise,
> To a haggling of wind and weather, by these lights
> Like a blaze of summer straw, in winter's nick.
>
> (CP, 420-21)

Here all the accustomed realities are known and accommodated to a summerlike brilliance in an icy world. Hölderlin would have called this poet a servant of the wine god, bearing all such care, seeing that blaze on behalf of all, imagining everything for them, including death. Knowing poverty ("His poverty becomes his heart's strong core" [CP, 427]) is the means to find a way through the world, which "Is more difficult to find than the way beyond it" (CP, 446). This is what Stevens calls the will to holiness. It is a favorite word of Hölderlin's. Wozu Dichter? They must dwell in their huts, their accustomed reality, framed by their commonplace thresholds and do all that angels can—intimate, by use of a perhaps delusive faculty, what lies beyond, the fullness of the encounter when Being has inched and edged its way to death. Santayana's choice of Rome as a place to die is a poet's choice; he seeks out this central city as affording the structures, the rituals, even the ritual compassions, that, out of accustomedness, the imagination confers on death. "These are poems," wrote Randall Jarrell of The Rock, "from the other side of existence, the poems of someone who sees things in steady accustomedness, as we do not, and who sees their accustomedness, and them, as about to perish."[5] Or, as Stevens himself puts it, "The thing seen becomes the thing unseen" (*Adagia, OP,* 167). Nevertheless, as he states elsewhere in the *Adagia,* "The poet is the intermediary between people and the world in which they live . . . but not between people and some other world" (*OP,* 162). Thus, in concerning himself with death, the poet must concern himself with the poverty of the accustomed, with the mystery of dwelling poetically in its midst. And perhaps, as Hölderlin remarked, "God's being missed in the end will help him." Perhaps it will also help him to see the poet's words comfortingly coated in the adventitious splendors of decorative bindings, rendered easy by sharp, clear type, the blessings of richness in poverty, of ease in the world of care.

Stevens was quite right to be curious about Heidegger and to want to know what the philosopher said about Hölderlin. The intense meditation on poetry that Heidegger produced in the series of works inaugurated by the 1936 essay on Hölderlin represents, in a way, the fulfillment of an ambition evident in Stevens' prose. Stevens could not achieve it fully for various reasons. The desire for ease could have been one. Then again, his philosophy, as he himself admitted, was a philosophy of collects, an amateur's philosophy. Heidegger was professional as well as incantatory; he thought as the pre-Socratics (or some of them) thought, poetically. But he thought accurately. Albert Hofstadter says that as a thinker Heidegger did what a poet does: *dichtet.*[6] Like the poet, he was concerned with "the saying of world and earth," with their conflict—not unlike the conflict of world and *mundo* in Stevens—and so with the place of all nearness and remoteness of the gods. "Poetry is the saying of the unconcealedness of what is. Actual language at any given moment is the happening of this saying." This is the *truth,* for Heidegger looked to the etymological meaning of *alētheia,* which is "unconcealedness." Thus, although it sets up a world, the work of art also *lets the earth be an earth.* "As a world opens itself the earth comes to rise up." And so it happens that "art

is the becoming and happening of truth." All art is in essence
poetry, a disclosure of the earth, a "setting-into-work of
truth." The appearance of this truth is beauty.[7]

There are times when Stevens would have recognized this
voice as that of a remote kinsman in poetry, for example, in
the "thinking poem" "Aus der Erfahrung des Denkens"
("The Thinker as Poet"):

> When the early morning light quietly
> grows above the mountains. . . .

> The world's darkening never reaches
> to the light of Being.

> We are too late for the gods and too
> early for Being. Being's poem,
> just begun, is man. . . .[8]

Or, one can just imagine these aphorisms occurring in the
Adagia:

> Poetry looks like a game and yet it is not.

> Poetry rouses the appearance of the unreal and of dream
> in the face of the palpable and clamorous reality, in which
> we believe ourselves at home. And yet . . . what the poet
> says and undertakes to be, is the real.[9]

Yet the affinity, I think, goes beyond these resemblances.
It is of course mitigated by differences of a kind at which
I have already hinted; Stevens was less bold, less willing to be
oracular than Heidegger. And then there is the matter of
those new typefaces and fine bindings: wear of ore for the
angel of accustomedness, precursors of a transfigured com-
monplace, patches of Florida in the world of books. Like-
wise, there are the *trouvailles* and the collects and the for-
tuities of dizzle-dazzle that interrupt disclosures of pure
poverty. But for all that, there is an affinity.[10]

If we think of the idea of dwelling and death we may come
to understand this affinity. "Poetically man dwells on this
earth," said Hölderlin. In the poverty of the Time Between,
one establishes this dwelling by finding the poetry of the

commonplace, in the joy of Danes in Denmark, in the cackle
of toucans in the place of toucans, in Elizabeth Park and
Ryan's Lunch. Stevens did it over and over again, observing
the greater brilliancies of earth from his own doorstep. He
dwelt in Connecticut as Santayana dwelt in the head of the
world, as if it were origin as well as threshold. He wanted to
establish Hölderlin's proposition, and every reader of Stevens
will think of many more instances of his desire to do so.
Freiburg, Fribourg, were elsewhere. The foyer, the dwelling
place, might be Hartford or New Haven, Farmington or
Haddam. The Captain and Bawda "married well because the
marriage-place / Was what they loved. It was neither heaven
nor hell" (CP, 401). It was earth, and the poetry of the
earth was what Hölderlin sought and Heidegger demanded.
Stevens was always writing it and naming the spot to which
it adhered. This is what poets are for in a time of need.
They provide a cure of that ground; they give it health by
disclosing it, in its true poverty, in the nothing that is. The
hero of this world, redeemer of being, namer of the holy,
is the poet. Stevens has many modest images of him, yet
he is the center. In that same central place Heidegger sets
Hölderlin and adorns him with words that have special
senses: *truth, angel, care, dwell.*

Heidegger gave the word "dwell" a special charge of
meaning. Drawing on an old sense of the German word, he
can say that "Mortals dwell in that they can save the earth,"
that is, "set it free in its own presencing," free, as Stevens
would say, of its man-locked set. There is much more to
dwelling,[11] but I will mention only that to dwell is to initiate
one's own nature, one's being capable of death as death,
"into the use and practice of this capacity, so that there
may be a good death." Furthermore, "as soon as man *gives
thought* to his dwelling it is a misery no longer"; so out of
its insecurity and poverty ("man dwells in huts and wraps
himself in the bashful garment," says Hölderlin;[12] "a single
shawl / Wrapped tightly round us, since we are poor . . . ,"
says Stevens [CP, 524]) he can build, can make poetry.[13] For
Heidegger is here meditating on Hölderlin's enigma, that we

dwell poetically on this earth, even in a time of destitution, and that our doing so is somehow gratuitous, independent of our merits, a kind of grace.

Where one dwells is one's homeland, and to return to it is to see it in its candid kind. Heidegger's first essay on Hölderlin is about the elegy "Homecoming," a poem of serenity and angels but also of the poet who names the town and makes it "shine forth." The angels are best summoned in one's homeland because the "original essence of joy is the process of becoming at home in proximity to the source."[14] The gods have failed, the poet "without fear of the appearance of godlessness . . . must remain near the failure of the god until out of that proximity the word is granted which names the High One." For he is the giant of the time that follows the default of the god. He is the first among men; others must help him by interpreting his word (which is the life of the world) so that each man may have his own homecoming.

In a second essay on Hölderlin, Heidegger deepens these apprehensions and speaks of the godlike power of his poet. Man has been given arbitrariness, and he has been given language, with which he creates and destroys and affirms what he is. What he affirms is that he "belongs to the earth and gives it being: Only where there is language is there world." (The "words of the world," says Stevens, "are the life of the world" [CP, 474].) The naming of the gods ("This happy creature— It is he that invented the Gods" [OP, 167]) was only the first act by which language—poetry—established Being. To dwell poetically is to stand in the proximity of being; when the essence of things receives a name, as the gods once received a name in the first poetic act, things shine out.[15] These things are commonplace and accustomed till thus named: only then is it the case that "The steeple at Farmington / Stands glistening and Haddam shines and sways" (CP, 533).

The completion and delimitation of Being come with death, with *my* death, for we cannot think authentically about the deaths of others. Heidegger had written much about this in *Being and Time,* and he thought about it in relation to poetry in essays written between 1947 and 1952, when Stevens' not dissimilar meditations were in progress and when he was saying he would like to read Heidegger. Only on the subject of care, on the necessity of speaking heavily and with radical plainness of being and ending, might he have found in the German a weight as of stones he chose not to lift.

But perhaps, after all, Stevens did know something about *Being and Time.* Perhaps it was knowing about it that sent him looking, in his seventies, for news of what that Swiss philosopher might have to say about his supreme poet. Heidegger wrestled with ideas we all wrestle with: the potentiality of no more being able to be there, he remarks, is the inmost, one might say the own-most, potentiality. We have many ways of estranging death; for example, we say, "Everybody dies," or "one dies." So we conceal our own "being-toward-death"; yet death is the "end" of Being, of *Dasein*— and the means by which it becomes a whole. To estrange it, to make it a mere fact of experience, is to make it inauthentic. Being understands its own death authentically not by avoiding that dread out of which courage must come but by accepting it as essential to Being's everydayness, which otherwise conceals the fact that the end is imminent at every moment. There must be a "running forward in thought" to the potentiality of death.

Only where there is language is there world, says Heidegger; and only where there is language is there this running in thought, this authentication of death. It is the homecoming that calls for the great elegy; it is "learning at home to become at home," as Heidegger says of the Hölderlin elegy.[16] "All full poets are poets of homecoming," he says. And he insists that Hölderlin's elegy is not *about* homecoming; it *is* homecoming. Stevens knew this, whether he learned it from Heidegger or not. He knew the truth of many of Heidegger's assertions, for example, about the nature of change in art. "The works are no longer the same as they once were. It is they themselves, to be sure, that we encounter . . . but they themselves are gone by."[17] The work of art "opens up a world and at the same time sets his world back again on earth."[18] The perpetuation of such truth is the task of an impossible philosopher's man or hero. Stevens' poet works in the fading light; the "he" of the late poems has to make his homecoming, has to depend on his interpreters to make it for themselves and understand that it is impermanent. The advent of the Supreme Poet, who would stop all this, is like the return of the god. Heidegger's most impressive meditation on this coming event is in the lecture on Rilke, "Wozu Dichter?" (1946). The time is completely destitute; the gods will return only when the time is free. Poets in such a destitute time must "sense the trace of the fugitive gods" and, in dark night, utter the holy. Of this night Hölderlin is the poet. Is Rilke such a poet? Certainly he came to understand the destitution of the time, a time when even the trace of the holy has become unrecognizable, and there is lacking "the unconcealedness of the nature of pain, death and love."[19] Certainly he understood the need for "unshieldedness" and the need to "read the word 'death' without negation." But it is not certain that he attained the full poetic vocation or spoke for the coming world era, as Hölderlin did.

The long, dark essay on Rilke is finally beyond the scope of Stevens. But Stevens knew that language makes a world of the earth and includes death in that world; he knew that it effects the unconcealment of the earth, that this is the poet's task in a time of destitution and seclusion. He could imagine a vocation for a supreme poet. Sometimes he could speak or chant of these things majestically enough, but in the last poems he would not dress the poet in singing robes. The poet is, mostly, at home and old, shambling, shabby, and human. He does not say " 'I am the greatness of the new-found night' " (OP, 93). But he accepts that what one knows "of a single spot / Is what one knows of the universe" (OP, 99). His Ulysses strives to come home; he seeks a new youth "in the substance of his region" (OP, 118), in its commonness, like that of the great river in Connecticut, which one comes to "before one comes to the first black cataracts" (CP, 533) of the other, Stygian river.

It should be added that the "he," the poet, of some of the last poems, can be a "spirit without a foyer" and search among the fortuities he perceives for "that serene he had always been approaching / As toward an absolute foyer . . ." (OP, 112). It is a different version of the running-toward-death, and Heidegger would have approved of that "serene," for Hölderlin used the word and his glossator turned it over many times in his mind. Is this ordered serenity too easy? When we climb a mountain "Vermont throws itself together" (OP, 115); Vermont does the work, provided, of course, that we climb the mountain. It is not quite easy, but it is of the essence that it is also not quite difficult. The greatest image of the being at the threshold of death is, I suppose, "Of Mere Being," a poem that is also, one may be sure, very late. It contains a foreign song and a foreign bird. There is dread in it. Heidegger, I dare say, would have admired it, but there is no reason to suppose that he would have been less severe on Stevens than on Rilke.

So one forces them together, Hölderlin-Heidegger in Freiburg or Fribourg, and Stevens in Hartford. But Stevens always draws back, as if to examine a binding or to keep some distance between himself and a mad poet or a very difficult philosopher. "Philosophical validity," he assured a correspondent in 1952, was no concern of his; "recently," he added, "I have been fitted into too many philosophic frames" (L, 753). Perhaps the Heidegger frame would have pleased him better than most; for one thing, Heidegger's thought is very different from any that Stevens was accustomed to think of as philosophical. But Stevens would have drawn back. Not to find a copy of *Existence and Being* was, in a way, to draw back, to seek Heidegger instead in Paris, where his bookseller knew the kind of book he liked, and it would arrive like something exotic. Then again, there was a crucial difference of origin: Stevens was an American in America,

Heidegger a German in Germany (not Switzerland), all life long. Part of this difference is reflected in varying styles of solemnity, in the fact that Heidegger is wholly without irony, while Stevens always has it within call.

There was an affinity between the ways they felt the world and understood poetry; between the truths they disclosed in the night of destitution by dwelling poetically in—that is, by saving—their worlds. Stevens had something of the quality that made Heidegger describe Hölderlin as himself having that third eye he attributed to Oedipus; he was virtually talking about it in the last lines of "The Auroras":

> he meditates a whole,
> The full of fortune and the full of fate,
> As if he lived all lives, that he might know. . . .
>
> (CP, 420)

But few could have refused more obstinately the fate of Hölderlin. For Stevens the world was by no means always a haggling of wind and weather or even of an *unheimlich* "serene." It was often, perhaps daily, a place of ease, of "Berlioz and roses" if that happened to be "the current combination at home" (L, 505), of postcards from Cuba, tea from Ceylon—fortuities of earth that solace us and make a world, or, like the Tal Coat painting that hung in his house in these years, an angel of reality. Such, too, though more elegant and more ornate, were the finely printed books of Mr. Hammer, a Viennese "without a foyer" but now growing accustomed to the reality of Kentucky, whence he might send surrogate angels to Connecticut. There dwelt the poet, watching the shining of the commonplace (occasionally, a distant palm, an unclassifiable, fire-fangled bird) and, for the most part, easy among his splendid books, though soon to die.

J. HILLIS MILLER

THEORETICAL AND ATHEORETICAL
IN STEVENS

IN AN ESSAY DESCRIBING THE CHANGES IN OCCIDENTAL thought associated with the names of Marx, Freud, and Nietzsche, Michel Foucault has said: "l'interprétation est enfin devenue une tâche infinie. . . . A partir du XIXᵉ siècle, les signes s'enchaînent en un réseau inépuisable, lui aussi infini, non parce qu'il reposent sur une ressemblance sans bordure, mais parce qu'il y a béance et ouverture irréductibles." Foucault relates this opening of an abyss of interpretation to the "refus du commencement" in Freud, Marx, and Nietzsche. The work of all three suggests that in the activity of interpretation it is impossible to go back to an unequivocal beginning that serves as the foundation of everything that follows. Whenever the interpreter reaches something apparently original, a genetic source behind which it is impossible to go, he finds himself, on the contrary, encountering something that is itself already an interpretation. The apparent source itself refers to something still farther back, and that to something behind it, ad infinitum. "Il n'y à rien d'absolument premier à interpréter, car au fond, tout est déjà interprétation, chaque signe est en lui-même non pas la chose qui s'offre à l'interprétation, mais interpretation d'autres signes."[1]

One example at this abyss of interpretation is the way many modern poems are poems about poetry. They contain within themselves discussions of what they are and of what they mean. They enact or embody in themselves that function of poetry about which they explicitly talk. Moreover, a poem like Wallace Stevens' "The Man with the Blue Guitar" or "A Primitive Like an Orb" does not express a single unequivocal theory of poetry. For Stevens, as for so many other modern writers, the theory of poetry is the life of poetry, and nothing is more problematical or equivocal than the theory of poetry. Stevens' poetry is therefore not merely poetry about poetry. It is a poetry that is the battleground among conflicting theories of poetry, as the poet tries first one way and then another way in an endlessly renewed, endlessly frustrated attempt to "get it right," to formulate once and for all an unequivocal definition of what poetry is and to provide an illustration of this definition.

The various theories of poetry that generate in their conflict the vitality of Stevens' poetic language are not, however, modern inventions. They are not tied to a particular time in history. Nor is it an accident that just those theories are present and that the poet cannot choose among them. The conflict among three theories of poetry is as old as our Western tradition. It goes back to Plato and Aristotle, and behind them to their precursors. It may be followed through all the languages and cultures that inherit the Greek tradition, the tradition, as it has been called, of Occidental metaphysics. Moreover, the conflict among these three theories of poetry is woven into the fabric of our language. It is present in the fundamental metaphors and concepts of our speech. To use that language is to be caught in a weblike interplay among terms that makes it impossible to adopt one theory of poetry without being led, willy-nilly, to encounter the ambiguous inherence within it of the other two. The three theories are not, then, alternatives among which one may choose. Their contradictory inherence in one another generates the meditative search for "what will suffice" in Stevens' poetry.[2]

One theory of poetry operative in Stevens' work is the idea that poetry is imitation, mimesis, analogy, copy. Truth is measured by the *adequatio* between the structure of words and the structure of nonlinguistic reality. Poetry is mirroring or matching at a distance, by analogy. The structure of the poem should correspond to the structure of reality. Things as they are on the blue guitar must match things as they are in nature. This "Aristotelean" theory of poetry as imitation has been dominant down through all the centuries since

Aristotle, for example, in nineteenth- and twentieth-century theories of realism in narrative fiction.

Already in Aristotle, however, the notion that poetry is imitation was inextricably involved with the theory of poetry as unveiling, as uncovering, as revelation, as *alētheia*. Poetry is not a mirror but a lamp. The words of poetry are that within which the truth comes to light. This assumes that reality, things as they are, is initially hidden. Language is what discovers things, that is to say, reveals them as what they are, in their being. Martin Heidegger's "Der Ursprung des Kunstwerkes" is a distinguished modern essay exploring the definition of art as *alētheia*,[3] but a key passage of Aristotle's *On the Art of Poetry* already turns on the conflict between poetry as imitation and poetry as revelation. "As to its general origin," says Aristotle,

> we may say that Poetry has sprung from two causes, each of them a thing inherent in human nature. The first is the habit of imitation; for to imitate is instinctive with mankind; and man is superior to the other animals, for one thing, in that he is the most imitative of creatures, and learns at first by imitation. Secondly, all men take a natural pleasure in the products of imitation. . . . The explanation of this delight lies in a further characteristic of our species, the appetite for learning; for among human pleasures that of learning is the keenest. . . .[4]

Imitation, argues Aristotle, is natural to man, part of man's nature, therefore part of nature, not opposed to it as the lie is to the truth. Imitation is not only natural to man. It is also natural for him to take pleasure in it. He takes pleasure in it because he learns by it. He learns by it the nature of things as they are, which without this imitation in words would be invisible. The *logos* as being comes into the open by way of the *logos* as words. The *logos* as the one is caught and expressed in the *logos* as the many, as differentiated, as dramatic action, as metaphor.

Poetry, according to this second theory, is an act. It is the act of the mind seeking a revelation through the words and in the words. Poetry is a revelation in the visible and reasonable of that which as the base of reason cannot be faced directly or said directly. Aristotle's example of that which cannot be shown directly on the stage because it is irrational is Oedipus' murder of Laius, the son's murder of the father. In the same way the poetry of imitation, the *logos* captured in language, is the annihilation of the *logos* as the hidden one. This annihilation cannot be shown directly, though it is the source of all poetry, for the moment of the origin of language cannot be shown in language: "in the events of the drama itself there should be nothing that does not square with our reason; but if an irrational element cannot be avoided, it must lie outside of the tragedy proper, as in the case of Sophocles' *Oedipus the King*."[5] In the same way, in stanza XXVI of "The Man with the Blue Guitar," Stevens speaks of "the murderous alphabet" (*CP*, 179). Poetry is the filial inheritor of the paternal energy or will in nature that will subjugate that father. As for Aristotle the murder of Laius cannot be shown directly, so for Stevens the "nothing that is" stands between the poet and the subject of his poetry. Both imagination and reality are liable at any moment to turn into this nothing, the "blank at the base." "Reality is a vacuum" in one of the *Adagia* (*OP*, 168). In stanza XII of "The Man with the Blue Guitar" the poet in his strumming picks up "That which momentously declares / Itself not to be I and yet / Must be. It could be nothing else" (*CP*, 171). In "The Snow Man" Stevens speaks of "Nothing that is not there and the nothing that is" (*CP*, 10). A movement of thought parallel to that of Aristotle in *On the Art of Poetry* may be found in stanza XIX of Stevens' "The Man with the Blue Guitar":

> That I may reduce the monster to
> Myself, and then may be myself
>
> In face of the monster, be more than part
> Of it, more than the monstrous player of

One of its monstrous lutes, not be
Alone, but reduce the monster and be,

Two things, the two together as one,
And play of the monster and of myself,

Or better not of myself at all,
But of that as its intelligence,

Being the lion in the lute
Before the lion locked in stone.

(CP, 175)

For Stevens, as for Aristotle, imitation is natural to man; therefore the imagination is part of nature or one of the forces of nature. In imitation, nature comes into language so that language is part of nature too. In poetry the *logos* or "being" comes to be in language. Poetry is the "intelligence" of nature. Stevens is not satisfied to produce poetry that is adjacent to nature or merely part of it. He must "reduce the monster," engulf him, appropriate the monster entirely to himself. When the two have become one, then poetry will not be "about" nature but will be the "intelligence" of nature speaking directly. Only then can the poet "be himself" in the face of the monster. Poetry is the destruction of things as they are when they are played on the blue guitar. It is the defeat of the lion in the stone by the lion in the lute.

In one of his letters to Renato Poggioli Stevens provides a commentary on stanza XIX of "The Man with the Blue Guitar":

Monster

= nature, which I desire to reduce: master, subjugate, acquire complete control over and use freely for my own purpose, as poet. I want, as poet, to be that in nature, which constitutes nature's very self. I want to be nature in the form of a man, with all the resources of nature = I want to be the lion in the lute; and then, when I am, I want to face my parent and be his true part. I want to face nature the way two lions face one another—the lion in the lute facing the lion locked in stone. I want, as a man of the

imagination, to write poetry with all the power of a mon-
ster equal in strength to that of the monster about whom
I write. I want man's imagination to be completely ade-
quate in the face of reality. (L, 790)

The Oedipal drama, the son's mortal battle with his father,
is muted in stanza xix itself, but emerges openly in the com-
mentary in the letter. The poet must face his "parent" na-
ture and appropriate his sexual power, "be his true part."
Only in this way can man's imagination be completely
adequate in the face of reality.

There is, however, still a third theory of poetry present in
Stevens' poems. This is the notion that poetry is creation,
not discovery. In this theory, there is nothing outside the
text. All meaning comes into existence with language and
in the interplay of language. Meaning exists only in the
poem. "The Man with the Blue Guitar" is poetry about
poetry. It is meta-poetry, a poetry of grammar in which what
counts is the play of words among themselves. Words are
repeated, grammatical forms change and alter, and the same
word is verb, adjective, noun, in turn.[6] "The Man with the
Blue Guitar" is poetry about poetry also in the sense that
the poem itself is the action about which it talks. The perva-
sive metaphor of a man playing the guitar is the action of the
poem itself as it takes shape. The true subject is the poem
as an activity. The words about guitars and tunes are the
construction blocks of a poem that accomplishes what the
metaphor only talks about. Language is always referential.
There must be real guitars in order for there to be a word
"guitar." Nevertheless, the word "guitar" in the poem, in its
interplay with all the other words, effaces any real guitar in
its poetic operation. As the word "guitar" is absorbed into its
interaction with other words and comes to draw its meaning
from that interaction, any referential base gradually disap-
pears and is finally abolished. Even the guitar of Picasso,
which seems as if it might be referred to by the central
image, is irrelevant. This may explain why Stevens in a letter
told Poggioli, gently but firmly, that he did not want Picas-

so's *Man with a Guitar* on the cover of Poggioli's Italian translation of a group of Stevens' poems (*L*, 786).

An interplay between metaphor and reality in which the two change places, like the hermetic egg mentioned by William Butler Yeats, which turns inside out constantly without breaking its shell, is characteristic of the structure of thought I am trying to identify. Plato, for example, must use the "metaphor" of "inscription" to describe the good kind of writing in the soul, though writing is for him secondary and derived.[7] In the same way, Yeats must use sexual metaphors to describe the intradivine life: "Godhead on Godhead in sexual spasm begot / Godhead."[8] Things below are copies," but that which is copied can come into language only by way of the transfers of metaphor. In that sense, things above are copies of what is below. Aristotle describes metaphor—"the application to one thing of the name that belongs to another"—as the fundamental instrument of poetry: "But most important by far is it to have a command of metaphor. This is the one thing the poet cannot learn from others. It is the mark of genius; for to coin good metaphors involves an insight into the resemblances between objects that are superficially unlike."[9] The difficulty, however, is to decide in the labyrinth of interchanges which is the metaphor, which the literal origin. In "The Man with the Blue Guitar," the "realistic level," that is, the words describing a man with a guitar, turns out to be the derived, metaphorical level. The words and images of the poem describe the activity of the poem itself. Moreover, the language of the poem is made up of the interplay between language about reality and language about the mind in which the two change places continuously. An example is all the terms for air, weather, or atmosphere, which describe not only the external weather but "air" as melody or as behavior. Words describing the world must be used to describe the mind, for there are no literal words for subjective events. Nevertheless, the things of the external world accede to language only through words. Words are products of the imagination, so that things as they are are things as they are said on the blue guitar, according to this third of the three theories of poetry that are woven inextricably together in the text of "The Man with the Blue Guitar."

My explanation of Stevens by way of the presence in his work of three traditional theories of poetry is, the reader will have noticed, an example of that interpretation by way of origins that I began by challenging, with the help of Foucault. Multiple origins are still origins and imply a causal accounting, however contradictory. The power of Stevens, the power in fact of any great writer, cannot be explained by any of its sources. Holly Stevens' recent *Souvenirs and Prophesies* is a presentation, with commentary, of her father's early journals and poems. It is a good place to investigate further this question of origins.

The interest of *Souvenirs and Prophecies* is partly anecdotal. If one admires (that is hardly the word) Wallace Stevens' poetry, one is interested in every scrap of information about Stevens the man. It is nice to know that the author of "Notes toward a Supreme Fiction" was once a somewhat mawkish, sentimental, moody, shy, socially awkward young man. This young man wrote indubitably bad verses ("Some of one's early things give one the creeps," he wrote in 1950). He earnestly exhorted himself to work hard and to rise in the world. He sometimes smoked too many cigars and drank too much, made resolutions about not drinking and smoking, and then broke them, recording the breakings with defiant verve in his journal, as in the entry for July 26, 1903, written soon after Stevens graduated from New York Law School and took up his clerkship in W. G. Peckham's office:

> I've just been reading my journal. A month or two ago I was looking forward to a cigarless, punchless weary life. *En effet*, since then I have smoked Villar y Villars & Cazadores, dine at Mouquin's on French artichokes & new corn etc. with a flood of drinks from crème de cassis melée, through Burgundy, Chablis etc. to sloe gin with Mexican cigars & French cigaroots. I have lunched daily on—Heav-

en's knows what not (I recall a delicious calf's heart
cooked whole & served with peas—pig that I am). . . .
(SP, 115-16)

The Stevens who emerges from these early journals is on
the whole an engaging youth. He is calculated to encourage
later youths to write more bad verses in the hope that these
may be, as Stevens' were, the prelude to greatness. But "hang
it," as Stevens says of the Frenchman who called the Cana-
dian Rockies low, "one wants more." Most readers will
search out *Souvenirs and Prophecies* for clues to the mean-
ings and sources of Stevens' mature poetry. We want to
know where that poetry comes from and how to read it.
Even in the light of the best secondary studies the major
poems remain to a considerable degree opaque. They speak
with indubitable authority and power. They have the accent
of greatness. Nevertheless, they resist analysis. The most pow-
erful attraction of *Souvenirs and Prophecies* is the reader's
hope that he may find some help in dissolving this opacity.
This is the lure of explanation by origins, the *post hoc ergo
propter hoc*. Somehow, where Stevens began must be capable
of explaining where he went.

To a considerable degree the reader's hunger for help is
satisfied. *Souvenirs and Prophecies* shows that the young
Stevens was already absorbed by the turn of the seasons; the
circuits of the sun and moon fascinated him. Already he saw
the sun as a king: "The day of the sun is like the day of a
king. It is a promenade in the morning, a sitting on the
throne at noon, a pageant in the evening" (April 20, 1904
[SP, 135]). Clouds, stars, flowers, birds, the whole panoply of
colors ("God! What a thing blue is!" he wrote on April 18,
1904 [SP, 133]), that abiding double fantasy of a green
mountain range on the one hand and "a warm sea booming
on a tropical coast" (SP, 145), on the other—all these are
already present in the early journals. There also are the vague
outlines of Stevens' particular version of the ancient Occi-
dental metaphysical system of concepts involving the pres-
ence of the present and the fleeting revelation of being in the

vanishing of the instant. This conceptual system is associated always in Stevens, as in the Western tradition generally, with the rising and setting of the sun. The reader will find evidence in Stevens' journals of his early interest in the tradition of the maxim: La Rochefoucauld, Pascal, Leopardi, "Schopenhauer's psychological observations" (*SP*, 160), etc. This interest flowered in the *Adagia* and in the aphoristic discontinuities so important in the poetry. Support would also be found in *Souvenirs and Prophecies* for a demonstration of Stevens' complex relation to the romantic tradition. He read Wordsworth, Shelley, Keats, Emerson, Whitman, and Santayana, but also Nerval, Schopenhauer, Nietzsche, and Leopardi. (This relation has been explored in Harold Bloom's distinguished book on Stevens, *Wallace Stevens: The Poems of Our Climate*.) The reader will find, finally, in what he learns in *Souvenirs and Prophecies* of Stevens' relations to his parents and of his courtship of Elsie Moll, the outlines of his version of the "family romance," a romance dramatized continuously in the later poetry.

All these relations between the Stevens of the early journals and poems and the Stevens of the great later poetry would support explanations by genetic cause. Nevertheless, the authentic voice of Stevens as a poet is not touched by such explanations. That voice is something unpredictable, savage, violent, without cause or explanation, irrational—as he always knew genuine poetry must be. It is both a voice and a way of writing. It is something continuous, a murmuring or muttering, sometimes a sing-song rhyme or a stammering alliteration. Continuously present, it is nevertheless a principle of discontinuity. It forbids explication by sources. It breaks both into the formal order of thought and into the formal order of shapely poetry. This voice appears intermittently and faintly even in these early journals and poems, as in the passage about the calf's heart quoted above. Of course it is much more evident in the poetry beginning with *Harmonium* and after, as in "Bantams in Pine-Woods" ("Chieftain Iffucan of Azcan in caftan / Of tan with henna hackles, halt!" [*CP*, 75]), or in "The Man with the Blue

Guitar" ("To strike his living hi and ho, / To tick it, tock it, turn it true, / To bang it from a savage blue, / Jangling the metal of the strings . . ." [CP, 166]), or in "Montrachet-le-Jardin" ("O bright, O bright, / The chick, the chidder-barn and grassy chives / And great moon, cricket-impresario, / And, hoy, the impopulous purple-plated past, / Hoy, hoy, the blue bulls kneeling down to rest. / Chome! clicks the clock . . ." [CP, 260]), or in "The Owl in the Sarcophagus" ("she that in the syllable between life / And death cries quickly, in a flash of voice, / Keep you, keep you, I am gone, oh keep you as / My memory, is the mother of us all . . ." [CP, 432]).

The intrusion of this doubling voice is figured in Stevens, among other ways, by the constant presence, just below the level of rational thinking, of the guitarist with his interminable strumming ("Nothing about him ever stayed the same, / Except this hidalgo and his eye and tune . . ." [CP, 483]), or it is figured in that other sail of Ulysses, doubling the first one and "Alive with an enigma's flittering" (OP, 105). The presence of this "enigma"—in the words and yet not directly named by the words—forbids any understanding of Stevens' poetry by way of origins in his family, in his reading, in the "Western tradition," in "Occidental metaphysics," in the landscapes of Pennsylvania, New Jersey, and Connecticut, or even in some intrinsic irrational property of language. In the end, the greatest value of Souvenirs and Prophecies is that now and then the early writing shows the first flitterings of this groundless enigma. Occasionally a strange voice appears between or behind the young Stevens' words. This is that austere and impersonal "Chome!" without which Stevens would not be the great poet he is.

To identify this disrupting element in Stevens' poetry, if it is neither imitation, nor "Being," nor merely the play of language, would require a full reading of his work. Even then, it may be that the identification would be a discovery of what cannot be named or identified in so many words, even figurative ones. In "A Primitive Like an Orb" the sun, "at the centre on the horizon" (CP, 443), the presumed literal object for which the rest of the poem is a series of figurative displacements strung in appositive chains, cannot be named directly, just as the sun cannot be looked at directly. To name the sun "literally" would falsify the perpetual movement of the "as" structure of the poem. According to this structure, whatever may be named or seen is "an illusion, as it was, / Oh as, always too heavy for the sense / To seize, the obscurest as, the distant was . . ." (CP, 441). The title of the poem, "A Primitive Like an Orb," exemplifies a linguistic structure in which the word "sun," if it were to be cited, would become in its turn only another figure for the "essential poem at the centre of things" (CP, 440). Only as not cited literally, as effaced, absent can the word "sun" retain its status as the literal name for something that can be perceived, viewed with the naked eye, "theoretically," taking "perceived" in both the etymological sense of "seen" and in the conceptual sense of "logically understood." If the theory of poetry is the life of poetry, it is also the case that "Poetry must resist the intelligence almost successfully" (OP, 171). The moment when the poem ceases to resist the intelligence and can be "seen through" theoretically may be the moment when the poem fails. It then fails any longer to bear a relation, even figurative, to that "Chome!" the essential poem at the center of things, which may be neither named, nor seen, nor possessed theoretically.

ROY HARVEY PEARCE

TOWARD DECREATION: STEVENS AND THE "THEORY OF POETRY"

TO THE MEMORY OF MICHAEL BENAMOU
(1929-1978)

> The theory of poetry is the theory of life.
> (*Adagia, OP*, 178)

COMING UPON THE WORD "DECREATION," STEVENS OF course came upon just that—a word, not a concept.[1] For the concept had been almost from the outset integral to what he came compulsively to call the theory of poetry. Compulsively, because that theory, could it be perfect, would support his need to solve in poems the romanticist subject-object problem, which was set for him by his understanding of the role of the poet in the modern world. Granting the presence, however varying, of the *concept* of decreation in Stevens' *oeuvre*, we must observe that the word "modern" is the operative term in the last sentence of this, the well-known passage in "The Relations between Poetry and Painting" (1951):

> This [new] reality is, also, the momentous world of poetry. Its instantaneities are the familiar intelligence of poets, although it has been the intelligence of another ambiance. Simone Weil in *La Pesanteur et La Grâce* has a chapter on what she calls decreation. She says that decreation is making pass from the created to the uncreated, but that destruction is making pass from the created to nothingness. Modern reality is a reality of decreation, in which our revelations are not the revelations of belief, but the precious portents of our own powers. (*NA*, 174-75)

Now, treating of the reality/imagination problem, as is well known, is Stevens' central concern at the level of theory in the essays he collected in *The Necessary Angel* (1951). But it had, at least immanently, been his central concern in the practice of poetry almost from the beginning. By 1947, setting himself straight in the first of his "Three Academic Pieces," he is at once bold and succinct:

> We have been trying to get at a truth about poetry, to get at one of the principles that compose the theory of poetry. It comes to this, that poetry is a part of the structure of reality. If this has been demonstrated, it pretty much amounts to saying that the structure of poetry and the structure of reality are one or, in effect, that poetry and reality are one, or should be. This may be less thesis than hypothesis. (NA, 80-81)

One way of looking at the development of Stevens' poetry, then, would be to trace the development of hypothesis into thesis. And here decreation—first as a condition of the working of the imagination, then as a process, and finally as an integral component of poetic realization—is primary in Stevens' theory of poetry and in the working of the poems themselves.

I have said that the operative word in the passage I have quoted from "The Relations between Poetry and Painting" is "modern." Stevens himself in this essay prepares us for his emphasis on the word as he earlier sketches a brief history of French classicism, in whose period reality was not that of decreation, precisely because "revelations" could in fact be those of "belief." So too in a passage in "The Noble Rider and the Sound of Words" (1942) [NA, 12-15]). So too in a number of poems—"Sad Strains of a Gay Waltz" (1935), "Mozart, 1935" (1935), the two parts of "Botanist on Alp" (1934, 1935), "Asides on the Oboe" (1940), and "Of Modern Poetry" (1940). The last named begins

> The poem of the mind in the act of finding
> What will suffice. It has not always had

To find: the scene was set; it repeated what
Was in the script.
          Then the theatre was changed
To something else. Its past was a souvenir.
It has to be living, to learn the speech of the place.
It has to face the men of the time and to meet
The women of the time. It has to think about war
And it has to find what will suffice. It has
To construct a new stage.

                    (CP, 239-40)

First Stevens defines the nature of poetry in the modern world, with its need to realize its special reality principle. Then he indicates that in the past, reality had somehow been different, during periods, to glance back at the passage I have quoted from "The Relations between Poetry and Painting," in which "revelations" of reality were indeed "revelations" of belief. What formerly sufficed no longer does, since finding is no longer repetition but rather what Stevens would come to call decreation—living by learning the speech of the place, itself uncreated, just perdurably there. The poems I have named were collected in *Ideas of Order* (1935) and *Parts of a World* (1942), a period during which intellectual historians were discovering a series of past *Weltanschauungen* in which cultures were understood to be integrated to the degree that men's imaginings of reality—because it was made out to be "created"—were virtually guaranteed to be accurate. For those realities, specifically because they were under the aegis of a single unifying power, were tightly and coherently ordered to the degree that there had to be a consonance of the imagination and reality, of (to use the Emersonian terms) the Me and the Not-Me. In a letter of December 10, 1935, Stevens—as so often, in accord with the scholarship of the period—finds the right technical word for this situation: "myth" (L, 300). And in a letter of June 3, 1953, thinking about "The Comedian as the Letter C" (1923) in long perspective, he concludes that it is after all an "anti-mythological poem" (L, 778). That poem of course was first published

in *Harmonium*. Stevens' comment on it indicates, as I have
noted, that early on he viewed modern reality not as some-
thing so ordered as to lead to mythic understanding—this
via the consonance of imagination and reality—but as indeed
a reality of decreation.

In the poems of *Harmonium* (1923) and of *The Man with
the Blue Guitar* (1937), decreation is a condition of the
imagination as it is operative on reality. The imagination
must be brought to grant that reality, given, in and of itself
exists prior to and independent of such transformations that
the imagination may and in fact does work on it. The imag-
ination cannot absorb reality, yet it cannot do what it must
do unless in so doing it acknowledges the absolute and sep-
arate existence of reality. The alternative at this stage is pro-
duction or reduction—seeing the world, and thus transform-
ing it, or thinking about it, and thus decreating it. Stevens'
method here, when decreation is involved, is quite simply the
method of reduction—or negation—as a way of thinking
about the world. But what is reduced/negated is not the
world, reality (for that is by definition impossible), but
rather the imagination itself. Such a reduction/negation is,
however, only temporary, a way on to a further stage; for as
I have said, quoting Stevens, in the course of projecting the
decreative process, the imagination discovers "the precious
portents of its own powers." The intention—it is as simple
as this—is to bring oneself to admit that there *is* a "reality,"
and so to conceive of the imagination in all its potential
freedom. Thus "Negations" (1918), which was originally
the seventh in the "Lettres d'un Soldat" sequence:

> Hi! The creator too is blind,
> Struggling toward his harmonious whole,
> Rejecting intermediate parts,
> Horrors and falsities and wrongs;
> Incapable master of all force,
> Too vague idealist, overwhelmed
> By an afflatus that persists.
> For this, then, we endure brief lives,

> The evanescent symmetries
> From that meticulous potter's thumb.
>
> (CP, 97-98)

Here the myth of the creator is rejected, proven wrong, ne-
gated, since no one can be "master of all force." What is left
is ourselves, facing up to the facts and conditions of our
"brief lives," which, in the necessarily short run, even if we
live beyond seventy, are our realities. The symmetries are
"evanescent," not, as Blake would have it, "fearful," precisely
because they are what Stevens, other poets, and writers about
poetry have come to call "myths."

In this stage of Stevens' "theory," then, decreation as a
condition of making poems marks a beginning, the accept-
ance of the limits of the imagination that is the necessary
condition of its exercise. At the end of "The Snow Man"
(1921) we are told what it would be like, not what it is, to
move all the way through the decreative process:

> the listener, who listens in the snow,
> And, nothing himself, beholds
> Nothing that is not there and the nothing that is.
>
> (CP, 10)

At the end of "Anecdote of the Jar" (1919) we are again
told, still analogically:

> It took dominion everywhere.
> The jar was gray and bare.
> It did not give of bird or bush,
> Like nothing else in Tennessee.
>
> (CP, 76)

And Stevens in the last section of "Nuances of a Theme by
Williams" (1918) addresses Williams' "ancient star" thus:

> Lend no part to any humanity that suffuses
> you in its own light.
>
> (CP, 18)

(It will be recalled that later, in 1934 and 1946, Stevens, for all his fondness for Williams' verse, found him somewhat too given to the "anti-poetic," and thus for a poet—for any man of imagination, as he was fond of saying—somewhat subservient to "reality" [OP, 254-58].)

A concern with decreation, and thus with the role of reduction and negation, is, to be sure, not the primary theme of the *Harmonium* poems. (In general, they portray and celebrate the imagination's productive transformations of reality.) But it is there often enough to let us see it as immanent even in Stevens' earliest work. I would cite as further examples "The Paltry Nude Starts on a Spring Voyage" (1919), "Fabliau of Florida" (1919), "Of the Surface of Things" (1919), "The Wind Shifts" (1917), and "The Indigo Glass in the Grass" (1919). And it is set forth with firmness and certitude in stanza v of "The Man with the Blue Guitar," as though the poet had once and for all, in his search for a theory of poetry, established for himself what is no less than a reciprocal relationship between decreation and creation:

> Do not speak to us of the greatness of poetry,
> Of the torches wisping in the underground,
>
> Of the structure of vaults upon a point of light.
> There are no shadows in our sun,
>
> Day is desire and night is sleep.
> There are no shadows anywhere.
>
> The earth, for us, is flat and bare,
> There are no shadows. Poetry
>
> Exceeding music must take the place
> Of empty heaven and its hymns,
>
> Ourselves in poetry must take their place,
> Even in the chattering of your guitar.
>
> (CP, 167)

The motif here—the capacity to face the sun-as-reality and its decreated earth ("flat and bare")—registers the full acceptance of man's (the imagination's, the mind's) condition vis-à-vis modern reality, a reality of decreation.

Since what is at issue in the *Harmonium* poems—and what is affirmed in "The Man with the Blue Guitar"—is acceptance, an affirmation of decreative condition, one could say that all this was Stevens' discovery, in his own "modern" terms, of Keats' "negative capability"—this as a condition of final "recreation." If so, it is appropriate to term Stevens' later emphasis on decreation as process and realization as moving, out of some historical necessity, into a "negating capability." That is, decreation is no longer just a stage or a state to be, however unflinchingly, taken into account. Now it has become a stage or a state to be worked through. On the way to what end? To authentic creation as in fact realization, recreation.

This is the end repeatedly emphasized in the essays collected in *The Necessary Angel*:

> The mind has added nothing to human nature. It is a violence from within that protects us from a violence without. It is the imagination pressing back against the pressure of reality. It seems, in the last analysis, to have something to do with our self-preservation; and that, no doubt, is why the expression of it, the sound of its words, helps us to live our lives. (NA, 36)

> Summed up, our position at the moment is that the poet must get rid of the hieratic in everything that concerns him and must move constantly in the direction of the credible. He must create his unreal out of what is real. (NA, 58)

> The accuracy of accurate letters is an accuracy with respect to the structure of reality.
>
> Thus, if we desire to formulate an accurate theory of poetry, we find it necessary to examine the structure of reality, because reality is the central reference for poetry. (NA, 71)

My final point, then, is that the imagination is the power that enables us to perceive the normal in the abnormal, the opposite of chaos in chaos. (NA, 153)

To create the unreal out of the real one must somehow come directly to know the real, not just accept and affirm its existence. This, I take it, is in general the end aspired to in the poems collected in *Transport to Summer* (1947). The central poem of those collected in that volume is of course "Notes toward a Supreme Fiction." Its centrality derives from the fact that, being one of the earliest published poems (1942) in the volume, it at once exemplifies and comprehends the place of decreation in the originative, initiating act out of which proceed virtually all the poems collected along with it. (I continue to think that "Esthétique du Mal" [1944] should be considered integral to the "Notes." Hence the titles of the sequence should read: "It Must Be Abstract," "It Must Change," "It Must Give Pleasure," and "It Must Give Pain.") If the intention of the "Notes" is to move us toward proposition-by-proposition understanding, then decreation is a necessary, mediating phase in the process. The first section of "It Must Be Abstract" commands:

> Begin, ephebe, by perceiving the idea
> Of this invention, this invented world,
> The inconceivable idea of the sun.
>
> You must become an ignorant man again
> And see the sun again with an ignorant eye
> And see it clearly in the idea of it.
>
> (CP, 380)

The young poet is instructed that he must grasp absolutely (per-ceive) the hard fact that reality (the "world") for him, even at its very source ("the sun"), can be known only as something discovered (in-vented, come upon), that for him it cannot be known as something created (conceived). What is at stake is accepting an even larger and harder fact, that of the nature of "invention" itself vis-à-vis what Stevens would come, in "The Relations between Poetry and Painting," to term "modern reality," that is, "invention" as in-vention, discovery, in no way as creation. And the necessary condition of such acceptance is a willingness to acknowledge that ignorance—the ignorance deriving from decreation—is a condition of whatever knowledge, whatever *kind* of knowledge, that poetry might in the long run generate. This granted, this affirmed, Stevens in the rest of the section can calmly and grandly proclaim that there is no "source" for reality, "modern reality": "Phoebus is dead. . . ." For us there can be no myths, chthonic or otherwise. And in what follows in "Notes toward a Supreme Fiction," Stevens, reminding us from time to time that decreation is a condition of the working of his poem, can as calmly and grandly maneuver his and our way toward that series of propositions that emerges from the parts of the "Notes" as their absolutely inevitable titles. Reality is "abstract," since to know it under the condition of decreation we must abstract from it the idea of a creator. "Change," "pleasure," and also "pain" are its attributes, since, once it is decreated, those are the affects of our "perceiving" it. Sponsored by no one, existing as nothing but uncreated *Ding an Sich*, reality necessarily yields to perception that at long last conceivable idea of a Supreme Fiction.

I have outlined elsewhere what I take to be the substance of the "argument" of "Notes toward a Supreme Fiction."[2] Here I mean to clarify further the mode of argument, and I am now ready to consider some poems in which decreation as process is explicitly the concern. For decreation as process is but implicitly the concern of the "Notes." Meditating on the real, Stevens is able to characterize its nature as the imagination (a violence within protecting us from the violence without, the agent whereby we may perceive the normal in the abnormal, the opposite of chaos in chaos), which lets us know and learn to live with it. Our God truly, in the words of one of the *Adagia*, turns out to be a postulate of the ego; yet reality—to look ahead—cannot in the "Notes" quite be conceived (discovered, de-created, and re-created) as the ground of our being, our Rock. "Notes toward a Supreme Fiction" is a powerful poem, perhaps a great poem. But it does not, as a poem, establish the conditions whereby a satisfactory (by Stevens' measure) theory of poetry could be generated. Indeed, I now see the poems collected in *Transport to Summer* (my notion of an extended "Notes" among them) as being preparatory for the transcending efforts of the poems collected in *The Auroras of Autumn* (1950) and the transcendent effort of the *Rock* sequence in the *Collected Poems* (1954).

Decreation as process is explicitly the concern of many of the post-"Notes" poems collected in *Transport to Summer*. (One should read "transport" in reference to both its old and new meanings.) In "The Motive for Metaphor" (1943) we (the poet addresses us as "you") are told why we shrink from decreative process; for would we/could we carry it through, we would have to bear "The weight of primary noon, / The A B C of being . . ." (*CP*, 288). In "No Possum, No Sop, No Taters" (1943) we are told that in this decreated scene, "It is here, in this bad, that we reach / The last purity of the knowledge of good" (*CP*, 294). In stanzas xx–xxii of "Chocorua to Its Neighbor" (1943), the mountain, decreating itself, addresses its shadow and discovers the source of its own being:

> Now, I, Chocorua, speak of this shadow as
> A human thing. It is an eminence,
> But of nothing, trash of sleep that will disappear
> With the special things of night, little by little,
> In day's constellation, and yet remain, yet be,
>
> Not father, but bare brother, megalfrere,
> Or by whatever boorish name a man
> Might call the common self, interior fons.
> And fond, the total man of glubbal glub,
> Political tramp with an heraldic air,
>
> Cloud-casual, metaphysical neighbor,
> But resting on me, thinking in my snow,

> Physical if the eye is quick enough,
> So that, where he was, there is an enkindling, where
> He is, the air changes and grows fresh to breathe.
>
> (*CP*, 300-301)

In "Crude Foyer" (1947), we are told

> That there lies at the end of thought
> A foyer of the spirit in a landscape
> Of the mind, in which we sit
> And wear humanity's bleak crown. . . .
>
> (*CP*, 305)

The motifs in these and other poems of their order in *Transport to Summer* are summed up in these lines from stanza v of "Repetitions of a Young Captain" (1944):

> On a few words of what is real in the world
> I nourish myself. I defend myself against
> Whatever remains.
>
> (*CP*, 308)

Not: I am master of all I survey. Rather: I can become master of all that surveys me.

What is at issue here is not only the decreative process insofar as the imgaination is capable of it or can bear it, but also the role of that process in the imagination's lifelong project of carrying out its task, at once realizing its own violence and somehow protecting itself against the realization:

> It is time that beats in the breast and it is time
> That batters against the mind, silent and proud,
> The mind that knows it is destroyed by time.
>
> ("The Pure Good of Theory," 1945 [*CP*, 329])

In "Credences of Summer" (1947), particularly in its seventh section (which, so he wrote in a letter of June 18, 1953 [*L*, 782], was one of his favorite parts of the poem), Stevens is quite explicit as regards the role of the decreative process:

> Far in the woods they sang their unreal songs,
> Secure. It was difficult to sing in face

Of the object. The singers had to avert themselves
Or else avert the object. Deep in the woods
They sang of summer in the common fields.

They sang desiring an object that was near,
In face of which desire no longer moved,
Nor made of itself that which it could not find . . .
Three times the concentred self takes hold, three times
The thrice concentred self, having possessed

The object, grips it in savage scrutiny,
Once to make captive, once to subjugate
Or yield to subjugation, once to proclaim
The meaning of the capture, this hard prize,
Fully made, fully apparent, fully found.

(CP, 376)

The singers have faced reality (the "object") and have re-
treated "far in the woods" to sing songs unreal because con-
ceived in the face of the real—in which, as they faced it,
they came to understand that they could not find themselves.
The dialectic (for that is what it is) of the making of their
songs is now understood to be of three stages: first, discovery
of the object as reality; second and alternatively, either sub-
jugating reality or being subjugated by it, that is, transfor-
mation or decreation; third, realization and celebration of
the meaning that man, having confronted reality either as
transformed or decreated, can give to his world. This last
stage, as it derives from the first alternative of the second
stage (transformation) yields poems of a dramatic or narra-
tive or purely lyrical nature, such as "Sunday Morning," "Le
Monocle de Mon Oncle," "The Emperor of Ice-Cream,"
"Bantams in Pine-Woods," and all the *Harmonium* poems
that are so easily available to us—easily, because as readers
we find it easier to work through the transformative than the
decreative mode. This last stage, then, as it derives from the
second alternative of the second stage (decreation), yields
meditative poems, ranging from cautious poems like "The
Snow Man" and "Anecdote of the Jar" to bold poems like

"Notes toward a Supreme Fiction," "Credences of Summer" itself, and the great work of *The Auroras of Autumn* and the *Rock* sequence—poems not easily available to us because, reading them, we must work through that decreative mode that requires denial and doubt as a condition of achievement and certitude.

Surely, by now we easily grant that Stevens is at his greatest as a meditative poet. Integral to the meditative mode, I suggest, is decreation. What makes Stevens' meditative poems so assuredly "modern" is precisely their attending to "modern reality" as a "reality of decreation." In them Stevens realizes the Carlylean proposition with which he had begun "The Well Dressed Man with a Beard" (1941):

> After the final no there comes a yes
> And on that yes the future world depends.[3]
>
> (CP, 247)

Whereas this poem ends with the statement that "It can never be satisfied, the mind, never," in the great later meditative poems the mind—working through the decreative process—can indeed find its satisfactions.

Increasingly, a criterion of formal excellence, of artistic achievement in Stevens' later poems becomes the *quality* of their dialectic, as much the analytic precision of their movement as the synthesizing capacity of their tropes, their language as *topoi*. Here, above all, the act of the mind is central. Stevens himself was, however uneasily, quite conscious of this fact. In a letter of May 3, 1949, he claimed that he had "never" had "any serious contact with philosophy," yet he went on to write:

> It may be that the title of my next book will be The Auroras of Autumn [the poem had been published about a year before], but this is some little distance ahead and I may not like that title by-and-by as much as I like it now. Nor is there anything autobiographical about it. What underlies this sort of thing is the drift of one's ideas. From the imaginative period of the Notes I turned to the ideas

of Credences of Summer. At the moment I am at work on a thing called An Ordinary Evening In New Haven. . . . But here my interest is to try to get as close to the ordinary, the commonplace and the ugly as it is possible for a poet to get. It is not a question of grim reality but of plain reality. The object is of course to purge oneself of anything false. I have been doing this since the beginning of March and intend to keep studying the subject and working on it until I am quite through with it. This is not in any sense a turning away from the ideas of Credences of Summer: it is a development of those ideas. That sort of thing . . . would have to do with the drift of one's ideas. (L, 636-37)

From this point on, what is paramount in Stevens' poems, the meditative poems, is precisely "the drift of [his] ideas," the "development of [his] ideas," variously moving through the three-stage dialectic of "Credences of Summer." If in decreation he can "purge [himself] of anything false," then, and only then, will he be able

> to proclaim
> The meaning of the capture, this hard prize,
> Fully made, fully apparent, fully found.
> (CP, 376)

I cannot understand the resistance of some of Stevens' exegetes to the fact of this dialectic and to the demands it put upon him, not to say them, to take with all seriousness poetry as "the act of the mind."

If we are to understand the poems collected in *The Auroras of Autumn* and the *Rock* sequence, we must above all attend to "drift" as it is transformed into dialectic, so as to achieve to the utmost possible limit a certain apodictic quality. "The Auroras of Autumn" (1948) succeeds marvelously in this mode. We are given successively, dialectically, a meditative lyric on evil itself figured as a serpent who is that Satan of "Esthétique du Mal" whom "a capital negation" (Satan: satan) had "destroyed," so that he must now be known as "uncreated," a fact of that reality which is life itself. Now, his true power and its locus admitted, he is truly *redivivus*, a violence among other violences. Then Stevens works through negations/decreations of a place and a situation, both of them warmly domestic, then a negation/decreation of what has just been negated/decreated:

> The cancellings,
> The negations are never final. The father sits
> In space, wherever he sits, of bleak regard,
>
> As one that is strong in the bushes of his eyes.
> He says no to no and yes to yes. He says yes
> To no; and in saying yes he says farewell.
>
> (CP, 414)

After the first four sections there follows a sequence in which there is announced that which is "fully made, fully apparent, fully found." In the last part of the final section Stevens writes:

> Turn back to where we were when we began:
> An unhappy people in a happy world.
> Now, solemnize the secretive syllables.
>
> Read to the congregation, for today
> And for tomorrow, this extremity,
> This contrivance of the spectre of the spheres,
>
> Contriving balance to contrive a whole,
> The vital, the never-failing genius,
> Fulfilling his meditations, great and small.
>
> In these unhappy he meditates a whole,
> The full of fortune and the full of fate,
> As if he lived all lives, that he might know,
>
> In hall harridan, not hushful paradise,
> To a haggling of wind and weather, by these lights
> Like a blaze of summer straw, in winter's nick.
>
> (CP, 420)

"[W]here we were when we began"—modern reality is a reality of decreation.

Stevens' control of the drift of his ideas is surest, I think, in "The Auroras of Autumn." There are of course other powerful poems in the volume named after that one, in particular "Large Red Man Reading," "The Ultimate Poem Is Abstract," "The Owl in the Sarcophagus," "A Primitive Like an Orb," "What We See Is What We Think," and, of course, "An Ordinary Evening in New Haven." And I would add to this list "The Course of a Particular" (1951). None of these, however, achieves, as regards the dialectical, meditative mode, the absolute precision and control of "The Auroras of Autumn." Suffice it to say nevertheless that they all quite systematically project that mode, again and again reaching triumphant and transcending conclusions, like the one from "A Primitive Like an Orb":

> That's it. The lover writes, the believer hears,
> The poet mumbles and the painter sees,
> Each one, his fated eccentricity,
> As a part, but part, but tenacious particle,
> Of the skeleton of the ether, the total
> Of letters, prophecies, perceptions, clods
> Of color, the giant of nothingness, each one
> And the giant ever changing, living in change.
>
> (CP, 443)

The "giant of nothingness" is at once lover, believer, poet, painter, altogether decreated, but by virtue of being decreated each is capable, should he work his fate all the way through, of being recreated and recreating.

Himself recreated and recreating, Stevens was able in the *Rock* sequence of the *Collected Poems* to achieve what I can only call transcendence. (We can count it among our worldly blessings that he lived long enough to bring the drift of his ideas to something of a stasis.) That sequence might well be called "Beyond Decreation." Although in the May 3, 1949, letter quoted above, Stevens denied that there was

anything "autobiographical" about the drift of his ideas, the
poems in the *Rock* sequence are autobiographical in a spe-
cifically American fashion, in which the poet, having moved
all the way through the stages of discovery, decreation, and
recreation, is now sure enough of himself, his role, and his
powers to discover himself for us as central, archetypal, fully
realizing "the precious portents of our own powers," because
they are the precious portents of *his* own powers.[4] In "The
Plain Sense of Things" (1952), which is marked by a mood
of calmness and certitude (transcendent as opposed to tran-
scending), he reviews the matter of the seventh section of
"Credences of Summer":

> After the leaves have fallen, we return
> To a plain sense of things. It is as if
> We had come to an end of the imagination,
> Inanimate in an inert savoir.
>
> It is difficult even to choose the adjective
> For this blank cold, this sadness without cause.
> The great structure has become a minor house.
> No turban walks across the lessened floors.
>
> The greenhouse never so badly needed paint.
> The chimney is fifty years old and slants to one side.
> A fantastic effort has failed, a repetition
> In a repetitiousness of men and flies.
>
> Yet the absence of the imagination had
> Itself to be imagined. The great pond,
> The plain sense of it, without reflections, leaves,
> Mud, water like dirty glass, expressing silence
>
> Of a sort, silence of a rat come out to see,
> The great pond and its waste of the lilies, all this
> Had to be imagined as an inevitable knowledge,
> Required, as a necessity requires.
>
> > (CP, 502-3)

The requirements of necessity, which derive from the require-
ments of decreation, are now known, if acknowledged and

lived through, to constitute the requirements, in the face of modern reality, of life itself: thus the component of auto-biography in these last poems.

Thus too, the actualizing of the ultimate poet, the hero, that possible, impossible philosopher's man. The Santayana of "To an Old Philosopher in Rome" (1952) is one such, because he knows and lives in the knowledge of

> The human end in the spirit's greatest reach,
> The extreme of the known in the presence of the
>   extreme
> Of the unknown.

Accordingly,

> It is a kind of total grandeur at the end,
> With every visible thing enlarged and yet
> No more than a bed, a chair and moving nuns,
> The immensest theatre, the pillared porch,
> The book and candle in your ambered room,
>
> Total grandeur of a total edifice,
> Chosen by an inquisitor of structures
> For himself. He stops upon this threshold,
> As if the design of all his words takes form
> And frame from thinking and is realized.
>   (CP, 508, 510-11)

Stevens' own transcendent certitude, the certitude of a man "seventy years later" reviewing his life—and in review-ing it first decreating and then recreating it—is fully made, fully apparent, fully found in "The Rock" (1954):

> It is not enough to cover the rock with leaves.
> We must be cured of it by a cure of the ground
> Or a cure of ourselves, that is equal to a cure
>
> Of the ground, a cure beyond forgetfulness.
> And yet the leaves, if they broke into bud,
> If they broke into bloom, if they bore fruit,

And if we ate the incipient colorings
Of their fresh culls might be a cure of the ground.
The fiction of the leaves is the icon

Of the poem, the figuration of blessedness,
And the icon is the man.

(CP, 526)

Modern reality, decreated, is no longer known just in terms
of its attributes (as in "Notes toward a Supreme Fiction").
Recreated, it is known directly, as man is at once integral to
and transcendent of it.

It is the rock where tranquil must adduce
Its tranquil self, the main of things, the mind,

The starting point of the human and the end,
That in which space itself is contained, the gate
To the enclosure, day, the things illumined

By day, night and that which night illumines,
Night and its midnight-minting fragrances,
Night's hymn of the rock, as in a vivid sleep.

(CP, 528)

But at the very end, surely, there is a cautionary note, a
suggestion of even the all-too-human limits of the poet as
hero. It is given only to old—and wise—men to integrate,
and thus to assuage, the violence within and the violence
without, to know modern reality directly, and that only
momentarily. In "The Bed of Old John Zeller" (1944; Zeller
was his grandfather, long since dead) Stevens had written:

It is more difficult to evade

That habit of wishing and to accept the structure
Of things as the structure of ideas. It was the structure
Of things at least that was thought of in the old peak
   of night.

(CP, 327)

In a poem on "the mythology of modern death," "The Owl
in the Sarcophagus" (1947), he had concluded of him who
would see deepest into reality:

It is a child that sings itself to sleep,
The mind, among the creatures that it makes,
The people, those by which it lives and dies.

(CP, 436)

In "Questions Are Remarks" (1949) he had written of one
who does not ask fundamental questions about reality:

He does not say, "Mother, my mother, who are you,"
The way the drowsy, infant, old men do.

(CP, 463)

In "Angel Surrounded by Paysans" (1950), the "angel of
reality," "the necessary angel of earth" in whose sight we
"see the earth again," tells us that he is "A figure half seen,
or seen for a moment . . ." (CP, 496-97). In "An Old Man
Asleep" (1947), the first poem in the *Rock* sequence, we are
instructed that only in sleep can the old man who is ad-
dressed know "The self and the earth—your thoughts, your
feelings, / Your beliefs and disbeliefs, your whole peculiar
plot . . ." (CP, 501).

Thus the passage from the last section of "The Rock,"
which I have quoted above, figures critically in the dialectical
drift of Stevens' ideas. In fact, the *Rock* sequence concludes
with "Not Ideas about the Thing but the Thing Itself"
(1954), the most direct of all of Stevens' accounts of the
immediate (as opposed to ultimate) result of the decreative
process.[5] The "new knowledge of reality"—or something
"like it"—that the poet so sharply celebrates comes to him
"At the earliest ending of winter":

He knew that he heard it,
A bird's cry, at daylight or before,
In the early March wind.

The sun was rising at six,
No longer a battered panache above snow . . .
It would have been outside.

It was not from the vast ventriloquism

Of sleep's faded papier-mâché . . .
The sun was coming from outside.

$$(CP, 534)$$

It is perhaps a direct vision, then, of reality, but in any case, only for an instant, and assuredly of something coming from outside, not a product of sleep, yet possible only immediately after sleep, as if it were the aftermath of a dream-vision. Decreation, in the end, does not yield a final yes. But it is not altogether a matter of the final no. It is rather a mode for him who would yield to his own capacity for a wise passivity—he who can, in his old man's wisdom, if only for a sleepy instant, achieve at least something "like" that "new knowledge of reality" whereby he may, waking, transcend himself. A "new knowledge of reality," achieved through decreation, is now understood to be penultimate to a new knowledge of self, as before it had been understood to be penultimate to the new knowledge that is poetry.

Thus, as it must now seem after the fact of Stevens' own life, the inevitability of "A Child Asleep in Its Own Life" (1954):

> Among the old men that you know,
> There is one, unnamed, that broods
> On all the rest, in heavy thought.
>
> They are nothing, except in the universe
> Of that single mind. He regards them
> Outwardly and knows them inwardly,
>
> The sole emperor of what they are,
> Distant, yet close enough to wake
> The chords above your bed to-night.

$$(OP, 106)$$

The *Adagia* entry immediately following the one I have quoted as the epigraph reads: "Reality is the object seen in its greatest common sense" (*OP*, 178). Common sense: decreation: reality: the theory of poetry: the theory of life. From "a child asleep in its own life" toward the "ultimate poem." From "the final no" to "a yes" on which "the future world depends." As Stevens wrote Richard Eberhart (January 20, 1954), "poetry is not a literary activity: it is a vital activity. . . . The good writers are the good thinkers" (*L*, 815).

JOSEPH N. RIDDEL

METAPHORIC STAGING: STEVENS' BEGINNING AGAIN OF THE "END OF THE BOOK"

> The idea of the book is the idea of a totality, finite
> or infinite, of the signifier; this totality of the signi-
> fier cannot be a totality, unless a totality of the signi-
> fied preexists it, supervises its inscriptions and its
> signs, and is independent of its ideality. The idea of
> the book, which always refers to a natural totality, is
> profoundly alien to the sense of writing.
>
> Jacques Derrida, *Of Grammatology*

> What a thing it is to believe that
> One understands, in the intense disclosures
> Of a parent in the French sense.
>
> And not yet to have written a book in which
> One is already a grandfather and to have put there
> A few sounds of meaning, a momentary end
> To the complication, is good, is a good.
>
> Stevens, "The Lack of Repose"

AT THE VERY BEGINNING (ALBEIT PSEUDO BEGINNING) of "Esthétique du Mal," a scene of writing:[1] someone (a poet?) "writing letters home / And, between his letters, reading paragraphs / On the sublime" (CP, 313). A double scene; a re-staging, as in the metaphors of another poem, "Of Modern Poetry": one scene/stage displacing/repeating another; a rupture in the scene of writing; a "modern" scene, as it were, reduplicating an ancient "catastrophe." The writer/reader sitting at his cafe table in Naples is one of the expeditionary forces of modern poetry, always in-between, homeless, the impoverished heir of Wordsworth and Mallarmé, sufferer of a "mal" that he can understand only in the mediations of a venerable "book." The "book" he reads, book of the "sublime" (Longinus' if you will, but in a sense, simply *the* book), arranges a world in its totality and accounts for nature and history as a fallenness, as "the most correct catastrophe." The book "made sure" of catastrophe, gives it place in the order of things. But the writer can no longer read its "correct" modulations. "He could describe / The terror of the sound because the sound / Was ancient" (CP, 314), because Vesuvius resounds (always already) in a Book of Nature that accounts for its sublimity, its significance. But the book cannot satisfy the "hunger" of a desire that has no object, an *angst*—the dis-ease that is marked by the exile of writing. The scene of writing that marks the beginning-again of "Esthétique du Mal" signifies a problematics of "modernism." It is not simply, as in "Of Modern Poetry," that an old "theatre" has ceased to be and a new one has come to replace it—a scene of representation in which a proper script is repeated, being replaced by a scene that composes its own stage in an "act of the mind" (CP, 240). For the old scene (book of the sublime or theater of representation) was already itself a fiction of fiction, an aesthetic of some proper fall or "mal," and the new stage can only repeat the necessity of representation. The modern scene of writing represents, as it were, the problematic scenario of representation. In a world from which the old gods have disappeared—or have, as Stevens says elsewhere and everywhere, become fictions—"The gaiety of language is our seigneur," we who are "Natives of poverty, children of malheur" (CP, 322).

The writer/reader of "Esthétique du Mal" confronts the problematical rupture that Stevens inscribed in another titular metaphor, in "Description without Place," of a writing without reference, of a "book" that organizes the world according to the "nostalgias." The book of the sublime may very well "describe / The terror of the sound because the sound / Was ancient," but it now accounts for a "total past" from which the writer is exiled. If the book makes "sure" of the "most correct catastrophe," of a nature and a history made orderly in the pattern of tragic fall, the book no longer feeds the hunger for such totalizations. Ex-centric, displaced, homeless, the modern writer signifies the exile of all writing. All the old books—the Book of Nature, the book of nostalgias, the truth of all "true sympathizers"—are displaced in the beginning-again of writing that is posed in "Esthétique du Mal." In the very first canto of the poem, the "self," that modern figuration of the logocentric idea of the author or authorizing presence, is suspended in the very gesture by which it displaces the old gods, the "over-human god" (CP, 315). With the end of the book of the sublime, the order of displacements, the hierarchy of signifieds, is radically disrupted. And, as in poem II, the writer's "pain" marks an unbridgeable abyss between himself and the "supremacy" of the "moon," between the self and its figural source.

It is just this self, this substitution of the modern (romantic) center for the ancient soul, this displacement of an "over-human god," "oldest parent" and "reddest lord" (CP, 315), by the "wholly human" (CP, 317), that is in question. The ex-centricity of the writer in "Esthétique du Mal" produces an instability; it disrupts our thinking of the chain of substitutions or orderly movement of centers that has allowed poetry to reimagine the unity of theology, history, and aesthetics. The third stanza of "Sunday Morning" traces the displacement of gods or centers from Jove to Christ to man and prefigures the ex-centric violence of "Esthétique du Mal." Every polarity—sun/moon; heaven/hell; God/Satan; metaphysical/physical—is reversed. But beyond the reversal, the notion of a stable polarity, of orderly reversal, of hierarchy succeeding hierarchy, is put into play and made to tremble. The master term, that which might govern or center all the others, is brought into question, decentered—placed "sous rature," under erasure, as we might now say.[2] "Esthétique du Mal" begins to plot a condition in which the self— that homeless and provisional center of the modern scene— becomes only another name of a center now lost or dispersed in a world without center. The question of the writer, how to begin to organize my world, to re-member it, to contain it in a "book," is doubled by the impossibility of asking the question. With the end of the "book" nothing commands the play between sun and moon except a certain "freedom." The "self" no longer mediates between heaven and earth, metaphysical and physical.

The self no longer governs language, but is governed by it. Language is no longer mediation but the law of the game: "Natives of poverty, children of malheur, / The gaiety of language is our seigneur" (CP, 322). The self is no longer at "the center of a diamond." The old mythology of moon / sun, of subject/object or inside/outside, no longer accounts for a language through which man, substituting for his "over-human god," regulates the world. No "Livre de Toutes Sortes de Fleurs d'après Nature" forms a "transparence" between two poles of reality. The "sentimentalist" fiction (the fiction of the transcendental subject) is undone (poem IV). The "inventions of sorrow" and the old "nostalgias" cannot be recuperated (poems V and X). "Panic in the face of the moon" (poem IX) ensues, an emptying out of all those follies of a "paradise of meaning" or transcendental signifieds that have accounted for the place of a self between sun and moon, as in a theater of proper images. Thus in poem VI, the spheric repetitions of the sun's day and the lunar month mark a "transmutation which, when seen, appears / To be askew" (CP, 318). They mark, that is, a temporal play that refuses the thinking, the notion of "perfection" and produces "desire." The sun "dwells" in a "consummate prime, yet still desires / A further consummation"; and the "big bird" (is it not the figure of the self as desire?) "pecks" at the sun as if to fulfill itself, to satisfy its "appetite." In this play of desires or appetites—a play, that is, of metaphor without correction—everything revolves by "curious lapses" or el-lipses. Everything moves in relation, asymptotically, desiring that "perfection" that it resists, postpones, refusing satisfac-tion, producing signs that are always beyond the pleasure principle.

The most famous canto (poem VIII) of "Esthétique du Mal" turns upon this double negation or eccentricity: "negation was eccentric" (CP, 319). The Satanic tragedy, the denial of Satan, the denial of the negative, is modern tragedy or doubling, since it is the denial of proper displacement, the circular fiction of decentering/recentering that leads from God to man and back again. The structure of "tragedy" is an orderly fall, and its disruption is a "capital / Negation" in the most precise sense, because the structure of the fall guarantees the proper displacement of fathers by sons, a displacement repeated and formalized in the history of "filial / Revenges." Tragedy, after all, is the stage of (Hegelian) history, of necessary "negation." But the negation of Satan is a double negation, the negation of negation, a disruption of the dialectic of history, and thus a negation of the "underground," where "phantoms" (fallen images) reside until they are returned to their origin or are reerected as capital figures once again.

Stevens meditates this myth of the restoration of "tragedy," which is to say, the epoch of man, as a remythologizing of the old, deconstructed fiction of proper negation or dialectic. Thus his "passion for yes," which overthrows the "mortal no," restores the play or scene of "tragedy." This "yes of the realist" is a "must," a necessity doubled in the awareness that it is a fiction. The "passion" for "yes" reveals the movement of writing as a death. The restoration of Satan in the "yes of the realist" is a "passion" of writing that fills in the old "vacancy" or absence and begins again the assassin's movement of a language of substitutions, displacements, or temporal movement.[3]

In "Esthétique du Mal" Stevens most vividly unveils the classical notion that affiliates writing and tragedy as a conundrum, or what Hart Crane called a "livid hieroglyph." The tragic structure is one of the old nostalgias, and sentimentalism is nothing more than its reversal. For example, the metaphors of poem XIII: the modern tragedy, in which the "son's life" is a "punishment" for the "father's," is only a "fragmentary tragedy"; the modern poem, no matter how it is condemned not simply to repeat or overcome by a kind of doubling the condition of classical tragedy, is an economy of delay that reassures its own self-overcoming, an ease of "desire." The negations of imagination have undercut the nostalgic and sentimental, caused "panic" in the "face of the moon" (poem IX) and undone the Book of Nature (poem IV). The imagination has divested itself, turning the structure of tragedy into the play of comedy (poems V and IX). The romantic displacement of the classical, the subject's ("in-bar") undermining of the object ("ex-bar"), as in poem V, has only produced the Nietzschean emptying out of the subject. Thus the figure of in-bar's poverty (poem V), of insatiable appetite (poem VI), of the irremediable wound of time (poem VII)—in short, the entire figuration of a system that is impoverished because its transcendental origin has been toppled like a "sky divested of its fountains" (poem IX)—signifies a displacement of the "book" by the "passion" of writing, by a dissemination of productive negations. As Michel Foucault might say, men's death has accompanied God's. Writing has replaced the "book," and writing is the "assassin's scene": "The assassin discloses himself, / The force that destroys us is disclosed . . ." (CP, 324).

"Esthétique du Mal" limns the margins of what poem XIV calls the "extreme of logic," the "illogical" that inhabits dialectical, historical, or tragical systems. An aesthetics of "mal" is a restaging of the "lunacy" of representation that underlies the historico-metaphysical stage. In this poem all logicians are "in their graves," entombed in their systems, which are, in their turn, systems inscribing and concealing a fictitious logos. To question these systems is to open the tombs, to expose the missing center. Or in the figuration of poem XIV, if a poem exceeds the "reasonableness" of lakes, which one can walk around (totalize), and if lakes are like minds or minds like lakes "with clouds like lights among great tombs" (CP, 325), then the poetic lunatic would double the logical lunatic in negating his one idea. This doubling exposes the simulacrum of the center. It re-marks insistently the tombs of logic, not simply the absence of the center but its doubleness, its lunacy, as a play of lights without origin.

"Esthétique du Mal" disrupts, both in its pseudo beginning and its pseudo end, the orderly movement of an aesthetics of representation or a poetics grounded in a "reality" or "physical world" and not in the "metaphysicals." The dispersed, illogical "physical" can never be totalized by the "book" but is marked by "life" as "desire." Desire and writing are a "living" that incorporates negation, death. They undo the "metaphysicals," the "book."

The writer's eccentricity or ex-centricity means that the scene of violence in which he begins is not a scene of nature but a text. He must rewrite the book of the sublime, and underwrite it. The poetic lunatic is a revolutionist who overthrows the "logical lunatic." The essay "Imagination as Value" offers us a gloss on this question of the poet's proper beginning:

> In the last analysis, it is with this image [the "chief image"] of the world that we are vitally concerned. We should not say, however, that the chief object of the imagination is to produce such an image. Among so many objects, it would be the merest improvisation to say of one, even though it is one with which we are vitally concerned, that it is the chief. The next step would be to assert that a particular image was the chief image. Again, it would be the merest improvisation to say of any image of the world, even though it was an image with which a vast accumulation of imaginations had been content, that it was the chief image. The imagination itself would not remain content with it nor allow us to do so. It is the irrepressible revolutionist. (NA, 151-52)

Writing destroys the nostalgia for a "chief image," a center, by exposing its fictionality. The "chief image," like a "first idea," is a belatedly produced fiction, an imaginary construct. It is neither original nor central but the mark of the imagination as nothing in itself, as a negation, a negating or revolutionary force. To displace the notion of a "chief image" is to destroy the "book."

Poem XXVII of "An Ordinary Evening in New Haven"

dramatizes the scene of writing in the image of a "scholar, in his Segmenta" who left the following "note": " 'The Ruler of Reality, / If more unreal than New Haven, is not / A real ruler, but rules what is unreal' "; and this "ruler," who is a " 'consort of the Queen of Fact,' " is a " 'theorist of life, not death, / The total excellence of its total book' " (CP, 485). The figure of the "total book" is so inscribed within quotation marks, within the scholar's "note," and thus within the fragmented writing of his "Segmenta," that it becomes the indelible mark of the false origin. The "book" of the "Ruler of Reality," signified in a scholarly footnote, is not the image of any absolute origin but the "drafting" of the fiction of the "ruler." Behind the "book" must be its author, an "unreal" of what is "real." The "book" is a "foremeaning" but also a late "image," a dream of totalization that can no longer be dreamed, except in a fiction that negates it.

The notion of the "book" was an early concern with Stevens. One has only to refer to the letter he sent to Williams, remarking the miscellaneous collection of Al Que Quiere, which protested that he, Stevens, hesitated to publish a volume because his poems to that point would not be ordered or centered into anything as coherent as a book.[4] Stevens' thinking of the book of poetry reflects, of course, Mallarmé's, and, analogously, Plato's book of philosophy, a notion that, as Derrida has shown us, bears within itself an *aporia*: the idea of the book prefigures or represents a unity that it at the same time produces and commands.[5] Like Crispin's "book of moonlight," which "is not written yet" (CP, 33), the idea of the book is the project of desire, to represent the coincidence of sun and moon. The notion of the book is always that of a book of imagination, or of the imaginary, a book always already written and never properly re-written—the "book" as an image, in Plato, of the soul, but an image, according to Derrida, in which the decision about whether the book initiates the soul or the soul the book is undecidable. In Stevens' poetry it is precisely this question of the ontological status of the "book"—of images and their origin, the imagination—that sets off those open meditations, pronouncing in the same word the authority of a "total book" or "chief image" and the ultimate deferring of such resolutions: "After all the pretty contrast of life and death / Proves that these opposite things partake of one, / At least that was the theory, when bishops' books / Resolved the world. We cannot go back to that" (*CP*, 215).

If modern man is a "Connoisseur of Chaos," it is because the "bishops' books" (which are only after-images of the idea of the book) have suffered the same fate as the book of the sublime. In "Notes toward a Supreme Fiction" the book is exposed in all of its doubleness as the "courage" (and poverty) of the "ignorant man, / Who chants by book" and "the heat of the scholar, who writes / The book, hot for another accessible bliss . . ." (*CP*, 395). If we "cannot go back" to the fiction of bishops' books, to the idea of the book as the image of unity or Truth, we might grasp the "accessible bliss"[6] of the *as if*, of aesthetic "balances that happen" and in that happening portend an end of the marginal writing of "notes." These "balances" prefigure, as always, deferred finality, realized as the end of interpretation, some future closure of the "war between mind and sky": "They will get it straight one day at the Sorbonne" (*CP*, 406). It is this closure or totalization (supreme fiction) that poetry repeatedly reinvents, and yet precludes in the "war" of its incessant, revolutionary writing.

"Notes toward a Supreme Fiction" is the great text of this writing against the "book." It is a philosophical poem, then, only in the eccentric sense that the "extremest book of the wisest man" (for which Plato's *Phaedrus* would, metonymically, be a model) is a master text to which all other texts are "notes" inscribed in its margin. But it is a master text that masters nothing. Poetry, then, writes itself (is written) in the margin of philosophy, even as it signifies the opposite, that philosophy plays always already in the margins of poetry. In either case, textuality is a question raised by a poem that proposes, like any text of the "supreme fiction," to achieve a "vivid transparence," to cleanse metaphor of all the "accent[s] of deviation" (*OP*, 96) and to "step barefoot

into reality" (CP, 423): "We seek / The poem of pure
reality, untouched / By trope or deviation, straight to the
word . . ." (CP, 471). But here the poem itself is the "pure
reality": "Part of the res itself and not about it" (CP, 473).
Such desire—for a "paradisal parlance" in which signifier
and signified are one, in which the poem goes "straight to
the word" and the word "Straight to the transfixing object,
to the object / At the exactest point at which it is itself, /
Transfixing by being purely what it is . . ." (CP, 471)—could
only marry word to word. Poems induce "pleasure" by fore-
shadowing, projecting, and deferring such fictions of a union
or adequate substitution, but also by deferring any closure or
completion of the line between word and thing. The figure
that would dissolve figuration, thus canceling the death sig-
nified by metaphor, is Stevens' "fiction of the leaves" (CP,
526): "The mobile and the immobile flickering / In the area
between is and was are leaves . . ." (CP, 474).

To follow the "argument" of a Stevens poem always de-
mands a kind of metaphorical detour like the preceding para-
graph, in which the problematic of "Notes" reverberates
through later texts—"An Ordinary Evening in New Haven"
and "The Rock"—in a way to suggest that they are mar-
ginalia of the earlier, notes produced out of the excess of the
earlier. The later poems do not complete the "Notes," but
signify its openness, its incompleteness, and therefore refuse
the earlier its priority as a "book." Similarly, "Notes" itself
appeals in its beginning to an earlier book, "the extremest
book of the wisest man" (CP, 380). (Plato's book, as pre-
viously suggested, for lack of another name?) "Notes," then,
begins in the margins of a book that one can say has always
been written, an "extremest" book, which the "ignorant
man" must forget and yet re-write in a gesture of writing
that simulates an "immaculate beginning" (CP, 380-82).

"Notes" opens with an imperative: a nameless father in-
sists to his "ephebe" that one can only recapitulate the fic-
tion of Adamic naming by using an old memory system (lan-
guage) to forget or overwrite that system, so as to overcome,
if only in a fiction, the belatedness signified by all naming.

Or, in other words, to name in such a way as to repress the problematic of naming (the "metaphor that murders meta- phor" [NA, 84]); to begin again in such a way that the be- ginning is marked as fiction, an original secondariness, as it were. This is only a strategy of marginalia to overcome the pathos of the pseudo beginning, to re-mark a beginning long since begun. Even the impossible-to-conceive first name of the sun, for which "Phoebus" is both a belated and out- moded substitution, was "A name for something that never could be named" (CP, 381). Even the "first idea" is incon- ceivable outside of a figure, a "sun," which the ephebe (as son) can only name by unnaming (forgetting). That is, the "first idea" itself is a metaphor, even if a first metaphor, that can only mark the absence of a "thing itself" that is never seen directly.[7] This beginning again can occur only with/in a representational system (metaphor) that is marked through and through by a contradiction. The system reveals itself as irreducibly figural, so that to think the "first idea" or the name of the origin of the system, one has first to think or be thought by the system.[8] Yet the representational or signi- fying or naming system, which Stevens calls variously the "poem" or "fiction," necessarily precedes what it is con- structed to represent: the pure "thing itself" or "supreme fiction." In the beginning was "notes toward."

Stevens' meditation on the anomaly of the "sun," which "Must bear no name, gold flourisher, but be / In the diffi- culty of what it is to be" (CP, 381), recapitulates a question of rhetoric posed in the *Phaedrus* of a naming or troping of a "first idea," an origin, that inaugurates every poem but has its be-ing only in the poem.[9] The "difficulty" of "to be," of the sun's be-ing outside any name it may be-ar, lies in the "project" of the "sun," that which casts images but itself exceeds all images. Any name of the sun is a metaphor that marks the discontinuity of perception and language. But the "sun" itself is irreducibly a name, for that idea cannot be perceived directly. Even the (impossible) perception of the sun is a metaphor, which the "ephebe" must forget if he is to ground his beginning in the truth of an origin (a "first idea") beyond the self, an "idea" itself original because it is without origin: "Never suppose an inventing mind as source" of the sun.[10] The "sun" seen "clearly in the idea of it" is a sun "Washed in the remotest cleanliness of a heaven / That has expelled us and our images . . . ," a sun never looked at directly but "seen" in the "cleanliness" of a figure that marks its absence. The "project for the sun" is that it "must bear no name." To begin is to forget the metaphoricity of the sun, to evoke the origin of poetry in a truth preceding language. It is to erase the sun/son.

If the ephebe is to begin (and hence escape slavish repetition), he must repeat the beginning as a forgetting.[11] The poem as a "fiction" of beginnings (hence "supreme fiction") "Inscribes a primitive astronomy / Across the unscrawled fores the future casts . . ." (CP, 383), producing the illusion of a moment when language and idea were one, satisfying "Belief in an immaculate beginning" and sending "us, winged by an unconscious will, / To an immaculate end" (CP, 382). The "candor" of the poem ("candor" and "candid," or light, amplify the fiction of "immaculate beginning") is that it inscribes the margin that always plays between philosophy's fall—its prosaic naming of the "first idea" or abstraction—and poetry's scattered representations of the "idea." A poetic language always plays between the pure notions of beginning and end, a "first idea" and its recuperation. The poem is the sign of the temporal and marginal, a play of differences, and of that "desire" for the idea signified in every erasure or every forgetting that the idea is already always a sign, another text. Thus the remarkable metaphors of section IV of "It Must Be Abstract":

> The first idea was not our own. Adam
> In Eden was the father of Descartes
> And Eve made air the mirror of herself. . . .
>
> .   .   .   .
>
> But the first idea was not to shape the clouds
> In imitation. The clouds preceded us

There was a muddy centre before we breathed.
There was a myth before the myth began,
Venerable and articulate and complete.
From this the poem springs: that we live in a place
That is not our own and, much more, not ourselves. . . .

                                        (CP, 383)

All beginnings take place in the "uncertain light" of a
"single, certain truth," to return to the verse prologue; all
beginnings begin by turning an earlier trope, a text of the
"idea" that was never "our own," of a "myth before the
myth began." Thus Plato's text is to that idea of "single,
certain truth" as Descartes' is to Adam's, a text of the ephebe
displacing his father, himself already an ephebe. It is not a
question here of the poem's marking in its beginning some
original fall, or giving access, even in a refreshed moment of
the "fiction," to a prelapsarian light. Even the myth of the
fall, of a heaven "That has expelled us and our images," is a
myth of "cleanliness" lately projected in the sun's detours,
its ellipses and eclipses: "the first idea becomes / The hermit
in a poet's metaphors . . ." (CP, 381).

The poem, then, becomes the temporary house (meta-
phor) of the "first idea." If man's truths are always meta-
phorical—the "celestial ennui of apartments"—it is this
sense of truth as fiction that produces the desire for truth,
that "sends" him "back" to the "first idea," motivating those
imaginations that displace the old images or names of the
"idea." Poem I has already warned the ephebe against think-
ing of "an inventing mind as source / Of this idea," or of
composing a "voluminous master." Later, poem VII will
evoke the satisfactions of thinking the idea "without the
giant, / A thinker of the first idea" (CP, 386). Like Nietzsche
warning of the linguistic reflex that projects a doer/thinker
behind the deed/thought, the Stevensian displacement of
the father by the ephebe skews the old paradigm. The "first
idea" as abstraction is a late invention. Revolved in the
analytic of a "poet's metaphors," it unveils the fiction of
original anteriority. "Notes" is an extravagant overwriting

of its own borrowed metaphors, those myths and texts that it boldly appropriates and revolves, those degraded images that it puts "sous rature."[12] The poetic movement that refreshens, if only for a moment, the first idea (poem III), thus producing the illusion of an "immaculate beginning" drawn to an "immaculate end," does not represent the cycle of the sun but is itself the text that lends a myth to the sun, naming it as the origin. Stevens' sun, which cannot be named, is already a figure that every poem must reinscribe and disguise in its beginning again.

The poem's dialectical movement performs a sequence of repetitions upon the more familiar figures of representation. If "Notes" has an *argument*, it occurs as a movement of negations, a dismantling and reworking of the venerable triad of metaphysico/poetics, the dialectics of subject/object that is mediated and regulated by the illusion of resemblance. "It Must Be Abstract" revolves the structure of every idealism and the dream of proper negation. If poetic reflection must think away the "giant" or "thinker of the first idea," revealing that the "academies" are "like structures in a mist" (CP, 386), it cannot think away the functional necessity of the subject. So the "major man," reduced to "expedient" and "crystal hypothesis," must replace the "giant," and this suggests a restoration of the very system that has been negated or reversed. Poem VIII of part one underlines the artifice, the machinery, of the restoration:

> Can we compose a castle-fortress-home,
> Even with the help of Viollet-le-Duc,
> And set the MacCullough there as major man?
>
> (CP, 386)

Like a Viollet-le-Duc restoration, the new structure will be more original than its predecessor. It is marked through and through as a fiction, a "machine" of "Swiss perfection," for it reveals that the thinker of the first idea has always been a figure laboriously reconstructed and installed within a system where it stands for the origin of the system. "Major man" as the "exponent" of the "idea of man" is clearly a propounded or invented figure, the abstraction (the clown of poem x) substituted for the sanctified giant or the transcendental fiction of thinker/author/god. The poet is always de-centered (poem v), suffering from the "celestial ennui of apartments" (poems II and v). But he dreams recurrently of restoring word to thing, of achieving a natural language (poems v and VIII), even if in a fiction he knows not to be true, as a metaphor that is "falseness close to kin" (poem VI).

"Notes," and "The Auroras of Autumn," after it, examines, revolves, and disrupts the orderly hierarchy of the authorial metaphor. As Michel Benamou has argued, it displaces parental space, since the parental or familial paradigm is the one that governs both philosophy and literature.[13] "It Must Change" examines the rigidity of the old abstraction in terms of prescription or ordination (the President of poem II, who "ordains the bee to be" and lives in a house where the "curtains" are arranged to a "metaphysical t") and in terms of the statue erected as a sign of a living past, a statue that can now only signify an absence, a "final funeral" (poem III). The old systems were governed by an absolute that stood outside the change it initiated and controlled, and is commemorated by a representation that marks the absence of presence (the statue). On the other hand, this section substitutes a new structure of marriage, of a balance of opposites that dissolves neither pole, in which the old negations are overcome in a perpetual play of substitutions, as in Nanzio Nunzio's espousal of Ozymandias (poem VIII). In "It Must Change" neither imagination nor reality, subject nor object, commands a scene in which both revolve as in a theater, a "Theatre / Of Trope" (CP, 397). And the marriages of "It Must Give Pleasure," like that portmanteau trope of the Captain and Bawda, who are married in Catawba, finally establish at the center, as a displacement of the statue, a "Fat girl" of reality who is neither singular nor nameable, but an "aberration" (poem x) that suspends all dialectical structures and especially the fictions of metaphoric truth.

As Stevens revolves the problematic of beginnings, his

doubling of the metaphysical fiction reveals the artistry of
the first installation, the first erection of the statue. "Notes"
reinscribes the fiction of the "immaculate beginning" (hence
the *telos* of fictions as they derive from Plato and Aristotle)
into a "Theatre / Of Trope," revealing that in the play of
"artificial things" the notion of an original thing itself from
which all images derive is itself a trope. If ideas, as Nietzsche
says, are the illogical equating of the unequatable, the revela-
tion of the strategy by which poems situate such inaugural
figures of origin (at once images of the idea and natural
images producing reflections) in turn reveals the "irrational"
force of poetry.[14] "It Must Give Pleasure" transcribes the
notion of a mimetic poetics (a poetics of the "good") into
a poetics of "play." In a sense, "Notes" deflects a poetics of
representation into a poetics of repetition, an eccentric repe-
tition that forever precludes the recuperation of an originary
or "first idea." "To find the real, / To be stripped of every
fiction except one, / The fiction of an absolute . . ." (CP,
404) is to acknowledge the origin of repetition in repetition,
the "absolute" as already always "fiction" or trope. Thus
"Mere repetitions" produce the "thing final in itself," those
works that signify the "good: / One of the vast repetitions
final in / Themselves and, therefore, good, the going round
/ And round and round, the merely going round . . ." (CP,
405). This circle, which has no beginning and no end, is not
a circle at all. Even the figure of "final good" (of a balancing
or equating of the unequal) can only reveal at the same time
the original difference and the fictive operation of equation.
The trope of the circle is not an original model representing
the dialectic but a figure always incomplete, an "eccentric
measure":

> And we enjoy like men, the way a leaf
> Above the table spins its constant spin,
> So that we look at it with pleasure, look
>
> At it spinning its eccentric measure. Perhaps,
> The man-hero is not the exceptional monster,
> But he that of repetition is most master.
>
> (CP, 406)

The "Fat girl" evoked in last poem of "It Must Give Pleasure" appears, on the contrary, as a figure of "difference," and not, like the statue, a figure of identity. She is a "moving contour, a change not quite completed," a "more than natural figure" and "soft-footed phantom, the irrational / Distortion" (CP, 406). She is always "more than" her image, a figure of excess. Neither the "master" of repetition, the "man-hero" who is always eccentric, nor the "Fat girl" is properly a center. The "Fat girl" is a name for a proliferation of images that will not reduce to one; she is "familiar yet an aberration" (CP, 406). She is metaphor itself.

"Notes" revolves, repeats, and parodies the "fiction of an absolute" (CP, 404), unveiling the ground of that fiction in the "aberration" of metaphor. And metaphor, in the Nietzschean terms that Stevens seems to echo, is "an identification of the non-identical."[15] By raising this "operation of the imagination," as Nietzsche called it, to the figural center of a fiction, however, "Notes" underscores the "more than rational distortion" that logic has repressed or forgotten. By returning us to a center that is a productive force of "difference," to metaphor as "irrational / Distortion," the poem reveals the "muddy centre" of our origins (CP, 383) to be not a "truth" that has expelled us (or from which we have fallen) but a "fluent mundo" of poetic language, the "Theatre / Of Trope."

The illogical margin between poetry and philosophy, as Stevens probed it in his later writings, is precisely the figural space where "supreme fictions" are written or figures of presence are inscribed, simulacra of the central identification, which turn out to be doubled and hence aberrational. Philosophy and poetry—always in their way interchangeable, if unequatable, polar fictions—are indeed "supreme fictions" that are written in the margins of two abstract and pure but always unwritten notions called poetry and philosophy, imagination and reality, moon and sun, or, as in the coda of "Notes," mind and sky. Poems, which are inscribed in this margin, are always "notes toward" and hence signs that the master text itself, the "extremest book," is composed upon the "eccentric measure" or "aberration" of metaphor and thus composes a "violent abyss" (CP, 404). Whether it is the "extremest book" of philosophy or the pure poem of the first idea, they are only texts made up of notes, marginalia. There is no proper word or master text and no master of repetition in this "war" of differences that plays in the margin that we can only call language. For the fiction of the absolute is irreducibly composed out of "every latent double in the word," and every speaker of the word—whether we call him author, poet, or major man—is, like the MacCullough, an "expedient" and a "crystal hypothesis," the "Logos and logic" that is signified by the installation (CP, 387) within an already completed system of the "form" that originated the system. The poles of imagination and reality are fabrications produced, sustained, and yet repeatedly displaced in the poetic repetition.

From Plato to Coleridge, any definition of poetry (or the poem) has always appealed to a concept of pleasure, a certain notion of pleasure that in its turn evoked the idea of closure or the "good." The third part of Stevens' "grand poem" acknowledges that notion and underwrites it. The "fiction of an absolute" repeats a certain closing of the circle and the installation of an "Angel"/author, or of an "I" that in its turn imagines the "angel." To imagine this closure and installation, however, is to imagine it as a fabrication, as "external regions" filled with "reflections, the escapades of death" (CP, 404-5). At the very moment of "Notes" where closure/pleasure is approached, where the figure of the author/angel is installed over "the violent abyss," the reflection empties out the dream of closure. He produces an "expressible bliss" by forgetting the "golden centre" (CP, 404). The poem of that "bliss" is the echo of a "violent abyss" filled with "reflections, the escapades of death."

The poem resounds in the abyss, bridges it over. But only momentarily. Stevens, who had to remind a correspondent that his figure of the "necessary angel" was a figure of "reality" and not the "imagination" (L, 852), underwrites and dispossesses the "angel" he has imagined as central to the "fiction of an absolute." The self (the "I" who "can / Do all that angels can" [CP, 405]), however, is revealed not as "exceptional monster" but as "he that of repetition is most master" (CP, 406). The self is not central but only a part of the "eccentric measure" of a "spinning" of the leaves (a writing) of a text long since begun, a book that will never close.

To expose this scene of writing, this "abysmal" scene, this "violent abyss," the poet has only to question his own place in the "vast repetitions"—his re-writing, as it were, of the fiction of the abyss from Milton to Yeats, in which the "abyss" can always be filled with a "gold centre" and "golden destiny," or fictions of the fall that is overcome, redeemed in some "expressible bliss." For the overcoming of the "abysmal" has always been a fiction of expressibility, of language overcoming its express limits, of stabilizing its play, its "fall," weaving together again "mind and sky." In a poem that ends by returning again to the dream of "proper words" and "faithful speech" (CP, 408), there is always a moment that reminds us that any such pairing of opposites takes place only in "shadows," in a "book in a barrack, a letter from Malay," or in a catalepsis. In the economy of "Notes," the play between a lover's desire for "accessible bliss" (CP, 395) and the repeated questioning of the "hour / Filled with expressible bliss" (CP, 404), an hour for which the poet has "No need," produces a poem without beginning or end.

Even the abyss does not exist outside of (in fact, it is produced by) the play of "Abysmal instruments" (CP, 384), which in an early section of "Notes" are clearly the "instruments" of the poet as "mimic." "Abysmal instruments" are, then, the machines by which the poet produces fiction out of fictions, the fiction that displaces myth, supplementing the already begun with his "sweeping meanings" (CP, 384). But this is an act of decentering, a displacement of the "giant" as "thinker of the first idea" with a figure of "major man" (CP, 386-87), and finally a disposing of the "golden centre" and the "solacing majesty" (CP, 405). "Notes" evolves a classical notion of "representation" of a "first idea" that "was not to shape the clouds / In imitation" (CP, 383)—only to reveal that the idea of a "muddy centre" or a "myth before the myth began," a myth of origins, complete and final in itself, can only itself be the idea produced by "Abysmal instruments."

The "violent abyss," like the "dumfoundering abyss" of "Saint John and the Back-Ache" (CP, 437), can only be bridged by figure, by poetry; it turns out to be the invention of the poem. The idea of "proper speech" is the product of language, of that excess of language called the poetic; it is not the idea that has produced language, compelling its abysmal fall, throwing it across the abyss into shadows. If the "first idea" is a "hermit in a poet's metaphors" and the "will to change" an "eye of a vagabond in metaphor" (CP, 381, 397), that "idea" of origins, which governs all representation and is itself unnameable, becomes a double name thrown into the "abyss." The abyss has no origin, nor is it an origin. It represents nothing, and is representable only in the nothing (the "vast repetitions") of the poem. From "The Snow Man" to the late discourses on discourse, Stevens projected a shudder through the "whole shebang" of representation, the fiction of the book. The "first idea," which can only be an origin of some original myth, could never have preceded language or been exterior to it. Nor could the imagination. Nor even the abyss, for it is nothing more and nothing less (hence "nothing itself") than the play of language, an originless origin, formed upon the familiar "aberration" of metaphor.

"[I]n respect to the general sense in which poetry and metaphor are one" Stevens wrote (NA, 81), poetry at its source is already metaphorical, as in the instance of Nietzsche's "First metaphor."[16] Poetry is the movement, change, revolution, troping of an abstraction: it is "to think of resemblances and of the repetitions of resemblances as the source of the ideal" (NA, 81). The ideal arrives very late, a concept of self-identification of which we have forgotten the illogical (aber-rational) origin. The search for resemblance is a search for pleasure (balances of differences, fictional equations), and pleasure is what we find in finding what we have erected and installed: a "transfiguration of ourselves" (NA, 80). Poetry is a certain narcissism, Stevens argues, and narcissism is "an evidence of the operation of the principle that we expect to find pleasure in resemblances" (NA, 80). Resemblance, however, is never the full equating of the non-identical. Resemblance is a mark of equivalence that also signifies the unequivocal, the irreducible. The realm of resemblance highlights reality as a "gradus ad Metaphoram," an abstraction grounded in the primary fiction of a "first idea." The self discovers itself, as in the mirror of resemblance, as a form of the ideal, situated in a linguistic field without origin or end. The self is poetic invention, the production of an identity by a marking of its nonidentity. Stevens refers to the figure of Narcissus, who, when he looked into the stream, found "in his hair a serpent coiled to strike" (NA, 79). He found not a simple reflection but the self as other, imaged in the serpent of discourse.[17] We will return, with Stevens, to this instituted serpent, to this excessive image, but only after a brief detour.

Two poems stand as examples (and supplementary modifications) of the prose section of "Three Academic Pieces" and indicate that the "gobbet" of every "abstraction" is so "thick" with "overlays, / The double fruit of boisterous epicures . . ." (NA, 85), that it produces the illusion of a "total reality" at the core. This totality (of the book centered in a chief image that is valorized and reified) cannot be attained by peeling away the layers, like a rind from a fruit. The poem/writing itself is just such a peeling, the very opposite of the poem that adds layer upon lower layer; but it never arrives at the unmetaphoric or even at a first idea that is pure abstraction. The core of the fruit is already doubled (it is of "earth / And water") at the very elemental center, already "distilled / In the prolific ellipses that we know . . ." (NA, 87). Indeed, as the poems revolve the argument, the core's plurality is a seedling fecundity, a seminal play. The sought-for "center of resemblance," if it exists, is found only "Under the bones of time's philosophers," and this provokes a radical question: "what heroic nature of what text. . .?" The "man" situated at "the center of ideal time" is always a "man" in the text. The subject that authors, orients, and governs the text is a product of the text, a Narcissus/serpent. The "tropic of resemblance," as Stevens meditates it, is a scene of tropes, of writing. The "total reality" is a "total artifice" (NA, 86-87). Like Nietzsche's, Stevens' search for a "realm" of resemblance, which begins in the distant planes of metaphor about metaphor, can never lead back to the "irreducible X" of the unrepresented or the identical. The image of resemblance is a hall of mirrors in which pleasure is never some rest, or a collapse of images back into some unimaged object, as in the shattering of the mirror. The point of X, the chiasmus of every origin, is "At the bottom of imagined artifice" (NA, 83), a "bottom" that is already figural.

Every poem, as in Nietzsche's parable of the creation, is a metaphor of a metaphor, a remove of one plane from another, one of the "prolific ellipses." The "irreducible" of each "imagined artifice" can only be an image/trace (not even a "chief image"), a figure not of that reality that precedes the "artifice" and is imaged or represented in the artifice, but the mark of every discontinuity that stands between any fiction and the "represented" it erases. Thus poetry is indeed a "prolific" ellipsis, a turning from nothing. There, in the "precious scholia," in the writing of the "scholar, captious," are produced the "incredible subjects of poetry": "there, where the truth was not the respect of one, / But always of many things" (NA, 85). The double sense of the "incredible" (that which is beyond words and yet is erased and displaced in every word) plays in the gap between "sound" and "meaning," the gap marked by plurality of a writing ("precious scholia") that will not reduce to "one" or be regathered into an "image certain." The "image certain" refracts, produces, multiplies in "casual exfoliations" that signify the "tropic of resemblance" as a movement of substitutions without origin. It is the "casual" and not the causal that plays throughout the grid of a "gradus ad Metaphoram" (NA, 81).

A text (poetry), which always begins by simulating a beginning, can only represent the "repetitions of resemblance"; it is a re-turn of the already always metaphoric. And in its turn it produces an "image certain" that divests "reality / Of its propriety" (NA, 86) and produces the "incredible" figure of a "truth" that is made of many things (a play of resemblances). Poetry images the imagination as "irrepressible revolutionist," writing as aberrational substitution. It produces the figure of a "cause" that is "casual," of an author/subject that produces a field of "exfoliations" that it does not command. The imagination itself is only a trope,[18] a disguise of the notion of an "immaculate beginning"; and as we have seen in "Notes," this notion is what the poem "restores" or invents. That is, the poem invents or re-invents the idea of its own origin by revolving (by disguising) a figure it appropriates from another poem.

After the inaugural beginning again, the troping of the pseudo beginning, there is only the "casual" and never the causal. The pseudo beginning thrusts the poem toward an intersection with reality, but a reality divested of "propriety." "The the" always turns out to be a figuration encrypted in "stanza my stone" (CP, 203), a "res itself" that is, like Nietzsche's "thing-in-itself," always in quotation marks or always inscribed upon a tombstone. To touch reality "Without evasion by a single metaphor" (CP, 373) is to arrive at the word as "sound" and not as "meaning." From Crispin of "The Comedian as the Letter C," who begins as a "general lexicographer" of his phantasy and ends up preferring "text to gloss" (CP, 28, 39), to the late "Things of August," the pure reality of Stevens' poem exists only in the folds of "A new text of the world" (CP, 494), one text displacing another. To unveil the "thing itself," and not ideas about it, as in the valedictory poem of Stevens' major collection, is to unveil the figuration of a pure outside, a "cry" that is "part of the colossal sun" and hence only a sign of the sun as master metaphor: "It was *like* / A new knowledge of reality" (CP, 534; italics added). That part or sign of the sun is always already the outside of an outside, a "choral" ring of that which is "Still far away" (CP, 534).

The "Thing Itself" of the title "Not Ideas about the Thing but the Thing Itself" would seem, then, to be the poem, or the constructed "thing," the representational system that produces an image, a "new knowledge of reality." Like "The Poem that Took the Place of a Mountain" or a "Description without Place," the poem is a text that produces "The exact rock where his inexactnesses / Would discover, at last, the view toward which they had edged" (CP, 512), a "recomposed" image and a displacement of mountain by word, or of one figure by another. Yet the "exact rock" produced in the metaphoric displacement is an image of fictive perfection, the projection of a need *to be* "complete." The poet's dream of his poem (or canon) as "The Planet on the Table," in which the "self and the sun were one," unveils the metaphoricity of "self." Like Mallarmé's "rock," Stevens' signifies a point where the word displaces meaning and reality becomes the ground as text, writing, and not meaning.

In "Saint John and the Back-Ache" Stevens locates this text of the world in the "dumbfoundering abyss / Between us and the object" (CP, 437), between the "mind" as "force" and the world as "presence." There the text is a "bridge," but presented in the figure of the folded twofold, the double figure of the "serpent." And the "serpent" is a configuration of the phallus, the signifier, whose meaning is never singular: it can only be celebrated "in our captious hymns, erect and sinuous, / Whose venom and whose wisdom will be one" (CP, 437). The irreducible doubleness of the serpent, a signature of what *"will be one,"* an ever-deferred closure or return, is Stevens' ultimate image of the productive "aberration" of poetry. At the deepest interior (the "nest") of any system of figuration, there is always inscribed a serpent, a figure of figures that cancels itself. It is not a figure of presence/absence, a cryptic sign, but the very figure of the "abyss" itself, "dumbfoundering." The "abyss" is not a form containing and concealing a master sign but a sign of the aberrant sign itself. Like Nietzsche's serpent, Stevens' is the figuration of a discourse, that which bridges two fictions: a mark, as it were, of the irreparable discontinuity between language and the "thing-in-itself."[19] The serpent is metaphor, ungovernable poetic play.

Stevens' great poem of the serpent, of course, is "The Auroras of Autumn," and it is appropriate to conclude this tracing of the path cut by Stevensian metaphors by pursuing the figure through a poem in which the movement of the serpent is so tantalizing. It is ironic that Stevens' most perplexing "philosophic" meditation is the one that some of his critics have chosen as a pure poem to set against more discursive and prosaic efforts like "An Ordinary Evening in New Haven." If "An Ordinary Evening" is Stevens' own epigrammatology,[20] "Auroras" exemplifies the issue and consequences of submitting a metaphorics to deconstruction or to a poetic reformulation of the realm of resemblance. If "An Ordinary Evening" anatomizes metaphor and hence breaks down the orderly margins between poetry and philosophy, "Auroras" begins in the uncertainty of the abyss produced by any demythologizing of logic. Like "Notes," the poem begins in a problematics of language shared alike by poet and philosopher who desire to free vision (the ideal) from the network of figuration (rhetoric) that signifies a degradation of idea (the order of the sign, the grammatical distribution of subject and object across a temporal abyss). But like Heidegger pursuing the original poetry and thought dispersed and fallen in grammar and logic, the poet finds the recuperation of truth impossible outside of the field of language, the play of images always already begun, which are like the flashings of lights without origin, more arbitrary even than the secondary images of logic. The auroras, like a "serpent body flashing without the skin" (CP, 411), are "light" without a proper origin, a natural aberration, flashings not of the sun but of the clashing play of unequal forces, a light of morning as cold as the end of an autumn's day. The "auroras" have no origin, and even their northern place is inconceivable outside of some eschatological fiction.[21]

There are indeed two serpents inscribed in the textual opening of "The Auroras of Autumn," or at least two of his "nests." The serpent at first appears to signify the order of two in one, projecting the return of two into one. It is the bodiless and the plurality of forms or bodies that signifies the essential polarities of any total form. But it is precisely this serpentine dualism that is undercut, or undercuts itself, in the poem's tentative opening. The "serpent," the "bodiless," "lives" only in its figuration; its "nest, / These fields, these hills, these tinted distances," is the text of nature, nature as a text, distributed among Plato's images:

> Or is this another wriggling out of the egg,
> Another image at the end of the cave,
> Another bodiless for the body slough?
>
> (CP, 411)

Like Nietzsche's disentangling (and skewed reversal) of the Platonic structure of essence and image, and hence subject/object, the poem unveils the original image as a trope already turned. The serpent, which in "another nest" of figuration is "the master of the maze," grounds or synthesizes the polarities of form and formlessness or "base" and "height"—"Of body and air and forms and images"—in an image that is irreducible to one. Like Plato's *pharmakon*, it is both a purgative and a poison, a figure turning in the sun, a figuration of the sun. He makes his "meditations in the ferns," and like every leaf of grass, every metaphorical turn toward the "sun" that seems to "make sure of sun," his flashings reveal him only as the colorations of the "sun." In the turnings of the serpent, a "serpent body flashing without the skin," the "master of the maze" is revealed as only another image, itself without origin. Its movement is a theater of trope, a scene of writing. The flashings of the serpent, like those of the auroras, are a pseudo sun or the images of sun as reflected in the "moving grass" of some venerable (narcissistic) text.

The three subsequent cantos of "The Auroras of Autumn" repeat in their opening phrase the sign of this movement as a cancellation, an erasure, an ellipsis: "Farewell to an idea . . ." (CP, 412, 413, 414; the elliptical marks are inscribed in the poem). Each beginning again is a turning of an image that repeatedly dismantles the "ancestral theme" of continuity, of the passage of truth from origin to end or from father to son. Successively, the poem elaborates and deconstructs the fiction of a chain of centers, of orderly displacements and substitutions. The fiction of purposeful change is revealed to be inscribed "blankly on the sand" or in the inevitable ellipses, which leave traces of every turning and hence every disappearance of the image. Successively, the images of "cabin," of "mother," and of "father" flash and are canceled, cancel the preceding image, but in "cancellings" or "negations" that "are never final" (CP, 414). Successively, the "velocities of change" are measured in a figuration that cancels and must be canceled. Only in these flashings, in the blanks or spaces of the cancellations, does the image of the "master" of change appear, that figuration of "the ever-brightening origin" that appears only as a writing, an inscription of something that has disappeared. The figure of the master, of the two folded in one, is, like the serpent itself, unveiled only in its shedding of another skin. The movement of the poem reveals, as in canto v, that all truths are images, rhetorical displacements, stories by "tellers of tales" who "mute much, muse much" (CP, 415).

Does philosophy cancel poetry or poetry philosophy? "The Auroras of Autumn" inscribes a "theatre floating through the clouds, / Itself a cloud" (CP, 416), a scene that represents nothing but its own theater of trope. Even as the poem asks the question of whether there is "an imagination that sits enthroned" (CP, 417), it reveals that imagination has always been enthroned in language or in that fiction of totalization, the book. The last cantos of "Auroras" examine the construction of the system for enthroning the center, a system that is not produced by its center but is, instead, produced to situate a center, the "imagination." Like a stele, the production inscribes its own tragedy, signifies its own displacement: "its stele / And shape and mournful making move to find / What must unmake it . . ." (CP, 417-18). The philosopher's need for a "time of innocence / As pure principle" (CP, 418) produces the fiction of the "book": that which is "Like a book at evening beautiful but untrue, / Like a book on rising beautiful and true" (CP, 418).

After "The Auroras of Autumn," all the old dreams, the nostalgias for recovering the "thing itself" or "things as they are" are put in quotation marks.[22] And the vision of a progenitive "central poem" or "poem of the whole" (a poem of poems never written but to be written; the paradigm of poems that is both origin and end) is revealed as the last installment in a chain of fictions. The figural origin of "lesser poems," the "central poem" is a figure produced by/in what it authors. Laboriously, patiently, but never too exactly, Stevens elaborates the installation of the "patron of origins" as a "centre on the horizon," a "giant of nothingness" belatedly inscribed in the system of language by a writing that kills. This "giant," like the thinker of the first idea in "Notes," is a necessary fiction, which can be maintained only historically, that is to say, rhetorically, by the ceaseless overwriting of writing, its "fated eccentricity" (CP, 443). This "giant," this decentered "patron of origins," must be at the same time sustained and displaced, reworked with each act of writing into a "total / Of letters" that is never finished. Poetry, which is at the origin of metaphysics, which produces and sustains the fiction of metaphysical closure, maintains the fiction only by disclosing and deconstructing its artifice—that is to say, the "total artifice" of the idea of totalization.

In a series of deconstructions of Nietzsche and Rousseau, Paul de Man has elaborated the linguistic or rhetorical basis of the *aporia* that binds literature and philosophy in a reciprocal deconstruction, the "endless reflection" of the one in the other, the repeated destruction of one at the hand of the other.[23] In one of the essays on Rousseau, he isolates an allegorical passage from the third section of Rousseau's *Essay on the Origin of Language* as a particularly crucial instance of this problematic.[24] The passage is Rousseau's parable of original naming, of the "origin" of the concept man, and hence of society, in the confrontation of two primitives. Out of "fear," one names the other "giants." Later, observing the similarity or resemblance between their sizes, the savage invents another name—"man"—to account for what is common between them. De Man's complex and decisive deconstruction of this parable bores in on the contradiction (or *aporia*) inherent in Rousseau's argument in the *Essay* that "man's first language had to be figurative" and his insistence in the *Second Discourse* that the "first nouns could only have been proper nouns." This incoherent notion of origins, which elaborates the difference between a so-called rhetorical and literary language and a so-called denominative or referential language, is a textual crux that can only be resolved by a patient and rigorous exploration of the turns in Rousseau's argument. It reveals for de Man the central blindness or "aberration" of linguistic narcissism. The inaugural metaphor of the "giant" becomes the denominational figure for the referential metaphor "man." And since the figure "giant" is a figuration of "fear," the inaugural figuration institutes an "error" that plays throughout all language, which is the play of a language about language in a dialectic that can never close.

Without pursuing the subtleties of de Man's analysis further, I would like to claim its applicability to Stevens' recent retelling of the anecdote of the giant. For while Stevens' parable seems to reverse Rousseau's and to argue that the notion of "giant," the "patron of origins," is a projection of figure behind the proper name of man, the invention and institution of the center that will allow the differences of proper naming, the reversal only produces or re-writes the original problematic, the problematic of origins. Poetry may replace philosophy in its argument for priority and originality, but only by grounding itself in itself, in a referential abyss that goes by the name subjectivity, self, or imagination. In "Notes," the giant, "thinker of the first idea," had to be abandoned and displaced by an idea of man, though a "major man." In "A Primitive Like an Orb," man in his "fated eccentricity" re-writes the "giant of nothingness" with every "particle" of his inscription. The "passion for yes" that reverses the "mortal no" (as in "Esthétique du Mal") is the movement of language, what de Man, analyzing the notion of "passion," calls in Rousseau a "blind metaphorization." The terms "reality" and "imagination" in Stevens are not the denominations of entities, things, places, or extralinguistic forces (a psyche) in Stevens, but the polar opposite of a linguistic field, an abyss in which a "serpent" repeats the changes of the "auroras," the metaphysical changes of a physical world.

"If all language," de Man writes of Rousseau, "is about language, then the paradigmatic linguistic model is that of an entity that confronts itself."[25] For de Man, appealing to Rilke for verification of the Rousseauistic structure, narcissism or self-reflection is not the name of "an original event but itself an allegorical (or metaphorical) version of an intra-linguistic structure."[26] If Stevens' figuration of Narcissus and the serpent of otherness has any meaning, it must be understood as the figuration of an intrapoetic (or metaphorical) structure. "It is a world of words to the end of it, / In which nothing solid is its solid self" (CP, 345), or, to recall a title, "Men Made Out of Words." Poetry has long since begun, not in an inaugural and proper event like the Adamic myth of naming, but in a curious and eccentric re-naming of itself. The "tropic of resemblance," to recall another figure, is not a field where language names and grounds the other, but the aberration to which conceptual or philosophical language presumably makes reference. "Poetry is the subject of the poem" (CP, 176), just as in Rousseau the first language was figural and for Paul Valéry the beginning was "fable." There is no pure or simple beginning but the aberrational play of narcissism, in which a figural language and a conceptual language tend to slide into each other or change places. The serpent and Narcissus cannot maintain an orderly and coherent distance. Stevens' poems, then, rework an old myth of origins, not by way of getting it "straight" at the Sorbonne, but in a manner to reveal that the origin, so fundamental to poetry's need to ground itself in unity or presence, is at bottom poetic and abyssal. It is abys-mal, serpentine, narcissistic, and blind, a beginning again that seems to promise as its project a certain closure. But it only delivers another violent troping to the fiction of the book.

NOTES

MARTZ. "FROM THE JOURNAL OF CRISPIN"

1. *The Autobiography of William Carlos Williams* (New York, 1951), pp. 146, 174.

2. Paul Rosenfeld, "American Painting," *The Dial*, 71 (1921), 649-70. Subsequent page references to this essay are included in the body of the text within parentheses. For an excellent view of this movement toward the "local" see Bram Dijkstra, *The Hieroglyphics of a New Speech: Cubism, Stieglitz, and the Early Poetry of William Carlos Williams* (Princeton, 1969), esp. chap. 4. It was a reading of this chapter that called my attention to the significance of the essay by Rosenfeld.

3. Williams, *Autobiography*, p. 174. Stevens sympathized with this drive for the "American thing": "I was in Charleston in July and while it is true that like any antiquated seaport it contains Armenian priests, Scotch Presbyterians and so on, nevertheless the place is beautifully and sedately the early and undefiled American thing. I love the south for this quality." Stevens to Harriet Monroe, Aug. 24, 1922, *L*, 228-29. "Approaching Carolina" reveals the quest for this quality.

4. For a detailed discussion of the figure of Crispin in French literature see A. Ross Curtis, *Crispin Ier: La Vie et l'oeuvre de Raymond Poisson comédien-poète du XVIIe siècle* (Toronto, 1972), pp. 75-113. For Stevens' relation to modern French poetry see Robert Buttel, *Wallace Stevens: The Making of "Harmonium"* (Princeton, 1967), and Michel Benamou, *Wallace Stevens and the Symbolist Imagination* (Princeton, 1972). An interesting relation to another aspect of French culture is suggested by Sidney Feshbach, "Wallace Stevens and Erik Satie: A Source for 'The Comedian as the Letter C,'" *Texas Studies in Literature and Language*, 11 (Spring 1969), pp. 811-18. Feshbach makes a convincing case for Satie as the inspiration for the opening account of man as "the Socrates / Of snails, musician of pears." He suggests that Stevens probably read an essay, "Satie and *Socrate*," by Paul Rosenfeld, which appeared in *Vanity Fair* in December 1921, and that this essay "figures importantly in the making of the poem."

5. For a strong account of the relation of the "Comedian" to American transcendentalism, especially to Emerson and Whitman, see Harold Bloom, *Wallace Stevens: The Poems of Our Climate* (Ithaca, N.Y., 1977), chap. 4.

6. *L*, 294; see also *L*, 351-52, 778.

7. This parallel has been drawn by A. Walton Litz, *Introspective Voyager: The Poetic Development of Wallace Stevens* (New York, 1972), p. 135. See also the important article by Richard P. Adams, " 'The Comedian as the Letter C': A Somewhat Literal Reading," *Tulane Studies in English*, 18 (1970), 95-114. Adams sees the poem as "a summing-up and a preparation, a putting behind of one way of seeing and working and a stepping stone from which to move toward another, somewhat different way" (p. 99).

8. See *L*, 214, 227, 276-77.

9. See Harold Bloom's excellent analysis of "The Snow Man" as an act of Emersonian reduction to the First Idea: Bloom, *Poems of Our Climate*, chap. 3. "Nuances" is also such a poem of reduction.

10. For Stevens' view of the term "romantic" see his comment with regard to his poem "Sailing After Lunch": "When people speak of the romantic, they do so in what the French commonly call a *pejorative* sense. But poetry is essentially romantic, only the romantic of poetry must be something constantly new and, therefore, just the opposite of what is spoken of as the romantic. Without this new romantic, one gets nowhere; with it, the most casual things take on transcendence. . . . What one is always doing is keeping the romantic pure: eliminating from it what people speak of as the romantic." Stevens to Ronald Lane Latimer, Mar. 12, 1935, *L*, 277.

11. *Kora in Hell: Improvisations* (Boston, 1920), pp. 17-18. The prologue is reprinted in Williams' *Selected Essays* (New York, 1954), pp. 3-26.

12. *Kora in Hell*, pp. 17-18.

13. Ibid., p. 16.

14. Quoted from "The Comedian as the Letter C" (*CP*, 33); see the end of section two of the "Journal" for interesting differences that stress Crispin's sense of freedom from established forms and modes of verse. In the quoted verses "the quintessential fact" was originally "the umbelliferous fact." I wish to thank Andrea Snell for valuable assistance in the preparation of this essay.

BRAZEAU. "A COLLECT OF PHILOSOPHY"

1. On October 2, 1951, Stevens wrote to Pearson, "I am going to read a paper at the University of Chicago in a month or two. Although it has been written, I am still going over it. Next it will be copied and after that I shall be glad to send what remains of it to you. . . . I do not have any old manuscripts whatever since I am an orderly person" (*L*, 730). What remained, except for possible preliminary notes, was apparently the essay in its stages of development from original manuscript to completion. The donation included: a pencil manuscript, 39 leaves, folio; a typescript, 4 leaves, quarto; and a carbon typescript,

23 leaves, quarto. By internal evidence it is possible to reconstruct the manuscript sequence as set out in this essay. I am particularly grateful to Holly Stevens and to the Beinecke Rare Book and Manuscript Library, Yale University, where this material is housed, for permission to publish the manuscript passages.

2. Revising this first draft was a comparatively minor process of erasing and rewriting a phrase or a line or two without disturbing the initial pattern. Most of the erased material is not legible. Some interesting variations can be deciphered, however, such as the original title of the essay, "A Collation of Philosophy."

3. See, for example, Stevens' letter of July 25, 1951, to Barbara Church (L, 721-22).

LITZ. PARTICLES OF ORDER

1. This sentence from the preface to Renan's *Souvenirs* was copied out by Stevens at the end of his first commonplace book, SUR PLUSIEURS BEAUX SUJECTS [*sic*] I, under the heading "Of journals."

2. Some of these volumes are in the Stevens collection at the Huntington Library; the majority are still owned by Holly Stevens, who graciously supplied me with a detailed list and useful information from the unpublished letters.

3. Among the titles are: *Les Proverbes François & Italiens*; *Cent Proverbes*; *Racial Proverbs*; *Wit and Wisdom in Morocco: A Study of Native Proverbs*; *Chinese Proverbs*; *Proverbs and Common Sayings from the Chinese*; *Japanese Proverbs and Proverbial Phrases*; *English-Japanese and Japanese-English Dictionary of Proverbs*; *A Collection of Hindustani Proverbs*; *A Collection of Proverbs, Bengali and Sanscrit*.

4. See ADAGIA entry 157.3(b) in the accompanying text. Numerical references indicate the page in *Opus Posthumous* on which each proverb appears and its position on that page; e.g., 157.3 means page 157, third entry. Entries omitted from *Opus Posthumous* are identified by parenthetical letters; e.g., 157.3(a) and 157.3(b) indicate that these aphorisms occur in the manuscript notebook immediately after the one printed in *Opus Posthumous* as 157.3.

5. Helen Vendler, *On Extended Wings: Wallace Stevens' Longer Poems* (Cambridge, Mass., 1969), pp. 69-70.

6. See Samuel French Morse, *Wallace Stevens: Life as Poetry* (New York, 1970), p. 129.

7. Paul Valéry, foreword to "Analecta" (1926), in *The Collected Works of Paul Valéry*, Vol. 14, *Analecta*, trans. Stuart Gilbert, Bollingen Series No. 45 (Princeton, 1970), p. 266.

8. Beverly Coyle, "An Anchorage of Thought: Defining the Role of Aphorism in Wallace Stevens' Poetry," *PMLA*, 91 (1976), 217.

9. When Stevens copied out a reflection by Georges Braque from

Verve No. 2 (159.10), he rejected the English version offered in the main text and transcribed the original French from the back of the journal. As Stevens once told René Taupin, "La légèreté, la grâce, le son et la couleur du français ont eu sur moi une influence indéniable et une influence précieuse." René Taupin, *L'influence du symbolisme français sur la poésie américaine* (Paris, 1929), p. 276.

TAYLOR. OF A REMEMBERED TIME

1. I should, perhaps, explain what suretyship is, since it was central to Stevens' responsibilities, and since confusion seems to arise easily around just what his role was. Brendan Gill, for example, refers to Stevens as purchasing and redeeming "millions of dollars' worth of bonds" (*Here at The New Yorker* [New York, 1975], p. 56). The word "bonds" might well be called a generic term, for it includes investment bonds, surety bonds, and fidelity bonds. But Stevens had absolutely nothing to do with investment bonds, which are issued and sold to finance corporate, state, federal, or municipal improvements. Stevens was occupied with surety and fidelity bonds.

With the exception of extremely large or unusual fidelity cases, Stevens spent his entire time on surety matters, which included the vast number of contract bonds (bonds on federal, state, municipal, and even private construction contracts). When the Hartford signed one of these, it guaranteed that the contractor would faithfully perform the work contracted for and that he would pay all the bills incurred in that performance. Then there is the vast segment of court bonds that are part of the surety field. These are bonds on executors, administrators, guardians, and conservators, or appeal and injunction bonds. And so the list grows, but never does it include investment bonds.

The idea of suretyship is ancient. From what I can discover, the first reference to a contract of suretyship has an early B.C. date and concerns the conveyance of a virgin daughter to a distant land to marry the man of her father's choice. It was not unusual for the father of the bride to extract from those doing the conveying a bond guaranteeing the continued virginity of the daughter. (One can imagine what the premium on such a bond would be today.) Holy Writ contains several allusions to suretyship. The Book of Solomon tells us that "He that becomes surety for thy friend is ensnared with the words of his mouth." And of course we know the part that a surety bond played in *The Merchant of Venice*.

BRAZEAU. A TRIP IN A BALLOON

1. *L*, 729-30. A glance at his correspondence shows that Stevens reserved the right to change his mind about the value of New York, as

he did about most subjects, though the underlying view in his letters was more typically the sentiment he expressed to Barbara Church in 1953: "one is always curious about the other side of the mountain, and it invigorates me, at least, to go to New York . . ." (L, 769). To Stevens, who felt that "One shrivels up living in the same spot, following the same routine" (L, 827), New York provided a most convenient opportunity for the occasional day away from the Hartford habits he also needed.

2. Unless otherwise noted, the quotations are excerpted from tapes recorded by the author with Stevens' friends, colleagues, and relatives. These tapes are the basis of a Stevens oral history-in-progress.

3. "The Third Little Show" was a 1931 revue starring Beatrice Lillie and Ernest Truex, with sketches by Noel Coward, S. J. Perelman, and Marc Connelly, among others.

4. Roofs were the rage when the Waldorf's Starlight Roof opened in May 1934. There Stevens may have danced to the exotic rhythms of Xavier Cugat or the more sedate tunes of Guy Lombardo, whose bands were among those playing at the Waldorf that summer.

5. CP, 160-61. Sending a copy of *Ideas of Order* to his young friends at Christmas 1935, Stevens wrote: "you and Mrs. Powers are named by name in one of the poems: A FISH-SCALE SUNRISE, which will be a souvenir, not so much of the bat we went on in New York as of the distorted state in which that bat left me" (L, 301).

6. A memorial exhibition of Walter Gay's seventeenth- and eighteenth-century interiors was held at the Metropolitan Museum in the spring of 1938.

7. A *Catalogue of a Few Fine and Scarce Prints Recently Purchased: Exhibited by H. Wunderlich & Co.* (New York, October 1900), in the Special Collections of the University of Massachusetts at Amherst, exemplifies young Stevens' detailed, and sometimes witty, responses to an exhibition. In it he penciled not only his reactions to certain prints but also a crude sketch of one of them.

8. Stevens was acting secretary of the annual stockholders' and directors' meetings in New York in 1917, 1919, and 1920. From 1938 until his death in 1955, Stevens was acting chairman of the annual meeting of stockholders.

9. L, 633. Because Stevens did not eat lunch on a daily basis in his later years, dining with his business friends every Wednesday noon at the Hartford Canoe Club or lunching with friends on his visits to New York became something of an important ritual, an occasion for good food and companionship.

10. "Paysage du Midi" and "Blue Bowl of Red Flowers" were the two Detthow paintings owned by Stevens.

11. To Irita Van Doren, Stevens wrote in 1954: "I like most to go to New York for a day and I like the ride to and fro, whether it is

in a train or in a car, almost as much as I like being in New York"
(*L*, 844).

LENSING. WALLACE STEVENS IN ENGLAND

1. *London Mercury*, 3 (January 1920), 330.
2. "Some Contemporary American Poets," *Chapbook*, 2 (May 1920), 29-30.
3. The four stanzas in the *Chapbook* correspond to stanzas I, VIII, IV, and VII of the original.
4. In "A Letter from America," published in the *London Mercury*, 4 (June 1921), 199, Aiken had quoted approvingly from the first stanza of "Sunday Morning" and predicted that "slowly will come a hearing" for Stevens in England, as well as for Fletcher and Bodenheim.
5. Holly Stevens' note in *L*, 311, that "The book was not published by the Dent firm; no correspondence relating to that possibility has been found by Mr. Church or the editor," is corroborated by a letter from Peter Shellard, director of J. M. Dent & Sons Ltd., to George S. Lensing, August 13, 1976.
6. (London, 1942), p. 80.
7. (London, 1946), p. vii.
8. Stevens to Moore, May 9, 1944. Unless otherwise indicated, the correspondence from Stevens quoted in this essay is unpublished. For permission to quote from it here, I am grateful to The Huntington Library, San Marino, California.
9. Stevens to Alfred A. Knopf, Sept. 14, 1944.
10. Knopf to Stevens, Sept. 21, 1944. (For permission to quote from this unpublished letter and the one from Knopf to Stevens of Nov. 1, 1945, I am grateful to Mr. William A. Koshland of Alfred A. Knopf Inc.)
11. Stevens to Tambimuttu, Sept. 23, 1944.
12. Stevens to Tambimuttu, Dec. 1, 1944.
13. Stevens to Moore, July 20, 1945.
14. Stevens to Moore, July 25, 1945.
15. Knopf to Stevens, Nov. 1, 1945.
16. Stevens to Knopf, Nov. 15, 1945.
17. Stevens to Oscar Williams, Nov. 20, 1945.
18. Stevens to Moore, Feb. 20, 1946.
19. Stevens to Henry Church, Mar. 11, 1946.
20. Stevens to Knopf, Nov. 8, 1946.
21. Stevens to Herbert Weinstock, Oct. 10, 1951.
22. Untitled remarks, *Trinity Review*, 8 (May 1954), 9.
23. Peter du Sautoy to George S. Lensing, Aug. 3, 1976.
24. "Sky Shades and Lamp Shades," *Irish Times*, Feb. 14, 1953, p. 6, cols. 3-4.

25. The Fortune Press had earlier issued *Poetry from Oxford, Michaelmas 1948 to Michaelmas 1949* in 1950, edited by Williamson and including three poems by him.

26. "Foreword," in *Selected Poems* (London, 1953), pp. 10-12.

27. Weinstock to Stevens, Feb. 27, 1953. These remarks are quoted in J. M. Edelstein, *Wallace Stevens: A Descriptive Bibliography* (Pittsburgh, 1973), p. 100. Edelstein incorrectly attributes the letter to Alfred A. Knopf instead of Weinstock.

28. Du Sautoy to George S. Lensing, Aug. 3, 1976.

29. Charles Skilton to George S. Lensing, Aug. 4, 1976.

30. "American Diction v. American Poetry," *Encounter*, 1 (October 1953), 65.

31. " 'Essential Gaudiness': The Poems of Wallace Stevens," *Twentieth Century*, 153 (June 1953), 455, 462.

32. *Times Literary Supplement*, June 19, 1953, p. 396.

33. "The Sound of a Blue Guitar," *Nine*, 4 (Winter 1953-1954), 50-51.

34. "An American Poet," *The Listener*, 49 (March 26, 1953), 521.

35. "Stevens in England," *Trinity Review*, 8 (May 1954), 43. Fourteen years earlier, Symons had written an essay commending *The Man with the Blue Guitar* as "one of the most notable poetic achievements of the last twenty years, an achievement that may be compared with *The Waste Land* or 'Mauberley.' " The essay goes on to fault Stevens for giving "an objective view of Mr. Stevens in various attitudes" instead of a "philosophy of life." "A Short View of Wallace Stevens," *Life and Letters Today*, 26 (September 1940), 215-24.

36. Du Sautoy to George S. Lensing, Aug. 3, 1976.

37. Stevens to Tambimuttu, Apr. 13, 1955.

38. *Trinity Review*, 8 (May 1954), 9.

ELLMANN. HOW STEVENS SAW HIMSELF

1. William James, *The Principles of Psychology*, 2 vols. (New York, 1890), 1:372.

2. William James and Gilbert Ryle, *The Concept of Mind* (New York, 1949), pp. 186-87.

3. Quoted in SP, 67.

4. Carlos Baker, *Ernest Hemingway: A Life Story* (New York, 1969), p. 28.

5. Harold Bloom's suggestion that the line in "Le Monocle de Mon Oncle," "Shall I uncrumple this much-crumpled thing?" refers to Stevens' penis is totally at variance with this view. To me the line means, "Shall I say what I have long brooded about?"

6. Harold Bloom, *Wallace Stevens: The Poems of Our Climate* (Ithaca, 1977), p. 2.

7. Quoted in Jerald E. Hatfield, "More about Legend," *Trinity Review*, 8 (May 1954), 30.

8. Compare, "Realism is a corruption of reality," as Stevens writes in the *Adagia* (OP, 166), and "the sense of reality makes more acute the sense of the fictive . . ." (L, 444-45).

9. Similarly, in *Carlos among the Candles*, Carlos, after extinguishing the candles, finds with pleasure "matter beyond invention" (OP, 150).

10. In "The Auroras of Autumn" he applies the same double nature to fire: "The scholar of one candle sees / An Arctic effulgence flaring . . ." (CP, 417).

11. Cf. A. Walton Litz, *Introspective Voyager: The Poetic Development of Wallace Stevens* (New York, 1972), p. 133.

12. Goethe, *Wilhelm Meisters Wanderjahre* (Zurich and Stuttgart, Artemis, 1948 ff.) I:14. "Many-sidedness merely prepares the element in which one-sidedness can effectively develop; for it is then that it is given sufficient space. Indeed, we do live now in a time of many-sidedness; he who understands this can achieve much for himself and others." (Translated by Erich Heller.)

13. His father continues: "Many seem so constructed that they will starve rather than dig the goobers under their feet unless somebody tells them they are there and how to dig and cook 'em but the chap who has gumption thinks for himself—plans according to his means—and keeps at it until he finally accomplishes great things." Unpublished letter, November 17, 1907, from Reading, in the Huntington Library.

14. Cf. "hundreds of eyes, in one mind, see at once." "An Ordinary Evening in New Haven" (CP, 488).

15. L, 218. The editors are grateful to Alfred A. Knopf, Inc., for permission to reprint this poem from *Letters of Wallace Stevens*, edited by Holly Stevens.

16. *The Palm at the End of the Mind: Selected Poems and a Play by Wallace Stevens*, ed. Holly Stevens (New York, 1971), pp. 395-96.

17. In "The Man Whose Pharynx Was Bad" (CP, 96), Stevens describes the world as posed lukewarmly between absolute summer and total winter.

18. "I shall explain The Snow Man as an example of the necessity of identifying oneself with reality in order to understand it and enjoy it" (L, 464).

19. Compare Emerson, "What is called a warm heart, I have not" (*The Journals and Miscellaneous Notebooks of Ralph Waldo Emerson*, Vol. 11, ed. W. H. Gillman, Alfred R. Ferguson, and Merrell R. Davis (Cambridge, Mass., 1961), 241 (April 18, 1824).

20. "Wallace Stevens' Ice-Cream," *Kenyon Review*, 19 (Winter 1957), 99-105.

21. Cf. "Le Monocle de Mon Oncle": "in our amours amorists discern / Such fluctuations that their scrivening / Is breathless to attend each quirky turn" (*CP*, 15).

22. Stevens, *Palm at the End of the Mind*, p. 366.

VENDLER. STEVENS AND KEATS' "TO AUTUMN"

1. See, for example, John Reibetanz, " 'The Whitsun Weddings': Larkin's Reinterpretation of Time and Form in Keats," *Contemporary Literature* 17 (Autumn 1976), 538-39. After noticing the echoes of Keats at the close of "Sunday Morning," Reibetanz remarks that Stevens uses "a similar landscape to capture and to convey a mood of mixed ripeness and decay that masterfully approximates the mood of Keats' poem, even as Stevens varies the tone to emphasize not so much the poignancy as the voluptuousness of the scene." All the items in this proposition seem to me false. Keats' landscape is domestic and agricultural, Stevens' represents the American wilderness; there is no decay (only harvest) in Keats, and no perceptible decay in this stanza of "Sunday Morning"; Stevens' berries, quail, pigeons, and deer are not "voluptuous" in any ordinary meaning of the word; and if Keats, as I believe, chastens his impulse to "poignancy," Stevens on the contrary makes poignancy the purpose of his closing line. Such a disagreement on two relatively brief passages exemplifies the difficulties of literary comparison.

2. Keats rejected the word "flock" for his swallows, as his draft shows.

3. H. W. Garrod was the first to identify "the songs of Spring" with the song of the nightingale, making the link through Ruth and the gleaner. Stevens' fantasia on this element of the autumn ode is found in "Autumn Refrain," where Stevens regrets the absence of "the nightingale . . . not a bird for me / But the name of a bird and the name of a nameless air / I have never—shall never hear" (*CP*, 160). What he hears instead is "Some skreaking and skittering residuum," which, while deriving from Keats' whistles and twitters, is less attractive than Keats' animal music. Cf. also "The Man on the Dump," where "*aptest eve*," "*Invisible priest*," and "*stanza my stone*" may derive from "tender night" in "Nightingale," "priest" in "Psyche," "priest," and "marble" in "Urn."

4. "Adieu" is present in "Psyche," "Melancholy," "Urn," "Nightingale," and "Indolence" (where "farewell" also appears), though not in "To Autumn." Its absence in "Autumn" (which in itself is one long adieu) is best explained by Stevens in his own poem "Waving Adieu, Adieu, Adieu" (a title that adds one more farewell than Keats offers to the nightingale). This poem equates "adieu" and "farewell" and says that neither phrase is necessary to the modern poet of disbelief:

In a world without heaven to follow, the stops
Would be endings, more poignant than partings, profounder,
And that would be saying farewell, repeating farewell,
Just to be there and just to behold.

.   .   .   .

Just to be there, just to be beheld,
That would be bidding farewell, be bidding farewell.

One likes to practice the thing. They practice,
Enough, for heaven. Ever-jubilant,
What is there here but weather, what spirit
Have I except it comes from the sun?

(CP, 127-28)

5. Here Stevens borrows from "Ode on a Grecian Urn," where the
panting lovers turn at the end into marble men and maidens.

6. Stevens had said, in "Like Decorations in a Nigger Cemetery,"
that "The album of Corot is premature." We could substitute, "the
album of Keats." Stevens continues: "A little later when the sky is
black [is the time proper for representation by the artist]. / Mist that
is golden is not wholly mist" (CP, 156). Keats' draft for the autumn
ode reads, "While a gold cloud gilds the soft-dying day": his "season
of mists" still keeps its mists golden.

MAC CAFFREY. WAYS OF TRUTH IN "LE MONOCLE"

1. A. Walton Litz argues in Introspective Voyager: The Poetic De-
velopment of Wallace Stevens (New York, 1972) that imagism "had
a catalytic effect on his art" (p. 36). Stevens himself remarked that
"when HARMONIUM was in the making there was a time when I liked
the idea of images and images alone . . ." (L, 288).

2. Vendler, On Extended Wings: Wallace Stevens' Longer Poems
(Cambridge, Mass., 1969), p. 65.

3. Litz, Voyager, p. 51. Vendler, however, calls it "both uncertain
and derivative" (Extended Wings, p. 63).

4. Litz, Voyager, p. 82.

5. Frank Kermode, Wallace Stevens (London, 1960), p. 45.

6. Voyager, p. 83.

7. Stevens, p. 45.

8. Daniel Fuchs, in The Comic Spirit of Wallace Stevens (Durham,
N.C., 1963), compares the lines with "the evolutionary regression fan-
tasy of Prufrock, who wished that he were a pair of 'ragged claws' "
(p. 26). The comparison reveals as many differences as similarities.
Stevens' speaker is talking about the involuntary processes of imagina-

tion as well as experiencing them, and his images lack the shocking force of Prufrock's unwitting self-revelations.

9. "The conflict between language and meaning" in Stevens has been noted by Joseph N. Riddel, *The Clairvoyant Eye: The Poetry and Poetics of Wallace Stevens* (Baton Rouge, La., 1965), pp. 88 ff.

10. Kenner, *A Homemade World: The American Modernist Writers* (New York, 1975), p. 80.

11. Donald Davie, in " 'Essential Gaudiness': The Poems of Wallace Stevens," *Twentieth Century*, 153 (1953), sees that "to get at the meaning, you have to go *behind* the poetry," but he argues that "Le Monocle" is traditionally "discursive" and interprets "meaning" reductively. "Understanding *Le Monocle* is a matter of groping through a dazzle, of stripping off the comparisons, until you come, behind the rhetorical magnificence, at a structure of plain sense that is quite lean and skeletal. It is possible to write a prose paraphrase of the poem, without quoting from it more than once" (pp. 456-57). One would like to see this paraphrase. "Stripping off the comparisons" would leave us with an argument made up of the explicit lines spoken by the persona; but one of the poem's subjects is the *relation* of this voice to its inventions—those parables or "comparisons" that Davie would strip away.

12. Riddel, *Clairvoyant Eye*, p. 88.

13. Preface to *Poems* (1815), in *Literary Criticism of William Wordsworth*, ed. Paul M. Zall (Lincoln, Nebr., 1966), p. 149.

14. *Stevens*, p. 44.

15. I am pleased that Harold Bloom's reading of "Le Monocle" in *Wallace Stevens: The Poems of Our Climate* (Ithaca and London, 1977), which I read when this essay was completed, is compatible with mine in a number of respects. He notes the analogy with Wordsworth's "Ode" on p. 39.

16. "The Nakcd Eye of the Aunt" is no more discerning. If Stevens did intend the stanzas printed by Morse in OP (p. 19) for "Le Monocle," one can only say that their self-conscious rhetoric confirms the sardonic point of view that he directs toward "twiddling *mon idée*" in the poem as a whole.

17. Helen Vendler, *Extended Wings*, pp. 60-61, perhaps comes closest to the truth of the stanza, but she exaggerates, I think, its "violence."

18. Cf. Ronald Sukenik, *Wallace Stevens: Musing the Obscure* (New York and London, 1967): "Figures whose sense is almost impermeable to the intelligence are expressed in forms that the intelligence is accustomed readily to grasp" (p. 40).

EHRENPREIS. STRANGE RELATION

1. Cf. the "shoo-shoo-shoo of secret cymbals," which is rejected

when Bawda marries a great captain in "Notes toward a Supreme Fiction" (CP, 401), because earthly marriage must not be ascetic or fleshless, as was that of St. Catherine.

2. See Frank Doggett's meticulous account of this poem in "The Transition from *Harmonium*: Factors in the Development of Stevens' Later Poetry," *PMLA*, 88 (1973), 128-29.

3. Cf. "An Ordinary Evening in New Haven" (CP, 471). For an interpretation of "Two Figures" based on the view that the speaker is a man, see Harold Bloom, "Wallace Stevens: The Poem of Our Climate," *Prose*, 8 (1974), 8-10.

4. Cf. Doggett, "Transition from *Harmonium*," p. 129.

5. See L, 783; cf. his explanation of "ai-yi-yi" ("The Man with the Blue Guitar," section xxv) in ibid., 784.

6. I presume that Stevens had a particular poet in mind. Schiller rhymes "Winde" with "linde" in "Laura am Klavier." Heine, in "Auf ihrem Grab da steht eine Linde," plays with "linde," "Aberwinde," and "so lind." But Stefan George sounds most likely. In poem after poem he juxtaposes the words used by Stevens: "Siedlergang," ll. 4 and 7 (winde, lau, blau); "Komm in den totgesagten park," ll. 3 and 6 (blau, wind, lau); "Ruckkehr," l. 8 (winde, lind); "Nicht forsche welchem spruch," l. 9 (gelind, lau); "Landschaft 1," ll. 22-23 (blau, wind, lau). George's symbolic use of seasons and weather is similar to that of Stevens. I am indebted to Dr. Raymond Ockenden of Wadham College, Oxford, for assistance in gathering this information.

7. Cf. Frank Doggett, "Stevens on the Genesis of a Poem," *Contemporary Literature*, 16 (1976), 463-77, esp. 468-71.

HOLLANDER. THE SOUND OF THE MUSIC

1. The internal rhyme connecting "she" and "sea" is given more significance by the way in which the initial *s* seems to "stir" in the initial *s*, and, thus, "sea" in "she."

2. See my "Spenser and the Mingled Measure," *English Literary Renaissance*, 1 (1971), 226-38; "Wordsworth and the Music of Sound," in Geoffrey Hartman, ed., *New Perspectives on Coleridge and Wordsworth* (New York, 1972); and *Images of Voice* (Cambridge, 1970).

3. I adopt, as elsewhere, Geoffrey Hartman's term, from *Wordsworth's Poetry, 1787-1814* (New Haven, 1964), pp. 95-98.

4. Emerson's famous phrase may come from Francis Quarles, *Hieroglyphics of the Life of Man*, Book II, 8: "The ploughman's whistle, or the trivial flute / Find more respect than great Apollo's lute." If so, Emerson's reworking of the image entails an implicit manifesto, as the bardic "harp" would have itself revised, in the history of English poetic emblem, the Renaissance anachronism of "Apollo's lute."

5. A journal entry of 1840, from Emerson, *Journals*, ed. A. W. Plumstead and Harrison Hayford, VII (Cambridge, Mass., 1969), 535. The whole passage is relevant: "Art is never fixed but flowing. The sweetest music is not in the oratorio but in the voice of tenderness or of truth + courage. The oratorio has already lost . . . but that persuading voice is in perfect tune with the blowing wind + the / growing plant / fall of the seed. All works of art should not be as now detached performances but extempore." Some aspects of Stevens' "The Creations of Sound" must be considered in the light of this theme.

6. Henry David Thoreau, *Journal*, ed. Bradford Torrey and Francis H. Allen, III (Boston, 1949), 332. See also Stanley Cavell's discussion of the "Sounds" chapter in *The Senses of Walden* (New York, 1972), 36-44.

7. Emily Dickinson, *Complete Poems*, ed. T. H. Johnson (Boston, 1969), nos. 1764, 157, 503.

8. The next step in the series of reworked figurations of remembered replayed music might be in Charles Ives.

9. Nature seems to echo the original scene of first-born flower or fruit here: in *Paradise Lost* (IV, 603-4), after the nightingale "all night long her amorous descant sang, / Silence was pleas'd."

10. See James Wright's graceful comments on this poem in "Whitman's Delicacy," in R.W.B. Lewis, ed., *The Presence of Walt Whitman* (New York, 1962), 178-80.

11. In this connection, see George Santayana's remark that music "deploys a sensuous harmony by a sort of dialectic, suspending and resolving it, so that the parts become distinct and their relation vital." "Music," from the abridgement of *The Life of Reason* by Santayana and Daniel Cory (New York, 1953), p. 317.

12. John Ashbery, "The Mythological Poet," from *Some Trees* (New Haven, 1966), p. 34.

13. Santayana, "Music," p. 315.

14. Consider the second stanza of "Variations on a Summer Day" (CP, 232) for an undersound that becomes an inscription.

15. Bloom, *Wallace Stevens: The Poems of Our Climate* (Ithaca, N.Y., 1977), p. 91.

16. Ibid., p. 92.

17. Stevens says in the *Adagia*: "There is no such thing as a metaphor of a metaphor. One does not progress through metaphors . . ." (OP, 179). This would so appear to deny the operation by which many of his own metaphors are generated, that we must conclude that a dead metaphor becomes a part of reality, like a corpse.

KERMODE. DWELLING POETICALLY IN CONNECTICUT

1. Margaret Peterson, "*Harmonium* and William James," *Southern Review*, (Summer 1971), 664 ff.

2. "Und keinen Waffen brauchts und keinen / Listen, so lange, bis Gottes Fehl hilft." Text and translation from Michael Hamburger's complete parallel text, *Friedrich Hölderlin: Poems and Fragments* (London, 1966), pp. 176-77 (translated from *Hölderlin: Sämtliche Werke* [Stuttgart, 1961]).

3. The prose poem "In lieblicher Bläue," from which these lines derive, is certainly not Hölderlin's own, but Heidegger treats it without question as authentic.

4. Thomson, "The City of Dreadful Night"; Whitman, "A Clear Midnight." Both quoted in NA, 119.

5. Jarrell, *The Third Book of Criticism* (New York, 1969), pp. 57-58.

6. Heidegger, *Poetry, Language, Thought*, trans. Albert Hofstadter (New York, 1971), p. x.

7. Heidegger, "The Origin of the Work of Art [Der Ursprung von Kunstwerkes]," in *Poetry, Language, Thought*, pp. 17-81.

8. "The Thinker as Poet," in *Poetry, Language, Thought*, p. 4.

9. Heidegger, "Hölderlin and the Essence of Poetry," trans. Douglas Scott, in Heidegger, *Existence and Being*, comp. Werner Brock (Chicago, 1949), p. 310.

10. Commentators on Stevens appear not to have interested themselves much in this affinity, always supposing that it exists. They have not, to my knowledge, spoken of Stevens in relation to late works of Heidegger (that is, from the 1936 Hölderlin essay on). But Richard Macksey freely alludes to *Sein und Zeit* (along with Husserl and Merleau-Ponty) to illuminate late Stevens. He observes, in part, that "Stevens grounds his poetics and defines his individuality in terms of a death which always *impends* even in 'the genius of summer' " (*CP*, 482). See his "The Climates of Wallace Stevens," in Roy Harvey Pearce and J. Hillis Miller, eds., *The Act of the Mind: Essays on the Poetry of Wallace Stevens* (Baltimore, 1965), p. 201. Heidegger argues that *my* death alone achieves and delimits wholeness of Being (cf. "Every man dies his own death" [*OP*, 165]); and the project of the late Stevens recalls Heidegger's *Sein zum Tode* (when *Dasein* reaches its wholeness in death, it simultaneously loses the Being of its 'there' "). Macksey cites as his epigraph Heidegger's favorite Hölderlin quotation ("dichterisch, wohnet der Mensch auf dieser Erde") but does not otherwise refer to the philosopher's later work. An essay by J. Hillis Miller in the same collection sounds as though Miller could have had these later essays in mind, but he does not allude to them explicitly.

11. In *Being and Time*, trans. John Macquarrie and Edward Robinson (New York, 1962), p. 80, Heidegger explains (though that is not the right word) that the word *innan* (*wohnen*) collects the senses of "to dwell" (*inn*) and "accustomed," "familiar with," and "look after

something" (*an*). But there is no substitute for a reading of that passage and related passages.

12. Quoted by Heidegger in "Hölderlin and the Essence of Poetry," p. 296.

13. Heidegger, "Building Dwelling Thinking," in *Poetry, Language, Thought*, pp. 143-62.

14. Heidegger, "Remembrance of the Poet," trans. Douglas Scott, in *Existence and Being*, p. 281.

15. Heidegger, "Hölderlin and the Essence of Poetry," pp. 293 ff.

16. Heidegger, "Remembrance of the Poet," p. 264.

17. Heidegger, "The Origin of the Work of Art," p. 41.

18. Ibid., p. 47.

19. Heidegger, "What Are Poets For?" in *Poetry, Language, Thought*, p. 97.

MILLER. THEORETICAL AND ATHEORETICAL IN STEVENS

1. Foucault, "Nietzsche, Freud, Marx," in his *Nietzsche* (Paris, 1967), pp. 187, 189.

2. In another essay I have tried to show that a similar irreconcilable conflict among concepts of poetry governs the thought of the important prose sections of the original version of William Carlos Williams' *Spring and All*. See "Williams' *Spring and All* and the Progress of Poetry," *Daedalus*, 99 (Spring 1970), 405-34.

3. In Heidegger, *Holzwege* (Frankfurt, 1950); also in a somewhat revised edition as *Der Ursprung des Kunstwerkes*, Universal-Bibliothek No. 8446/47 (Stuttgart, 1960). For an English translation see "The Origin of the Work of Art," in *Poetry, Language, Thought*, trans. A. Hofstadter (New York, 1971), pp. 17-87.

4. Aristotle, *On the Art of Poetry*, trans. Lane Cooper (Ithaca, N.Y., 1947), pp. 9, 10.

5. Ibid., p. 50.

6. See Mac Hammond, "On the Grammar of Wallace Stevens," in *The Act of the Mind: Essays on the Poetry of Wallace Stevens*, ed. Roy Harvey Pearce and J. Hillis Miller (Baltimore, 1965), pp. 179-84.

7. See Jacques Derrida, "La Pharmacie de Platon," in his *La Dissémination* (Paris, 1972), pp. 71-197. For a discussion of the play in Aristotle's thought between imitation as copy and imitation as revelation see the second and third sections of Jacques Derrida, "La Mythologie blanche," in his *Marges de la philosophie* (Paris, 1972), pp. 274-302.

8. "Ribh in Ecstasy," in *The Collected Poems of William Butler Yeats* (New York, 1958), p. 284.

9. *On the Art of Poetry*, p. 74.

PEARCE. TOWARD DECREATION

1. I am of course developing here the analysis of "decreation" and its significance for Stevens' work set forth in my *Continuity of American Poetry* (Princeton, 1961), pp. 412-13. As will be quite apparent, my present understanding of that significance differs somewhat from my earlier one, as it also does from Frank Kermode's, in his *Continuities* (London, 1968), pp. 75-77. My apologia simply is that over the past few years I have learned something and wish to communicate it here. It will also be apparent that I think it a capital error to confuse "decreation" with "deconstruction" and to make Stevens' use of the concept an occasion to "deconstruct" Stevens' poetry in particular and modernist poetry in general. For examples of this, as I take it, error, see, among others: Joseph N. Riddel, *The Inverted Bell: Modernism and the Counterpoetics of William Carlos Williams* (Baton Rouge, 1974), particularly pp. 214-16; J. Hillis Miller, "Williams' *Spring and All* and the Progress of Poetry," *Daedalus*, 99 (Spring 1970), 405-34, and "Stevens' Rock as Criticism and Cure," *Georgia Review*, 30 (1976), 5-31, 330-48; and Michel Benamou, "Displacements of Parental Space: American Poetry and French Symbolism," *Boundary 2*, 5 (1977), 471-86.

2. *Continuity of American Poetry*, esp. pp. 395-400.

3. I take it that the Carlyle of the Everlasting Nay/Yea is in fact *the* "Well Dressed Man with a Beard." For Stevens' early interest in Carlyle, see *L*, 82.

4. I have charted the American mode of archetypal autobiography in "Whitman: The Poet in 1860," in my *Historicism Once More: Problems & Occasions for the American Scholar* (Princeton, 1969), pp. 200-239.

5. The title and the thrust of this poem of course indicate that to the end Stevens insisted in his polemic against William Carlos Williams on the relationship of the imagination to reality—which is to say, the power and place and possibility of the decreative process. For the title and also the substance of the poem are variations on the title and substance of Williams' "A Sort of a Song" (1926), in which there twice occurs the refrain, "Say it, no ideas but in things," a theme and locution that dominate Williams' *Paterson*.

RIDDEL. METAPHORIC STAGING

1. The phrase "scene of writing" does not refer to a specific event, but is a metaphor for a certain notion of writing that has been elaborated by the French philosopher Jacques Derrida. The poem does evoke a writer and a place of writing, so that the notion of writing here is a "scene of writing" within a "scene of writing." Scene implies staging, hence a metaphor for a certain idea of writing, or a metaphor

of metaphor. Thus writing implies more than either the physical act or the literal notion of script. Writing is always staged, already always a scene, not simply a broken immediateness, but a rupture of any notion of the immediate. Writing involves the whole movement of language— displacement, substitution, repetition, which puts in question the classical concept of representation, of the production of signs that represent, as a double, some thing, event, idea, "thing itself," etc. Similarly, the notion of the "book" implies, as in the epigraph from Derrida, a philosophical concept of closure, or the organization and totalization of signs (surfaces) around a center, subject, presence, meaning, which the signs express or represent. Hence, the "book" implies the figuration of inside/outside, of depth and centrality, of a meaning that is at once concealed and revealed through and by an opaque exteriority. A "text," in contrast to the "book," is a surface, a place of heterogeneous, and thus uncentered, signs, a surface without depth.

2. See Jacques Derrida, *Of Grammatology*, trans. Gayatri Spivak (Baltimore, 1976), for the implications of this notion of erasure, which runs through Derrida's prolific writing. Spivak discusses the notion in her long introduction. To put a concept "under erasure" means to submit it to a rigorous questioning in a manner that reveals the figuration of the concept, that it is grounded in a reference that is no less metaphorical, and so on. The erasure of a concept (or crossing it out) nevertheless leaves an imprint or trace of it, so that far from simply negating or vanquishing the notion to the status of a fiction or false idea, erasure reemploys the concept as a problematic or illogical notion, a functional nonconcept, a splitting or pluralizing of its illusory univocity or its singular, referential meaning. One of the methodological chapters of this text is entitled, "The End of the Book and the Beginning of Writing."

3. Cf. Derrida *Of Grammatology*, p. 234, on "passion," writing, and supplementation in Rousseau's *Essay on the Origin of Language*. In the "Thus Spake Zarathustra" section of *Ecce Homo*, Nietzsche reflects on the "passion" of epigrams, the thrown-forwardness of eloquence, which overcomes or disrupts metaphoric continuity. Then he writes of Zarathustra: "The psychological problem in the type of Zarathustra is how he that says No and *does* No to an unheard-of degree, to everything to which one has so far said Yes, can nevertheless be the opposite of a No-saying spirit; how the spirit who bears the heaviest fate, a fatality of a task, can nevertheless be the lightest and most transcendent . . . how he that has the hardest, most terrible insight into reality, that has thought the "most abysmal idea," nevertheless does not consider it an objection to existence, not even to its eternal recurrence—but rather one reason more for being himself the eternal Yes to all things 'the tremendous, unbounded saying Yes and Amen.' —'Into all abysses I still carry the blessings of my saying Yes.'" Quoted from *On the*

Genealogy of Morals and *Ecce Homo*, trans. Walter Kaufmann (New York, 1969), p. 306.

4. "Prologue—*Kora in Hell*," in Williams, *Imaginations*, ed. Webster Schott (New York, 1970), pp. 14-16.

5. See Derrida, *Of Grammatology*, pp. 15 ff. and passim.; and Derrida, "La Double séance," in his *La Dissémination* (Paris, 1972), pp. 199-317.

6. Recall "Sunday Morning," where the lady's desire for some "imperishable bliss" (*CP*, 68) is explored as a contradiction; and "Le Monocle de Mon Oncle," where "anecdotal bliss" (*CP*, 13) is rejected as a transcendental dream and folly. In "Notes," as we shall see, the metaphors of "accessible" and "expressible" bliss (*CP*, 404, 395) link the desire to language. And in "Esthétique du Mal" the desire for "So great a unity, that it is bliss" (*CP*, 317) is to be permitted only within the "actual, the warm," which is not a unity or a transcendentality but an otherness.

7. I borrow here from Nietzsche's early essay on rhetoric, "Truth and Falsity in an Ultramoral Sense" (sometimes translated as "Of Truth and Falsity [or Error] in the Extra-Moral Sense"), in *The Philosophy of Nietzsche*, ed. Geoffrey Clive (New York, 1965), pp. 503-15. (This text is taken from Oscar Levy's 18-volume translation of Nietzsche's *Complete Works*.) In this, the only completed section of his *Philosophenbuch*—an essay largely ignored by philosophy until this last decade, when it has become the model for deconstructive analysis—Nietzsche radically situates the notions of essence and truth, located as it were in the "thing-in-itself," in the evasions and discontinuities of language that are taken for "truth" because the origins of truth in metaphoric accident have been forgotten. For Nietzsche, even a percept is a "first metaphor," discontinuous with the unknowable stimulus that provoked it; and language, or the sign (sound or script) of the percept is a metaphor of a metaphor, a "second metaphor" at best. There can be no movement of essence or presence through these discontinuous planes, hence no access to a "truth" or its "origin," the "thing-in-itself," by a regression from late to earlier metaphors.

8. Harold Bloom, *Wallace Stevens: The Poems of Our Climate* (Ithaca, N.Y., 1977), p. 49, finds Stevens' notion of the "first idea" most relevantly anticipated in C. S. Peirce's "Idea of Firstness," which locates that idea in trope, indeed, in the figure of heliotrope. Also see Derrida, "La Mythologie blanche," in his *Marges de la philosophie* (Paris, 1972), pp. 247-324 (translated as "White Mythology," *New Literary History*, 6 [Autumn 1974], 5-74).

9. See Derrida, "Le Supplement du copula," *Marges*, pp. 209-46 (translated as "The Supplement of the Copula," *Georgia Review*, 30 [Fall 1976], 527-64).

10. Hence Stevens' deconstruction of the subject/imagination, which echoes Nietzsche's in *The Will to Power* and elsewhere.

11. In an essay on Nietzsche and the Heideggerean reading of Nietzsche, first titled "La Question du style" and later "Eperons—les styles de Nietzsche" (English title, "Spurs—Nietzsche's Styles"), Derrida explores the philosophical question of "forgetting" with regard to the question of style, or styles as he insists on the plural. "Eperons" has been reprinted as a text, including Italian, German, and English translations, edited and with introduction by Stefano Agosti (Venice, 1977). Nietzsche's "Truth and Falsity" links the movement of metaphor to forgetting.

12. See n. 1 above.

13. Benamou, "Displacements of Parental Space: American Poetry and French Symbolism," *Boundary* 2, 5 (Winter 1977), 471-86.

14. See Nietzsche, "Truth and Falsity," p. 507: "Every idea originates through equating the unequal."

15. Quoted by Derrida in "The Supplement of the Copula," 528-29. Derrida in turn takes the phrase from a bilingual (French-German) edition of Nietzsche's *Das Philosophenbuch*.

16. See n. 7 above.

17. In "Truth and Falsity" Nietzsche refers to the proper name of the serpent as an example of linguistic or metaphorical abstraction, of the word that is not only discontinuous with the "thing" but is at least three removes from any assent it evokes by a powerful reduction of individual to concept. The serpent, of course, is a recurring figure in Nietzsche, not a symbol as such but a problematics of the symbol, one of the signs of Zarathustra. Students of Stevens will probably insist on some relation of his serpent to Paul Valéry's, either the silent serpent of "La Jeune parque" or the figure of "Ebauche d'un serpent."

18. In *Poems of Our Climate*, p. 396, Bloom asserts that "Every notion of the will that we have is itself a trope, even when it tropes against the will, by asserting that the will is a linguistic fiction."

19. See n. 17 above.

20. See Geoffrey Hartman, "Monsieur Texte: On Jacques Derrida, His *Glas*," *Georgia Review*, 29 (Winter 1975), 759-97, and "Monsieur Texte II: Epiphony in Echoland," *Georgia Review*, 30 (Spring 1976), 169-97. Hartman puns on Derrida's grammatology as an epigrammatology.

21. In a letter to Mona Van Duyn, Stevens remarks that "the auroras of autumn are not the early autumn mornings but the aurora borealis which we have now and then in Hartford, sometimes quite strong enough to attract attention from indoors. These lights symbolize a tragic and desolate background (L, 852).

22. Again, see "Truth and Falsity," p. 507, where Nietzsche writes of the "thing-in-itself" that "it is just this which would be the pure ineffective truth," an "enigmatical x" for which every name is a metaphysical equation.

23. Paul de Man, "Nietzsche's Theory of Rhetoric," *Symposium*, 28 (Spring 1974), 33-51, and "Action and Identity in Nietzsche," *Graphesis*, Yale French Studies, 52 (1975), 16-30.

24. De Man, "Theory of Metaphor in Rousseau's *Second Discourse*," in David Thornburn and Geoffrey Hartman, eds., *Romanticisms: Vistas, Instances, Continuities* (Ithaca, N.Y., 1973), pp. 83-114.

25. Ibid., p. 110.

26. Ibid., p. 106n.

NOTES ON CONTRIBUTORS

Peter A. Brazeau, under grants from the American Council of Learned Societies and the National Endowment for the Humanities, is completing an oral biography of Wallace Stevens' mature years. He is Associate Professor of English at St. Joseph College, West Hartford, Connecticut.

Irvin Ehrenpreis is Linden Kent Memorial Professor of English Literature at the University of Virginia and editor of *Wallace Stevens: A Critical Anthology* (1972). He has held several fellowships, including a Guggenheim, and has published, along with his work on Swift and other eighteenth-century subjects, *Literary Meaning and Augustan Values* (1974).

Richard Ellmann, Goldsmiths' Professor of English Literature at Oxford University, is the author of several books on Joyce and Yeats. He has also edited the *New Oxford Book of American Verse* (1976) and coedited the *Norton Anthology of Modern Poetry* (1973). His earlier essay on Wallace Stevens, "Wallace Stevens' Ice-Cream," appeared in the *Kenyon Review* in 1957 and was reprinted in R. M. Ludwig, ed., *Aspects of American Poetry* (1962).

John Hollander teaches English at Yale University. His most recent books are *Spectral Emanations: New and Selected Poems* (1978), *Blue Wine*, and *The Figure of Echo* (1979), a study of allusion.

Frank Kermode is the author of *Wallace Stevens* (1960) and several essays on the poet. He has also written *Romantic Image* (1957), *The Sense of an Ending* (1967), and *The Classic* (1975). At present he is King Edward VII Professor of English Literature at Cambridge University.

George S. Lensing is Associate Professor of English and Assistant Chairman of the English Department at the University of North Carolina at Chapel Hill. He is coauthor of *Four Poets and the Emotive Imagination* and has published essays on Wallace Ste-

vens in various books and journals. He is review editor of the
Wallace Stevens Journal.

A. Walton Litz, the author of *Introspective Voyager: The Poetic
Development of Wallace Stevens* (1972), has also published
two books on James Joyce and a study of Jane Austen. In addi-
tion, he has edited a number of anthologies, most recently *Eliot
in His Time* (1973), *Major American Short Stories* (1975),
and the *Scribner Quarto of Modern Literature* (1978). Chair-
man of the English Department at Princeton University, he has
received fellowships from the National Endowment for the
Humanities and the American Council of Learned Societies. In
1972 the Danforth Foundation awarded him the E. Harris Har-
bison Award for gifted teaching.

Isabel G. MacCaffrey was Kenan Professor of History and Litera-
ture at Harvard University. At the time of her death in the
spring of 1978 she was preparing a book of essays that was to
include the essay on Stevens that appears in this volume. Her
earlier essay on the poet, "The Other Side of Silence: 'Credences
of Summer' as an Example," was published in *MLQ* (Septem-
ber 1969). A former Guggenheim Fellow, she was, of course,
a highly regarded scholar in Renaissance studies, her chief con-
tributions in that field being *Paradise Lost as "Myth"* (1959)
and *Spenser's Allegory: An Anatomy of Imagination* (1976).

Louis L. Martz is Sterling Professor of English at Yale Univer-
sity. His interest in Stevens began in 1933, when Theodore
Roethke, his teacher at Lafayette College, urged him to read
Harmonium (the 1931 edition, then newly acquired by the col-
lege library). "I read it from cover to cover," he reports, "and
have been a Stevensian ever since!" He is the author of *The
Poem of the Mind* (1966), which contains two essays on Ste-
vens, *The Poetry of Meditation* (1954), which won the Chris-
tian Gauss Award, and *The Paradise Within* (1964).

J. Hillis Miller is the Frederick W. Hilles Professor of English
at Yale University. An essay on Wallace Stevens is included in
his *Poets of Reality* (1965), and more recently he has published
"Stevens' Rock and Criticism as Cure" in the *Georgia Review*
(Spring-Summer 1976). He is the author of *The Disappearance
of God: Five Nineteenth-Century Writers* (1963) and has writ-
ten on Dickens, Hardy, and other Victorian novelists.

Roy Harvey Pearce has served at the University of California,

San Diego, as Professor of American Literature, as Chairman of the Department of Literature, and as Dean of Graduate Studies. His 1951 PMLA article, "Wallace Stevens: The Life of the Imagination," marked the beginning of his continuing concern with Stevens. The recipient of numerous fellowships, including one from the Guggenheim Foundation, he is the author of *The Savages of America: A Study of the Indian and American Mind* (1953), *The Continuity of American Poetry* (1961), which was awarded the prize for criticism of the Poetry Society of America in 1962, and *Historicism Once More: Problems & Occasions for the American Scholar* (1969). Among the numerous works that he has edited is *The Act of the Mind: Essays on the Poetry of Wallace Stevens* (1965), which he coedited with J. Hillis Miller.

Joseph N. Riddel is Professor of English at the University of California, Los Angeles. The author of *The Clairvoyant Eye: The Poetry and Poetics of Wallace Stevens* (which was awarded the Explicator Prize for 1965), he has also written books on C. Day Lewis (1971) and William Carlos Williams (1974), as well as publishing essays on numerous modern poets and on poetic and critical theory. He is presently at work on a study of American poetics.

Holly Stevens, daughter of the poet, has edited *Letters of Wallace Stevens* (1966) and *The Palm at the End of the Mind: Selected Poems and a Play by Wallace Stevens* (1971), and she is the author of *Souvenirs and Prophecies: The Young Wallace Stevens* (1977), which incorporates the journals that Stevens kept as a young man. She has presented numerous papers on the poet and readings of his work.

Wilson E. Taylor was for many years a friend and business associate of the poet, first when he worked in the New York office, and then in the San Francisco office, of the Hartford Accident and Indemnity Company. Over the years the two colleagues maintained a personal correspondence. The letters that Mr. Taylor received are now in the Stevens archive at the Huntington Library. Mr. Taylor resides with his wife in Menlo Park, California.

Helen Vendler is Professor of English at Boston University. She is the author of *On Extended Wings: Wallace Stevens' Longer Poems* (1969) and has also written books on Yeats and Herbert. She reviews contemporary poetry for *The New Yorker* and other journals, and is working on a book on the odes of Keats.

Library of Congress Cataloging in Publication Data

Wallace Stevens: a celebration.

Bibliography: p.

1. Stevens, Wallace, 1879-1955—Addresses, essays,
lectures.   2.   Poets, American—20th century—Biography—
Addresses, essays, lectures.   I. Doggett, Frank A.
II. Buttel, Robert.

PS3537.T4753Z84   811'.5'2   79-18877
ISBN 0-691-06414-8